Studies in Logic
Logic and Argumentation
Volume 33

Conductive Argument
An Overlooked Type of Defeasible Reasoning

Volume 22
The Axiom of Choice
John L. Bell

Volume 23
The Logic of Fiction
John Woods, with a Foreword by Nicholas Griffin

Volume 24
Studies in Diagrammatology and Diagram Praxis
Olga Pombo and Alexander Gerner

Volume 25
The Analytical Way: Proceedings of the 6th European Congress of Analytical Philosophy
Tadeusz Czarnecki, Katarzyna Kijania-Placek, Olga Poller and Jan Woleński, eds.

Volume 26
Philosophical Aspects of Symbolic Reasoning in Early Modern Mathematics
Albrecht Heeffer and Maarten Van Dyck, eds.

Volume 27
Inconsistent Geometry
Chris Mortensen

Volume 28
Passed Over in Silence
Jaap van der Does

Volume 29
Logic and Philosophy Today, Volume 1
Johan van Benthem and Amitabha Gupta, eds

Volume 30
Logic and Philosophy Today, Volume 2
Johan van Benthem and Amitabha Gupta, eds

Volume 31
Nonmonotonic Reasoning. Essays Celebrating its 30th Anniversary
Gerhard Brewka, Victor W. Marek and Miroslaw Truszczynski, eds.

Volume 32
Foundations of the Formal Sciences VII. Bringing together Philosophy and Sociology of Science
Karen François, Benedikt Löwe, Thomas Müller and Bart van Kerkhove, eds.

Volume 33
Conductive Argument. An Overlooked Type of Defeasible Reasoning
J. Anthony Blair and Ralph H. Johnson, eds.

Studies in Logic Series Editor
Dov Gabbay   dov.gabbay@kcl.ac.uk

Conductive Argument
An Overlooked Type of Defeasible Reasoning

Edited by

J. Anthony Blair

and

Ralph H. Johnson

© Individual author and College Publications 2011.
All rights reserved.

ISBN 978-1-84890-030-1

College Publications
Scientific Director: Dov Gabbay
Managing Director: Jane Spurr
Department of Informatics
King's College London, Strand, London WC2R 2LS, UK

http://www.collegepublications.co.uk

Original cover design by orchid creative   www.orchidcreative.co.uk
Printed by Lightning Source, Milton Keynes, UK

All rights reserved. No part of this publication may be reproduced, stored in a retrieval system or transmitted in any form, or by any means, electronic, mechanical, photocopying, recording or otherwise without prior permission, in writing, from the publisher.

Contents

Preface vii

Introduction

Ch. 1 Conductive Reasoning/Arguments: A Map of the Issues 1
J. Anthony Blair

Part I The Concept of Conduction

Ch. 2 The Structure of Pro and Con Arguments: A Survey of the Theories ... 10
Rongdong Jin
Ch. 3 Notes on Balance-of-Considerations Arguments 31
H.V. Hansen
Ch. 4 The Relationship between Pro/Con and Dialectical Tier Arguments ... 52
Ralph H. Johnson
Ch. 5 Why Argumentation Theory Should Differentiate Types of Claim ... 62
Christian Kock
Ch. 6 An Attempt at Unifying Natural Language Argument Structures ... 74
Frank Zenker

Part II Evaluating Conductive Arguments

Ch. 7 Weighing Considerations in Conductive Pro and Con Arguments ... 86
Thomas Fischer
Ch. 8 Weighing Evidence in the Context of Conductive Reasoning ... 104
Robert C. Pinto
Ch. 9 Evaluating Conductive Arguments in Light of the Toulmin Model ... 127
James B. Freeman
Ch. 10 Guidelines for Reaching a Reasoned Judgment 145
Mark Battersby & Sharon Bailin

Part III Case Studies and Special Topics

Ch. 11 Ranking Considerations and Aligning Probative Obligations ... 158
Fred Kauffeld
Ch. 12 Conductive Arguments and the Toulmin Model: A Case Study ... 167
Derek Allen
Ch. 13 Conductive Arguments in Ethical Deliberation 191
Douglas Walton
Ch. 14 A Misleading Model for the Analysis of Pro- and Contra- Argumentation ... 210
Harald Wohlrapp
Ch. 15 Conductive Arguments: A Meta-Argumentation Approach ... 224
Maurice Finocchiaro

Afterword

Ch. 16 Conductive Arguments: Overview of the Symposium 262
Trudy Govier

About the Authors 277
References 280
Indexes 292

Preface

The University of Windsor's Centre for Research in Reasoning, Argumentation and Rhetoric (CRRAR), then Directed by Hans V. Hansen, organized a two-day symposium on the topic of conductive argument, held on 30 April–1 May, 2010. This book contains the revised proceedings of that symposium, plus two added papers.

The participants were asked simply to address any issues related to the concept of conductive reasoning or argument. The terms 'conduction' and 'conductive' were coined in 1971 by Carl Wellman, in *Challenge and Response: Justification in Ethics*, as deliberate contrast terms to 'deduction' and 'deductive,' and 'induction' and 'inductive.' Wellman's thesis is that there is a distinctive kind of reasoning and argument involved in the justification of many ethical judgments, among others, that is neither deductive nor inductive. Wellman's views were brought to the attention of the nascent community of informal logic argumentation scholars in 1979 by Trudy Govier in a critical review of *Challenge and Response* in the *Informal Logic Newsletter* (Govier 1979). Govier herself has introduced a slightly modified conception of conduction in her textbook *A Practical Study of Argument* (2010) and in a chapter in her anthology, *The Philosophy of Argument* (1999). Hitchcock (1981, 1994) has also published papers on conductive argument. However, apart from these authors, conductive argument has received little scholarly attention. The objective of publishing these papers is to launch conductive argument as a topic for the attention of theorists of reasoning and argumentation, informal logic and logic in general.

Besides CRRAR fellows Anthony Blair, Ralph Johnson, Robert Pinto, Douglas Walton and visiting scholar Rongdong Jin (Shanghai Normal), Hansen invited, from elsewhere in Canada: Derek Allen (Toronto), Trudy Govier (Lethbridge), David Hitchcock (McMaster); from Europe: Frans van Eemeren (Amsterdam), Christian Kock (Copenhagen), Harald Wohlrapp (Hamburg), Frank Zenker (Lund); and from the United States: Maurice Finocchiaro (Nevada–Las Vegas), Thomas Fischer (Houston), James Freeman (Hunter College, CUNY), Jean Goodwin (Iowa State) and Fred Kauffeld (Edgewood College). Van Eemeren and Goodwin were unable to attend due to prior commitments and Allen, Govier and Hitchcock attended but did not present papers. Following the discussions at the symposium and in later email exchanges, all the presenters revised their papers for publication in this volume. Allen and Govier have written papers expressly for this volume.

The papers in this volume provide a comprehensive picture of the theoretical issues raised by and related to Wellman's concept. These include: historical antecedents of conductive argument, problems with Wellman's account, various conceptualizations of conductive argument, whether conductive arguments constitute a distinct class, the structure of conductive arguments, problems involved in the conceptual ingredients of conductive arguments, the domain(s) of conductive arguments, how conductive arguments might be diagrammed, how conductive arguments might be evaluated, and case studies of conductive arguments. A more detailed account of the issues dealt with in the volume is provided in the Introduction.

The editors are most grateful to College Publications's Scientific Director, Dov Gabbay, and for the assistance and patience of its Managing Director, Jane Spurr.

J. Anthony Blair & Ralph H. Johnson
Centre for Research in Reasoning, Argumentation and Rhetoric
University of Windsor
September 2011

I – INTRODUCTION

Chapter 1

Conductive reasoning/arguments: A map of the issues

J. ANTHONY BLAIR

1. Introduction

This introductory chapter maps the issues that need attention in order to have a theory of conductive argument or conductive reasoning. It identifies many of the questions that need answers, and for each it refers the reader to locations in the book where other authors have discussed it in detail.

There seem to be several broad questions about conduction, each of which harbors several others. (1) *Issues of definition.* What are the distinguishing properties of conductive reasoning and of conductive argument? (Are the two different? If so, how?) Wellman's definition (see below) has not been followed, and there are different deviations from it past literature and in this volume. (2) *Issues of conceptualization.* What is the nature of the illative relation between the reasons or grounds and the conclusion of conductive reasoning or arguments? How is conduction related to deduction and induction? How is conduction related to similar reasoning or arguments (such as risk-benefit analysis in decision making)? What is the (proper) domain of conduction; to what kinds of subject matter does it apply? (3) *Issues of analysis.* How are conductive reasoning or conductive arguments to be analyzed? How are they to be diagrammed? How are "con" considerations to be handled (as premises?)? Is it possible and if so, useful, to analyze or model conductive reasoning or conductive arguments as dialogues? (4) *Issues of assessment.* What constitutes probatively good conductive reasoning and what constitutes a probatively good conductive argument? What are the conditions of conductive adequacy? Can pros and cons to be weighted or valued and can they be weighed against each other? If so, how? If not, why not? (Is quantitative weighting and summing possible or useful?) (5) *Issues of originality and connection.* If there is a distinct kind of reasoning or argument such as Wellman alleges, it would be surprising if it had not been noticed before 1971. Have other, earlier theorists noticed this sort of reasoning?

2. Definition: What is conductive reasoning or argument?

2.1 The definition

What is *conductive* X? That is, whether it is reasoning or argument that is the substantive term, what is *conduction* as it relates to the referent of that term?

Here we start with Wellman's canonical definition:

> Conduction can best be defined as that sort of reasoning in which 1) a conclusion about some individual case 2) is drawn non-conclusively 3) from one or more premises about the same case 4) without any appeal to other cases. (Wellman 1971, p. 52.)

That definition has features that have not been congenial to everyone.

First, if arguments are different from reasoning, can there not be conductive arguments too? Wellman's answer is to *define* reasoning in terms of argument. "Reasoning" he proposes, "is using one or more arguments" (1971, p. 102), while by 'argument' he says we can mean either "a bit of language consisting of one or more premises, a conclusion, and an implicit claim to validity" (p. 102) or else "that which is formulated in the language" (103), so that "reasoning applies to both public and private forms, both conversations in which some speaker presents an argument and thinking in which he does not make any utterance" (103). The articles in this volume follow Wellman in making nothing of this distinction.

However, does nothing rest on the difference between reasoning and argument? Reasoning starts from givens, with the outcome unknown or undecided, and works towards some outcome as the literal conclusion of the process. Arguing starts with the end-point or "conclusion" stated or given, and seeks or offers support for it.[1] Reasoning and arguing in these senses are events. Wellman, as noted, is aware of a possible equivocation on the term 'argument,' namely the shift from the sense in which the term denotes the verbal expression of any step of reasoning—the sense in which Copi (1982, p. 6) claims that corresponding to every possible inference there is an argument—to the sense in which 'argument' denotes a set of reasons adduced in support of a claim. And one can always invite others to share in or accept one's reasoning, thereby using an argument in the first sense as an argument in the second sense. Still, it strikes me that advice about how best to think through (i.e., to reason) to a decision or judgment might be different from the criteria of a well-thought-through and so well-supported (i.e., well-argued) decision or judgment. For the first, one needs a coach or trainer; for the second, a rule-book or a referee. "Cross the finish line first" (the criterion of winning a race) is useless as coaching advice about how to accomplish that feat. When Battersby and Bailin (Chapter 10) offer guidelines for reaching a reasoned judgment, they are making suggestions about how to reason conductively oneself—offering advice about how to reason well conductively. When Freeman (Chapter 9) addresses evaluating conductive arguments, he is proposing how we may assess conductive arguments that have been expressed by others—offering criteria for good conductive arguments. Is there, then, a difference between conduction as a particular way of figuring out conductively what data imply or suggest (reasoning conductively) and conduction as a particular way of defending or justifying a claim (arguing conductively)?

A second point, about article 1) of Wellman's definition: Cannot this type of reasoning be about *types* of cases, such as policies, as well as about individual cases, such as what *this person* should do *in this situation*. Every author in this book who addresses this question advocates giving up Wellman's restriction. Govier was the first to do so (1987, p. 69), and in this volume is followed explicitly by Freeman (Chapter 9) and Finocchiaro (Chapter 15), and implicitly by others. Wellman himself, in a later book, *Morals and Ethics* (1975, 2nd ed. 1988) offers what look like "conductive" arguments in some respects for a number of social policies, for instance in favour of civil disobedience and of genetic engineering under certain limiting conditions.

A third point about Wellman's definition, regarding articles 3) and 4): *Must* the premises be all about the same case without any appeal to other cases? For instance, can they not include generalizations? Wellman wanted to distinguish arguments from analogy from conductive arguments, and this restriction accomplished that end. For, as he says:

---

[1] Of course this is not the order always found in presented arguments; the point is that the conclusion of an argument is known to the arguer at the moment of arguing.

> Another way of drawing a conclusion about a particular case ... is reasoning by analogy. ... The point of this appeal to analogous cases is that in these cases experience has shown that certain characteristics ... have gone together with another characteristic .... But in conduction the link between premises and conclusion is not established on the basis of the experience of analogous cases; it is entirely a priori." (1971, p. 53)

It seems, though, that arguments from analogy can be distinguished from conductive arguments without ruling out generalizations as possible grounds for their conclusions. Wellman was also concerned to distinguish conduction from deduction, and restricting the scope of the former to arguments without generalizations among the premises was a way to rule out some deductive arguments, but not all. In any case, it seems one might appeal, as Ross does, to a *prima facie* duty as a ground (e.g., lying is *prima facie* wrong) for a particular moral judgment (I shouldn't fail to declare this lecture fee on my income tax form). Wellman himself cites Ross's move with approval (Wellman 1988, p. 21), so either he is not consistent, or he changed his mind on this point, or he would not label such reasoning and arguments conductive, even though they are neither deductive nor inductive.

In the end, only the "non-conclusive" requirement, article 2), seems on the face of it essential. However, if the other requirements are not included in the definition of induction, then what distinguishes conduction from, for instance, induction? If the definition is altered, then do arguments and reasoning of the third pattern (see below) become like other kinds of argument and reasoning? For instance, if the conclusion can be about more than a single case, then it looks like policy decision-making reasoning or argument. Or if the premises can be about other cases, then there seems no bar from analogies with other cases to count as reasons for or against the conclusion. These overlaps might or might not be welcome. The point is that changing the definition offered by Wellman can have ramifications for theorizing the concept of conduction.

2.2 The three patterns of conduction

Wellman's *definition* makes no reference to the three "patterns of conduction" that he introduces. He describes these as follows. Pattern [I]: "a single reason is given for the conclusion" (1971, p. 55). Pattern: [II] "several considerations, each of which may be independently relevant, are brought together into a unified argument from which a single conclusion is drawn" (p. 56). Pattern [III]: "that form of argument in which some conclusion is drawn from both positive and negative considerations ... reasons against the conclusion are included as well as reasons for it" (p. 57). These patterns are variations in the form that arguments or reasoning with the defined properties of conduction listed in 1.1 can take. In Wellman's hands, none of these patterns is definitive of conduction; they represent different forms that conduction can exhibit.

Nevertheless, those who have discussed conductive reasoning and arguments have tended to focus on just the second or the third of these patterns, and some even seem to identify conduction with arguments or reasoning of the third pattern exclusively. Wellman himself encourages that understanding. For he says of the first pattern, that "Although only one reason is advanced in this pattern, there are always (or almost always) other relevant considerations that might have been mentioned" (p. 55). In other words, instances of the first pattern are usually—"always (or almost always)"—truncated versions of the second one. Moreover, of the second pattern Wellman says that, "Here, also there are likely to be relevant considerations, particularly on the other side, that are not mentioned" (p. 56). In other words, usually instances of the second pattern are in turn truncated versions of the third one. It seems to be Wellman's own position that although arguments will be found exhibiting each of the three patterns, the typical situation is represented by the third pattern. That is, whether an arguer expresses his or her reasoning fully, typically the he or she reasons that there are several considerations (or at least more than one) that independently support the conclusion, and there are considerations that independently tell against it, and the former are stronger than the latter.

Some (thus) seem to want to reserve the term 'conductive' for this third "pro and con" pattern of argument or of reasoning. In that case, though, the first two patterns would seem to need their own labels, since they are distinctive if they accord with the definition offered. All of the authors in this book take the reasoning, or arguments, of the third pattern to be the most interesting, and most focus on it exclusively.

Govier (2001, p. 392) has said that all conductive arguments are convergent, but that is already a departure from Wellman, who allows for single-reason conductive arguments (which therefore cannot be convergent). Shall convergence be part of the definition? If so, the controversies about what constitutes a convergent argument become germane. And what is the relation between conductive and non-conductive convergent reasoning or arguments? Govier's position is that all conductive arguments are convergent (thereby rejecting Wellman's first pattern, or perhaps following Wellman in treating it as a truncated version of the second pattern), but, notice that since there can be deductive and inductive convergent arguments, not all convergent arguments are conductive.

While Wellman invented the labels 'conduction' and 'conductive,' it would be surprising if no one had noticed this pattern of reasoning and argument before him. Freeman (Chapter 9) notes that W.D. Ross's examples in *The Right and The Good* (1930) of moral arguments with conflicting *prima facie* duties exhibit Wellman's pattern III conductive arguments, and Hansen (Chapter 3) shows how in *The Philosophy of Rhetoric* (1776) George Campbell's (1776) notion of moral reasoning is match for pattern III conductive reasoning.

3. Conceptualization

There are other questions related to how to understand "conduction" that are not aspects of its definition, but are implied by it.

One of these is, what is the nature of the conductive "inference" or premise-conclusion link? According to Wellman, it is "non-conclusive," and in this respect it is different from a deductive premise-conclusion relation. Moreover, the premises of a conductive argument are not empirically related to its conclusion, and in this respect it is different from a scientific inductive premise-conclusion relation. Given these features, one wants to know how conductive inferences are related to other categories of inference discussed in the literature that share these two features, such as those called "presumptive," "plausible," "*prima facie*," "*pro tanto*," "proviso'd" or "defeasible." Indeed, how is each of these related to the others? This is a local variant of what (2000, pp. 21-23) called "the network problem," namely, the problem of how related concepts are connected to one another.

Some theorists in this book take the concept of a warrant introduced by Toulmin (1958) to explain the conductive premise-conclusion linkage. Freeman in particular (Chapter 9), followed by Finocchiaro (Chapter 15), understand Wellman's examples, such as "You ought to help him for he has been very kind to you" (1971, p. 55), as inferences that are justified just when there is a defensible, albeit defeasible, generalization licensing the inference from the premise(s) to the conclusion. Allen (Chapter 12) takes this approach in his case study as well.

Another question that arises in conceptualizing conduction relates to its domain. What is the subject matter of conductive reasoning and argument? Is it appropriately applied only to certain types of topics? Wellman was particularly interested in "ethical arguments which infer some ethical statement about some particular case from factual premises about that case" (pp. 53–54), but he held that conduction arguments also occur outside ethics: "Wherever some descriptive predicate is ascribed on the basis of a family resemblance conductive reasoning takes place" (p. 54), and more generally, it occurs when "factual conclusions about some individual case are drawn from information about the case" (p. 54). We have already noted that the authors in this volume do not consider that the domain of conduction is restricted to judgments about particular cases, nor do they consider it restricted to ethics. It would seem that conductive arguments could be appropriately applied to prescriptions and evaluations of any kind, to interpretations of meaning or significance, and to classifications—perhaps among other things.

Is "conductive" a property that belongs to the same category as "deductive" and "inductive"? Skyrms (1999), Hitchcock (1980), Ennis (2001) and others have proposed that the latter are best understood as types of criteria for evaluating the premise-conclusion link or inference in reasoning or arguments, and *not* as types of reasoning or argument. If that conceptualization is accepted for deduction and induction, does conduction, too, represent a criterion of evaluation, and not a type of reasoning or of argument? That is not the way Wellman introduces the concept. He introduces "conductive" as referring to a type of reasoning or argument, not a norm. But if he is followed, then, accepting the Skyrms *et al.* approach, "conductive" is not an appropriate contrast term to "deductive" and "inductive." Perhaps 'deduction,' 'induction' and 'conduction' all name distinctive types of implication relationship.

What are related kinds of reasoning or argument? It seems that problem-solving (reasoning to the best solution to a problem) and decision-making (deciding what is the best act to perform or policy to institute), both of which have large literatures, look a lot like instances of conductive reasoning. Are they? Johnson (Chapter 4) takes up the question of how Wellman's pattern III (pro and con) conductive arguments relate to arguments in which the arguer anticipates and responds to criticisms and objections—arguments with what he has called a "dialectical tier" (see Johnson 2000).

Kock (Chapter 5) makes a case that it matters a good deal whether an argument's conclusion is an assertion (about what is true) or a prescription (about what to do), and that if Wellman's conception of conduction is to be applied to ethics, he had best abandon his meta-ethical cognitivism. In Chapter 6, Zenker explores the relation between deductive, inductive and conductive argument structures, and suggests a reversal of the standard way of viewing their connection.

4. Analysis: How is conductive reasoning or argument to be analyzed? How are they to be diagrammed?

The analysis of reasoning or arguments of the first pattern identified by Wellman seems unproblematic: reason supports claim. Will a simple circle and arrow diagram or some variant of it not serve? No, for such a diagram fails to distinguish an argument with a conductive inference from one premise from an argument with a deductive inference from a single premise or from one with an inductive inference from a single premise.

For the second pattern: reason or consideration #1 supports a claim, and (independently) reason or consideration #2 supports that claim, and so on for all the n reasons or considerations. Why is there one argument rather than n arguments if the reasons independently support the conclusion? It seems the second pattern of conductive arguments requires some further property, some combinatory, corroborational or cumulative property shared by the reasons. (This is, to be sure, a problem for convergent arguments in general.)

Moreover, if there can be more than one deductively valid argument for a given conclusion, or more than one inductively strong argument for a given conclusion, then there is in a typical "convergent argument" diagram—one with a separate arrow pointing to the conclusion from each argument's group of premises—nothing to distinguish them from a conductively strong argument with more than one consideration supporting its conclusion.

For the third pattern: reasons pro-#1 to pro-#n are considerations in favor of the conclusion, and reasons con-#1 to con-#m are considerations against the conclusion. How are the "con" considerations to be treated in "pro and con" conductive arguments? If they are to count as "premises" do we not then require a new concept of (negatively relevant) premise, since in its standard sense a premise is a proposition *supporting* the conclusion? If the con considerations are not premises, what are they? And if the "con" considerations cannot count as "premises," can the "pro" considerations count as premises? But if not, how are they to be conceived?

These questions are addressed in several chapters of this book—by Jin (Chapter 2), Hansen (Chapter 3), Freeman (Chapter 9) and Govier (Chapter 16).

Perhaps we should model pro and con conductive arguments as three separate but related arguments, with the pro considerations constituting a convergent argument in favour of some claim, the con considerations constituting a convergent argument in favour of the contradictory of that claim, and a third argument to the effect either that the pro argument is stronger or weightier than the con argument (hence the claim) or that the con argument is stronger or weightier than the pro argument (hence the contradictory of the claim). If so, what is the nature of that third argument?

And if not, then how should we model such arguments? Here's another possibility: Premise 1—There are pro reasons for C and con reasons against C; premise support for Premise 1—P1A: the pro reasons for C for the first conjunct of P1; and P1B: the con reasons against C for the second conjunct of P1. Then, Premise 2 (version Pro)—The pro reasons for C outweigh the con reasons for C; Conclusion (version Pro)—C. Or else, Premise 2 (version Con)—the con reasons against C outweigh the pro reasons for C; Conclusion (version Con)—not-C. If that model is not acceptable either, then how else might these arguments be modeled?

And, in any case, how is "Pro (or Con) reasons or considerations X are *weightier* than [or *outweigh*] Con (or Pro) reasons or considerations Y" to be analyzed?

A completely different question: Is it possible, and if possible is it useful, to model conductive reasoning or arguments as dialogues? What seems to make a conductive argument dialogue different from the standard interchange between dialogue partners is that the proponent's concession of a criticism of his standpoint by the opponent does not (necessarily) count as a refutation of the standpoint that the proponent is defending. The proponent can concede, "Yes, that is a good argument against my standpoint," and yet, without inconsistency, assert, "But you haven't refuted my standpoint" or "But it does not follow that my standpoint is false." So the modeling of a conductive argument dialogue requires distinctive dialogue rules. Presumably these can be formulated. Is there a gain promised by going to the trouble to do so? (Perhaps here is a place where the reasoning/argument distinction has traction, with reasoning best modeled as monological and argument as dialogical. But perhaps reasoning is best modeled dialogically too?) Govier comments on this matter in Chapter 15.

5. Assessment: What constitutes good conductive reasoning? What constitutes a good conductive argument?

This question will need to be answered for each type or pattern of conductive argument.

For Wellman's Pattern I arguments, for which the reason offered provides *pro tanto*[2] justification (since the conclusion is drawn non-conclusively), there will be at least four, and possibly five, evaluative questions: (i) is the premise true (or otherwise acceptable)? (ii) assuming the acceptability of the premise, does it indeed provide a *pro tanto* reason for the conclusion (that is, if other things are equal, has it probative weight or force?)? (iii) are there other considerations besides the premise offered that support the conclusion? and (iv) assuming affirmative answers to the first two questions, are other things indeed equal, or is there one or more countervailing consideration telling against the conclusion? Questions (i), (ii) and (iv) check whether the argument is weak in various ways; question (iii) checks whether the argument could be stronger than it was in its original formulation. If the answer to question (iv) is affirmative, then a fifth question must be raised: (v) do the countervailing considerations override the presumptive force of the stated premise or of the stated premise plus other possible supporting premises?

If there is an affirmative answer to question (iii), the argument is transformed into a Wellman pattern II conductive argument. The same questions apply to pattern II arguments, except now there must be reference to more than one premise. If there is an affirmative answer to question (iv), the argument is transformed into a Wellman Pattern III conductive argument, and question (v) then becomes germane. To be sure, the argument can start off in Pattern II if the arguer offers more than one supporting consideration, or in Pattern III if the arguer offers at least one supporting consideration and at least one countervailing consideration.

Question (v) is the tricky one. To my knowledge there is no consensus about how to go about answering it. There seem to be at least three different issues that need to be resolved in order to answer question (v) for Pattern III arguments. One is, how are the pros and cons to be weighted, or how is their probative strength or force to be determined? That is, how is it to be decided what weights, strengths or values to assign to each of them? The second issue is, how are the considerations on each side, pro and con, to be added together or summed? And the third issue is, how are the weights, strengths or values on each side to be compared or balanced against each other? These questions are addressed by the papers in Part III by Fischer (Chapter 7), Pinto (Chapter 8), Freeman (Chapter 9) and Battersby and Bailin (Chapter 10) as well as by Finocchiaro (Chapter 15) and Govier (Chapter 16). Wohlrapp (Chapter 14) and and Zenker (Chapter 6) are skeptical of the weighing metaphor.

In cases in which numerical values can reasonably be assigned, perhaps the mathematics of summing and counter-balancing are straightforward. But is it always reasonable to

---

[2] "A pro tanto reason has genuine weight, but nonetheless may be outweighed by other considerations. Thus, calling a reason a pro tanto reason is to be distinguished from calling it a prima facie reason, which I take to involve an epistemological qualification: a prima facie reason appears to be a reason, but may actually not be a reason at all" (Kagan 1989, p. 17).

assign numerical values? It seems that at least in some cases it is not. (For example, how do you assign a number to a father's promise to take his daughter to the circus and to his countervailing obligation to help a friend move into a new apartment?) To be sure, items on lists of reasons, either pro or con, can be ranked relative to each other by a series of pair-wise comparisons. If numbers cannot reasonable be assigned, then these questions become especially vexing. Wellman more or less threw up his hands over this question, as did Ross before him[3]; but as Hitchcock (1994, p. 60) has observed, that is hardly a satisfactory response. Fischer (Chapter 7) has some positive suggestions, and he responds to the criticism of Wohlrapp (Chapter 14) and Zenker (Chapter 6).

6. Cases of conductive reasoning or argument

It is all very well to speculate in the abstract about conductive reasoning or arguments, working with imagined examples. What to cases of conductive reasoning and arguments "on the hoof" look like? Several chapters in the volume offer answers to that question. Hansen (Chapter 3) finds an example in an application of the "notwithstanding" Clause of the Canadian Charter of Rights and Freedoms. Kauffeld (Chapter 11) finds such arguments in the arguments of the Federalist Papers in which Hamilton, Jay and Jefferson advocated for the ratification of the American Constitution. Allen (Chapter 12) finds them in the arguments of two Canadian Supreme Court justices in their respective rationales for their opposed judgments in a case involving the interpretation of the Charter of Rights and Freedoms to a law prohibiting hate propaganda. Walton (Chapter 13) takes up an example that Wellman himself used in his ethics textbook, *Morals and Ethics*. And Finocchiaro (Chapter 15) analyses as conductive the argument in a 2009 op-ed piece by *New York Times* columnist David Brooks criticizing the Obama government's health-care plan as well as Galileo's argument on the motion of the earth.

7. Concluding remarks

The book ends with a chapter by Wohlrapp (Chapter 14) expressing strongly skeptical reservations about the concept of conductive argument, a meta-analytic approach and review of the literature on conductive arguments by Finocchiaro (Chapter 15), and a response to the papers presented at the symposium from which the book originated by Govier (Chapter 16), the theorist most responsible for the revival of interest in Wellman's concept of conduction.

This Introduction has not been a survey of the work that has been done on conductive reasoning or argument, although it has clearly been written with at least some of that work in mind. An extensive survey is to be found in Finocchiaro's chapter. With a few excep-

---

[3] See Wellman, *Challenge and Response*, p. 79: "But by and large there is no way to judge the validity of these basic ethical arguments but by thinking them through and feeling their logical force"; and see Ross, *The Right and The Good*, p. 31: "... [T]here is no principle by which we can draw the conclusion that is on the whole right or on the whole wrong. In this respect the judgment as to the rightness of a particular act is just like the judgment as to the beauty of a particular natural object or work of art. . . . Both in this and in the moral case we have more or less probable opinions which are not logically justified conclusions from the general principles that are recognized as self-evident."

tions, this introduction does not describe or discuss the solutions to some of the questions listed that some have proposed.

The intent, rather, has been to provide an at least tentative framework for the discussions gathered in this book. The general idea is that we need to be clear in (at least) three areas. We need to be clear in each case what conception of conduction we are addressing (what exactly we mean by 'conduction,' whether it applies to reasoning or argument, and whether it be pattern I, II or III, or something else), and what exactly we mean by 'conduction.' We need to be clear about how we identify, describe or analyze the reasoning or the arguments we call conductive. And we need to be clear about what constitutes good (and bad) conductive reasoning or argument and about how to go about deciding its merits in each case. The chapters in this book provide such clarification. Then they proceed to develop substantive positions on the issues they address.

II – THE CONCEPT OF CONDUCTION

Chapter 2

The Structure of Pro and Con Arguments: A Survey of the Theories

RONGDONG JIN

1. Introduction

'Pro and con argument'[1] in this paper is used to mean the third pattern of conductive arguments discussed by Wellman (1971), a subtype of balance-of-considerations arguments described by Hitchcock (1983), and what Govier (1999b, 2010) may call the typical conductive arguments. One of the common characteristics of arguments under these different names is that they can accommodate both reasons for a conclusion (*pros*) and reasons against the same conclusion (*cons*); in other words, a conclusion can be reached from both positive and negative considerations in these kinds of arguments.[2]

The focus of this paper is on the structure rather than the evaluation of pro and con arguments. From section 2 to section 4, I reconstruct in turn how Wellman, Hitchcock and Govier deal with this issue in as much detail as possible. The reconstruction is carried out by means of the following analytical framework, consisting of five questions:

1) What is an argument?
2) What are basic component parts of arguments?
3) What is the status of counterconsiderations in pro and con arguments?
4) How are positive considerations, counterconsiderations and conclusions connected in pro and con arguments?
5) How can this kind of connection or structure be diagrammed?

Along with reconstructing their answers to these questions, I subject them to careful scrutiny, examining their respective self-consistency, applicability, explanatory power and other theoretical features. Then, in section 5, I venture my own solutions to some of questions listed above. Section 6 is the conclusion.

2. Wellman on the structure of pro and con arguments

Wellman defines 'argument' in terms of reasoning. This means he more or less has touched upon the issue of the relation between argument and reasoning. When Wellman claims that

---

[1] There are some other terms similar to 'pro and con argument,' such as 'pro aut contra' arguments (Naess 2005), 'pro/con argumentation' (Zenker 2009d, 2010b), 'pro- and contra-discussion' (Wohlrapp 2008a). These terms do not share a same and exact meaning partly because those theoreticians take different approaches to conceptualizing arguments, for example, a product-based one or a process-based one, and partly because there are different understandings of whether an argument of this kind is a simple argument or includes multiple arguments.

[2] When describing how Wellman and Hitchcock understand the structure of pro and con arguments, I will, following Govier, call negative considerations or reasons against a conclusion "counterconsiderations" no matter whether it is used by them.

"the unit of reasoning is an argument" (p. 90)[3] and that "reasoning is using or following arguments" (p. 110),[4] he seems to treat arguments as constituent parts of reasoning. Then what is reasoning? It is the kind of activity in which a speaker presents considerations to defend one of his statements against the challenges of his audiences, and it "can always become transformed into the give-and-take of discussion…a contest of mutual persuasion" (p. 102). Clearly Wellman here adopts a dialogical approach to reasoning, but he does not elaborate this point any further.

Reasoning is a kind of dialogue—that does not mean that arguments are also necessarily dialogical. An argument Wellman has in mind is "a bit of language consisting of one or more premises, a conclusion, and an implicit claim to validity" (p. 90). This concept of argument is obviously based upon a product point of view that typically defines arguments as a type of discourse or text that consists of a designated set of propositions, one of which is put forward on the basis of the others. Although arguments can be used in reasoning as a kind of dialogue, for example, discussion or mutual persuasion, Wellman does not conceptualize them from a process point of view. He does not see arguments as a kind of dialogue that moves through different stages towards a collective goal, based on collaborative conversational postulates that govern how moves are made during the process (Reed and Walton 2003).

Taking argument as product, Wellman maintains that any argument has three components, namely, premise, conclusion and a claim to validity that indicates that the conclusion is thought to follow validly from the premises. Considering that the claim to validity is usually implicit and closely related to the evaluation of arguments, we can leave it aside when describing the structure of arguments and take premises and conclusions as the basic components of arguments. Put it another way, Wellman actually conceives of arguments as having a premise-conclusion structure.

As we might know, either in ordinary language or in logical textbooks, the term 'premise' is usually used to mean a proposition that supports or is supposed to support a conclusion. For example:

> (A premise is) a proposition upon which an argument is based or from which a conclusion is drawn. (*The American Heritage Dictionary of the English Language*)

> The *conclusion* of an argument is the proposition that is affirmed on the basis of the other propositions of the argument, and these other propositions, which are affirmed (or assumed) as providing support or reasons for accepting the conclusion, are the *premisses* of that argument. (Copi and Cohen 1990, p. 6; italics in original)

According to this prevailing usage of 'premise,' propositions that count or are supposed to count against a conclusion cannot function as premises. Wellman, however, does not think so and gives us an odd, even anti-intuitive explanation of the meaning of the term in question:

> A premise is any consideration (that is, anything that can be considered or attended to) which counts or is thought to count *for or against the conclusion*. The conclusion is something that ostensibly is to be accepted on the basis of the premises. (p. 90; italics added)

---

[3] Unless otherwise indicated, all page references in this section are to Wellman (1971).
[4] Govier (1980a, p. 14) argues that Wellman fails in distinguishing between reasoning and arguments.

Here, premises are not thought to be composed exclusively of considerations in favor of a conclusion, considerations that would oppose a conclusion—counterconsiderations—can also play the role of premises in arguments.

Besides deductive and inductive argument, according to Wellman, there is another *sui generis* type of arguments called conductive argument. He identifies three patterns of conductive arguments, each of them is a sort of reasoning in which "1) a conclusion about some individual case 2) is drawn non-conclusively 3) from one or more premises about the same case 4) without any appeal to other cases" (p. 52). It is the third pattern of conductive arguments "in which a conclusion is drawn from both positive and negative considerations" (p. 57) that constitutes what I call pro and con argument in this paper.

Here is an example of pro and con arguments [A1] made by Wellman:

> Although your lawn needs cutting, you ought to take your son to the movies because the picture is ideal for children and will be gone by tomorrow. (p. 57) [5]

In [A1], "You ought to take your son to the movies" is the conclusion, "the picture is ideal for children" and "the picture will be gone by tomorrow" are put forward as supporting the conclusion. Introduced by "although," "your lawn needs cutting" represents a consideration that would count against the conclusion. In this case, the arguer admits the truth or acceptability of counterconsideration and does take it into account, but the conclusion shows that the positive considerations finally prevail over the negative one.

Since both positive and negative considerations are included in pro and con arguments, a question arises naturally: what is the status of counterconsiderations in pro and con arguments? As mentioned above, putting aside what Wellman calls the implicit claim to validity, we can identify only two components in any of three kinds of arguments: premise and conclusion. According to his own definition of 'premise,' Wellman does not think counterconsiderations belong to a third category that is neither premise nor conclusion. In realty, they function as part of premises. This understanding of the status of counterconsiderations is clearly contradictory to the ordinary meaning of 'premise,' as I indicated before, but entirely compatible with his own definition of the term at issue as well as his conception of components of arguments.

The key issue of the structure of pro and con arguments is how positive considerations, counterconsiderations and conclusions are connected, but Wellman does not explore this problem, so we can only make some conjectures from his description of the second pattern of conductive arguments. Let us look at an example [A2] offered by Wellman:

> You ought to take your son to the movie because you promised to do so, it is a good movie, and you have nothing better to do this afternoon.

[A2] is an instance of the second pattern of conductive arguments. What differs [A2] from pro and con arguments is that its premises involve only positive considerations. In this pattern of conductive arguments, summarizes Wellman, "several considerations, each of which may independently relevant, are brought together into a unified argument from which a single conclusion is drawn" (p. 56).

There are two points merit attention concerning the structure of the second pattern of conductive arguments. First, its premises are independently relevant to the conclusion. This means arguments of this kind have two or more independent lines of support, since their

---

[5] It is necessary to point out that I am not claiming that all arguments cited in this paper are good ones, but am only claiming that they are arguments of some kind.

premises are made up exclusively of positive considerations. Second, in this kind of arguments, it is not any single premise itself but "the logical convergence of evidence" that forms the basis upon which the conclusion is drawn. In order to reach a conclusion the arguer should think all independent premises together or "hold them together in the mind" (p. 57). It is clear that the structure of the second pattern of conductive arguments falls into the category of convergent structure of arguments.

After indicating that several positive considerations are given for the conclusion in the second pattern of conductive arguments, Wellman adds, "there are likely to be relevant considerations, particularly on the other side, that are not mentioned" (p. 56). Suppose that some unmentioned relevant considerations that are on the other side—counterconsiderations—have already been incorporated into a given instance of the second pattern of conductive arguments, this means we have a new argument of the third pattern or a pro and con argument, just like [A1]. In this argument, two conflicting groups of premises can be easily recognized: one is composed of positive considerations, the other counterconsiderations. In contrast to the second pattern of conductive arguments where the conclusion is based upon the logical convergence of positive considerations, the arguer encounters a totally different problem when making a pro and con arguments—how to estimate "the relative logical force of the pros and cons, the reasons for and the reasons against the conclusion" (p. 59). That is to say, in pro and con arguments the basis upon which a conclusion is drawn is neither the logical convergence of positive considerations nor the logical convergence of counterconsiderations, but "how much logical force the reasons for the conclusion have in comparison to the reasons against the conclusion" (p. 68). Against this background, is each single premise of pro and con arguments, whether it is a positive or negative consideration, still independently relevant to the conclusion, just as in the second pattern of conductive arguments? In what kind of way does the group of positive considerations as a whole relate to the group of counterconsiderations? Unfortunately, Wellman shows no interest in these important issues of the structure of pro and con arguments and devotes a lot of space to discussing how to evaluate arguments of this kind.

To sum up, Wellman adopts a product approach to arguments in general and pro and con arguments in particular, and takes premises and conclusions as the basic components of arguments. He not only views counterconsiderations as part of pro and con arguments, but also makes them qualify as premises of arguments. This understanding of the status of counterconsiderations is obviously consistent with his own definition of 'premise' as well as his conception of components of arguments. On the other hand, the meaning of 'premise' he puts forward seems different from, even contradictory to its ordinary or conventional meaning. With regard to the issues of how positive considerations, counterconsiderations and conclusions are connected and how to diagram this kind of connection, he does not touch upon them.

3. Hitchcock on the structure of pro and con arguments

In Hitchcock's terminology, pro and con arguments come into the category of what he calls balance-of-considerations arguments. As I will indicate soon, all pro and con arguments, according to his theory, are balance-of-considerations arguments, but the converse is not true. Only some of balance-of-considerations arguments can be classified as pro and con arguments.

Focusing on argument as product,[6] Hitchcock defines the term 'argument' as:

---

[6] Hitchcock (2007, pp. 102-103) distinguishes between the reason-giving and the disputational senses

a set of claims, one of which is put forward on the basis of the rest, these claims being termed respectively the *conclusion* and the *premises*. (p. 31; italics in original)[7]

Clearly the arguments Hitchcock has in mind are also of the premise-conclusion kind, or have premises and conclusions as their basic components. But from this definition it is still unclear whether premises can accommodate counterconsiderations. Let us look at an example used by Hitchcock to illustrate the differences between argument and explanation: "He contracted lung cancer because he smoked two packs of cigarettes a day for 30 years." Hitchcock believes that this statement is not an attempt to persuade that the person in question contracted lung cancer (it has already been known), but an attempt to explain why he contracted it. As it stands, this causal statement is just an assertion that one event or state of affairs causes another, "with no supporting evidence"; whereas an argument is an attempt to convince somebody of something on the basis of reasons (p. 34). What Hitchcock emphasizes here is that arguments must include supporting evidence, or arguers should provide supporting evidence when convincing somebody of the conclusion. At this point, only considerations in favor of a conclusion have the license to function as premises, counterconsiderations that would count against the conclusion do not have.

Hitchcock offers a description of the structure of balance-of-considerations arguments in the following passage:

> (It) has several reasons, each having some weight but operating in conjunction with one another to provide more support for the conclusion than any single reason could do. We might call such argument structures ones in which there are *independent but mutually enhancing reasons for a conclusion*. (p. 51; italics in original)

Regarding this characterization I want to stress three points. First, it is several positive considerations that make up the premises of this kind of arguments. Second, each premise gives independently some support to the conclusion. Finally, the conclusion is reached on the basis of the conjunction of all independent premises, which provides stronger support for the conclusion than any single premise could do. It is easy to see that the argument structure in question is the same as that of the second pattern of conductive arguments characterized by Wellman. In other words, balance-of-considerations arguments also have a convergent structure.

Following the previous description, Hitchcock concludes, "We will refer to all arguments of this type, *whether or not they include negative factors among the premises*, as balance-of-considerations arguments" (p. 52; italics added). Here Hitchcock seems to divide implicitly balance-of-considerations arguments into two subtypes: one is identical to what Wellman calls the second pattern of conductive arguments where only positive considerations function as premises; the other is the third pattern of conductive arguments in which both positive and negative considerations are included into premises.[8] Therefore,

---

of 'argument' and 'argue,' and holds that informal logic studies arguments in the reason-giving sense. In my opinion, this differentiation can be viewed as being on the basis of the distinction between the product and the process approach to arguments.

[7] Unless otherwise indicated, all page references in this section are to Hitchcock (1983). See Hitchcock (2007) for a more sophisticated definition of argument. However he has not mentioned yet whether it can be applied to characterize the structure of pro and con arguments.

[8] According to Hitchcock's definition of balance-of-considerations argument, there cannot be such kind of subtype which is equivalent to what Wellman calls the first pattern of conductive arguments

only part of balance-of-considerations arguments, that is, those of second subtype, can be classified as pro and con arguments.

To my mind, Hitchcock's understanding of the status of considerations in pro and con arguments can be approached from the following two angles. First, it looks as if he has differentiated counterconsiderations from objections. Hitchcock talks about counterconsiderations in section 4-5 and considers them only as those factors or reasons that would count against the conclusions. In section 4-9 he comments that a common technique in advancing an argument is to defuse possible objections by explicitly stating them and responding to them. Then what are objections? Unfortunately he does not provide us with a definition of the term at issue, just mentions several possibilities of the focus of objections. For him, objections can be raised against either the premises, or the inference, or the conclusion of arguments (p. 60). Clearly the scope of objections is greater than that of counterconsiderations, and the latter only makes up a particular kind of objections—objections against the conclusion. So it seems to me that Hitchcock could never agree that objections are identical with counterconsiderations.

Second, Hitchcock acknowledges that balance-of-considerations arguments may include among their premises counterconsiderations, this means counterconsiderations can function as part of arguments, for example, in pro and con arguments. But what kind of role do they play? I find there is a kind of inconsistency in Hitchcock's theory. On the one hand, it is impossible for counterconsiderations to qualify as premises since premises are, by Hitchcock's definition, claims that support the conclusion, not claims that would oppose the conclusion. On the other hand, when claiming that balance-of-considerations arguments may "include among their premises considerations against the conclusion" (p. 52), he actually takes counterconsiderations as part of the extension of 'premise.' So I think his definition of 'premise' is indisputably contradictory to his actual use of this term. In brief, it remains unclear how Hitchcock understands the status of counterconsiderations in pro and con arguments.

As to the way that positive considerations, counteconsiderations and conclusions are connected, Hitchcock seems to take it for granted that pro and con arguments, as a subtype of balance-of-considerations arguments, share the same structure of balance-of-considerations arguments in general. Now let us look at whether his description of the structure of balance-of-considerations arguments in general is a useful tool for characterizing the structure of pro and con arguments.

First, Hitchcock claims that "we can capture the structure of these so-called *balance-of-considerations arguments* in ordinary English by writing each separate consideration as an argument supporting the conclusion 'other things being equal'..." (p. 51; italics in original). As a subtype of balance-of-considerations arguments, pro and con arguments accommodate not only positive considerations but also counterconsiderations. This fact is apparently inconsistent with Hitchcock's description of the premises of balance-of-considerations arguments which involve positive considerations only. Moreover, it means when we capture the structure of pro and con arguments it is not the case that each consideration can be written as an argument supporting the conclusion "other things being equal." On the contrary, some

---

where a single reason is given for the conclusion. When Govier says that "in a conductive argument, *one or more premises* are put forward as reasons supporting the conclusion" (1999b, p. 155; italics added), she seems to admit the legitimacy of the first pattern of conductive arguments. However, when she claims that "in conductive arguments the support for the conclusion is always convergent" (2010, p. 352), she actually excludes this pattern from her own conception of conductive argument since it is impossible for one premise to provide convergent support for the conclusion.

considerations, that is, counterconsiderations, must be written as independent arguments opposing the conclusion "other things being equal."

Second, Hitchcock argues that each premise in balance-of-considerations arguments provides independently some support for the conclusion. Is this still the case in pro and con arguments? As mentioned above, pro and con arguments involve two conflicting groups of considerations: one is composed of positive considerations, the other counterconsiderations. It is not difficult for us to find out that in pro and con arguments individual considerations can still be independently relevant to the conclusion just within the group to which they belong. So there is not only independent support for the conclusion within the group of positive considerations but also independent objection to the conclusion within the group of counterconsiderations. However, a further question comes up — do two conflicting groups of considerations still relate to each other independently?

Let me probe into this question by considering the simplest type of pro and con arguments. It is such kind of arguments where, except the conclusion, two groups of considerations include only one member respectively. Here is an example [A3] adapted from Wellman (1971, p. 51):

> Because of ① his underlying kindness, I think ② he is still a morally good man, even though ③ he is tactless.

In [A3], are positive consideration ① and negative one ③ independently relevant to the conclusion? Would the relevance of ① (or ③) to the conclusion not be affected if ③ (or ①) were removed, just as in those balance-of-considerations arguments where the premises involve only positive considerations? My answer is "No." By nature pro and con arguments must accommodate both positive and negative considerations; otherwise they will not be pro and con arguments any more. In [A3], if ① were removed, the conclusion could not be drawn from ③ since it is a consideration that would count against the conclusion. If ③ were removed, it seemed that ① could still provide some support for the conclusion, however it would be the case only in another argument — "He is still a morally good man because of his underlying kindness" — which is exactly not a pro and con argument, but belongs to what Wellman calls the first pattern of conductive arguments. In my view, both ① and ③ are needed and indispensable for drawing the conclusion in [A3] as a pro and con argument. To prove likewise, in all pro and con arguments, both groups of considerations, no matter how many individual considerations they may have, are needed and indispensable for drawing the conclusion, even though single considerations can continue to support or oppose the conclusion independently within the group to which they belong.

Finally, Hitchcock believes that in balance-of-considerations arguments all premises operate together to provide stronger support for the conclusion than any single premise could do. To my mind, however, it does not have to be this way in pro and con arguments. Within the group of positive considerations, it is true that the conjunction of all positive considerations provides stronger support for the conclusion than any single positive consideration could do. Within the group of counterconsiderations, however, what the conjunction of all counterconsiderations provides is not stronger support for but stronger objection to the conclusion. When making pro and con arguments, one of the most important things the arguers should know is how much logical force the group of positive considerations has in comparison to the group of counterconsiderations. That is to say, what the arguers concern most is not whether there are "mutually enhancing reasons" or "cumulative support" for the

The Structure of Pro and Con Arguments: A Survey of the Theories

conclusion, but whether "the positive considerations outweigh the negative ones" (p. 51), "whether the factors supporting the conclusion outweigh those opposing it" (p. 130).

From the above analysis and discussion, I think it is clear enough that Hitchcock's description of the structure of balance-of-considerations arguments in general is not fully applicable to pro and con arguments.

Unlike Wellman who does not deal with the issue of how to diagram the structure of pro and con arguments, Hitchcock introduces a method for showing how positive considerations, counterconsiderations and conclusions are connected. The basic idea of his method is that "we can diagram such arguments by introducing each consideration by a plus sign if it is positive and a minus sign if it is negative, and by bracketing the total as supporting the conclusion" (p. 51).

Hitchcock's method can be illustrated by considering an example [A4]:[9]

> ① We should avoid building nuclear power stations. Because ② a meltdown of their core could have catastrophic consequence, and ③ there is no proven solution to the problem of disposing safely of their radioactive wastes. Even though ④ there is no danger of them blowing up, and ⑤ they will not make global warming more serious.

[A4] has five component propositions: ② and ③, introduced by "because", represent two considerations that are put forward as giving independent support to the conclusion; ④ and ⑤, following "even though", represent two considerations that are acknowledged by the arguer as counting independently against the conclusion; ① represents the conclusion which is reached on the basis of the outweighing of ② and ③ against ④ and ⑤; Thus [A4] can be diagrammed as shown in figure 1.0:[10]

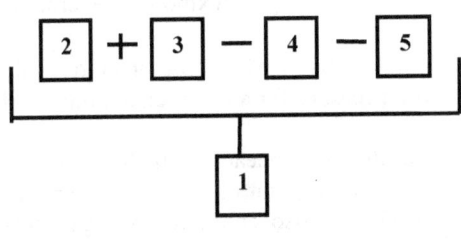

Figure 1.0

It seems to me that this kind of diagram has at least three strengths. First, it shows well that the conclusion is drawn from both positive and negative considerations by indicating them respectively with plus sign or minus sign. Then by bracketing all the considerations this diagram represents well that in order to draw the conclusion all considerations should be thought together. Finally, it displays to some extent that the conclusion is based upon the arguer's weighing positive considerations against counterconsiderations since plus sign and minus sign can also be taken as a metaphor for weighing or balancing. However, Hitchcock's diagram also has some weaknesses. For example, it cannot represent pictorially how single considerations are independently relevant to the conclusion. That is to say, it is un-

---

[9] This example is adapted from Hitchcock (1983, p. 132).
[10] A similar method for diagramming arguments involving counterconsiderations can be found in Scriven (1976, p. 42).

able to picture how ② and ③ provide independent support for the conclusion, nor how ④ and ⑤ count independently against the conclusion.

To conclude, Hitchcock also takes a product-based approach to conceptualizing arguments, and regards premises and conclusions as the basic components of arguments. With regard to the status of counterconsiderations in pro and con arguments, he is clearly self-contradictory when defining 'premise' in terms of positive considerations only on the one hand, and including counterconsiderations into the extension of 'premise' on the other hand. As to the structure of pro and con arguments, his description of the structure of balance-of-considerations arguments in general appears inapplicable to pro and con arguments, even though the latter actually makes up a subtype of the former. Unlike Wellman, Hitchcock introduces a method to diagram how positive considerations, counterconsiderations and conclusions relate to each other. This method has several noticeable disadvantages as well as some notable advantages.

4. Govier on the structure of pro and con arguments

Govier (1980a) first draws attention to the significance for informal logic and argumentation theory of Wellman's idea of conductive arguments. Since then she has made a number of presentations of conductive arguments. Just like Wellman and Hitchcock, she does not use the term 'pro and con argument' either, but she has realized to some extent the connection between this term and what Hitchcock calls balance-of-considerations arguments.[11]

Govier is aware that some arguments actually occur in the form of dialogues, but against the process-based approach to arguments, such as the pragma-dialectics of the Amsterdam school (Eemeren and Grootendorst 1984, 1992) and the related multi-dialogue model of Walton and Krabbe (1995). She stresses that arguments, even those addressed to mass audiences, cannot be usefully reduced to or modeled as dialogues (1999b, pp. 183-201). In her well-received and widely adopted textbook, the term 'argument' is defined as:

> An argument is a set of claims in which one or more of them—the premises—are put forward so as to offer reasons for another claim, the conclusion. (2010, p. 1)

This definition is very close to that one appears in Hitchcock (1983). It reveals that Govier prefers a product rather than a process point of view in conceptualizing arguments. Just as Wellman and Hitchcock do, Govier also conceives of arguments as having a premise-conclusion structure and takes premises and conclusions as the basic components of arguments. She states this point explicitly: "Arguments have two basic parts: premises and conclusions" (2010, p. 20).

With respect to the nature of the relationship of premises and conclusions, Govier lays great attention on the feature of supporting and being supported. For her, an argument is composed of the supporting claims and the supported claim, and premises are the kind of claims that are put forward as providing support for conclusions. In some places, she also explains the nature of this kind of support in terms of relevance. "In a cogent argument, the premises must be positively relevant to the conclusion. That means they must count in fa-

---

[11] According to Govier, "the name balance of consideration arguments has also been used, because often in these arguments factors supporting the conclusion (pro) have to be balanced, or 'weighed' against factors that would count against it (con)" (2010, p. 353). The use of 'often' shows that she does not think that all balance-of-considerations arguments are pro and con arguments.

vor of the conclusion; if true or acceptable, they must provide evidence or reason that the conclusion is true or acceptable" (2010, p. 174).

As pointed above, Wellman identifies three patterns of conductive arguments and the third pattern is identical to pro and con argument. Hitchcock seems to divide balance-of-considerations arguments into two subtypes and the second subtype which includes among premises both positive and negative considerations is the same as pro and con argument. At first glance, Govier does not touch upon the issue of the typology of conductive arguments; however she mentions more than once the so-called "common characteristic" of conductive arguments. For example:

> A common characteristic of conductive argumentation is that the arguer may acknowledge points that actually or apparently count against the conclusion. Such *counter-considerations* are claims negatively relevant to the conclusion.... Counter-considerations may be strongly or weakly acknowledged. To strongly acknowledge a counter-consideration is to allow the claim really is acceptable and really does count against the conclusion. To weakly acknowledge a counter-consideration is to allow merely that others have taken that claim to be acceptable and to count against the conclusion. (1999b, pp. 155-156; italics in original)[12]

Here Govier seems to treat those conductive arguments with above-mentioned common characteristic as the typical conductive arguments, so I think it is justifiable to call conductive argument of this kind "pro and con argument."[13] The passage cited above actually highlights three points. First, Govier uses explicitly the term 'counter-considerations' to call negative considerations or reasons that would count against a conclusion. Second, in contrast to premises that are positively relevant to the conclusion, counterconsiderations are negatively relevant to the conclusion. Third, there are two different ways by which counter-considerations can get involved in conductive argumentation—to be strongly or weakly acknowledged. In my opinion, only arguers' strongly acknowledging counterconsiderations can result in pro and con arguments. To weakly acknowledge counterconsiderations, however, cannot produce pro and con arguments, for the arguers themselves do not admit the truth or acceptability of these considerations, and an argument cannot by definition be a pro and con argument if counterconsiderations fail to enter into the same inferential process with positive considerations.

Now let us look at how Govier understands the focus of counterconsiderations and their status in pro and con arguments.

What is the focus of counterconsiderations or against what material in arguments are counterconsiderations directed? Wellman and Hitchcock do not use the term 'counterconsideration,' but they both believe that counterconsiderations are put forward as being directed against the conclusion of arguments. In the passage cited above Govier indubitably

---

[12] The same point is also mentioned in Govier (2010, p. 114): "Typically, in conductive arguments, we deal with matter on which there are various considerations pros and cons that count for and against the conclusion."

[13] In my view, Govier may agree that not all conductive arguments are pro and con arguments because there actually are those conductive arguments that only involve positive considerations. But Zenker seems to consider both as the same thing, especially when he maintains that "the conductive structure is also known as the pro/contra argument form..." and that "the conductive structure is characterized most markedly by its conclusion being arrived at through *a weighing of pro reasons against counter-considerations*" (Zenker 2010b, p. 3; italics in original).

shares the same view with them—it is only conclusion, not premises or the inference from premises to conclusion that constitutes the focus of counterconsiderations.

Closely related to 'counterconsideration' is the term 'objection' used by logicians to characterize the structure of arguments. Objections seem to be differentiated from counterconsiderations in Govier (1999a, Ch. 13). There she offers a definition of 'objection' and develops in a somewhat systematic way a doctrine of types of objections. She first defines an objection as "any *claim* alleging a defect in the argument or in its conclusion ...," then says that "an objection is an *argument*, a *consideration* put forward, alleged to show either that there is something wrong with the conclusion in question or that there is something wrong with the argument put forward in its favour" (1999b, p. 229; italics added). Although it remains unclear whether an objection is a claim (or a consideration) or an argument, the focus of objections is definitely greater than that of counterconsiderations. According to her typology of objections, there are at least five categories of objections, one of which is objections raised against the conclusion. As far as these accounts are concerned, I think Govier is inclined to believe that objections are not the same as counterconsiderations.

In Govier (2010), however, she offers another sort of accounts of the relation of objections and counterconsiderations. In the section "Counterconsiderations in Other Contexts" of Chapter 12, Govier suggests that "considering *counterconsiderations or objections* is a crucial aspect of evaluating and constructing any argument" (p. 370; italics added), but does not explain what an objection is. At the end of that chapter where she provides some reviews of the terms introduced in that chapter, she answers the question—"What is an objection?"—with "See Counterconsideration," and defines 'counterconsideration' as "a claim that is negatively relevant to the conclusion of an argument" (p. 375). Here, Govier obviously considers objections and counterconsiderations as the same thing and takes the view that both are directed against the conclusions of arguments.[14] It is clearly enough that this view is inconsistent with her own position in Govier (1999a, Ch. 13) that objections are not the same as counterconsiderations and the latter only makes up one of five categories of the former.

As to the focus of counterconsiderations, on page 375 of Govier (2010) she shares the same idea with Govier (1999a, Ch. 13) and views counterconsiderations as claims that are negatively relevant to the conclusion, but on the same page she also expresses a broader understanding of the focus of counterconsiderations:

> The notions of counterconsiderations, objections…apply not only to conductive arguments but also to all the other sorts of arguments discussed in this book. Counterconsiderations are, in effect, objections that may be stated against *any claim* or *argument*. (Italics added)

Here the focus of counterconsiderations has undoubtedly been broadened. According to Govier's analysis in that section, given that a cogent argument must satisfy the ARG conditions, we are told that counterconsiderations can not only be made to the conclusion but also bear on the premises (the A condition) or the inference from the premises to the conclusion (the R and G conditions). This kind of understanding is completely different from

---

[14] It is surprising that besides 'counterconsideration' Govier also gives considerations against the conclusion another name—'counterargument.' She maintains explicitly that "a crucial aspect of evaluating conductive arguments is thinking of *counterarguments*—factors or reasons that would count against the conclusion" (2010, p. 90; italics in original). As cited above, when articulating the same point in Govier (2010, p. 370), the term she uses is 'counterconsideration.'

what Wellman and Hitchcock think of counterconsiderations, and also totally incompatible with her own definition of the term 'counterconsideration' offered in Govier (2010, p. 375).[15] It seems to me that Govier is to a large extent unclear about the focus of counterconsiderations as well as the relation of counterconsiderations and objections.

Now let us fix the meaning of 'counterconsiderations' on claims that are negatively relevant to the conclusion. In pro and con arguments, arguers not only acknowledge the truth or acceptability of counterconsiderations but also include them into the same inferential process with considerations supporting the conclusion. As part of pro and con arguments,[16] what is the status of counterconsiderations? By nature counterconsiderations cannot function as conclusions. Does it mean they can play the role of premises? As we have known, Govier argues that premises must be put forward as being positively relevant to the conclusion, but counterconsiderations are negatively relevant to the conclusion. Therefore "counterconsiderations do *not* stand in the role of premises of an argument" (2010, p. 356; italics in original). We can find a further elaboration on this point in the following passage:

> Counter-considerations are not premises in the argument, because they are not put forward as supporting the conclusion. They are objections to the conclusion, strongly or weakly acknowledged by the arguer. One might think of counter-considerations as *anti-premises*. (1999b, p. 156; italics added)

For Govier, counterconsiderations are neither premises nor conclusions, but any argument has premise and conclusion as its basic components, so clearly counterconsiderations do not belong to the category of basic components of arguments. Do they fall into a category of non-basic components of arguments? As a matter of fact, Govier (2010) does mention some non-basic components of arguments, such as indicator words, but so far I have found no textual evidence that she has talked about counterconsiderations as a kind of non-basic components when addressing the issue of the components of arguments. Anyway Govier's excluding counterconsiderations from premises is undoubtedly compatible with both her own definition of 'premise' and the ordinary meaning of this term.

In the field of informal logic and argumentation theory Govier has probed deeply into the issue of the structure of conductive arguments, but in my view, she has not really touched upon the issue of how positive considerations, counterconsiderations and conclusions relate to each other in pro and con arguments. Since she believes that a common characteristic of conductive arguments is that arguers may acknowledge counterconsiderations and take them into account, it is natural for us to presume that her characterization of the structure of conductive arguments is applicable to pro and con arguments. But is that true?

According to Govier, "in conductive arguments in which there are several premises, those premises support, or are put forward as supporting, the conclusion *convergently*" (1999b, p. 156; italics in original). Put it another way, "in conductive arguments, the support for the conclusion is always convergent" (2010, p. 352).[17] Then what kind of support is convergent?

---

[15] Zenker seems to share the same broader understanding of the focus of counterconsideration when he stresses that "among its premises, conductive arguments feature counterconsiderations *against premises, conclusion or both*" (2010b, p. 1-2; italics added). But he limits the focus of counterconsiderations to the conclusion of arguments in Zenker (2009d).
[16] Govier (1987b, p. 68) comments that "conductive arguments…naturally admit counterconsiderations as part of the argument."
[17] Govier does not think the converse is true. See Govier (1999b, p. 179; 2010, p. 376) for a detailed discussion about this issue.

(It is) a kind of support where premises work together in a cumulative way to support the conclusion, but are not linked. The bearing of one premise on the conclusion would be unaffected if the other premises were removed; however, the argument is strengthened when the premises are considered together, since more evidence is then offered. (2010, p. 55)

It is easy to see that the convergent pattern of support is essentially the same as that of the second pattern of conductive arguments characterized by Wellman or that of balance-of-considerations arguments described by Hitchcock. Analogous to the case of Hitchcock, here I have three reasons to argue that Govier's characterization of the structure of conductive arguments—convergent support—is also an unsuitable tool for capturing the structure of pro and con arguments.

First, the convergent pattern of support cannot accommodate counterconsiderations. According to Govier's definition, convergent support is such kind of support where premises—positive considerations—work in a cumulative way to support the conclusion. This means it is a kind of relationship that exists exclusively between positive considerations and conclusion, so there is no room for counterconsiderations—that are negatively relevant to the conclusion—to get involved in the convergent support.

Second, the independent relevance of considerations to the conclusion cannot be applied to describe the structure of pro and con arguments. Pro and con arguments involve two conflicting groups of considerations. Although individual considerations can still be independently relevant to the conclusion within the group to which they belong, it is not the case that the two groups of considerations themselves are independently relevant to the conclusion. This means that both groups of considerations are necessary and should work together for establishing the basis upon which the conclusion is drawn. If one group of considerations were removed, the arguments would not be pro and con arguments any more.

Third, the convergent pattern of support cannot represent how a conclusion is drawn from both positive and negative considerations. It is true that by means of convergent support positive considerations can provide cumulative support for the conclusion, which is more than any single positive consideration could do. However, in order to reach the conclusion in a pro and con argument, the arguer should not only consider how strongly the group of positive considerations supports the conclusion and how strongly the group of counterconsiderations counts against the conclusion. More importantly, she should consider whether the former outweighs the latter. Clearly this kind of weighing cannot be achieved within the frame of convergent support.

Just like Hitchcock, Govier also introduces a method for diagramming the structure of pro and con arguments. This method is based on how to represent the convergent pattern of support. Let me illustrate the latter first. Here is an example [A5] offered by Govier:

① She never takes her eyes off him in a crowd, and ② she is continually restless when he is out of town. ③ At any opportunity, she will introduce his name in a conversation. And ④ no other man has ever occupied her attention for so long. You can tell ⑤ she is in love with him. (2010, p. 352)

We number the component propositions ①–⑤ respectively. Among them, ①–④ are premises, each of which is separately and positively relevant to the conclusion ⑤. Thus the structure of [A5]—the convergent pattern of support—can be diagrammed as shown in figure 2.0:

The Structure of Pro and Con Arguments: A Survey of the Theories

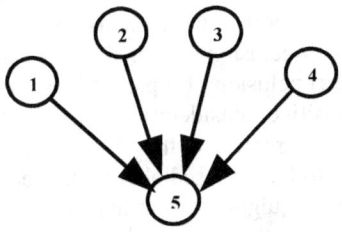

Figure 2.0

Then let me take the following example [A6] to show how Govier diagrams the structure of pro and con arguments.

> I think ① Bill is annoyed, because ② he seems to tense up whenever he sees me and ③ he never invites me for coffee the way he used to. Even though ④ he still says hello and ⑤ we work fairly effectively together, ① he just seems annoyed. (2010, p. 355)

In [A6], proposition ① is the conclusion and stated twice; ② and ③ are considerations that give independent support to ①; ④ and ⑤ represent considerations that would count against ① independently. Different from using straight arrows to display the connection from positive considerations to conclusion, Govier pictures the connection from counter-considerations to conclusion by means of wavy arrows. Thus we can diagram [A6] as shown in figure 3.0:[18]

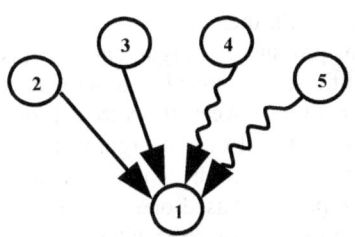

Figure 3.0

Since Govier's method of diagramming pro and con arguments stems from how to represent the convergent pattern of support, to my mind, a significant advantage of this method is, compared to Hitchcock's diagram, that it can represent pictorially how individual considerations are independently relevant to the conclusion. For example, we can easily read out from figure 3.0 that ① and ③ are put forward as providing independent support for ①, ④ and ⑤ are put forward as counting against ① independently. Closely related to this

---

[18] In Thomas (1973, pp. 163-164; 1981, pp. 195-196) he has introduced a similar diagram to show "all the reasons, pro and con, relevant to an option," even though he does not mention the term of 'pro and con argument' or 'conductive argument.' In his diagram, the arrow used to connect a reason against an option to the conclusion is different from Govier's wavy arrow, but a dashed one.

merit, this diagram can also show to some extent how single positive considerations work convergently to give stronger support to the conclusion, and how single counterconsiderations cumulate to oppose the conclusion. As mentioned above, Hitchcock's diagram can show to some degree that the conclusion of a pro and con argument is based upon arguer's weighing or balancing the positive considerations against the counterconsiderations; Govier's method, however, cannot represent this kind of weighing. Furthermore, it often makes readers of the diagram to be confused about whether the conclusion has really been reached, since both straight and squiggly arrows appear at the same time above the conclusion and the diagram itself fails to show explicitly whether the positive considerations outweigh the counterconsiderations.

In short, Govier also theorizes about arguments from a product point of view, and sees premises and conclusions as the basic components of arguments. Govier is to a large extent unclear about the focus and the status of counterconsiderations and the relation between counterconsiderations and objections, but her excluding counterconsiderations from premises is entirely consistent with her own definition of 'premise' and the ordinary meaning of this term. With regard to the structure of pro and con arguments, her idea of convergent support is not fully applicable to characterizing how positive considerations, counterconsiderations and conclusions are connected, even though pro and con arguments are claimed to be typical of conductive arguments. Govier's method of diagramming pro and con arguments has the ability to show how single considerations are independently relevant to the conclusion, but still has some weaknesses in displaying the structure of pro and con arguments accurately and explicitly.

5. Further discussion

From the above analysis and discussion, I think I have shown clearly that some aspects of Wellman's, Hitchcock's and Govier's theorizing about the structure of pro and con arguments are either inconsistent within their respective theories or unsuitable for capturing or diagramming the structure of pro and con arguments. In this section, I will bring forward my own solutions to some of those questions listed in the introduction.

For some time, the distinction between the verbal process and the textual product of arguments has been taken as a useful one in argumentation theory and informal logic,[19] accordingly there have been two different approaches to arguments: one is the process-based approach, the other the product-based one. The former views arguments as dynamic entities in the form of dialogues, whereas the latter sees them as static entities having a premise-conclusion structure. Thus far Blair (1992) and Wohlrapp (1998, 2008a) and others have argued that the nature of conductive arguments or pro and con arguments can be better understood when taking up a dynamic view (in addition to the structural view) or modeling them as a kind of dialogue, Wellman, Hitchcock and Govier among others, however, prefer a structural or product-based approach.[20] Here I also focus on the structure of pro and con arguments from a product point of view.

---

[19] O'Keefe's 'argument$_1$' and 'argument$_2$,' and Habermas's 'argumentation' and 'argument,' among others, have helped to define and characterize this distinction. See O'Keefe (1977) and Habermas (1984, p. 18).
[20] Closely related to the discussion about the structure of conductive arguments, when the linked/convergent distinction concerning argument structure is addressed, the product perspective is also distinguished from the process perspective. Cf. Walton (1995) and Freeman (2001).

5.1 Counterconsiderations and their status in pro and con arguments

Counterconsiderations play a constitutive role in pro and con arguments, but their nature and status in pro and con arguments remain controversial among informal logicians and argumentation theorists. My tentative solution to this issue includes three points:

(1) *A claim is a counterconsideration if and only if it is put forward as being negatively relevant to a conclusion and functions with consideration(s) for the same conclusion in the inferential process which would lead to that conclusion.* From this new definition of 'counterconsideration,' compared to the unclearness and inconsistency of Govier's theory, a clearer understanding of the relation between counterconsiderations and objections or rebuttals (Freeman, 1991) can be achieved. On the one hand, objections or rebuttals are really somewhat similar to counterconsiderations, for one kind of objections or rebuttals would also be raised against the conclusion of an argument. On the other hand, counterconsiderations are actually different from objections or rebuttals in at least three aspects. First, the focus of counterconsiderations is smaller than that of objections or rebuttals since the latter can also be directed against other materials of an argument, such as the inference from premises to conclusion. Second, counterconsiderations function in the illative core of a pro and con argument. That is to say, they, together with positive considerations, play an argument-generating role that would finally lead to the conclusion. Objections or rebuttals, however, function in the dialectic tier of an argument, and the function that they perform is argument-criticizing rather than argument-generating. Finally, counterconsiderations, acknowledged by the arguer and outweighed by positive considerations, would not really weaken the case or undermine the force of a pro and con argument, but by nature objections or rebuttals are put forward to undermine or undercut the force of an argument.

(2) *Counterconsiderations can be designated a role of distinctive non-basic component of arguments if the ordinary usage of "premise" is kept.* In pro and con arguments, counterconsiderations are explicitly acknowledged and taken into account by the arguer, so I strongly disagree with this opinion that counterconsiderations are just background material and "do not constitute some additional category of argumentative element" (Freeman 1991, pp. 173-174). Counterconsiderations do have a role in pro and con arguments, but what is it? Govier argues that counterconsiderations are not premises, and an advantage of this treatment is its according with the sense of 'premise' used in ordinary language and most of logic textbooks. Since premises and conclusions make up the basic components of arguments, counterconsiderations actually do not come into the category of basic components. If we want to keep the ordinary usage of 'premise' when talking about the structure of arguments, I think it is better to designate counterconsiderations a role of distinctive non-basic component. Of course, the appropriate place to mention their status in arguments is, I want to say, not in the specific discussion of the structure of pro and con arguments but the general formulation of the theory of argument structure.

(3) *Counterconsiderations can also play the role of premises in pro and con arguments, provided a stipulative definition of 'premise' is laid down.* Wellman shows us another way to settle the issue being discussed, that is, to include counterconsiderations under a stipulative definition of 'premise.' If we see 'premise' as a technical word used by logicians more than a word used in ordinary language, the word actually has a long history that can go back to Aristotle's word *protasis*. In this tradition, "a premise is that *from which* an argument starts, i.e. that *from which* the conclusion is presented as following" (Hitchcock 2003, p. 71; italics in original). So, either considerations in favor of a conclusion or those against a conclusion can function as that from which an argument starts or that on which one bases her conclusion. By this definition, counterconsiderations can be called "negatively relevant

premises" or "con premises", and premises in ordinary sense, "positively relevant premises" or "pro premises" (Hitchcock 1994). [21]

5.2 The complex structure of pro and con arguments

As to the structure of pro and con arguments, my own view is that pro and con arguments have a complex structure. The structure manifests itself through two different levels, which correspond to the following two basic facts about pro and con arguments: one is that all pro and con arguments involve two conflicting groups of considerations; the other is that each group has one or more considerations. Now let me call the group of positive considerations "PC", the group of counterconsiderations "CC", and the conclusion "K."

Related to the first basic fact, I am inclined to believe there contains a quasi-linked structure at the level of the connection among PC, CC and K. As proved in section 3, in the simplest type of pro and con arguments, a single positive consideration and a single counterconsideration are both needed and indispensable for drawing the conclusion. Analogously, both PC and CC are also indispensable and should work cooperatively in the inferential process which would lead to K. It is this factor that makes me to believe pro and con arguments have a structure among PC, CC and K, which is similar to the linked pattern of support. What distinguish the former from the latter are the different consequences of the removal of premises. In an argument with the linked structure, if one or more premises were removed, no single remaining premise can give any support to the conclusion. In a pro and con argument, however, if PC were removed, it would not be a pro and con argument any longer, and K would not be reached since CC is by nature put forward as opposing K; if CC were removed, it would not be a pro and con argument either, but K could continue to receive support from PC. That is why I call the way in which PC, CC and K are connected with each other "a quasi-linked structure."

Related to the second basic fact, I think there also contains a convergent structure at the level of the relation between the individual members of PC or CC and K. As we know, PC and CC usually include several considerations as their members that are independently relevant to K. Let us recall the example [A6]. There are two positive considerations (② and ③) within PC, and two counterconsiderations (④ and ⑤) within CC. In PC, ② and ③ are put forward as giving independent support to K. If either of them were removed, the relevance to K of the rest would be unaffected. It means that ② and ③ work convergently to support K. In CC, however, ④ and ⑤ are put forward as counting against K independently. If either of them were removed, the relevance to K of the rest would be unaffected too. This means ④ and ⑤ also function convergently in order to oppose K.[22] Unlike Govier and other logicians who consider the convergent structure and the convergent pattern of support as the same thing, here I use the term 'convergent structure' in a broad sense. That is to say, the convergent pattern of objection that exists between the individual members of CC and K also forms part of the extension of this term.

From the above discussion, I think it is justifiable to say that pro and con arguments actually contain two types of structure or a complex structure, which can be approached from two different levels of the relation between argument components. Therefore it seems

---

[21] Zenker (2009d, p. 3) seems to agree this when he claims that "any premise will fall in either of two groups: for or against the conclusion." But he does not mention explicitly the stipulative definition of 'premise.'
[22] Note: The conception of convergent structure will be inapplicable if PC or CC has only one member.

The Structure of Pro and Con Arguments: A Survey of the Theories

to me it is misguided to think that pro and con arguments, as a particular type of conductive arguments, have only one type of structure, such as the convergent structure.[23]

5.3 How to diagram pro and con arguments

Since pro and con arguments contain more than one type of structure, a good method to diagram them must be capable to show well this kind of complexity. As argued above, Hitchcock's method fails to represent how single considerations are independently relevant to the conclusion, so I would like to take Govier's method as the foundation of my further discussion. But there are still two significant weaknesses in her method: First, it is unable to display the quasi-linked structure among PC, CC and K; even though it can picture how individual members of PC or CC are independently relevant to K. Second, both straight and squiggly arrows—indicating the negative relevance of members of CC to K—appear at the same time above K, and the diagram itself fails to show explicitly whether PC outweighs CC, so it often makes readers to be confused about whether K has really been reached.

Now let me make some revisions to Govier's method so that those two disadvantages can be removed. When talking about how the conclusion of a pro and con argument can be reached, both Wellman and Hitchcock have mentioned that the basis on which the conclusion is drawn is the outweighing of PC against CC. Govier provides us with more details about this point:

> If we deem a conductive argument *cogent*, we commit ourselves to the judgment that the reasons in the premises, considered together, provide good reasons for the conclusion—even in the light of counterconsiderations constituting reasons against that conclusion. That is, we commit ourselves to the judgment that, on balance, the pros *outweigh* the cons, and do so to a sufficient degree that there are good grounds for the conclusion. (1999b, p. 170; italics in original)[24]

This means that we are led to K not only by considering the cumulative support of PC for K and the cumulative objection of CC to K, but also by the judgment that the cumulative support of PC for K outweighs the cumulative objection of CC to K. I think we should take this judgment as a consideration that is indispensable for drawing K in pro and con arguments, and give it a name "on-balance consideration" (OBC).

Both Zenker (2009a) and Hansen (2010b) call this judgment "on-balance premise" and claim that it should be written into the standard form of pro and con arguments. It seems to them that the OBC functions as a premise or a missing premise. To my mind, the OBC is not that from which a pro and con argument starts or that on which one bases her conclusion, hence it is not a premise or a missing premise. The OBC functions in effect at a meta level of pro and con arguments. What I mean here by a "meta level" is that it works in a similar way that Toulmin's warrant does: it is not a part of argument, but licenses or permits the inferring from premises to conclusion. So the role that the OBC plays is to justify the step from both PC and CC to K. Only under the condition that PC outweighs CC—this is what the OBC expresses—can K be reached from PC and CC.

---

[23] I agree with Goddu (2007) that the terms 'linked,' 'convergent,' etc., are better used to modify 'structure' rather than 'argument.' It means that an argument can contain more than one type of structure.

[24] In Govier (2010, pp. 355-356) she also says that "If an arguer explicitly acknowledges counterconsiderations but nevertheless still claims that her conclusion is supported by positively relevant premises, she is judging that her positively relevant premises outweigh the counterconsiderations."

Generally speaking, when picturing the structure of an argument, we need not display in the diagram the warrant used by the arguer, since it is not a premise, even a missing premise. But the OBC seems to be an exception. As I will indicate soon, picturing the OBC in the diagram of pro and con arguments can help us to overcome those two weaknesses of Govier's method mentioned above.

As to how to represent the OBC or the outweighing of PC against CC, I think we can follow the example of how Hitchcock diagrams objections (1983, p. 60). Let us look at figure 4.0:

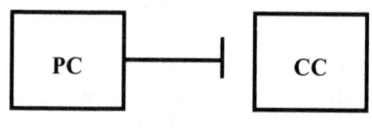

Figure 4.0

This figure shows how the OBC of pro and con arguments is generally diagrammed as PC "shunting aside" CC. If we integrate this figure into Govier's diagram, the structure of pro and con arguments can be fully and clearly displayed. Let me use again [A6] analyzed in section 4 as an example. First, we standardize and rewrite [A6] as follows:

    K: ① Bill is annoyed.
    PC: ②Bill seems to tense up whenever he sees me.
         ③ Bill never invites me for coffee the way he used to
    CC: ④ Bill still says hello.
         ⑤ We work fairly effectively together.

So far [A6] can be diagrammed as shown in figure 3.0 by means of Govier's method. Then we make its implicit OBC explicit and articulate it as follows:

    OBC: PC (② and ③ taken together) outweighs CC (④ and ⑤taken together).

The OBC of [A6] can be diagrammed as shown in figure 4.0. Now we integrate figure 4.0 into figure 3.0, remove "PC" and "CC" written in the former, and let two quadrilaterals to enclose respectively all the members of PC and CC. Thus the structure of [A6] is fully shown in figure 5.0:

The Structure of Pro and Con Arguments: A Survey of the Theories 29

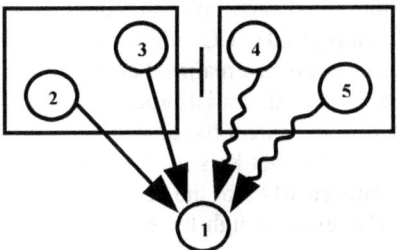

Figure 5.0

This figure pictures clearly that there are two considerations (② and ③) supporting independently the conclusion ①, and two considerations (④ and ⑤) opposing ① independently. Even ④ and ⑤ are acknowledged by the arguer, ① is still supported by ② and ③ because their cumulative support outweighs the cumulative objection of ④ and ⑤.

As mentioned above, PC or CC may include only one member, thus there will be no convergent structure between PC (or CC) and K. These kinds of possibilities can be diagrammed as shown in the following figures. For instance, figure 6.0 represents the simplest type of pro and con arguments such as [A3] analyzed in section 3. Since arguments of this type involve only one positive consideration ① for the conclusion ② and one counterconsideration ③ against ②, clearly there is no need to use quadrilaterals to enclose respectively ① and ③. So the outweighing of PC against CC can be directly diagrammed as ① "shunting aside" ③.

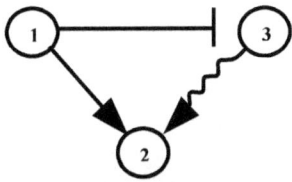

Figure 6.0

Figure 7.0 tells us that this pro and con argument includes two positive consideration (② and ③) supporting the conclusion ① independently and one counterconsideration ④ that would count against ①, so we need a quadrilateral to enclose ② and ③. Then the outweighing of PC against CC can be diagrammed as ② and ③, taken together, "shunting aside" ④.

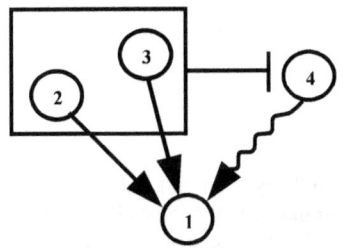

Figure 7.0

By picturing the OBC into the diagramm of pro and con arguments, those figures have an additional part—PC "shunting aside" CC—than Govier's diagrams. In my opinion, it is with the help of this part that readers can realize that both PC and CC are indispensable and actually work cooperatively in the inferential process which would lead to K. This means these diagrams can display to some extent the quasi-linked structure among PC, CC and K. Moreover, they can show explicitly that K is reached from PC and CC since the part of PC "shunting aside" CC represents clearly that the cumulate support provide by PC outweighs the cumulate objection of CC, even though there are still two conflicting kinds of arrows above K.

6. Conclusion

What I have tried to do in this paper is to subject the existing discussions of the structure of pro and con arguments found in Wellman (1971), Hitchcock (1983) and Govier (1999b, 2010) to careful scrutiny. Although these theoreticians have contributed a lot to capturing the structure of pro and con arguments, undeniably there are some significant weaknesses in their respective theories. In this paper I argue that counterconsiderations should be differentiated from objections or rebuttals, and that pro and con arguments actually have a more complex structure than the convergent structure, and also introduce a new method to diagram the structure of pro and con arguments. If this paper achieves nothing else, I hope it raises the issue of the need to rethink the existing theories of conductive arguments in general and pro and con arguments in particular.[25]

---

[25] I am particularly indebted to J. Anthony Blair and Ralph H. Johnson for critical comments on earlier drafts of the paper. And I would like to thank James B. Freeman, Trudy Govier, David Hitchcock and Robert C. Pinto for their insightful comments and suggestions. The paper has been significantly improved as a result of the feedback from each of these individuals.

Chapter 3

Notes on Balance-of-Considerations Arguments

H.V. HANSEN

1. Introduction

Each of the following sections of this chapter is a short essay about some aspect of balance-of-considerations arguments (third-pattern conductive arguments). Section 2 recovers a passage from an eighteenth century text that identifies a kind of argument very similar to conductive arguments. Section 3 attempts to give a proof that every reason for the conclusion in a conductive argument is negatively relevant to every counter-consideration and vice-versa. The fourth and fifth sections are concerned to understand the structure of conductive arguments as they might be pictured in an argument diagram. Section 4 considers the place of counter-considerations and Section 5 takes up problems related to on-balance premises. Section 6 is a study of the "even-though" relation that is a distinctive feature of conductive arguments and Section 7 is an attempt to understand the application of the "Notwithstanding Clause" of the Canadian Charter of Rights as an instance of conductive arguments.

2. Campbell on moral arguments

In *An Essay Concerning Human Understanding*, David Hume famously distinguished two kinds of reasoning, that which is about relations of ideas and that which is about matters of fact and existence (Hume 1748, sec. iv, pt 2). His examples of reasoning involving relations of ideas were the Pythagorean theorem and mathematical statements. In contrast, reasoning about propositions like "the sun will rise tomorrow" or "your friend is out of the country" were his examples of reasoning about matters of fact. Hume termed reasoning about relations of ideas *demonstrative reasoning*, and that concerning matters of fact *moral reasoning*. We shouldn't confuse *our* meaning of 'moral reasoning' (which is pretty-well equivalent to 'reasoning about moral issues') with the eighteenth century's meaning of 'moral reasoning'. Stroud explains how Hume means the term 'moral' in this context.

> 'Moral' philosophy, in Hume's sense, is to be contrasted with 'natural' philosophy, which deals with objects and phenomena in the world of nature. Natural philosophy is roughly the same as what is now called physics, chemistry and biology. Of course, men are objects of nature too, and are therefore part of the subject-matter of natural philosophy. ... Moral philosophy differs from natural philosophy only in the *way* it deals with human beings—it considers only those respects in which they differ from other 'objects of nature'. Men think, act, feel, perceive and speak, so 'moral subjects' deal with human thought, action, feelings, perception and language. (Stroud 1977, p. 2)

Moral reasoning, then, takes as its subject matter human nature, not physical nature. But not only is human nature the object of moral reasoning, it is also a defining factor in moral reasoning since, as Hume argued, moral reasoning ultimately rests on habits and customs, a foundation made by human nature.

When in 1776 James Boswell went to visit the dying David Hume, he found him with his countryman George Campbell's newly published *The Philosophy of Rhetoric* before him (Walzer 2003, p. 12). Campbell shared Hume's distinction between demonstrative and moral reasoning, sometimes expressing it as a distinction between deductive and moral evidence. He found four points of contrast between these two kinds of evidence or reasoning. The first pertained to subject matter: deductive (or demonstrative) evidence concerns "invariable properties or relations of general ideas" whereas moral evidence is about the "variable connexions subsisting among things," a distinction we might well recast as one between what is knowable *a priori* and *a posteriori*. The second difference concerned the comparative strength of the two kinds of evidence. Demonstration does not admit of degrees of proof: "it is either mere illusion . . . or absolutely perfect" according to Campbell (1776, p. 44); however, moral evidence, although it is never conclusive, does admit of degrees of proof. These two points of difference between demonstrative and moral reasoning are familiar to us from Hume's first *Enquiry*, but the next two points that Campbell adds go beyond the basic distinction that characterizes Hume's fork.

A third difference between demonstrative and moral reasoning that Campbell observed has to do with the fact that moral reasoning—unlike demonstrative reasoning—may have multiple grounds. Demonstrative reasoning is such that a single proof is sufficient to establish a proposition and further proofs, although they may be interesting, add nothing to the strength of the first proof. Demonstrative reasoning, therefore, consists of a single line of argument whereas moral reasoning tends to consist in what Campbell called "a bundle of independent proofs."

> In moral reasoning . . . there is often a combination of many distinct topics of argument, no way dependent on one another. Each has a certain portion of evidence belonging to itself, each bestows on the conclusion a particular degree of likelihood, of all which accumulated the credibility of the fact is compounded. The former [demonstrative reasoning] may be compared to an arch, no part of which can subsist independently of the rest. If you make any breach in it, you destroy the whole. The latter [moral reasoning] may be compared to a tower, the height whereof is but the aggregate of the heights of the several parts reared above one another, and so may be gradually diminished, as it was gradually raised. (Campbell 1776, pp. 45-46)

Reasoning consisting in a "combination of distinct topics" that are in "no way dependent on one another" describes what we have come to call convergent reasoning or convergent argumentation.[2] A number of different reasons *converge* on a conclusion. This kind of reasoning can be weakened or strengthened by the subtraction or addition of more lines of argument "each belonging to itself"; that is, lines of argument which are independent of the other lines of argument. Campbell wants to emphasize that this kind reasoning is unlike demonstrative reasoning and he illustrates the distinction by comparing demonstrative and moral reasoning, respectively, to an arch and a tower. These are appropriate similes for linked and convergent arguments as well. Linked arguments are those whose premises depend on each other as do the stones in an arch; convergent arguments are those whose strength can be increased or diminished by adding or taking away premises just as towers are heightened and lowered by adding stones or taking them away.

The fourth difference between demonstrative and moral reasoning that Campbell

---

[2] By a *convergent argument*, I mean an argument whose premise set may be divided into two or more proper subsets each of which is meant to offer support for the conclusion independently of the other proper subsets.

identified concerns the observation that unlike demonstrative reasoning, moral reasoning includes the consideration of contrary evidence:

> There are contrary experiences, contrary presumptions, contrary testimonies to balance against one another. In this case [moral reasoning], the probability, upon the whole, is in the proportion which the evidence on the side that preponderates bears to its opposite. We usually say, indeed, that the evidence lies on such a side of the question, and not on the reverse; but by this expression is only meant the overplus of evidence, on comparing both sides. In like manner ... we do not scruple to say ... This is more probable than that; or, The probabilities on one side outweigh those on the other. (Campbell 1776, p. 45)

This is in contrast with demonstrative reasoning in which there cannot be proofs both for and against a conclusion—if there were, one of the two proofs would be "fallacious and sophistical." Hence, Campbell saw it as characteristic of moral reasoning that with few exceptions "there is always real, not apparent evidence on both sides" and he thought that such moral reasonings were to be decided by weighing the probability of the evidence on each side of the question. In summary, Campbell distinguishes demonstrative and moral reasoning in four ways: by subject matter, by argument strength, by the possibility of multiple independent reasons for the conclusion, and by the existence of reasons opposed to the conclusion.

3. Balance-of-considerations arguments

In 1971 Carl Wellman. introduced 'conductive argument' as a technical term for three patterns of argument that were neither deductive nor inductive (1971, Ch. 3). The third of these patterns has the same characteristics as what I mean by balance-of-considerations arguments. In such arguments the reasoning, before issuing in a conclusion, takes into account considerations against the conclusion in addition to the reasons or considerations supporting the conclusion. These are *counter-reasons* but, following Govier, we will call them *counter-considerations*.

> A common characteristic of conductive argumentation is that the arguer may acknowledge points that actually or apparently count against the conclusion. Such counter-considerations are claims negatively relevant to the conclusion. ... Counter-considerations may be strongly or weakly acknowledged. To strongly acknowledge a counter-consideration is to allow that the claim really is acceptable and really does count against the conclusion. To weakly acknowledge a counter-consideration is to allow merely that others have taken that claim to be acceptable and to count against the conclusion. (Govier 1999, pp. 155-156)

The distinction Govier has introduced here between strongly and weakly acknowledged counter-considerations can be made as a distinction between two kinds of third-pattern conductive arguments: those in which the counter-considerations are treated only as appearing to be reasons against the conclusion but not taken into account in the reasoning, and those third-pattern conductive arguments that admit the counter-considerations as being negatively relevant to their conclusions and do take them into account in the reasoning. The former we may call weak third-pattern conductive arguments and the latter strong third-pattern conductive arguments. It is with the strong version of third-pattern conductive argument that I am especially concerned in the rest of this essay. From now on, I will call this kind of a conductive argument, a *balance-of-considerations argument*, or, a *BC-argument*.

In BC-arguments the counter-considerations are negatively relevant to the conclusion. One proposition is negatively relevant to another if the truth of the one is evidence that the other one is false. If there is more than one counter-consideration, we may suppose that each of them is independent of the others, just as the premises in convergent arguments are independent of each other. If that is the case, then each counter-consideration should be negatively relevant to each sub-argument for the conclusion. On the assumptions that contraposition, obversion and transitivity (for at least a limited number of steps) hold for propositional relevance, it should be the case *that every reason in support of the conclusion is negatively relevant to every counter-consideration, and vice versa.* This can be shown as follows.

Let '+$R(p, q)$' mean "p is positively relevant to q," and '–$R(p, q)$' mean "p is negatively relevant to q." Assume the following principles:

+$R(p, q) \equiv$ +$R(\text{not-}q, \text{not-}p)$ (Relevance contraposition)
+$R(p, q) \equiv$ –$R(p, \text{not-}q)$ (Relevance obversion)
+$R(p, q)$ & +$R(q, r) \rightarrow$ +$R(p, r)$ (Relevance transitivity)

Suppose a BC-argument with one or more independent premises of which we arbitrarily select P, and with one or more counter-consideration of which we arbitrarily pick C. Let the conclusion of the argument be K. Then, to prove that P is negatively relevant to C and C is negatively relevant to P, proceed as follows:

1. +$R(P, K)$ assumption
2. –$R(C, K)$ assumption
3. +$R(C, \text{not-}K)$ 2, obversion
4. +$R(\text{not-not-}K, \text{not-}C)$ 3, contraposition
5. +$R(K, \text{not-}C)$ 4, double negation
6. +$R(P, \text{not-}C)$ 1, 5, transitivity
7. –$R(P, C)$ 6, obversion
8. +$R(\text{not-}K, \text{not-}P)$ 1, contrasposition
9. +$R(C, \text{not-}P)$ 3, 8 transitivity
10. –$R(C, P)$ 9, obversion
11. –$R(P, C)$ & –$R(C, P)$ 7, 10, conjunction
12. –$R(P \equiv C)$ 11, Df '≡'

Since P and C are arbitrary, every premise is negatively relevant to every counter-consideration and every counter-consideration is negatively relevant to every premise. QED.[3] Moreover, on the assumption that if P and Q are independently negatively relevant to C, then the conjunction of P & Q will jointly be negatively relevant to C, it will follow that the set of all the premises of a BC-argument, (or any independent subset of them) will be negatively relevant to each counter-consideration, and vice versa. Moreover, by parity of

---

[3] The Achilles heel of this argument might lie in the problem that relevance doesn't hold for contraposition, as observed by R.C. Pinto in a personal communication to me.

reasoning, we may conclude that the conjunction of the counter-considerations, or any subset of them is negatively relevant to each of the premises. And then, assuming that if P is negatively relevant to C and also to counter-consideration D, then P is negatively relevant to C & D, we may reach the conclusion that the set of premises in a BC-argument is negatively relevant to the complete set of the argument's counter-considerations.

Because none of the evidential relationships in BC-arguments is necessary, the truth of the premises necessitates neither the truth of the conclusion nor the falsity of the counter-considerations. In fact, the set of counter-considerations in a BC-argument must be consistent with the set of its premises; that is, it must be possible for all the premises and all the counter-considerations to be true at the same time. This is a defining characteristic of BC-arguments.

4. The place of counter-considerations

BC-arguments diverge from the general conception of argument in two crucial ways. The one is that they allow that there can be multiple independent reasons in support of a conclusion. Independent reasons are complete reasons and so if we are wont to individuate arguments on the basis of one-reason per argument, then BC-arguments will appear to be cumbersome unnatural logical kinds. This may give us cause to think that convergent arguments should be separated into several arguments and each separately evaluated. However, this is something that both Wellman and Govier oppose since what the strength of a convergent argument depends on is the accumulated force of the several independent reasons taken together (Wellman 1971, p. 57; Govier 2005, pp. 394-395). Thus, if we cut up convergent arguments into n non-convergent arguments on the basis that there are n independent reasons for the conclusion, we would just have to combine the n arguments again when we wanted to evaluate the convergent argument.

The other way in which BC-arguments differ from the traditional conception has to do with the role of counter-considerations. It is unclear how they can be parts of arguments. Let us consider some possibilities.

Possibility 1. Counter-considerations are premises. The first proposal to consider is that a BC-argument is one that *includes* both reasons for the conclusion and reasons against the conclusion. There is a concept of argument that can accommodate both reasons for and

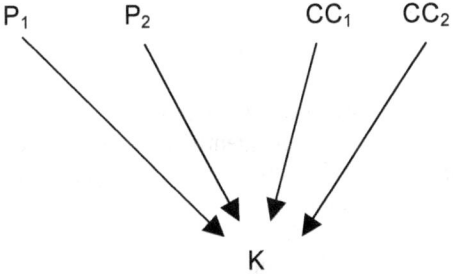

Diagram 1

against a conclusion. It is that of a *social argument*, a debate or a discussion, in which there are two disagreeing parties advancing their own positions and arguing *against* each other. Here, unless the argument is especially degenerate, there will be reasons both for and against a conclusion. But that is not the kind of argument Wellman and Govier have in mind. When they propose BC-arguments as an alternative to deductive and inductive arguments, they mean that they are the premise-conclusion kind of argument, typically defined as a set of claims (or propositions) of which one is the conclusion and the remainder are put forward as reasons in support of the conclusion. In this kind of argument a person argues *for* something but not necessarily *with* or *against* someone, and anything that is negatively relevant to the conclusion could not function as a premise. Govier in fact says that "One might think of counter-considerations as anti-premises" in a reasons-for kind of argument (Govier 1999, p. 156) and further elaborates the point in her textbook, saying that "Counter-considerations are not premises of an argument because they are not put forward by the arguer as supporting the conclusion" (2005, p. 397). Hence, we must seek some other way to understand the role of counter-considerations in order to find their place in BC-arguments.

Possibility 2. Counter-considerations are background knowledge. If the counter-considerations are not premises of BC-arguments, then perhaps they are background knowledge. All nonconclusive arguments are to be understood and appreciated against a background tapestry of unstated knowledge and assumptions (see Diagram 2). But since counter-considerations are explicitly identified and taken into account in the reasoning, relegating them to a background role fails to allow for their impact in BC-reasoning. Counter-considerations are not just latently present but explicitly acknowledged; hence, the idea that they are merely background beliefs or assumptions misrepresents their role in BC-arguments.

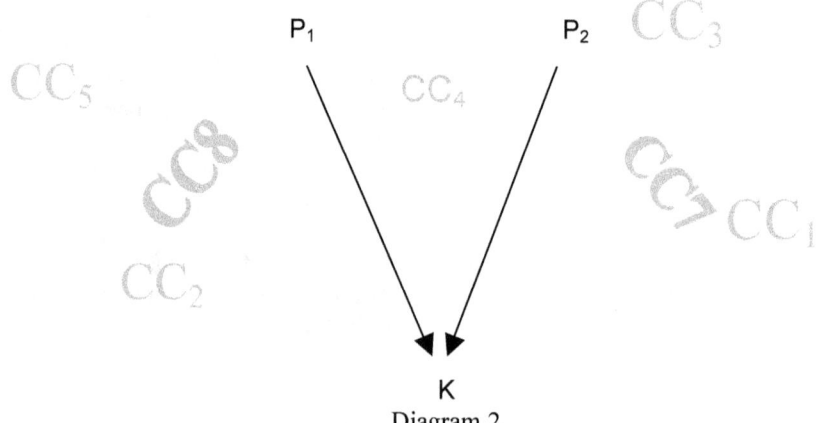

Diagram 2

Possibility 3. Counter-considerations are parts of arguments as expressions of reservation about the conclusion. Govier identifies a number of linguistic indicators associated with BC-arguments, words like 'though,' 'although,' 'even though,' 'despite the fact that,' 'notwithstanding the fact that,' which serve to introduce counter-considerations (2005, p. 397). (These will be examined in more detail in Section 6.) Perhaps the counter-considerations can be included in BC-arguments by using one of these conjunctive operators as shown in the following argument:

[A1]
Premise 1: Taking the plane to Chicago is faster than taking the train.
Premise 2: We can depart nearly any time of day (there are so many flights).
Conclusion: We should take a plane to Chicago *even though* taking the train is (a) cheaper and (b) more comfortable.

Notes on Balance-of-Considerations Arguments

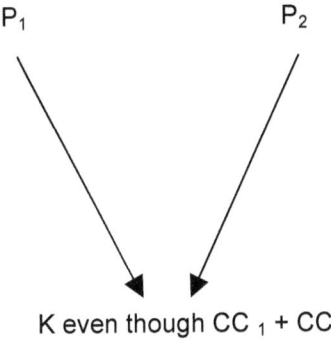

Diagram 3

This way of considering BC-arguments overcomes the difficulties with the previous two suggestions, but even so, it cannot be the right structure of BC-reasoning (see Diagram 3). First, in BC-arguments we reason *from* the premises and counter-considerations taken together, not *towards* the counter-considerations as is the case in [A1]. So, neither the counter-considerations nor their significance in relation to the reasons for the conclusion are inferred *from* the premises as they appear to be in [A1]. Second, 'even though' (and the other linguistic operators serving the same function) are conjunctive operators, so sentences of the form "*p* even though *q*" imply, by simplification, "*p*" and "*q*." This means that the conclusion in [A1] is really a conjunction that can be broken down into two distinct propositions, (i) "we should take a plane to Chicago," and (ii) "taking the train to Chicago is cheaper than taking the plane to Chicago, and taking the train to Chicago is more comfortable than taking the plane to Chicago" (and this second conjunct itself divides into two more conjuncts). But the two premises of [A1] do not lend support to the second conjunct in the conclusion, and this makes [A1] a very bad argument, much worse than we think it should have turned out.

Diagram 4

Possibility 4. Counter-considerations are the premises of a counter-argument. It is suggested by the term 'anti-premise' that a BC-argument really consists of two arguments, one whose premises are reasons for the conclusion, K, and another which employs the counter-considerations as premises for the conclusion, not-K (see Diagram 4). But to have two opposing arguments is not to have a single argument with one conclusion, which is what a BC-argument is. The present proposal might well amount to what is called *collective defeat*, "where we have a set of two or more arguments and each argument in the set is defeated by some other argument in the set" (Pollock 2006, p. 455). Each argument cancels out the other. Perhaps BC-reasoning has its genesis in the recognition of the existence of opposed arguments; however, it moves beyond mere recognition of the opposition, deciding, if possible, which of the two sets of considerations to favour. Therefore, there must be something in the argument that gives expression to the view that the disagreement presented by the two opposing arguments has been overcome.

Possibility 5. Govier (2005, p. 396) pictures BC-arguments by using straight arrows from the supporting premises to the conclusion and squiggly arrows from the counter-considerations to the conclusion (see Diagram 5). Such diagrams make it clear that the premises are independent and also that the counter-considerations are independent as well. We can tell from the quality of the conclusion (it is positive) that the premises have been taken to outweigh the counter-considerations. If the quality of the conclusion was changed (from positive to negative) we should read the diagram as conveying the information that the counter-considerations had outweighed the premises (we might then consider the counter-considerations to be the premises and the premises to be the counter-considerations). In diagramming arguments we give a pictorial representation of their standard form and, as Govier remarks (2005, p. 26), "standardization ... helps to indicate how the author reasoned from the premises to the conclusion." However, the proposed kind of diagram (with squiggly lines, etc.) does not show the reasoning that is unique to BC-arguments because that the premises have been judged to *outweigh the counter-considerations* is left implicit in this way of picturing BC-arguments.

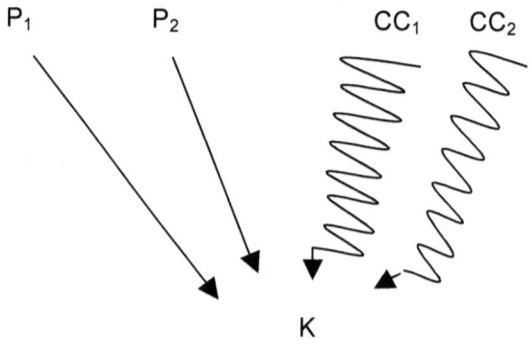

Diagram 5

Possibility 6. Counter-considerations are claimed to be outweighed in an on-balance premise. Wellman remarked that it is the reasoning leading to the judgment that makes BC-reasoning unique, and Govier, commenting on the way BC-arguments are diagrammed, writes:

> A person who explicitly acknowledges counter-considerations and nevertheless still claims that her conclusion is supported by positively relevant premises is committed to the judgment that the positively relevant premises outweigh the counter-considerations. (Govier 2005, p. 397)

In light of this, let us consider again how we might describe BC-reasoning in general terms. We are led to a conclusion by considering each of the independent supporting reasons and their amassed force, and by the judgment that taken together those reasons outweigh the counter-considerations taken together. If we make that judgment part of the reasoning, then the BC-argument we are considering could have this structure:

[A2]
Premise 1: Taking an airplane to Chicago is faster than taking the train.
Premise 2: Unlike the trains, flights leave for Chicago several times a day, making flying more convenient.
Premise 3: The reasons given in premises 1 and 2 *outweigh* the counter-considerations that (i) taking the train is cheaper, and (ii) more comfortable.
Conclusion 1: Hence, we should take an airplane to Chicago *even though* (i) taking the train is cheaper, and (ii) more comfortable.

What we have here is an argument that goes from the observation that one set of considerations outweighs a second set—the counter-considerations—to the conclusion that some claim is reasonable even though the counter-considerations are true, or acceptable. It is an inference from *p outweighs q* to *p even though q*. For convenience let us call the third premise in this argument the "on-balance premises." I am suggesting that all BC-arguments may be viewed as having such an implicit on-balance premise. But there will be more to the argument than shown so far; a second inference must follow, namely that

Premise: We should take an airplane to Chicago *even though* (i) taking the train is cheaper, and (ii) more comfortable.
Conclusion: Hence, we should take an airplane to Chicago.

This second part of the argument is a matter of simplification from a sentence of the form '*p even though q*' to '*p*', an inference that is truth-functionally valid. The general schema for BC-arguments would then look something like this (with 'CC' abbreviating 'counter-consideration'):

[S]
P_1: Independent reason$_1$ (for conclusion K)
. . . .
P_n: Independent reason$_n$ (for conclusion K)
P_{n+1}: The reasons in P_1 to P_n taken together *outweigh* the independent counterconsiderations to K, CC_1 to CC_n taken together (value judgment)
Conclusion: K even though CC_1 & . . .& CC_n (inference to 'even though')

Premise: K even though CC_1 &. . . & CCn
Conclusion: K (simplification)

This way of structuring BC-arguments overcomes the shortcomings of the other possibilities we looked at. (i) The counter-considerations are not presented as parts of the argument for the conclusion but they still find their way into the argument as subject of the on-balance premise; (ii) they are not mixed in with other background knowledge, but neither are they stated on their own as premises; (iii) they are not given the role of qualifying the conclusion, yet they have a place that shows they are relevant to the conclusion; (iv) although they are not placed in the role of being premises in a counter-argument, they are recognized as being negatively relevant to the conclusion; and (v) the counter-considerations are not just stated without resolution along with the reasons for the conclusion. The inclusion of the implicit on-balance premise acknowledges the weighing of premises and counter-considerations as an essential part of BC-arguments.

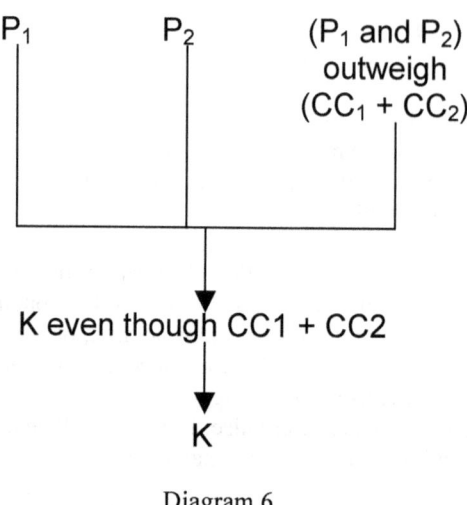

Diagram 6

Overview of the Hypotheses

	Hypothesis	Response
1	Counter-considerations are premises.	No. Only statements that are positively relevant to the conclusion can be premises of an argument.
2	Counter-considerations are background knowledge.	No. They are mentioned and considered in the argument.
3	Counter-considerations are qualifications about the conclusion.	No. It is the reasoning for the conclusion, not the conclusion, that is qualified.
4	Counter-considerations are the anti-premises of a counter-argument.	No. A BC-argument is one argument, not two.
5	Counter-considerations and premises are both relevant to the conclusion.	Yes. But there is more to a BC-argument than identifying reasons for and against the conclusion.
6	Counter-considerations are said to be outweighed in an on-balance premise.	OK. But this means giving up the thesis that BC-arguments have convergent premises.

5. Problems related to the on-balance premises

This inclusion of the on-balance premise in the structure of BC-arguments is not occasioned by the need to include *all* relevant background information or *every* assumption made for the argument, nor is it included because of a desire to make deductive arguments out of non-deductive arguments. The reasons for its inclusion is that identifying a set of opposing considerations without indicating that they have been weighed against each other and a judgment made about their relative strengths, amounts to no more than indicating that there are two sets of reasons each supporting an opposite conclusion. The presence of the on-balance premise is needed to allow the reasoning to go forward to the even-though conclusion, an intermediate step *en route* to the final conclusion. However, viewing the structure of balance-of-considerations arguments as having an on-balance premise raises a number of problems, two of which I will briefly discuss here.

Problem 1: Since it makes reference to all the other premises in the argument, the on-balance premise is not independent of those other premises—if those premises were not there the on-balance premise would have no referents. Thus, the on-balance premise is dependent on the other premises. If that is so, then BC-arguments are not convergent arguments with independent premises, but rather arguments with linked, dependent premises. This result is at odds with how Wellman and Govier characterize BC-arguments. Is it then the case, that if their premises are linked, BC-arguments give conclusive, non-defeasible support to their conclusions? The answer is No. Although having linked premises is a necessary condition for two-or-more-premise valid arguments, it is not a sufficient condition. There are arguments with linked, dependent premises, that are defeasible (non-conclusive) arguments, inductive syllogisms being the most obvious example.

> Most married women are mothers.
> Ms. Woolf was a married woman.
> So, Ms. Woolf was a mother.

The premises depend on each other, but the reasoning is defeasible as we find out when we are told that Ms. Woolf's first name was Virginia.

What kinds of new information would give us reason to change our evaluation of a BC-argument? The argument might be made *stronger* either (i) by the addition of more premises supporting the conclusion or (ii) by finding information that would undercut one or more of the counter-considerations. In the first case we add the premise to the argument and rewrite the on-balance premise to make reference to the new premise; in the second case we just re-write the on-balance premise leaving out the dismissed counter-consideration. A BC-argument would be made *weaker* either (iii) by the discovery of undercutting defeaters for one or more of the supporting premises or (iv) by additional counter-considerations (rebutting defeaters) coming to light. Taking account of such possible changes involves either withdrawing the defeated premise from the argument and then removing reference to it in the on-balance premise or adding the new counter-consideration to the on-balance premise. Anyone of these four changes to a BC-argument would lead to a change in the strength the premises provide in support of the conclusion. Suppose, for illustration, that we chance upon new information, namely, that our friends are taking the train to Chicago, that baggage at the Chicago airport often gets lost, and that the security checks for passengers at our local airport are becoming increasingly invasive. We incorporate these new counter-considerations into the argument [A2] as follows:

[A3]
Premise 1: Taking the plane to Chicago is faster than taking the train.
Premise 2: Flights leave for Chicago several times a day.
Premise 3: The evidence presented in premises 1 and 2 is outweighed by the counter-considerations (i) that taking the train is cheaper, (ii) that it is more comfortable, (iii)

that our friends will be on the train, (iv) that luggage often gets lost at the Chicago airport, and (v) that the security inspections at our local airport are becoming too invasive.

Conclusion 1: We should take the train to Chicago even though taking a plane would be faster and flights depart several times a day.

Conclusion 2: We should take the train to Chicago.

Thus, the introduction of balance-of-consideration premises does not change the defeasible character of BC-arguments. (When the balance of considerations changes it would be natural to redesignate the components of the argument.)

Problem 2: It has been suggested (Possin 2010) that the introduction of the on-balance premise starts an infinite regress of premise add-ons as was envisioned in Lewis Carroll's famous essay, "What the Tortoise said to Achilles" (1894). This objection does have some plausibility since on-balance premises, like the premises the tortoise in its conversation with Achilles kept on demanding should be included, are linked to the other pre-existing premises. Hence what the tortoise in effect wanted was another inference rule, but I don't think on-balance premises, although they fill in the gaps in inferences in BC-arguments, are inference rules. This is because they are particular propositions intimately tied to the circumstances of a unique argument rather than general propositions as inference rules are. Moreover, with the on-balance premises included in BC-arguments a certain problem is solved (that of relating the premises to the counter-considerations), and once this is done the same problem no longer exists, whereas the tortoise cannot get rid of his problem, no matter how many times he adds a new rule. For this reason, it seems to me that the inclusion of the on-balance premise as part of the structure of BC-arguments does not open the gate to an infinite series of more on-balance premises. Hence, the second problem turns out not to be a problem at all.

6. The "even-though" relation

Not all uses of 'even though' are in the context of argumentation. For example, the sentences, "We made it home safely even though the roads were icy" and "They stayed married for 40 years even though towards the end they had little to say to each other." When 'even-though' is used to express argumentation, however, it signals the presence of (a) argument-parts that are reasons for the conclusion (premises), (b) other parts that are reasons against the conclusion (counter-considerations) as well as (c) a conclusion itself. Linguistic premise indicators are well-known (e.g. 'since,' 'because,' 'for the reason that') and so are linguistic conclusion indicators ('therefore,' 'hence,' 'it follows that,' etc). Linguistic counter-consideration indicators have not been discussed as widely nor as often, but Trudy Govier (Govier 2005, p. 397) has presented the following list: *though, although, even though, despite the fact that, notwithstanding the fact that, while granting that, even granting that* and *even allowing that*. All these linguistic operators have a similar functional role and meaning in argumentative contexts.

Like 'and,' 'but,' and 'however,' the expressions 'even though' and 'although' are natural language conjunctive operators. These conjunctive operators, however, have different nuances and communicational implications. Quine made the following observations:

> ... in ordinary language conjunction is expressed not only by 'and' but also by 'but', by 'although', by unspoken punctuation, and in various other ways. Consider-

ation of 'but' and 'although' is instructive, for it brings out a distinction between what may be called the logical and the rhetorical aspects of language. We are likely to say:

Jones is here but Smith is away.

rather than:

Jones is here and Smith is away.

because of the contrast between being here and being away; or, if the contrast between 'Jones is here' and 'Smith is away' attains such proportions as to cause surprise, as it might, e.g., if Jones is not in the habit of coming except to see Smith, we are likely to say:

Jones is here although Smith is away.

But the circumstances that render the compound true are always the same, viz., joint truth of the two components, regardless of whether 'and', 'but', or 'although' is used. Use of one of these words rather than another may make a difference in naturalness of idiom and may also provide some incidental evidence as to what is going on in the speaker's mind, but it is incapable of making the difference between truth and falsehood of the compound. The difference in meaning between 'and', 'but', and 'although' is rhetorical, not logical. (Quine 1952, pp. 40- 41)

Goldfarb, another Harvard logician, echoed these thoughts fifty years later, writing:

The differences among "and", "but", and "although" are rhetorical rather than logical. Each of the statements

Churchill voted "Aye" and Asquith voted "Nay."
Churchill voted "Aye" but Asquith voted "Nay."
Churchill voted "Aye" although Asquith voted "Nay."

is true just in case both constituents are true. We would use the statement with "but" if we wish to emphasize the contrast between the divergent votes, and we would use "although" if the contrast is dramatic and surprising—for example, if Churchill had previously always agreed with Asquith. Use of one rather than another expresses an attitude toward the relevant facts, but involves no difference in truth-value. (Goldfarb 2003, p. 29)

In saying that the differences between these three conjunctive operators is rhetorical and not logical, Quine and Goldfarb mean that each operator has a non-truth-functional meaning over and above their truth-functional meaning (conjunction). The extra-logical meaning of *although* in "p although q" according to Goldfarb, is that it is dramatic and surprising that while q is the case, p is also the case. Other logicians have commented on these differences as well, Rubin and Young, add to the analysis as follows:

A person who says "It's raining, but the sky is blue" expresses some surprise that it's raining while the sky is blue. And a person who says, "Although it is raining, the sky is blue" expresses the same surprise, but emphasizes the point that the sky is blue while deemphasizing the point that it's raining. (Rubin & Young 1989, p. 93)

Here the element of surprise is said to belong to *but-conjunctions* as well as *although-conjunctions*. What is distinguished for the role of 'although' is that the conjunct following it (or 'even though') is downplayed in importance while the other conjunct is emphasized. Two conjuncts are thus rhetorically unequal when they are joined by 'even though.'

That part of its meaning is given in terms of truth-conditions suggests that 'even though' is short for 'even though *it is true that*.' But depending on subject matter and metaphysical inclinations it may also be taken as an abbreviation of 'even though *it is correct that*' or 'even though *it is acceptable that*' or 'even though *it is conceded that*.' The conjunctives 'notwithstanding,' 'despite' and 'in spite of' are naturally completed by the expression *the fact that*, which may be taken as synonymous with *that it is true that*. Use of these conjunctives signals that there are "obstacles or opposing conditions"[5] taken into consideration. This is a unique character of BC-arguments: (a) they explicitly acknowledge the existence of counter-considerations, and (b) they do not dismiss them or attempt to refute them, but (c) take them into consideration in the reasoning towards their conclusions. The expression '*p* even allowing that *q*' is perhaps somewhat of an exception to this, implying that the considerations in place of *q* have the status of assumptions, or that they may be known to be false but have to be considered for the sake of discussion.[6]

Ducrot (1996, pp. 44 and 108) points out that the conjunctive operator 'but' invariably connects utterances that have "opposite orientations." By an 'orientation' is here meant a direction of informal implication suggested by the conventional meaning of a word that will lead us to infer one conclusion rather than another. Ducrot's observation is that when *but* joins two propositions the consideration of either conjunct inclines us towards a conclusion that is incompatible with the conclusion to which we are led by considering the other conjunct. For example, in response to the suggestion to take a walk, it may be answered that,

(1) The weather is beautiful but I'm tired.

Here the segment "the weather is beautiful" is oriented towards agreeing to the walk and the segment, "but I'm tired" is oriented towards declining the invitation. According to Ducrot, "the overall movement of an *X but Y* string is the same as that of *Y*" (1996, p. 46). Let us say that in compound propositions of the form "*X* but *Y*" the proposition that follows *but* is in the *scope of 'but.'* Ducrot's thesis may then be stated as saying that *in but-conjunctions the overall direction of implication is that implied by the proposition in the scope of 'but'*. The "overall movement" of (2) is therefore towards not going for a walk because "I'm tired" is in the scope of 'but'. Used as a conjunctive, 'however' seems to have very much the same function as 'but.' What is in the scope of 'however' is the stronger consideration.

We can extend Ducrot's interests to 'even though.' It is like 'but' and 'however' in that it connects statements with opposite orientations and represents them as being of unequal

---

[5] Entry on 'notwithstanding', *The Random House College Dictionary*, revised edition, 1975.
[6] Thanks to Jean Goodwin for this observation.

strength. 'Even though' differs from the others in one respect, viz., *in even-though-conjunctions the overall direction of implication is opposite to that implied by the proposition in the scope of 'even-though.'* This is confirmed by Rubin and Young's observation above. Thus, in the formula "p even though q," p and q have opposite orientations and q, which is nested in the scope of *even though*, is represented as weaker than p. Thus, the argument schema "k even though q; because p" implies (i) that k is a conclusion and q is a set of reasons oriented against, or away from k, and (ii) that p is a set of reasons oriented toward k, and (iii) that p is a stronger consideration than q.

According to Adler (1992, p. 25), understanding the construction 'even though' presupposes understanding 'even.' Let us then consider the outline of his analysis of 'even' and then see whether it can further our understanding of 'even though'.

Adler identifies a class of arguments that he calls *even-arguments* in which 'even' occurs in premises as an operator affixed to singular or general terms like 'Elisabeth II', 'Lakehead University', or 'conservatives'. This is an example of an "even argument":

(2) *Even* conservatives are in favor of taxing carbon emissions.
 Therefore, we ought to impose such a tax.

It is a stronger argument than it would be if 'even' were taken out of the premise. Why is that? Adler's answer is that 'even' signals that it is 'contrary-to-expectation' that the term to which it is attached ('conservatives') would have the property predicated (being in favour of taxing carbon emissions). The idea of being 'contrary-to-expectation' is explained by reference to a pragmatic scale:

> The pragmatic scale supplies the source for why even-sentences implicate something's being contrary-to-expectation. ... The fact stressed by "even" is contrary-to-expectation because it is located at or near an extreme on a scale. Therefore, ... anyone or anything at positions removed from that extreme are more assured of having the property (or having it to a higher degree), and it is thus less surprising that they do have it. (Adler 1992, pp. 23-24)

Consider then a spectrum of those who have an attitude towards taxing carbon emissions. The environmentalists will be the least inclined to resist such a tax, followed (let us say) by socialists, liberals and conservatives, in that order. The conservatives we expect to be firmly against a tax on carbon emissions and therefore we position them at the opposite end of the scale (or near to it) to where we have positioned the environmentalists. So, when it is asserted that "*even* conservatives are in favour of taxing carbon emissions," what is asserted is that a group of people who are most expected to be resistant to the tax are supporting it, and it is implied that others who are less resistant to the tax—those towards the middle of the pragmatic scale and those at the end furthest from the conservatives—will also support it. Without the use of *even* the background assumption of a pragmatic scale ordering of attitudes towards the tax would not be invoked, hence, some refer to 'even' as a scalar operator (e.g., Kay 1990, p. 62). In this case, 'even' enables the implication that groups not mentioned are also inclined to support the tax.

Ducrot had earlier identified the scalar aspect of uses of 'even.'[7] He observed that in sentences of the form "p and even q" the components p and q are oriented in the same

---

[7] Ducrot's published work in French on argumentative linguistics antedates that of Adler's 1992 article.

direction as they are in "*p*, moreover *q*" and "*p*, furthermore *q*." What is noteworthy about *even*, according to Ducrot, is that it represents *p* and *q* as being of different strengths. The scalar aspect of "*p* and even *q*" is that *q* is represented as being a stronger consideration than *p* (Ducrot 1996, p. 116) as in, perhaps, "The liberals support the carbon tax and even the conservatives support it."

The other observations Adler makes about 'even' concerns what he parenthetically calls its rhetorical uses.[8] Like Quine and Goldfarb, he appears to mean by a "rhetorical use" a non-logical communicational use and not a deceitful or vacuous use. He says that 'even' is used rhetorically "to ward off doubts about the truth of the assertion minus 'even'," and to signal that "the speaker acknowledges recognition of that reason for doubt," and, consequently to communicate that "the speaker acknowledges that he or she can allay [the doubt]" (Adler 1992, p. 23). Adler's observations here seem reasonable because if something is subject to doubt, then that it is proposed or actually happens will be contrary to expectation. Thus, when a speaker makes a statement of the form "even α has *P*" this will normally be in a context where there is reason to doubt that "α has *P*" and by using the form of expression "even α has *P*" the speaker shows that s/he is aware that there are reasons for doubt. Moreover, to advance the claim "even α has *P*" when there is doubt that α has *P* is reckless unless one has evidence in support of the contrary-to-expectation claim. Thus, with the assertion of the form "even α has *P*" the speaker implies (conversationally) that s/he is able to give a sufficient reason for the claim that "α has *P*."

Are these insights about the meaning of 'even' helpful in understanding the meaning of 'even though'?

To review, we find first a syntactic difference between 'even' and 'even though'. 'Even' is a scalar operator attaching to terms and modifying the meaning of sentences; 'even though' is a binary operator used to form compound sentences from other sentences. We next observe their semantic functions. A claim of the form "α has *P*" is made stronger by affixing 'even' to the subject, ("even α has *P*")—stronger in the sense that it increases premise sufficiency with respect to a given conclusion. 'Even though' has a number of semantic functions. It is used to form compound sentences that are true from component sentences that are true. Another of its semantic functions—one that it shares with *but*—is that *even though* can only be used to conjoin propositions with opposite orientations (*à la* Ducrot). Therefore, a sentence like, "We must save for our retirements *even though* we will need money when we no longer have our jobs," is not well-formed because its conjunctive operator is 'even though' and both its components are oriented in the same direction. A third semantic characteristic of 'even though' is that the sentence in the scope of 'even though' is indicated as a weaker consideration than the conjunct outside the scope of 'even though.' Thus, sentences of the form "*p* even though *q*" will be false if the consideration nested in 'even though' is stronger than the one without.

The other dimensions of the meaning of 'even' and 'even though' get lumped together as rhetorical meaning. There are three interlocking components of this rhetorical meaning and they have to do with doubt, surprise and having reasons.

The use of "even α has *P*" is a recognition that there is an element of doubt associated with "α has *P*," that in fact there are reasons to think that "α has *P*" is false. Hence, it is unexpected when someone asserts a claim of the kind, "even α has *P*." Similarly, that the expression "*p* even though *q*" is used at all is an explicit recognition of the fact that there are reasons, worthy of recognition, to doubt that *p* is the case; those reasons are represented

---

[8] Adler puts 'rhetorical' in parentheses (1992, p. 23).

by q.

In sentences of the form "p even though q" an element of surprise is attached to the assertion of p (this was noticed by Quine and Goldfarb). What makes it surprising (at least mildly) when p is asserted in sentences like that is that there are reasons to doubt that p. Adler explained the surprise as being due to the fact that it was contrary-to-expectation that the subject had the property attributed to it, and we may extend this observation to say that given the sentence nested in 'even though' (q) it is surprising that the other sentence (p) is asserted. Consider the statement,

(3) We should impose a tax on carbon emissions *even though* it will be an unpopular measure.

Here we may explain the unexpectedness or surprise of "we should impose a tax on carbon emissions" by seeing that its orientation is opposed to "a carbon tax will be an unpopular measure," a proposition which is favoured by presumption. (There is a presumption in favour of the way things normally go, and for popular, widely held beliefs.) In general, then, our analysis of "p even though q" sentences will include the hypothesis that the presumption for q creates a presumption for *not-p*. This will explain why there may be resistance to p and this in turn explains why the assertion of p is surprising. So, the surprise

Comparison of the roles of 'even' and 'even though'

	even ("even α has P")	even though ("p even though q")
a	used to modify a term (a subject). [*Syntactical role*]	a sentential connective. [*Syntactical role*]
b		"p even though q" is true just in case p and q are both true; [*Semantic role 1*]
c	not relevant to this comparison	*Orientation*: p and q have opposite orientations. [*Semantic role 2*]
d	"even α has P" is a weightier reason than "α has P." [*Semantic role*]	p is represented as stronger than q. [*Semantic role 3*]
e	*Doubt*: by using 'even α has P' a speaker acknowledges that there are some reasons to think "α has P" is false; it is thus a context in which doubt exist. [*Rhetorical role 1*]	*Doubt*: by using 'p even though q' the speaker acknowledges to her audience that there are reasons opposed to p; it is thus a context in which doubt about p exist. [*Rhetorical role 1*]
f	*Unexpectedness*: use of 'even' implies that it is contrary-to-expectation that the subject α would have the property P predicated of it. [*Rhetorical role 2*]	*Unexpectedness*: use of 'p even though q' implies that p is surprising or unexpected in light of the fact that q is true; (perhaps because there is a presumption for q). [*Rhetorical role 2*]
g	*Justification*: by using 'even α has P' in a context in which doubt exists, the speaker claims to be able to allay the reasons for doubting "α has P." [*Rhetorical role 3*]	*Justification*: by using 'p even though q' in a context in which there is doubt about p, the speaker implies that s/he has a good reason for p. [*Rhetorical role 3*]

element accompanying "*p* even though *q*" can be explained by the fact that *p* is contrary to what we presumed to be the case. There is no threat of inconsistency here since "there is a presumption for *not-p*" and "*p*" can both be true. We could also say this about even-sentences. In the sentence, "Even conservatives are in favour of taxing carbon emissions," the contrary-to-expectation factor is due to there being a presumption that the conservatives will not support such a tax.

Finally, to assert something that we expect others to doubt and find surprising, is to put ourselves in a position of having to defend the claim with reasons. Thus sentences of the form "*p* even though *q*" that merely appear to make a claim will implicitly imply an argument of the form "*p* because *r*, even though *q*," where *p* holds the place of the conclusion, *q* the presumptive reason against the conclusion, and *r* holds the place of the reasons for the conclusion. This implicit commitment to having reasons for *p* in "*p* even though *q*" dovetails with a general normative requirement of having to give reasons for *p* if *not-p* has presumptive status. These extensions of Adler's analysis of 'even' to 'even though' do not seem forced to me: the insights regarding 'even' are easily adapted to 'even though' and they fill in our understanding of the latter expression.

7. A case in point: The "Notwithstanding Clause" of the Canadian Charter of Rights and Freedoms

In this section of the essay I want to show that taking 'even though' to mean the same as 'notwithstanding' helps us to understand an important part of the *Canadian Charter of Rights and Freedoms*, passed in 1982. The Charter contains a celebrated clause that has come to be called the "Notwithstanding Clause." It occurs in the final substantial section of the Charter; it is backward-looking to earlier sections.

> 33. (1) Parliament or the legislature of a province may expressly declare in an Act of Parliament or of the legislature, as the case may be, that the Act or a provision thereof shall operate notwithstanding a provision included in section 2 or section 7 to 15 of this Charter.

The effect of the clause is that governments in Canada (federal and provincial) can temporarily pass laws even though they are inconsistent with some of the rights or freedoms guaranteed by the Charter. The most famous use of the Notwithstanding Clause was by the provincial government of Quebec in 1988. Here is how it came about.

In 1977 the government of Quebec passed a law (Bill 101) that required that all commercial signs within the province be in French only. Bill 101 was voided by the Supreme Court of Canada in 1988 which said it was "an unreasonable limitation on the freedom of expression" contrary to section 2 of the Charter. Later that year the Quebec government passed a law (Bill 178) declaring that only French could be used on exterior commercial signs and, mindful of the Supreme Court's earlier ruling, invoked the Notwithstanding Clause of the Charter (which had come into effect in 1982) to protect its restrictive law from the possibility of being overruled.

Two of the restrictions governing the use of the Notwithstanding Clause are of interest. The one is that a legislature must "expressly declare" through legislation that it is invoking the clause (this prevents secretive uses of the Clause); the other restriction is that legislation depending on the Clause expires after five years unless it is re-enacted by another application of the Notwithstanding Clause (section 33.(3) of the Charter). However, in Canada there must be elections at least every five years, and this means that when any legislation depending on the Notwithstanding Clause comes up for renewal, it will be by a government that has been elected since the Notwithstanding Clause was first invoked, a government that may possibly have a different or modified political agenda. This is what happened to Bill 178. In December 1988 it was originally brought in, by the Liberal Government, under the Notwithstanding Clause. There was an election in 1989 in which the Liberals lost seven seats (and 7 per cent of the popular vote) and which saw the election of four members of the Equality Party, a party created to defend the rights of English speakers in Quebec. This election result, which returned the Liberals to power with a reduced majority and a democratic reminder of the strength of the English minority, may well have been a factor in the government's decision to introduce a less restrictive language law (Bill 86) requiring only that French lettering must be at least twice as large as English lettering on exterior signs, a bill which did not contradict the Charter of Rights and Freedoms. Bill 86 did not come into effect, however, until December of 1993 when Bill 178 ceased to be valid when its protection under the Notwithstanding Clause, invoked five years earlier, expired.[9]

What does 'notwithstanding' mean in this context? Although the Charter is a legal document, 'notwithstanding' is not given a special stipulated or technical meaning; still, the word is obviously used deliberately and very carefully. Since we are hypothesizing that 'notwithstanding' means the same as 'even though', let us review the use of the Notwithstanding Clause in support of Bill 178 under the analysis we made of 'even though.'

(A) *Syntactically*, 'notwithstanding' has the role of conjoining two sentences, for example:

(5) (i) the government of Quebec may pass a law that only French may be used on exterior signs in Quebec,
(ii) the Charter of Rights and Freedoms states that all Canadians have a right to freedom of expression.

when conjoined by 'nothwithstanding' yield:

(6) The government of Quebec may pass a law that only French may be used on exterior signs in Quebec *notwithstanding the fact that* the Charter of Rights and Freedoms states that all Canadians have a right to freedom of expression.

(B-D) *Semantic considerations*. Here there are three things to consider. First, sentence (6) is true because both the conjuncts 5(i) and 5(ii), joined by *notwithstanding,* are true (or acceptable, etc.). Second, 5(i) and 5(ii) have opposite orientations: the one that the Quebec government has a right to limit freedom of language use, the other that all Canadians have a right to freedom of language use. Third, the use here of 'notwithstanding,' like the use of 'even though,' indicates that the one component of the conjunction is weaker than the other, in this case the one nested in the scope of 'notwithstanding,' that the Charter states Canadians have a right to freedom of expression.[10]

---

[9] I have checked my facts against an article by R. Hudon in *The Canadian Encyclopaedia*, "Bill 86," www.thecanadianencyclopedia.com, accessed 2009-01-12. Also "Quebec General Election," 1989, *Wikipedia*.
[10] That it is both the case that only French may be used on exterior signs in Quebec and that the Charter specifies a right to freedom of expression, appears to be inconsistent. The apparent inconsistency arises because the right to freedom of expression is taken as an absolute right. In effect, what the Notwithstanding Clause does is that it divides charter rights into two kinds: those that are absolute and those that are *prima facie*. There are some absolute rights in the Charter (e.g. the right of

(E) There are three *rhetorical* roles of 'notwithstanding' to consider. The first concerns a context of doubt in which the notwithstanding clause can be invoked. It would have been doubted that it was morally and legally possible to pass a law in Quebec, or Canada, that would limit the right to use the English language—this was doubted, at least by many members of the anglophone population inside and outside Quebec. The reason for the doubt might have been that there was a widespread belief that freedom of speech is an absolute right; this would yield a natural presumption that freedom of speech could not be limited. In addition, the right to freedom of expression is recognized in the Charter, which means that there is a legal presumption for freedom of speech. Thus Bill 178 was the kind of law whose legitimacy may have been doubted because of its clash with presumptions. That it was eventually brought in under the Notwithstanding Clause is evidence that the reasons against adopting it were recognized by the Bill's proponents.

(F) The second rhetorical role of 'notwithstanding' is that sentences of the form, "q notwithstanding p," mark that something unexpected, or surprising attaches to "p." This goes hand-in-hand with the prior recognition that doubt attaches to p. In the present case, because there is a presumption for freedom of speech it is unexpected that Bill 178 would be introduced. That Bill 178 should become law *notwithstanding the fact that* it explicitly contravened one of the Charter rights, was an exceptional and surprising development.

(G) Lastly, that a government would propose to employ the Notwithstanding Clause to support a piece of legislation in a context where there is doubt as to its legitimacy implies that the government must have good reasons for that legislation—that it believes it can justify the legislation. In the case of Bill 178 that justification—advanced as a reason in the Quebec legislature and made public in the media—was that passing the law would protect the French language and Québecois culture in the province of Quebec. So, by invoking the Notwithstanding Clause the Quebec government commits itself to an argument, not just a claim.

> (8) The government of Quebec may pass a law that only French may be used on exterior signs in Quebec *notwithstanding the fact that* the Charter of Rights and Freedoms states that all Canadians have a right to freedom of expression *because* such a law will protect the French language and Québecois culture in the province of Quebec.

This justification, or something very much like it, did in fact accompany the introduction of Bill 178. We see that it naturally lends itself to reconstruction as a BC-argument, following the structure outlined in Section 4 above.

> *Premise*: A law that only French may be used on exterior signs in Quebec would protect the French language and Québecois culture in the province of Quebec
> *On-balance premise*: The consideration that such a law would protect the French language and Québecois culture outweighs the counter-consideration that the Charter of

citizens to vote in elections), but the freedom-of-expression right is not one of them. Due to its inclusion under the Notwithstanding Clause the freedom of expression right is but a *prima facie* right, one that can be outweighed by another right, namely the right of a government to override it for a period of five years, providing it can get the support of its legislature. The sentence in (6) can thus to be understood as:

> (7) The government of Quebec may pass a law that only French may be used on exterior signs in Quebec *notwithstanding the fact that* the Charter of Rights and Freedoms states that all Canadians have a *prima facie* right to freedom of expression.

Rights and Freedoms states that all Canadians have a right to freedom of expression.

Conclusion 1: The government of Quebec may pass a law that only French may be used on exterior signs in Quebec *notwithstanding the fact that* [even though that] the Charter of Rights and Freedoms states that . . . .

Conclusion 2: The government of Quebec may pass a law that only French may be used on exterior signs in Quebec.

Thus, the meaning of the word 'notwithstanding' in the *Canadian Charter of Rights and Freedoms* appears to be the same as the meaning our analysis uncovered for 'even though' in its syntactical, semantic and rhetorical roles. And the justification of the use of the Notwithstanding Clause by the Quebec Government fits the pattern that was suggested for BC-arguments in Section 4 above.

The Charter case is interesting for a number of additional reasons. One is that it specifies that the duration of any law passed under the protection of the Notwithstanding Clause is five years. This suggests an awareness that employment of the Clause may be controversial, that it will involve issues where public opinion may fluctuate and where there might well be a change of mind within a short period of time. This is to admit more than that the "even-though" arguments that can be developed under the Charter are defeasible, it is to anticipate that there may be attempts to overturn them. The other point worth noting is that presumptions involved in arguments directed against Charter rights will include legal presumptions since the Charter is a legal document. Outside the law "p even though q" turns largely on natural, non-legal presumptions.[11]

---

[11] Earlier versions of this chapter were presented at the Rhetorical Citizenship and Public Deliberation conference at the University of Copenhagen (2008), the Centre for Research in Reasoning, Argumentation and Rhetoric (CRRAR) at the University of Windsor in September 2009, and to the Association for Informal Logic and Critical Thinking (AILACT) at the American Philosophical Association mid-western division meetings in Chicago in February 2010. I am grateful to J.A. Blair for his helpful comments on the original draft.

Chapter 4

The Relationship between Pro/Con and Dialectical Tier Arguments

RALPH H. JOHNSON

1. Introduction

In this chapter I investigate the relationship between pro/con arguments and arguments with a dialectical tier, both of which appear to be types of conductive argument.

So far as I know, there is no agreed-upon understanding of just how to characterize conductive arguments, except perhaps to say that they should be distinguished from deductive and inductive arguments (and notwithstanding the reservations of those who do not believe that arguments can/should be sorted into types). Still it does seem clear that most of those working on this matter recognize as one important type of conductive argument what are called "pro and con" arguments ("pro/con" arguments, "pro and contra" arguments). Such arguments are, I believe, also often referred to as "balance of considerations" arguments.[1]

In this important type of argument, the arguer presents reasons for the conclusion, then presents reasons against the conclusion (sometimes called counterconsiderations (Govier, 2010), then offers some additional reasoning in which the arguer defends the claim that the reasons for outweigh reasons against, and then draws the conclusion. The way in which the conclusion "follows" here is understood to be neither deductive nor inductive. The main issue appears to be how to give an account of the weighting process, how such weighting claims are to be justified. Other papers in this volume deal with that issue.

The dynamic in a pro/con argument seems very much like what occurs in what I called an argument with a dialectical tier (2000a). This is an argument in which the arguer, after laying out the grounds for the conclusion (what I called the illative core), then attempts to anticipate and defuse objections that might be raised against the argument (the dialectical tier).

Both types of argument seem to be transparently dialectical in my sense of the term (2000a, p. 161)—in that what I call the voice of the Other is given presence within the argument. In one case, the arguer takes note of [though does not assert] reasons that the Other might cite as going against the conclusion. In the other case, the arguer mentions objections that might be raised by the Other.

To understand the relationship between these two types of argument, we need to ask and answer the question: What is the relationship between an objection and a counterconsideration? Some, Govier would be one, seem to equate (or conflate) objections and counterconsiderations (see below, p. 52). But it seems to me important to distinguish between an objection and a counterconsideration, and to distinguish both of them from terms that refer to other sorts of dialectical material: e.g., alternative positions. More on this in Section 4.

At this point, I want to cite J. L. Austin in "A Plea for Excuses" where he says that:

> ...our common stock of words embodies all the distinctions that men have found worth drawing... in the lifetimes of many generations: these are surely likely to be more numerous, more sound ... are more subtle.... than any that you or I are likely

---

[1] Here I assume that "pro and con" arguments and "balance of consideration" arguments are the same.

to think up in our arm-chairs of an afternoon—the most favoured alternative method. (p. 182)

What I take from Austin's words is that we should not be too quick to conflate what our common stock of words has distinguished, at least granting such distinctions a *prima facie* status. And that is how I will proceed, by assuming that there is a distinction between an objection and a counterconsideration.

To observe this distinction, one must be prepared to characterize, or define, what an objection is, and what a counterconsideration is. We come now to what I regard *a striking fact*. As important as this issue of what counts as an objection is, there was, so far as I know, no serious attempt by argumentation theorists or logicians to take this problem in hand until Govier's 1997 paper, "Progress and Regress on the Dialectical Tier." Think about that for a moment. We all recognize that part of the very life-blood of argumentation is anticipating and responding to objections. Indeed, Perelman has said:

> The strength of an argument depends upon the adherence of the listeners to the premises of the argument; upon the pertinence of the premises; upon the close or distant relationship they may have with the defended thesis; *upon the objections; and upon the manner in which they can be refuted.* (1982, p. 140, emphasis added)

Yet very little explicit theorizing has been done on this important issue. We have had plenty of theoretical work on other important concepts involved in the analysis of arguments. Think of the work devoted to the concept of a warrant, or to presumption. But almost no work has been done on the concept of an objection. Is that because its meaning is so transparent? I think we will see that this is not the case.

One author who has given thought to these matters is Govier. In the next section, I begin by reviewing Govier's definitions of 'objection' and 'counterconsideration,' after which I offer some further reflections on the relation between them.

2. Govier on objections and counter-considerations in conductive arguments

In her (1997/2009) paper, "Reasoning with Pros and Cons," about conductive arguments, Govier mentions both counter-considerations and objections:

> But in either case, counter-considerations are not premises in the argument, because they are not put forward as supporting the conclusion. They are objections to the conclusion, strongly or weakly acknowledged by the arguer. One might think of counter-considerations as anti-premises. (p. 156)

Note that counter-considerations are here spoken of as "objections to the conclusion." Here is how Govier introduces the idea of counterconsiderations in the 7th edition of *The Practical Study of Argument* (2010):

> In a cogent conductive argument, the premises must be positively relevant to the conclusion. How strongly they support that conclusion can be determined only by considering them together and estimating their collective strength, but when we do this, we also have to take into account points that are negatively relevant to the conclusion. These negatively relevant points are called **counterconsiderations**. (p. 355)

Throughout the section that follows, she also refers to objections (pp. 357, 362). In the section "Counterconsiderations in other Contexts," she brings the two ideas together as follows:

> Given that conductive arguments are designed to deal with pros and cons, it is easy to see how counterconsiderations are important for their evaluation. However it is not only for conductive arguments that counterconsideration are important. *Counterconsiderations, or objections,* may arise for every type of argument.... Considering *counterconsiderations or objections* is a crucial aspect of evaluation and constructing any argument. (p. 370, emphasis added).

In the "Review of Terms Introduced," the entry for 'Objection' says: "See Counterconsideration" (p. 375).

These texts suggest to me that Govier regards the two terms as pretty much equivalent. It seems to me, however, that there is, at least at first glance, a striking difference between them. A counterconsideration occurs within an argument, in what I call the illative core. On the other hand, an objection, I will argue, need not occur in an argument, but it does makes its appearance as a comment on some other argument. The making of an objection presupposes the existence of some other argument to which it is directed. So here is one difference between these two terms on the basis of how and where they occur.

Govier is not alone in having a tendency to conflate/identify these terms. In Meiland's *College Thinking* (1981), for example, one can find a conflation of 'objection' with 'counterargument.' In Chapter 3, Meiland provides a definition (of sorts) of an objection in his opening discussion of argument:

> What is an argument? Reasons for beliefs constitute *arguments* for those beliefs. When you give an argument for a certain belief or position, you are said to *argue* for it. There can also be arguments *against* a certain belief or position. These arguments against a belief or position are called *objections* to the belief or position. (p. 30)

For Meiland, then, an objection is an argument against a belief or a position. This comes very close to what many would call a *counterargument, (or alternative position)*. So here we have a potential conflation of 'objection' with 'counterargument.'

It seems to me likely that this conflating tendency and the failure to mark distinctions are related phenomena. In the next section, I make a case to support the distinction.

3. Some distinctions

In this section, I attempt to support the Austinian view about respecting the distinctions implicit in our ordinary stock. Both 'counterconsideration' and 'objection' appear in that stock.

If we follow Austin here, we should recognise the distinction between them, at the very least by not conflating them. It seems to me that there is a role here for definition, which could help support the distinction. That is, one way in which one might support a distinction is by introducing definitions that help make clear fundamental differences. If we have decent definitions of 'counterconsideration' and 'objection,' the distinction between them should become clearer.

In my judgement, the crucial step is to define what is meant by an objection. Here one cannot do better than to begin with Govier's (1999) paper. That will lead into my own definition of 'objection'—after which I will offer definitions for 'counterconsideration' and 'counterargument.'

3.1 Defining 'objection'

Govier's position. In Chapter 13 of *The Philosophy of Argument* (1999), "Progress and Regress on the Dialectical Tier," Govier offers one of the first attempts that I am aware of to think through the question of just what an objection is, and to develop in a somewhat systematic way a doctrine of types of objection. This occurs in Section 3: "Theorizing about Objections." Although I am not in complete agreement with her views, they are an excellent start on thinking about a seriously underdeveloped topic in the theory of argument and she is to be congratulated on having taken the initial steps on this important matter.

Govier begins by presenting an intuition: "an objection is an allegation that there is something wrong with the position of the arguer" (p. 229). My own sense is that this is too strong a claim, that raising an objection is more like issuing challenge than alleging a wrongdoing. It is a kind of test of the argument. Having discussed the focus of an objection, Govier now offers this broader account:

> [A]n objection is (a) any claim alleging a defect in the argument or its conclusion; (b) which, insofar as it does not compete for the same intellectual and social space as that conclusion, does not constitute an alternative position to the conclusion; and is either (c) raised by the audience to which the argument is addressed or (d) might plausibly be raised by that audience; or (e) might plausibly be raised by a rational person to whom the argument might plausibly be addressed. (p. 229)

This account is important for a number of reasons. First, to the best of my knowledge *this is the first definition[2] of an objection to be found in the scholarly literature by argumentation theorists about argument.* Second, clause (b) explicitly distinguishes between an objection and an alternative position (whereas Meiland tended to conflate these). In the spirit of Austin cited earlier, I support this distinction. Indeed, I want to propose that we take the next step and distinguish between an objection and a criticism, but I do not undertake that task in this paper.[3] Third, Govier's account contains the clear recognition that an objection proceeds out of Otherness; it is a concern raised by someone in the audience, or one's interlocutor. Fourth, Govier sees an objection as a form of resistance to the argument—a claim alleging a defect in the argument or its conclusion. Here I think Govier's position is too limiting. I will explain why shortly. Govier now offers a more succinct characterization of an objection:

---

[2] I am calling this a definition. Perhaps Govier would not use that term here, although she does offer a definition of 'alternative position' on p. 227. Nevertheless I am inclined to proceed down the path of searching for a definition. The path is beset by hazards. The first is: Do you really need or want a definition? The best that I can say in reply is that because of the conflation associated with this term, it seems to me that there is a role for definition. The second is: What kind of definition will this be? The answer to this question is complicated because there is not anything like consensus about the various types of definition. I can say that it is not a lexical definition, nor a stipulative definition. Perhaps it is what Hansen (2002, p. 273) called a theoretical definition.

[3] In *Dialectical Adequacy: A Study of Dialectical Obligations* (forthcoming from Cambridge University Press), I hope to make the case for the distinction.

> An objection is an argument, *a consideration* put forward, alleged to show either that there is something wrong with the conclusion in question or that there is something wrong with the argument put forward in its favour. (p. 229, emphasis added)

This account contains an important "amendment," for here Govier seems to require that an objection be itself an argument, in the sense that some reasoning must support the objection. I say "seems" because she uses both 'argument' and 'consideration' here, and the latter might seem to allow for an unsupported statement to qualify as an objection. But that issue seems to be settled by what she then says:

> Implicitly, if not explicitly, one who raises an objection is either saying "O; therefore there is something wrong with conclusion C" or "O; therefore there is something wrong with the argument in support of C." Here "O" refers to the substantive considerations which constitute *the premises of the objection*." (p. 229, emphasis mine)

This passage suggests to me that Govier requires that there be reasons that support the objection, which means that for Govier, an objection *must* take the form of an argument.

I have some reservations about this aspect of her account. For it does not seem to accord with the way in which many use the term "objection" in argumentative discourse, where it is often used to denote a claim or a statement which is not itself argued for, as I shall shortly show. However, there are severe limits to the weight of this point, given that our ordinary usage here seems to exhibit conflicting tendencies. More important is that her account is too limiting. On her view, a question as such cannot constitute an objection. Govier gives an example to support her point. Suppose, she says, someone is defending a theory about the construction of Stonehenge and claims that the rocks serve to assist ancient peoples in making astronomical predictions. On p. 229, Govier writes:

> Then someone in the audience pops up to ask "How much do we know about the mathematical ideas of people living in Britain in 5000 BC?" This question may be purely a request for information. If so, it does not constitute an objection to the lecturer's case.

But it may not be. It may pose a challenge, a request that the arguer elaborate his position. Govier goes on to allow that such a question may be rhetorical and hence "a truncated argument," in which case it would count as an objection. But "[a] question in and of itself does not constitute an objection either to a conclusion or to the argument put forward on its behalf" (p. 230). However, suppose the question had been: "Then how do you account for the religious totems found there?" It seems to me that the person who asks this question is putting forth a challenge to the arguer, is raising an objection by means of the question, even though she has not made an assertion, much less an argument.

It may prove helpful reflect for a moment on the question of why someone raises an objection. It seems to me that the intention behind raising an objection is often not *to assert* that there is something wrong with the argument, but rather merely to probe the argument, to offer a challenge to the arguer to find out how the arguer will handle it. Thus, the objector may only be "sounding out the argument" by saying something like: "How would you respond to the statement that P?" Or, the objector may ask: "But then how do you distinguish between X and Y?" without intending to *show* that any defect exists in the argument. In such cases, the objector need not be construed as *claiming* anything at all, much less that there is a defect, but only as probing or testing the argument, perhaps seeking clarification before attempting an assessment. Or, the objector may simply be asking for elaboration. It seems to me to make sense to allow such responses to count as objections, even though they aren't presented in the form of an argument, as required by Govier. Thus, when someone raises an objection in the form of an assertion, it seems to me that that person should be seen as raising an objection, even if no support or defence is provided. In his book, *The Fragmentation of Reason*, Steven Stich writes in a section entitled "Objections to Pragmatism":

> For along with the virtues of the view, there were a pair of obvious objections, each of which initially seemed quite overwhelming. The first *objection* is that pragmatism leads to relativism. And relativism is to be avoided at all costs. The *second objection* is that pragmatism is viciously circular, since there is no way we could show that our cognitive system is pragmatically preferable without using the very system whose superiority we are trying to establish. (pp. 24-25)

Of the two objections cited by Stich, the first does not take the form of an argument. The objection is the claim that "pragmatism leads to relativism," but this claim, though it is part of an argument, is not itself argued for. In the second case, the objection [pragmatism is viciously circular] is supported by a line of reasoning [since there is no way...]. His use reflects the variability of usage of the term in common discourse.

In my view, then, requiring that an objection take the form of an argument is unduly restrictive. Further, it seems to me desirable to distinguish clearly between various types of dialectical material: between an objection and alternative position, and between an objection and criticism. And the definition I will shortly propose will pave the way for such a distinction, whereas if we take Govier's path there is no real difference between an objection and a criticism.

3.2 A new definition of 'objection'

In this section I attempt to improve on Govier's account. Let me start by touching base with *The American Heritage Dictionary* which defines 'objection' as "... 2. a statement or other expression offered or presented in opposition; an adverse contention; 3. A ground, reason, or cause for expressing opposition or disagreement" (p. 905).

Two points. First, this definition seems to understand an objection as consisting of statement rather than an argument. Second, it seems to me that this definition could also apply to 'counterconsideration'—so for my purposes, it is not helpful.

Let us then consider the etymology. Our word comes from the Latin—*objicere* which means to put something in the way of something. Etymology thus suggests that an objection is an obstacle of some sort that one puts in the way of the arguer. The objector understands the arguer may well overcome that objection, like a hurdle in a race which is there to pose a test for the runner but is not intended to stop the runner. Thus, we may view an objection as a kind of dialectical challenge or test posed to an argument, typically to a premise, or perhaps to the conclusion (in which case we may rather be looking at an alternative position—to be taken up shortly) but there are other forms an objection may take, such as targeting an assumption; viz., "Your argument rests on the assumption that *p*..., but you have not yet given any defence of *p*." (Let me point out that this example gives us a reason to be leery of any attempt to classify objections on the premise-inference-conclusion approach. An objection could target an assumption of the argument and an assumption, at least as I understand it, is neither a premise nor an inference nor the conclusion.)

Next consider the question of how one raises an objection. It is fairly typical that one raises an objection by indicating what one is up to: "I want to raise the following objection:

....." However, such a preface is not necessary. There are many other ways of signalling/making this sort of intervention. One might say: "But how then do you distinguish between X and Y?" Or: "What do you say to those who argue that P?" Or: "But if we accept that, then don't we open the door to Z"? Or: "But doesn't your argument assume that A"? All of these, it seems to me, are ways of indicating that one is raising an objection.

On the basis of this discussion, let me then propose the following definition:

> An *objection* is: (1) a response to an argument that (2) contains an expression of a propositional content that (3) presents a challenge, difficulty or a possible impediment to the argument's achieving its purpose (however that is understood) (4) by challenging some part (whether explicit or implicit) of the argument.

I now offer some comments on each of the four elements of the proposed definition.

(1) An objection, in the sense that concerns us in this context,[4] is a response to an argument. Another way of putting this is to say that an objection only exists in a *dialectical environment*.[5] No statement or assertion is an objection in and of itself. It only takes on that status when it is directed toward a specific argument. (That is not to deny that objections can exist in advance of an argument—viz., the standard objections.)

(2) An objection has propositional content that is typically presented in a statement or an assertion, but need not be. A question can be used to present an objection: "But how do you handle this situation?" Thus the reference to propositional content is intended to avoid restricting objections to statements. I seek here to avoid one further limitation, in that, unlike Govier, I do not require the propositional content to take the form of an argument.

(3) The propositional content in some way challenges the argument--whether by raising a question or posing a potential problem. It need not *assert* the existence of a flaw or a problem because the one raising the objection may only be testing of the argument. The objector may wish to see how the arguer, using the argument thus far presented, can respond to the objection. On the other hand, it is also often the case that the one who raises the objection thinks that the objection has the potential for undermining the argument. That is, the future life of an objection could be as a criticism, where I take a criticism as an allegation that the argument is deficient in some specified respect where that allegation is supported.

(4) The objection may be directed to an explicit part of the argument--a premise, or an inference or even the conclusion. "I object to your premise that p because..." But it need not be. It seems quite common that the objection is directed against something that the objector believes is *assumed* or *implied* by the argument, as indicated above.

There are two immediate payoffs to this definition. First, we do not rule out as an objection a statement that is not supported by any reason. Other accounts of "objection" (Meiland, Johnson and Blair, possibly Govier) seem to rule out this possibility. Second, such a definition can help us distinguish between an objection and other forms of dialectical material—counterconsiderations and counterarguments—if, as I suspect, there is an important difference between an objection and a counterconsideration. And it can pave the way for a clear distinction between an objection and a criticism, as indicated above.

---

[4] One can object to many sorts of things: statements, proposals, etc. I am interested here in its role in argumentation.

[5] The rough idea here is that each argument is located in what might be referred to as argumentative space and around each argument gathers "dialectical material" in what I call the "dialectical environment". Thus a host of objections and criticisms now populate the dialectical environment surrounding the co-called "pain and private language argument" in Wittgenstein's *Philosophical Investigations*.

3.3 Defining 'counterconsideration'

What is a counterconsideration? Here is how Govier explains this term in her (2010):

> A claim that is negatively relevant to the conclusion of an argument. Counterconsiderations may be explicitly acknowledged by an arguer, as is reasonably common in conductive argument. (p. 375)

I like this definition, and it is clear from this definition, and from my definition of "objection," that they are different types of dialectical material. How so?

The issue has to do with the negative relevance condition. This condition applies to a counterconsideration but it cannot be applied to "objection" (howsoever defined). To be precise, negative relevance cannot be a necessary condition for an objection. It is too strong. Let me explain why. Clearly, the person who raises "O" takes it to be negatively relevant. But she may well be wrong, and the arguer may be able to show that although O *appears to be negatively relevant*, it is **not** negatively relevant at all. In his (2003), speaking about one of the objections I raised to the definition I proposed, Finocchiaro writes: "…Is this objection relevant? (p. 38)" The very question suggests that something could be objection and not be relevant. Yet it seems to me that even if O is not relevant, O remains an objection (though it probably would not be a good objection). For there is no contradiction in saying that even though O is not negatively relevant, it is nevertheless an objection. Thus the most that can be claimed is that the *objector takes O to be negatively relevant*. Negative relevance, then, cannot be a necessary condition for an objection.

However, negative relevance is a necessary condition for a counterconsideration. It makes no sense to say that even though C is not negatively relevant, it is nevertheless a counterconsideration.

Here then it seems to me we have a *crucial difference* between an objection and a counterconsideration that provides a basis for the distinction between the two and that our definitions of each would need to honor. Negative relevance must be considered a defining feature of a counterconsideration, but it is not a feature of any kind in an objection.

3.4 Defining 'counterargument'

A counterargument would be an argument with a conclusion which is in some fashion "opposed" to the conclusion it opposes. Thus it is a contextual notion. On this view, if C is the conclusion I am urging, then a counterargument to my argument would be argument for not-C: P4–P5–P56 → ~C.[6] The phrase "in some fashion opposed to" is vague but likely should not be made more precise.

It seems clear that, so defined, a counterargument is very much like what has been called an alternative position, but I do not here undertake the task of making the distinction between the two. (For an analysis of the term 'alternative position,' I recommend Govier, 1999, pp. 223-228).

In this section I have proposed an account of 'objection,' 'counterconsideration' and (to a lesser degree) 'counterargument' that supports their distinction. In the next section, I offer some additional comments about these matters.

---

[6] There are other forms a counterargument may take, but I cannot go into details about that here.

4. Some additional thoughts about these matters

In the wake of this attempt to preserve the distinction, I want to address two issues that have emerged for me in thinking about these matters.

4.1 Types of dialectical material

I thought it might be useful to provide a list of the many and various types of dialectical material that have been mentioned in the literature.

Objection, criticism, rebuttal, refutation—these types are fairly standard. Also fairly standard are these terms: counterconsideration, counterargument, and alternative position. Somewhat newer to the inventory are two terms that appear to have originated with Pollock(1995): undermining defeater and rebutting defeater. They have proven their value particularly in discussions of what has come to be known as defeasible reasoning (inference, argument). Somewhat wider afield, Blair (1998) mentions "qualifications," "provisos, " "distinctions," and "objections." We could add "replies," "challenges," "difficulties," "observations," "requests for clarification," etc.—indeed any sort of material which might be directed at the argument, whether as challenge or support.

I call all such "dialectical material"—"dialectical" because such material typically occurs as part of the give-and-take, the back-and-forth between the arguer and the Other, whether that other be an audience, an interlocutor(s), a respondent(s), etc. I use the term "material" rather than "response" because there is a kind of material that collects around an argument which, though pertinent to the argument, is not necessarily a response to that particular argument. The standard objections often collect about a certain issue so that anyone who addresses that issue in an argument would have a *prima facie* obligation, in my view, to deal with them.

Not all responses to an argument have an equal claim on the attention of the arguer. Some responses are more important than others, have a greater claim on the arguer's attention than do others. Thus, in a work in progress,[7] I propose the following principle:

> The arguer has a *prima facie* duty to respond to all dialectical responses to his or her argument. Priority should be given to responses in proportion to their perceived capacity to undermine the argument.

In my view, strong criticism typically poses the gravest threat to the argument, and so would have a stronger claim on the arguer's attention than would an objection. I cannot here debate the wisdom or the justification of this principle, but wish rather make the point that the ability to deploy it (or something like it) will call for the arguer's judgment about the relative strength of the responses he received; and in my judgement, one of the factors in that judgement will be the type of response it is. For example, in my own account as given above, I distinguish between a criticism and an objection. I take the view that the former is more likely than the latter to post a grave threat, and therefore typically has a stronger claim on the arguer.

One benefit, then, of the survey of types of dialectical responses I have been discussing is that such a list could help provide a principled basis for helping the arguer sort out and prioritize what his obligations are in a given case.

---

[7] *Dialectical Adequacy: A Study of Dialectical Obligations*, forthcoming from Cambridge University Press.

4.2 Imagining objections and counterconsiderations

There is, it seems to me, an important difference between anticipating an objection (or counterconsideration) and dealing with an objection (or counterconsideration) that has been posed by someone else. Usually the objections that one can anticipate are also those that one has some sense of how to respond to. My experience is that the objections that have really given me pause, and posed the greatest challenge to my argument, are those that come from another mind. They're the ones I react to by saying: "In a million years, I never would have thought of that objection." We all have cognitive and epistemic blind spots—and that is where the strongest objections often reside.

This point says something about the task of developing counterconsiderations and about imagining objections. The arguer can enhance his ability to do this by immersing himself in the mindset of those who disagree with his views, by getting to know how their minds work on the issues. This point applies to my idea of a dialectical tier in which the arguer does his best to anticipate and defend against objections. In *Manifest Rationality,* I was able to anticipate some of the objections that would be made to my conceptualization of "argument." But there were objections that I did not, and I am inclined to say could not, have raised; e.g., the objections raised by Finocchiaro in his 2003 OSSA keynote.

I believe that same point applies to pro/con reasoning/argument. If I am "pro," there is a real danger that in my own formulation of the "cons," I will come up with cons that are not as strong as the cons that a real opposer would list. Thus it seems to me that the best "pro and con" reasoning efforts, just as in the case of argument, are joint efforts rather than solo outings, dialectical rather than monolectical (to use terminology I am not fond of but which I think helps make the point).

5. Conclusion

My focus in this paper has been what I have called dialectical material—that is material that collects in the dialectical environment that forms around an argument.[8] More specifically my intention has been to argue for the importance and value of maintaining distinctions, particularly the distinction between "objection" and "counterconsideration." I have attempted to provide a definition for "objection" which both supports the distinction and overcomes limitations in Govier's account.

There is one important consequence to which, in conclusion, I would like to call attention: If I am right, then, arguments with a dialectical tier are not reducible to "pro and con" arguments; hence, they constitute a distinctive type of conductive argument. Hence the criteria for the evaluation of arguments with a dialectical tier will be different than those for "pro and con" arguments.[9,10]

---

[8] Not all arguments receive the sort of attention that constitutes what I call a dialectical environment. As most of us know, some of our arguments generate no response at all, not even the sound of one hand clapping. Very few of us are deluged in the way that Searle reports (Johnson, 2000b).

[9] For one attempt at formulating criteria for evaluating an arguer's response to objections, see my (2003) where I argue that the response should be evaluated by the criteria of accuracy, appropriateness, and adequacy (pp. 49-50).

[10] Thanks to Tom Fischer and Rongdong Jin who read earlier versions of this chapter and offered stimulating and helpful comments.

Chapter 5

Why Argumentation Theory Should Differentiate between Types of Claim

CHRISTIAN KOCK

1. Introduction

Argumentation theory needs a typology of *types of claim* (where 'claim' means that for which an arguer argues). This view is in line with the Wittgensteinian idea of multiple '*Sprachspiele*' and with the notion of different fields with different types of warrant, etc., in Toulmin (who was, incidentally, Wittgenstein's student).

The main reason that necessitates such a typology is that much which can be said theoretically about argument for one type of claim is misleading when said about argument for claims of other types; neglecting the differences between these types is a pernicious Platonic fallacy, against which philosophical argumentation scholars should be warned.

One important type distinction, as I have argued repeatedly elsewhere, is that between theoretical or epistemic reasoning (i.e., arguing for the truth of propositions) and practical reasoning (i.e., arguing for the adoption of proposals); although some argumentation theorists have recognized this distinction, they have not, I believe, fully understood the amount and the depth of the differences it implies.

In general, there is no lack of recognition that not all the claims we argue about in real-life argument are about philosophical truth. But the distinctions most often applied are, I suggest, either too vague or directly misleading. For example, we often hear a distinction between necessary and contingent propositions, where a contingent proposition is one that is neither necessarily true nor necessarily false. But as this definition makes clear, all claims are still seen as propositions which are to be assessed with regard to their truth or falsity. Another related, insufficient distinction depends on the concept of probability: some claims, it says, are about something being true, others about something being merely probable. This distinction, for example, is seen by Brockriede and Ehninger as an important reason to adopt Toulmin's argument theory for the teaching of practical argument:

> Whereas in traditional logic arguments are specifically designed to produce universal propositions, Toulmin's second triad of backing, rebuttal, and qualifier provide, within the framework of his basic structural model, for the establishment of claims that are no more than probable (1960, p. 46).

However, I would argue that the concept of probability misleads us regarding the nature of the claims we argue about in practical reasoning. To say that something is probably the case is an epistemic claim just like the claim that something is definitely the case. To say that the ongoing global warming is probably to a large extent man-made is such a claim. But to say that the EU should reduce its CO_2 emissions by 30 percent is not a claim or proposition about what is "no more than probable"; it is not a proposition at all, but a proposal to the EU to make a decision and implement it.

Just as the concepts of contingency and probability are insufficient to identify the differences between the types of claim that we may argue about, they are also insufficient for another task, namely that of demarcating what rhetoric is about. Although rhetoric has been defined, at least since Aristotle, as argument centered on issues in a certain domain, that domain is not properly defined by means of concepts like the contingent or the probable, nor is that what Aristotle did, as we shall see below.

Jeanne Fahnestock and Marie Secor are rhetoricians who, in a number of papers and textbooks over several years, have made a proposal for a typology of claims or arguments, based on a reinterpretation of ancient *stasis* theory. One recent version of their proposal (Fahnestock and Secor, 2003) distinguishes between the following types of argument: What is it? (definition arguments); how did it get that way? (causal arguments); is it good or bad? (evaluation arguments); what should we do about it? (proposal arguments). An earlier version (Fahnestock and Secor, 1988) proposed that what they call the stasis of an argument could belong to five types, according to whether it concerns an issue of fact, definition, cause, value, or action.

Basically, my proposal in this paper is not new and adds nothing to such an approach as far as the notion of different types of claim is concerned. Rather, my intention is to point to the necessity of making this kind of typological distinction at all, and to show that the differences between types are deeper than generally assumed by most contemporary theorists of argumentation. As a consequence, we will find that many irreducible theoretical differences emerge, in particular between "theoretical," truth-oriented argument on the one hand and practical, action-oriented argument on the other.

2. A spectrum of types

However, I do not wish to set up what might be a misleading dichotomy. Nor am I eager to commit myself to a fixed number of distinguishable "types," whether four or five or another number, as in Fahnestock and Secor's theory and pedagogy. Rather, I suggest that we need to think about the relevant differences in terms of a spectrum. It would have purely theoretical (truth-oriented, "alethic") claims at one end and purely practical ones at the other. In between, and probably with intermediary areas separating the "types," there should, at least, be types like interpretive claims (next to theoretical claims) and value claims of different kinds (next to practical claims). My basic concern is to heighten an awareness of differences.

I believe the point I want to make here is highly apposite because contemporary argumentation theorists, in my view, give far too little attention to these differences, assuming too blithely that argumentation is about one homogeneous kind of thing, and that, for instance, all argumentation is basically about showing the truth of something. As the example of Fahnestock and Secor shows, scholars with strong practical and pedagogical leanings are far more aware of the usefulness of making these distinctions.

What this has to do with conductive argument is that the closer you move toward the "practical" end of this spectrum, the more will conductive argument be the natural and inevitable order of the day. Some of the corollaries of this are these: at this end of the spectrum, good arguments are rarely, if ever, logically valid; the "goodness" of arguments is gradual, multidimensional, and in certain respects relative to individuals; and inference, in the strict, traditional sense of that term, does not exist.

It should be added that rhetoricians such as Aristotle, Cicero, and many others, have always, in some form or other, recognized these views (or most of them), although not many rhetoricians after Aristotle have theorized them. However, philosophically trained argumentation scholars have, at best, only recognized them very reluctantly, or not at all. So I am also trying to add the weight of an "authority" argument to my case when I base it, in particular, on Aristotle. To spell out one important difference between the two ends of the spectrum I turn to Aristotle's theory of the will and related subjects, including his theory of practical reasoning; i.e., reasoning about what to do, as propounded by the British philosopher Anthony Kenny (1979).

3. The logic of practical reasoning

One important insight in Aristotle that Kenny has helped clarify is that in practical reasoning we argue as it were backwards; that is, we start with the valuable goal or result that we want to bring about, for example, health; thus, if health is a good thing, it follows that what brings health is also good, and since exercise is something which brings health, it follows that exercise is good; moreover, if I bicycle to work rather than drive, I get exercise, so bicycling to work is good. Bicycling to work is an available means to this good, i.e., it is in my powers to do. So I may decide to do it. Before I decide to do it I may engage in deliberation (with myself and possibly with my family) on whether that is what I will do.

What we see here is that in practical reasoning, and hence in practical argumentation (we leave aside for the moment the relation between these two terms) we begin with the goal or the end, i.e., the value we wish to promote. Given that the end is good, we look for a means to bring about that end, because that means will also, in that respect, be good. So we look for steps in reasoning that will transfer or *preserve goodness* from the end to the means.

If we compare this kind of reasoning with reasoning about propositions, we see that there we look for steps in reasoning that will *preserve truth*. For that purpose we need truth-preserving rules, whereas in practical reasoning what we need is something that could be called goodness-preserving rules. But these two kinds of rules are quite different. Kenny makes clear that whereas Aristotle himself managed to formulate truth-preserving rules for propositions, he did not even try to formulate a parallel set of goodness-preserving rules for practical reasoning, nor has anyone else attempted to do so, let alone succeeded. The reason is that practical reasoning is much more complicated, and so are the goodness-preserving rules that would be required to codify it. Because practical reasoning works as it were backwards from the desired effect or good to an available means, whereas reasoning about propositions works forward from the truth of one to proposition to the truth of another that follows, we may notice the following:

> If a proposition is true, then it is not also false; but if a project or proposal or decision is good, that does not exclude its being also, from another point of view, bad. Hence, while truth-preserving rules will exclude falsehood, goodness-preserving rules will not exclude badness. (Kenny 1979, p. 146)

As an example of this "backwardness," we might take the following piece of reasoning:

More nuclear power means reduced CO_2 emission ($p \Rightarrow q$).
$\Rightarrow$
Reduced CO2 emission is good $\Rightarrow$ More nuclear power is good (q good $\Rightarrow p$ good).

Notice the backward, goodness-preserving reasoning from the desired goal to an available means. What should be remembered, however, is that more nuclear power may be good *from this point of view*—but possibly bad from other points of view. So it does not simply follow deductively that we should have more nuclear power because we want reduced CO_2 emission, i.e., no such "inference" is valid. The notion "practical inference," if understood as a piece of reasoning on which a certain purposive choice follows as a deduction or entailment from the recognition of a certain goal, is a phantom; other means to the same goal might be available and indeed preferable, and there might be other goals that might be interfered with if we chose to aim for this particular goal. It is no improvement on the notion of "practical inference" to speculate that practical inference is an entailment that is "presumptive"; what this amounts to is essentially to saying that when a good reason for a given choice has been offered, the inference is accepted, but as soon as a counter consideration is brought forward, it is cancelled—and so on *ad infinitum* (see Kock 2007a).

Practical reasoning is modeled in Figure 1 (on page 64). The rectangles are available means or courses of action, while the circles are the goals or ends, that is to say, the goods that we wish to promote. Triangles are means that happen to be unavailable. A straight arrow between a means and a goal indicates that this means will promote this goal, while a dotted arrow indicates that the means will counteract the goal. The point is that for any goal there is more than one available means; and any means that promotes some goal will at the same time counteract at least one other goal. As for the means represented by triangles, all their effects are desirable, i.e., they promote several of our goals and counteract none; sadly, however, these means are unavailable.

To this complicated structure is added the further complication that when we are engaged in practical reasoning, what we have to do first is consider a goal we want to promote, and then look backwards along the straight arrows at the various means that might promote it. Some of these, as we saw, happen to be unavailable, and among the ones that are available we find that they also have dotted arrows leading towards other goals; that is, although they may be good from the point of view of the goal we began our reasoning with, they counteract other goals and are thus bad from other points of view.

The backward logic by which we reason from ends to means is called by Kenny, in an early paper (1966), a "logic of satisfactoriness," as opposed to the "logic of satisfaction." The former is concerned with the way a satisfactory end or goal transfers its satisfactoriness backwards to the choices that will promote it, while the latter is concerned with the way a proposition's state of satisfaction, i.e., of being satisfied, is transferred forwards to another proposition.

If we could reduce practical reasoning to inferences from the truth of certain propositions to the truth of others that follow, things would be simpler; but we are not reasoning about truth. If I want to stay healthy and therefore choose, in light of that premiss, to pursue the habit of bicycling to work, then that decision cannot be called true, nor is it false. It may be true that this kind of exercise may enhance my health, but that is not the same thing as saying that the decision to pursue it is a "true" decision. Kenny, interpreting Aristotle, says: "if the conclusion of a piece of practical reasoning has the imperative form 'Pursue this' or 'Avoid that' it is not something which can itself be straightforwardly described as true or false" (Kenny 1979, p. 94).

Another way of stating the same difference is this: Truth is a one-dimensional thing, often even a dichotomous thing; for many propositions it is indeed the case that they are either true or false. Goodness, by contrast, is a multidimensional thing (see Kock 2003; 2006). That is why there is no goodness-preserving rule that excludes badness. My decision to bicycle the twelve miles to work may be good from the point of view of my personal fitness; but it may be bad from another point of view: it might imply that I cannot find the time or energy to do my work properly, or to walk my dog in due time after work, or maybe I risk being run over by cars or mugged on the way, or catching pneumonia in the rain, or over-exercising and thereby permanently damaging my weak knee. Also, there is the fact that I may find exercise of any kind, including bicycling, so dreadfully boring that is significantly reduces my quality of life.

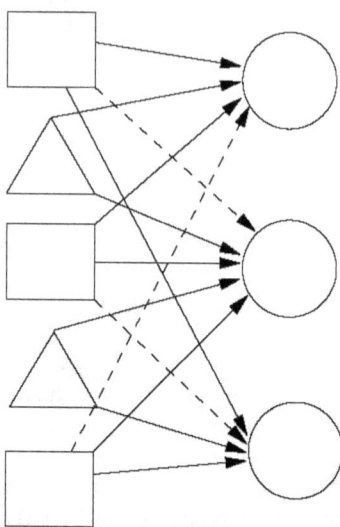

Figure 1: Practical reasoning illustrated.

The rectangles are available means or courses of action, while the circles are goals, that is to say, goods that we wish to promote. Triangles are means that happen to be unavailable. A straight arrow between a means and a goal indicates that this means will promote this goal, while a dotted arrow indicates that the means will counteract the goal.

Thus it is clear that we must stop theorizing as if all claims people may argue about are claims about something being true. Some claims are claims for a purposive choice, or in Aristotle's term, for a προαίρεσις. And a προαίρεσις is not a proposition expressing a belief or an opinion (a δόξα). The *Eudemian Ethics* in particular makes that very clear:

> it is manifest that purposive choice is not opinion either, nor something that one simply thinks; for we saw that a thing chosen is something in one's own power, but we have opinions as to many things that do not depend on us, for instance that the diagonal of a square is incommensurable with the side; and again, choice is not true or false [ἔτι οὐκ ἔστι προαίρεσις ἀληθὴς ἢ ψευδής]. Nor yet is purposive choice an opinion about practicable things within one's own power that makes us think that we ought to do or not to do something; but this characteristic is common to opinion and to wish. (1226a)

Carl Wellman, the originator of the concept of conductive reasoning, seems to take an ambiguous position on the question of whether what we argue for in practical reasoning can be true or false. In several of his ethical writings he declares himself an ethical objectivist, in the sense that ethical judgments in his view can indeed be true or false; but on the other hand a statement like the following seems to accept that truth or falsity is not what we argue about in practical reasoning:

> Too often reasoning is conceived of as a logical operation upon propositions, statements, sentences, or beliefs only. Reasoning must be so restricted, it is alleged, because the validity of an argument is tied to the truth-value of the premises and the conclusion. Where there is no truth or falsity, as in the case of exclamations or imperatives, there can be no reasoning. But if this were so, there could be no such thing as practical reasoning; reasoning that does not arrive at practice or action in the end is not genuinely practical (1976, p. 545).

So practical reasoning is ultimately about action, not about beliefs that may have truth or falsity. But could we not say that after all purposive choice *is* a kind of belief, namely to the effect that one *should* do something? Aristotle specifically addresses this question and answers it in the negative. His reasons include the following: The object of such a belief is a goal, e.g., to be healthy; by contrast, the object of purposive choice is a means, e.g., exercise. Moreover, one can believe that one should do something without acting on that belief or even intending to. Other observations in Aristotle that refute the identification of a purposive choice with a belief are these: We choose *to* do something or avoid it; we believe *that* something; a choice is judged as good because of its object is good, i.e., it is a choice of the right object, whereas a good belief is judged as good because is the right kind of belief, i.e., a *true* belief; and finally, belief has gradations, whereas purposive choice is dichotomous: you either choose to do a thing or you don't (*Nicomachean Ethics* 1112a2-14; Kenny 1979, p. 72).

4. Deliberation, rhetoric and conductive reasoning

In Aristotle's thinking on practical reasoning, the concept of purposive choice is wedded to that of deliberation. The domain of deliberation is demarcated in exactly the same way as that of purposive choice. A purposive choice is one that is preceded by deliberation on the object of that choice. This is where we may notice a link in Aristotle's thinking that has not been sufficiently explored yet, not even by Kenny, namely the link between his ethical thinking and his rhetoric. It is precisely the concept of deliberation that connects them. Deliberation (βούλη; verb: βουλεύειν) is the kind of reasoning that concerns our ethically relevant choices; but it is also the kind of reasoning that rhetoric is made of. What distinguishes rhetoric from ethical reasoning is the fact that rhetoric is speech in front of audiences about the things on which we deliberate in public, i.e., the purposive, collective choices of the polity; moreover, the function of such reasoning is not to achieve consensus between the discussants but to influence the members of the audience, whose role (as Aristotle makes clear) is to act as judges.

Let me add that the expression 'influence the members of the audience' reflects the function of rhetoric from the point of view of the public speaker; from the point of view of the polity as such, the function of rhetoric is to supply the available reasons the decisions being considered. (More on social deliberation as the domain of rhetoric in Kock 2009a; more on the social function of rhetoric in Kock 2007c, 2007d.)

Moreover, it is clear that as soon as we are looking at claims for something being the best choice, we are dealing with conductive reasoning. This is precisely because any purposive choice, although it may be good from some point of view, might still be bad from another point of view. In fact these other points of view are always relevant—or shall we say, in the standard case they are. Admittedly, it is also true that Aristotle in his discussions of practical reasoning and practical inference has pretty consistently limited himself to cases where only one end is taken into consideration and only one available means to bring it about is considered; thus one might get the false impression that in practical reasoning, as in deductive reasoning, the normal case is that we are able to establish a chain of reasoning which necessarily leads us to a conclusion, namely a claim regarding what one should do. That is to say, we might get the false impression that there is something we might call practical inference which is structurally very similar to deductive inference, and we might be tempted to introduce the term 'practical syllogism,' although there is no such expression in Aristotle, and although the examples of practical reasoning we find in him are hardly ever syllogisms in form, but are much more complex.

Two further claims that I made at the outset should also be explained, namely these: "goodness" of arguments is gradual, and that it is, in certain respects, relative to individuals. Both of these claims are based on the multiplex structure of practical reasoning. Nuclear power plants may help us reduce CO_2 emission, and that is a good reason for building them—but *how* good? That of course depends on what can be said *against* building them, i.e., it depends on what other goals might be adversely affected, and what alternative means might also be available to promote the same goal. For example, the risk connected with radioactive waste from nuclear power plants is a well-known reason that speaks against them, and so is the cost of building them, running them, demolishing them, etc.

What we have here is clearly a case of conductive reasoning, insofar as there are, in Govier's terms, "separately relevant non-sufficient factors" as well as "counter considerations" (Govier 1987a, p. 69). But once we recognize the presence of separately relevant factors and counter considerations, we must necessarily ask how strong these factors and considerations are, i.e., "how much support they give to the conclusion" (Govier 1987a, p. 70)—in other words, we must recognize that their strength is a matter of degrees. And along with that insight comes the insight that the strength of the reasons and counter considerations is, at least in some respect, relative to individuals. How could it be otherwise? If we recognize that the weight of reasons and counter considerations is assessed by individuals along continuous scales, how likely would it be that all individuals would assign exactly the same weight along these scales to all these reasons and counter considerations?

In the example of the nuclear plants this problem of indeterminate degrees is obvious: just *how* strong is the counter consideration about radioactive waste disposal? Experts can give us figures about radioactive decay and the likelihood of accidents now and in the future—but how much weight these considerations will have in our deliberations on whether to choose to build more nuclear power plants is still, and unavoidably will be, relative to individuals. Some will decide that the counter considerations outweigh the pro considerations, others that it does not. There is no objective answer to the question—which amounts to saying that the answer is relative to the individuals who have to decide.

This is so not only because of the fact that individuals must be assumed to assign weight to any given factor along a continuous scale, but also because of the fact that there is no intersubjectively recognized *commensurability* between the scales that will be involved. For example, just how much weight will risks affecting future generations have in relation to risks affecting the present generation? What part should be played here by ethical considerations? And how much weight will risks as such have when held against the putative benefits in regard to the prevention of climate change, especially when these benefits are only putative and of uncertain magnitude—just as are the predicted climate changes? Moreover, what about the financial costs of making certain choices now, held against the putative future costs of not making them? And what about risks and costs held against benefits?

My point is not that we should not try to hold all these considerations together and against each other, because we have to, and that is what deliberation is all about; but the point is that there is not and cannot be any authoritative and intersubjectively demonstrable way or doing so.

5. The vexed subjectivity issue

The issue I have just addressed is one that, in my view, constitutes a sore tooth in philosophy and philosophically based argumentation theory. It is an issue that you had better not touch, or you risk an outcry of pain and rage. Philosophers, at last those coming from logic and epistemology, seem so wary of being associated with any sort of "subjectivism" or "relativism" that they, as I see it, will blithely deny the testimony of an overwhelming bulk of everyday experience. Even those few philosophers, such as Wellman, Govier, and other informal logicians who have been bold enough to reject deductive validity as the one criterion of good argument, and who have given us a three-dimensional method of assessing arguments (e.g., Govier's 'ARG': Acceptability, Relevance, and Good Grounds/weight)—even these thinkers have been extremely wary, or blankly unwilling, to concede the property that seems to me to follow with necessity from the admission of relevance and weight as aspects of a good argument: namely the fact that both of these aspects, and in particular weight, are subject to ineliminably differential judgment.

Wellman's vacillation on this issue is representative. He insists that the "validity" of arguments in conductive reasoning is not governed by rules or criteria, where, we should remember, the "validity" of an argument does not mean deductive validity, but simply that it offers "good reasons for its conclusion" (1971, p. 21). Yet both in *Challenge and Response* and elsewhere he professes ethical objectivism and says, e.g., "that there can be one and only one correct answer to any ethical question and that which answer is correct is independent of anyone's acceptance or rejection" (1968, p. 98). Although he insists that no objective weighing can take place, as in an actual pair of scales, his basic position is that "we" will weigh the arguments in conductive reasoning as if we were one person; the way to find the "correct" answer is to continue our discussion, because such "disagreement can be overcome by further reasoning" (1975a, p. 220). His view of validity "projects an ideal of universal agreement" (1971, p. 96)—with one restriction "built into the claim": "a valid argument will, through the process of criticism, remain or become persuasive *for everyone who thinks in the normal way*" (ibid.).

We may remark, in passing, that this "restricted" view of validity would seem to place Wellman in the company of Perelman and his "universal audience." But in any case, I suggest that even if we accept the claim that valid arguments in ethics (and other instances of conductive argument) will be persuasive for anyone who thinks "in the normal way," this does not prove the stronger claim that "there can be one and only one correct answer to any ethical question" (or similar claims in different phrasings). For what is a "valid" argument to Wellman? It is simply a good one; but it is not one that *entails* its conclusion. And even if we all (or at least all those of us who are "normal") were to agree that an argument is "good," this may not lead to the same conclusion for us all, for it does not *entail* its conclusion.

There is, for one thing, the matter of just *how* good the argument is, i.e., the matter of its *weight*, and even more importantly, of its *relative* weight when held against the counter considerations. Of these "weights" Wellman, Govier, and others have clearly said (and I could not agree more) that they *cannot* be "calculated," "measured" or the like. In fact, Wellman himself, almost inadvertently as it appears, concedes that the "weighing" may not lead to the same result for everyone; the whole "calculation" idea "suggests too mechanical a process as well as the possibility of everyone reading off the result in the same way"; so assuming that everyone would do that is apparently erroneous, and furthermore we should avoid "suggesting any automatic procedure that would dispense with individual judgment" (1971, 58).

This is possibly the only reference to individual judgment in the book, but it represents, I would say, an inevitable insight that many philosophers have sought to repress because they feel about it the same way one feels about a sore tooth. In ethical assessment, there *is* individual judgment involved, certainly in the sense that the relative *weight* of a consideration when "weighed" against other considerations, pro and con, is subject to individual judgment. As I said, even if we do admit that we may have universal agreement among all normal people that an argument is "valid" (i.e., good)—and we may admit that for the sake of the argument—we would still, to reach the one "correct" answer together, also have to agree on the *relative* weight on this consideration when "hefted" against all the others (to use the term Wellman suggests). And why and how could we assume that this quasi-universal agreement on the relative weight of all relevant considerations would come about? To claim that it would is an empirical hypothesis that, as I see it, is challenged by a massive amount of daily experience. Do disagreements of this nature generally get resolved by prolonged discussion between people holding different ethical and political views? Have recurring disagreements of this kind generally been settled by centuries of discussion among philosophers? These, obviously, are "rhetorical" questions: they answer themselves.

Most of those who happen to read this paper are probably academics who routinely serve as examiners in their institutions. In my own country, many exams are graded by two examiners—one "internal" (the instructor who has taught the course) and one "external" (an experienced expert in the field, coming from outside the institution). Often in grading a paper or an oral presentation these two will disagree on the "conclusion," i.e., the grade to be given. Both may agree on all the noteworthy properties of the student's effort, the good one as well as the not so good ones; so there will be agreement on which considerations are acceptable and relevant to the assessment. Yet we may still disagree on the relative weight of these considerations, and often do; for example, the fact that the student does not spell very well will undoubtedly count as a "negative" factor for both of us, but in the eyes of the external examiner this shortcoming is perhaps weighty enough to cause the grade to be a C, all things considered, whereas to me it is not quite as weighty as that, given the "positive" considerations, to which I assign more relative weight.

In such cases we naturally discuss things for a while, but let us say that this does not bring agreement. We also look at rules and regulations, but although there is a clause about "formal" factors such as spelling having some weight in the assessment, there is no rule to help us decide whether this degree of bad spelling is enough to land this effort in the C category, or whether it should still be a B. Yet rules dictate that we should find agreement.

What I believe this example shows, along with countless others in everyday disagreements in the domains of ethics, politics, education, etc., is that there *is* no "one and only one correct answer" as to the merit of the student's paper. The external examiner and I both disapprove of bad spelling; it just happens that, in this particular case, he disapproves more strongly than I do. To generalize, the circumstance that different individuals may legitimately differ as to how much relative weight they assign to relevant considerations when making practical decisions such as this one, is an undeniable and ineradicable fact of life, and moreover, I suggest, one that no one could really *wish* would go away.

6. The problem of many dimensions

Moreover, while this example highlights a problem that could hardly be seen as ethical, the argument I have made could be made in an analogous manner for issues with clear ethical considerations involved. Let us imagine a student who does rather badly at an exam. The external examiner wants to fail her; I lean towards letting her scrape through. I first point out that she is eight and half months pregnant and poor as well; in fact, she comes from a disrupted family with a history of drug abuse, crime, sexual abuse, etc. The external examiner seems unmoved. I now change tactics and point out that the department depends for its survival on the number of graduates we turn out, and every "pass" grade counts. Silence. I further inform my co-examiner that the young woman, if she passes this exam, will have finished her final degree, and incidentally that her whole family, or what is left of it, is eagerly waiting at home to start the celebrations, but also she already has a been offered a rather nice job, provided she gets her degree; however, if she fails to get it, and thus the job, her residence permit will expire, and she will be expelled from the country, to which she came as a fugitive from Afghanistan, and where she worked her way up through the educational system, studying at day and washing floors at night. Back in Afghanistan, by the way, there's a good chance that she will be caught by fundamentalist thugs and killed.

What would you say if you were the external examiner in this case? Would you say that *all* these considerations are absolutely irrelevant and should not have been cited, and we should simply assess the young woman's performance at its merit and fail her? Or would you say that one or two of these considerations, especially the last one, might after all be relevant to what you decide, and if relevant, it is also weighty enough for you to let her pass? (Even so, you would probably say that the internal examiner—that is, me—"doth protest too much.") Or would you say that the first considerations I mentioned are perhaps relevant, but surely not weighty enough to let her pass, but the last ones are?

What I believe the example shows is a number of things: (1) It is also true of *ethical* considerations that they may legitimately be assigned different relative weights by different individuals. (2) Moreover, it is quite possible that also the *relevance* of given considerations in ethical and other practical issues may legitimately be differently assessed by different individuals. (3) In relation to a given decision, such as grading an exam, there may be considerations belonging to different *dimensions* of judgment—considerations which are not compatible because they are incommensurable. In academic exams, grading is supposed to be determined only by professional (i.e., scholarly) considerations; but who can deny that, at least in extreme cases, other considerations, such as ethical and humanitarian ones, to say nothing of economic ones, may legitimately be cited?

Even if, in deliberating on a given choice, we did not have multiple and incommensurable factors to deal with, and even if we could have some kind of objective quantification of just *how* much good that choice would do in relation to a given goal or value, and even if that choice could objectively be said to do a lot of good, it would still be categorially wrong to call it a "true" choice. Truth value is one thing, but the kind of value that a good choice brings is another.

7. The spectrum of claims

I have now tried to show that argumentation scholars should distinguish between claims about beliefs and claims about choices. But instead of advocating a dichotomy I wish to suggest that our typology of claim types should probably be more like a spectrum. It would have purely theoretical (truth-functional or alethic) claims at one end and purely practical ones (choices) at the other. In between, and probably with intermediary areas separating the "types," should, at least, be types like interpretive claims and value claims of different kinds.

A hasty version of such a spectrum or continuum might look like this:

Claim type	Factual (alethic, theoretical) claims	Claims about social facts, such as norms	Claims about values	Evaluations	Claims about choice of interpretive claims	Stipulative claims	Practical claims (i.e., about purposive choice of action)
E.g.s of Claims	There is water on Mars; "Look, Sire, the peasants are revolting!"	This nation is a multicultural one	Multiculturalism is good; Charity is the greatest good	Hubble was the greatest astronomer in the 20th Century; Picasso sucks; "Yuck! The peasants are *revolting!*"	Let's do Deconstructionism rather than mainstream literary history	Pluto is henceforth not a 'planet', but a 'dwarf planet'	Let us send an expedition to Mars
E.g.s of reasons given	The channels we see could not be caused by anything but water	Everyone keeps saying it	Multiculturalism makes for a more peaceful world	Hubble's discovery of the expanding universe is mind-blowing	It's more interesting and will get us more graduate students	It is more practical that way	It will make us top nation again and generate a lot of great technology

Some of the points I wish to make are these:

There are intermediary gradations between pure factual (alethic) claims and pure claims of choice. Norms and values are in a third position in between; they are not facts about the world as such, nor are they pure arbitrary choices. Aristotle sees them as intuitions underlying claims of choice.

Wellman, it might be added, is another philosopher who thinks that practical claims are distinct from epistemic ones, and also that there are additional subtypes and intermediary types of claim or argument that ought to be distinguished. Some claims or arguments are more practical than others: "The most practical arguments, I suppose, are those that conclude with judgments of what ought to be done or ought not to be done; only one step more remote from practice are those conclude with value judgments setting up goals worthy of pursuit or evils to be avoided" (1976, p. 531). So Wellman too sees value judgments in some intermediary position between epistemic claims and "real" practical arguments.

Specific evaluations are more like choices than abstract values are; using abstract values as warrants, we make specific evaluations of acts, people or objects in our world.

Interpretive claims as a category seem to me to resemble choices even more. We choose a paradigm or a theory in scholarship not simply because we think it is truer but because it addresses other issues, generates more valuable insight, more interesting discussions, more perspectives—in short, we think it yields more value along several dimensions. (For example, I think it generates more value to look at practical argumentation as conductive rather than as presumptive, deductive, abductive, or what other alternatives there might be.)

Stipulative claims are almost like interpretive claims; they are purposive choices, and as such they cannot have truth value, but we make them because we think they bring other kinds of value, such as being are more practical.

Finally, the purely *practical claims* about purposive choices are similarly made by people who think that on balance the values, purposes or goals they subscribe to are more strongly promoted by a certain choice than by others (for example, *not* making the choice they consider)—but as we saw, because of the complexities of practical choices, including their ineliminable relativity to individuals, it is categorically misleading to describe them as either true or false.

In conclusion, my aim has been to demonstrate that argumentation theory should abandon all attempts to look at all claims as if they were of one and the same type, namely propositions which may be true or false. Instead of seeing truth value as the only kind of value that is relevant for argumentation theory, we should recognize that there are many values—in fact, an open set of them—that are relevant in argumentation, and that it ought also to be so in argumentation theory. The difference I have highlighted between propositions and proposals for purposive choice is basically a reflection of distinctions recognized not only in Aristotle but in modern philosophy as well, notably in the distinction in speech act philosophy between assertives on the one hand and directives, commissives, etc., on the other (Searle 1975, 1983), or he distinction set up by Austin (1953), Anscombe (1957), and others between utterances with a word-to-world "direction of fit" and those with a world-to-word direction of fit (such as directives and commissives).

Understanding the importance of this difference will make the need for a developed theory of conductive argument more obvious, for argumentation for purposive choice is necessarily conductive. If argumentation theory insists on neglecting these insights, it makes a bad choice.

Chapter 6

Deduction, Induction, Conduction:
An Attempt at Unifying Natural Language Argument Structures

FRANK ZENKER

1. Introduction

At the top level of what might be called the most entrenched ontology of natural language argument, normally at least two structures are distinguished: the *deductive* and the *inductive* one (Rehg 2009, Sinnot-Armstrong & Fogelin 2010, Snoeck Henkemans 2001). The first may be characterized as an information-*preserving* transition from premise(s) to a conclusion, the latter as an information-*enlarging* transition. Oftentimes, 'truth' or 'content' may be substituted for 'information.'

It might too early to say if *abduction* has lost the race for recognition as a third top-level category. Should it lose, then presumably that will be because its structure appears to be too similar to (reverse) deduction. Another candidate is *conduction*, proposed by Wellman (1971, 1975) and revived by Govier (1987a,b, 1999, 2001; also see Hitchcock 1981, 1994). Among its premises, conductive arguments feature counter-considerations against pro-reasons, against the conclusion, or against both. Generally, the conductive structure is filled out by an accumulation of individually non-decisive reasons. It is empirically instantiated in deliberative (Scriven 1981) and interpretative contexts (Allen 1993, Ball 1995), and has also received attention in legal studies (Aqvist 2007, Feteris 2008).

With Wellman, we hold that the conductive structure should be treated as a variant of neither the deductive one nor the inductive one.[1] If the conductive structure were treated as a token of the deductive structure, well-accepted properties of the deductive structure would beare lost—which is undesirable.[2] Further, if the conductive structure were treated as a token of the inductive structure, then the distinction between "a premise being accepted *simpliciter*" and "a premise being accepted *and weighed* (or valued in importance)" would be leveled—which is at least equally undesirable.

Moreover, we claim that reducing the conductive to the inductive structure is more promising than a reduction of the conductive to the deductive structure, but nevertheless mistaken. Instead, we investigate the (presumably unorthodox) attempt of reversing this process, and understand the inductive as a limiting case of the conductive structure. We think there is a case to be made, and also the deductive structure might be understood as a limiting case of the conductive structure.

In Section 2, the conductive structure is introduced, and the deductive, inductive and conductive ones are distinguished on the criteria *information content* and *support dynamics*. The introduction of weights serves to explicate evaluative criteria (Section 3) and allows

---

[1] "[I] must admit that the reasons for a moral judgment do not logically entail it; that is, the logical connection between factual premises and moral conclusions cannot be deductive. Those who hold that all reasoning is deductive, or even either deductive or inductive, must reject my view of moral knowledge because the sort to thinking involved in weighing the pros and cons is neither deductive nor inductive" (Wellman (1988, p. 292).
[2] This is opposed to Bickenbach and Davies's (1998, pp. 321f.) claim: "If conduction were straightforwardly a matter of weighing (...) the argument would be either deductive or inductive."

An Attempt at Unifying Natural Language Argument Structures

for a reductive treatment (Section 4). Further evaluative constraints are discussed (Section 5) before closing with a summary and outlook (Section 6).

2. The conductive structure introduced and distinguished

2.1 The conductive or pro/con structure

By 'conductive structure' we refer to the abstract properties of those natural language arguments (as opposed to their contents) that are reconstructable such that:

(1) Pro-reasons and counter-considerations form (normally two) groups, the elements of which are partially ordered on some scale capturing the notion comparative importance.[3]

(2) Pro-reasons confer positive and con-reasons negative support to the conclusion or some group element.

(3) An on balance principle (OBP) indicates that support for the conclusion is based on or comes about by considering more than one group.[4]

The above three conditions appear sufficient to identify a conductive structure, but they are perhaps not necessary.

The conductive structure is also known as the "pro/contra" argument form (Naess 2005). Wellman (1971) considered it in the context of case-by-case (ethical) reasoning; Govier later revived the idea in informal logic. The conductive structure is characterized most markedly by its conclusion being arrived at through a *weighing of pro reasons against counter-considerations*. On Wellman's view, "[t]o claim that a statement is true is to claim that the reasons for it outweigh the reasons against it (...)" (1971, p. 192).[5] Presently, a weaker claim is accepted in the context of pro/con argument: To claim that a proposal (not a statement) is acceptable (not true) is to claim that the reasons for it outweigh the reasons against it.

Several disciplines (e.g., economics, jurisprudence, political science, psychology, philosophy) acknowledge a weighing of considerations as an indispensable feature of deliberation.[6] However, little is known about the processes or mechanisms (if any) that sustain it. Since the 1960s, mathematical modeling is regarded as having established the principled impossibility of *always* arriving at a unique aggregated preference order (*Arrow's theorem*).[7] Should results transfer, this goes at least some way towards explaining why little

---

[3] The notion *comparative importance* is adopted from Gärdenfors (1984).
[4] The on balance principle (OBP) can be added in the reconstruction process or might appear as an overt discourse item. Typically, it will be a variation on: "While I/we *acknowledge* your reasons for X, I/we hold that ... ."
[5] The sentence continues: "(...); to claim that an argument is valid is to claim that it would be persuasive after indefinite criticism" (Wellman 1971, p. 192f).
[6] Kock (2007, p. 185) presents the classical virtues *prudence, social instinct, courage, temperance*, then cites Cicero: "[I]t is often necessary in deciding a question of duty that these virtues be weighed against one another" (*De Officiis* 1.63.152).
[7] Arrow (1950) derived his theorem from comparatively weak assumptions. Reference to *values* was purposefully avoided. Instead, the (presumably less charged) term 'preference' is used. The theorem suggests that Arrow's assumptions may be strengthened. Rather than working with comparative pref-

attention has been paid to the conductive structure. Moreover, along with Wellman, many are of the opinion that there is no formal or general logic that could be used to evaluate conductive arguments in the same sense that deductive- or inductive arguments may be evaluated. This view is often based on the grounds of a principled distinction between *practical* and *theoretical* reasoning (e.g., Kock 2009a, b).

Addressing evaluative standards at the end, we are mainly concerned with relations between deduction, induction and conduction. Our starting point is to question the usefulness of the practical/theoretical distinction for argument structures.

2.2 Information content and support dynamics

For the purpose of distinguishing the conductive from the deductive and the inductive structure, two criteria will be employed.

(1) The comparative difference in information content of the premise-set *vis à vis* the conclusion (*information content*).[8]

(2) The dynamic behavior of the support relation between premise and conclusion under premise-revision (*support dynamics*).

By *support relation* we designate what is also called *argumentative strength* or *justificatory force* (see, e.g., van Eemeren and Grootendorst 2004). By *dynamic behavior* we designate the effect suffered by this support relation upon premise retraction or premise addition.[9] By *premises* and *conclusion*, we designate natural language sentences and their (descriptive or normative propositional) contents. '$P_n \therefore C$' shall mean that C *is* a consequence of a set with n premises, and *is not* such a consequence when "$\therefore$" is starred ("$*\therefore$"). Deductive, inductive and conductive consequences are indicated by the subscripts DED, IND and CON.

If one employs these criteria, differences are obtained when comparing paradigmatic instantiations ("toy examples") of the three argument structures. These differences provide support for the claim that the *weighing of pros and cons* is not merely an accidental feature of the conductive structure—a feature one would dispense with carelessly when treating pro/con arguments under the reconstructive standards of the deductive or inductive argument form.

2.3 The deductive structure

If a conclusion is a *deductive* consequence of a group of premises, then the information content of the premise group, $I(P_n)$, is equal to the information content of the conjunction of the premise-group and the conclusion, $I(P_n \wedge C)$. We can allow the conclusion to be a

---

erences (*ordinal scale*), at cardinal value (*interval scale*) unique social welfare functions become more expectable. Also see Scriven (1981).

[8] 'Information content (difference)' should be understood informally; we do not offer a formal measure (likewise for 'relevance', below). Information may be understood as semantic content, the Bar-Hillel/Carnap distinction into *factual* and *instructional* content being basic (see Floridi 2005, section 3).

[9] These operations are adopted from the AGM approach which models the dynamics of deductively closed and consistent sets of sentences. See Alchourón, Gärdenfors and Makinson (1985) and Gärdenfors (1984, 1988, 2003, 2005).

An Attempt at Unifying Natural Language Argument Structures

premise-repetition (copy), yet require that premises are individually and jointly consistent[10] as well as relevant to the conclusion. Expressed concisely:

(1) If $P_n \therefore_{DED} C$, then $I\,(P_n \wedge C) = I\,(P_n)$

It is a different question whether the premise group P_n is (externally) consistent to some other premise group, e.g., background knowledge. However, P_n must be internally consistent, otherwise any conclusion would follow deductively (*ex falso quodlibet*).

As for dynamics, in the *deductive* case, premise addition is without effect upon the support that premises lend to a conclusion, since *monotony* holds. Monotony means: If a set of premises deductively entails a conclusion, C, then the logical conjunction of this set and any premise deductively entails C. In contrast, premise deletion literally "destroysucts" the argument, once it is required that the premise group features no irrelevant premises. With '&' for addition and '–' for retraction, we can write:

(2) If $P_n \therefore_{DED} C$, then $P_n \,\&\, P_m \therefore_{DED} C$ and $P_n - P_m * \therefore_{DED} C$

As a paradigmatic (meta-level) example of a deductive structure, consider the following instantiation of disjunctive exploitation (*p* or *q*; *p* is not the case; therefore *q*).

Example of a Deductive Argument

(P1) An argument is either deductive or defective.
(P2) This argument is not deductive.
(C) This argument is defective.

This is a meta-level instantiation, since both premises are *un*acceptable. After all, (P1) states a non-exhaustive dilemma and (P2) states a factual falsehood. Nevertheless, the premises deductively imply (C), which is an acceptable conclusion: "This argument is defective." (This example can easily be replaced with a less loaded one.)

Under the above constraints (internal consistency, relevance), and for reasons of deductive logic, there can be no premise (P3), the addition of which would render (C) anything less than the deductive consequence of (P1) and (P2). In other words, *via* premise addition, one cannot change the conclusion of a deductive argument. Moreover, upon deletion of (P1) or (P2) from the premise group, (C) could remain a deductive consequence only if (P1) or (P2) are replaced. So, in order to *maintain* deductive support for (C), premise deletion incurs premise revision.

In summary, in the deductive structure, *premise weakening* does not come in degrees. A conclusion either is a deductive consequence of some premise set or it is not. Moreover, premise *addition* does not strengthen the premises in the sense that "including new information" suggests. This means, a conclusion which is to remain a deductive consequence of a group of old and new premises will be *supported* by the entire premise group only if new and old information has (somehow) been "integrated."

The above considerations set the stage for the claim that, if the conductive structure is a limiting case of some other structure, then it seems implausible to assume that the reducing structure will be deductive.

---

[10] Consistency means that instantiations of '$p \wedge non\,p$' do not occur.

2.4 The inductive structure

If a conclusion is the *inductive* consequence of a group of premises, then the information content of the conjunction of the premise-group and the conclusion is at least as great as the information content of the premise group alone. In other words, the transition to the conclusion may be *ampliative*.

(3) If $P_n \therefore_{IND} C$, then $I(P_n \wedge C) \geq I(P_n)$[11]

As for dynamics, in the inductive case, both premise addition and premise deletion will necessarily *influence* the support that the premises lend to conclusion. Below, this influence is indicated by a subscripted '+/-,' and holds under the same constraints as in the deductive case (consistency, relevance).

(4) If $P_n \therefore_{IND} C$, then $P_n \& P_m \therefore_{+/-} C$ and $P_n - P_m \therefore_{+/-} C$

As a paradigmatic (object-level) example of an inductive argument, consider the following. It is a simplified version of an example from Toulmin (1958). Copi and Cohen (2001) call it *statistical* syllogism, since (P2) is not general. (Ignore for the moment that (P2) is untrue; presently, most Swedes do not commit to any religion.)

Example of an Inductive Argument

(P1) Peter was born in Sweden.
(P2) 90% of Swedes are Protestants.
(C) Peter is a Protestant.

Under the above constraints (consistency, relevance), there may—for empirical reasons—be a premise (P3), addition of which ceases to render (C) the inductive consequence of (P1) and (P2), e.g.:

(P3) Peter's parents emigrated from China 15 years ago.

So, *adding* information to the premises of an inductive argument can weaken the premise-conclusion support. In the two-premise example above, premise-deletion will likewise destroy the argument; this mirrors the deductive case. However, for inductive arguments with more than two premises, premise addition or deletion normally affects support in a less drastic way: premise change will strengthen *or* weaken the inductive support lent to the conclusion. Only in cases of unexpected new information would support be drastically reduced. If so, then the negation of (C) is supported.[12]

---

[11] By choosing '≥,' we also account for *enumerative induction* (e.g., "This marble is black, so is this, and this, etc.; therefore: All *these* marbles are black."), where the information content of the conclusion is equivalent to that of premises (compare the deductive structure). In contrast, "If $P_n \therefore_{IND} C$, then $I(P_n \wedge C) > I(P_n)$" captures cases of inducing content which goes *beyond* the premises. The induced content may be considered *new information* relative to this premise group.
[12] In probabilistic terms, this is expressed by taking a conclusion, C, (rather than non C) to be inductively supported as long as its (objective or subjective) probability value is within the]0.5, 1[interval. Wellman (1971, p. 269) mentions cases in which supporting and support-undermining reasons can

2.5 Reasons against the conclusion vs. reasons against the premises

In the above example, (P1) and (P2) are reasons *for* the conclusion, (C), while (P3) is a reason *against* (C), possibly in conjunction with a premise that China's population is not predominantly Protestant. Furthermore, for any con-reason to undermine the conclusion of a deductive argument the consistency requirement levied onto the premise group must be undermined. Therefore, a reason against a deductive consequence is also a reason against at least one premise. As (P3) shows, in the inductive case, this is not so: (P1-P3) are jointly consistent.

In the three- premise inductive example (P1—P3), the geographic origin of one's family is not logically inconsistent with one's own nationality and that nation's religious proportions. (P1—P3) are logically independent. Rather, the Chinese heritage of Peter's parents, as expressed in (P3), provides a reason against the conclusion (Peter is a Protestant) receiving inductively strong support from the premises. (P3) is not a reason undermining a group element (P1, P2). Likewise,

(P4) Peter has dark eyes and black hair.

may be construed as a reason against the conclusion (though not a decisive one), possibly in conjunction with a premise expressing that China's population is predominantly black-haired and dark-eyed.[13]

Finally, the order in which information is received matters at least to some extent. For example, the support (C) receives from (P1) and (P2) does not seem to be affected when (P4) is added. However, support for (C) is affected negatively when (P4) is accepted along with (P1–P-3). The Chinese family heritage is relevant insofar as hair and eye color follow particular distributions in a population.

2.6 The conductive structure

If a conclusion is the *conductive* consequence of a group of premises, then the information content of the conjunction of the premise-group and the conclusion is larger than the information content of the premise group. This mirrors the inductive case in which the transition to the conclusion is ampliative.

(5) If $P_n \therefore_{COND} C$, then $I(P_n \wedge C) > I(P_n)$[14]

Unlike the inductive case, the pro and the con premises groups *can*, but they need not be jointly consistent. Moreover, adding or retracting a relevant premise from either the pro or the con group *can*, but need not result in a difference with respect to the support conferred by the premises upon the conclusion. So, a conductively supported conclusion will not necessarily be less supported when a reason is retracted, nor necessarily more supported when one is added. This feature holds under the relevance constraint on premises.

(6) If $P_n \therefore_{CON} C$, then $P_n \& P_m \therefore_{CON} C$ and $P_n - P_m \therefore_{CON} C$

"balance out," i.e., the 0.5 point. He holds that, occasionally more than one conclusion may be equally supported.
[13] Here is a natural contact point with defeasible reasoning (Pollock 2010, Woods 2010) which, presently, I cannot develop. For details, see Pinto (this volume, Ch. 8).
[14] Weakening this to "If $P_n \therefore_{COND} C$, then $I(P_n \wedge C) \geq I(P_n)$," as suggested for enumerative induction, might also be reasonable. See note 11.

The distinct support behavior under premise-change can be explained by the independent relevance of the premises for the conclusion,[15] and by an arguer not only retracting or expanding premises, but also updating[16] the *importance* of premises. Both explanations do not exclude, but rather complement, each other. The odd connection between premise revision and support-strength appears to be the most marked difference between the conductive and the inductive structure.

As a paradigmatic example of a conductive argument, consider the following. Here, (CC) stands for *counter-consideration*, (PR) for *pro-reason* and (OBP) for *on-balance premise*; order and numbering are presumed to be arbitrary.[17]

Example of a Conductive Argument

(CC1) Aircraft travel leaves a large environmental footprint.
(CC2) Aircraft travel is physically exhausting.
(CC3) Aircraft travel is comparatively expensive.
(CC4) Airports do not always route baggage correctly.

(PR1) Aircraft travel is comparatively fast.
(PR2) I am overworked and likely able to sleep on the plane.
(PR3) My department reimburses travel expenses.
(PR4) Environmental footprint-differences can be compensated by purchase.

(OBP) (PR1–PR4) outweigh/are on balance more important than (CC1–CC-4)

(C) It is OK[18] to travel to the conference by aircraft (rather than by train).

The near-triviality of this example is on purpose.[19] (PR3) could be retracted, e.g., upon coming to learn that the department cannot reimburse 100% of travel cost. This would constitute (CC5). Also (CC2) could be retracted and modified, e.g., upon coming to learn of a first class ticket. Finally, a family member's illness could be a counter-consideration against a presumption of the conclusion (namely, to attend the conference), *without* pertaining to any pro reason.

In this example, (PR2–PR4) counter (CC1–CC3), while (PR1) is not addressed by a counter-consideration ("is open"). It is difficult to discern how (PR1) could be addressed,

---

[15] This is suggested in Govier (2001). She ranks pro-reasons and counter-considerations as part of argument evaluation. Importantly, not the premises are ranked (e.g. according to importance), but each premise's associated conditional generalization according to the size of its exception class (a.k.a., the scope of its *ceteris paribus* clause). I find it more natural to rank the "individuated reasons," i.e., "$Fa \to Ga$" rather than "CP $[\forall x \, (Fx \to Gx)]$." On Govier's method, see Wohlrapp (2008, pp. 316-334), translated in Zenker (2009a), and Zenker (2009b).
[16] See Wohlrapp (2008) for an account of such updating. He assumes that premise importance is a function of how an issue is subjectively constituted ("framed"), and holds that continued discussion can lead to a correct (or ultimate) framing.
[17] I owe the core of this example to Hans Hansen. Considerations of persuasive effect may pertain to the order in which pro and con reasons are presented, e.g., "pro followed by con, etc., conclusion" or *vice versa* or "pro/con, pro/con, etc., conclusion." Here, I can neither address these, nor any dialectical considerations.
[18] Instead of 'it is OK' (Pinto 2009), 'apt' or 'adequate' could be used.
[19] Deciding on aircraft travel is trivial compared to socio-political issues such as global warming, population growth, genetic engineering, aging societies.

other than by cancelling the above presupposition, in which case (PR1) would be rendered irrelevant. Moreover, (CC4) remains unaddressed by any pro-reason. It might be countered by stating that the objective probability of *my* baggage (as opposed to a piece of baggage similar to mine) being routed incorrectly on *my* flight (as opposed to a flight similar to mine) is epistemically inaccessible to me. Hence, the accessible probability of a baggage loss event is a subjective credence value. This *should* be less important than considerations which do not depend on subjective credence, such as the environmental footprint.

In summary, featuring both pro *and* con reasons, the conductive argument structure, as described here, bears a stronger resemblance to the inductive than to the deductive structure. For reasons of consistency and monotony (above), to respect the pertinence of counter-considerations appears not possible in the deductive structure.

2.7 Closure principle vs. On balance principle

As a necessary evaluative condition, the "principle of total evidence" associated with induction demands that a conclusion count as inductively supported *only if* all relevant reasons appear in the premise group.[20] Some of these may be counter-considerations.

This inductive closure principle resembles the 'on balance principle' of a conductive argument. However, the total evidence principle serves a different purpose. Like the conductive principle, it signals that the transition to the conclusion is based on a finite premise group. Additionally, it spells out the normative demand that this group be *exhaustive* or complete with respect to relevant considerations.

In contrast, the on balance principle indicates at most a descriptive truth, namely that the transition from the premises to the conclusion occurs on the basis of (at least) two particular groups of premises, the pro and the con group. But there is usually no indication that these groups satisfy additional normative standards. Rather, if such a requirement is imposed on the argument, this occurs when evaluating the argument.

It seems natural to assume that various specifications of the on balance principle can give rise to distinct evaluative constraints. I return to this in Section 3.

2.8 The dynamics of the premise groups

Premise groups of a conductive structure may (in principle) be thought of as dynamic. More precisely, the groups of premises claimed to be positively or negatively relevant to a conclusion may be understood as *dynamic* in two senses.

In a *simple sense*, groups are dynamic because new reasons pro/con a given conclusion can be added to the premise set (Wohlrapp 2008). This at least holds in principle. However, it is not clear (to me) to what extent the presumed openness of the pro/con premise groups translates into *qualitatively new* reasons.[21] Clearly, new reasons may again relate favorably or unfavorably either to the conclusion or to the premises. This, however, is also the case in the inductive structure.

In a *less simple sense*, the group of premises in a conductive structure remains dynamic with respect to the positive support conferred by the pro-reasons upon the conclusion and the negative support by the con-reasons undermining it, as each reason in the pro and the

---

[20] It is another matter if one can *know* that the principle is sufficed. But it is a correct criterion nevertheless. *Ex ante* knowledge of the reference class of a future event is an independent problem, unless total evidence would include information we currently do not know how to access or assess.
[21] For example, the debate on the permissibility of abortion and human embryonic stem cell research (Zenker 2010) normally features *exactly four* entrenched con-reasons (a.k.a. "SCIP arguments") for species, continuity, identity, potentiality).

con group can be assigned (what may most generally be called) an *evaluative mark*. This mark can, but it need not be represented by a numeral. If it is, one speaks of a *weight, w*. It may be captured as a function assigning a positive real number[22] to a premise.

(7) $w\,(P_n) \rightarrow R+$

Thus, over and above (positive or negative) support for a conclusion, the differential support-*contribution* of a premise for a conclusion is indicated.

3. Towards evaluative criteria

Given the above, the support which the conclusion of a conductive structure receives from the premises may be captured as the sum of aggregated weights of pro and con reasons. In other words, for one conclusion (rather than another) to be the conductive consequence of a group of *pro and con* premises, a comparison must yield a weight-*difference*.[23] If such aggregation is a mere matter of summation, this yields:

(8) If $Pro_n, Con_n \therefore_{CON} C$, then $\sum w\,(Pro_n) / \sum w\,(Con_n) \neq 1$

The comparative importance of a reason *vis à vis* a counter-consideration cannot be represented in the inductive case—at least not without leveling the distinction between "a premise being accepted *simpliciter*" vs. "a premise being accepted *and weighted in a particular manner*." Indications of a premise's importance for a conclusion appear to be different from and are, perhaps, independent from, indications of its probability. After all, (im)probable premises can, but need not amount to (un)important considerations.

Through the assignment of comparative importance (*via* weights), and through the distinction of weights from probabilities, then, the inductive and the conductive argument structure come apart. The weight-update suffices to explain that conductively supported conclusions may cease to be supported upon retraction or addition of relevant premises; and it also suffices to explain that conductively supported conclusions may be maintained upon premise change.[24]

The above shall support the claim that the notion *comparative importance* can give expression to a reasonable evaluative constraint for pro/con arguments featuring an on balance principle. We return to the evaluative aspect below. First, we demonstrate that *comparative importance* in conjunction with *information content* and *support dynamics* can feature in a unified treatment of the deductive, inductive, and conductive structures.

4. Two-step reduction

The following objection is immediate: On the present understanding, a conductive argument is but an inductive one in which the premises are consistent, relevant, etc., and each premise bears a weight reflecting its comparative importance for (supporting) the conclu-

---

[22] One might further restrict this range, depending on the particular case.
[23] This difference could go above some threshold, to indicate its significance.
[24] So, by allowing weight updates, one may account for the observation that, despite a premise having been retracted, a proponent may still maintain her conclusion.

An Attempt at Unifying Natural Language Argument Structures

sion. Therefore, one might say, the conductive structure reduces to the inductive one in the limiting case where the assigned weights all take some constant value.

While *prima facie* plausible, it is a reduction in the opposite direction that harbors the potential for unifying argument structures. That is, rather than view the conductive as a limiting case of the inductive structure, one might view the inductive as a limiting case of the conductive structure.

If this move is accepted, the possibility for extending the reduction to the deductive structure arises. That is, one may try to understand both the inductive and the deductive structure as *successively reached* limiting cases of the conductive structure. The conductive structure would then be the richest of the three structures.

In the first step, to generate the inductive from the conductive structure, the range of assignable weights is constrained (here: from R+) to a constant value. In the second step, to generate the deductive from the inductive structure, the information content difference is constrained from $I(P_n \wedge C) \geq I(P_n)$ to $I(P_n \wedge C) = I(P_n)$.

The two sufficient (though perhaps non-necessary) criteria, *information content* and *support dynamics*, continue to distinguish the three structures. The principled difference between the conductive and the inductive structure is that weights can be updated upon premise change in the conductive, but not in the inductive (or the deductive) structure. Further, we can have information increase between premises and conclusion in the conductive and the inductive, but not in the deductive structure.

Dropping some of the subscripts, the following summarizes the desiderata. (Ps) indicates constraints on the acceptability of premises (Freeman 2005).

Conductive
(C1) If $P_n \therefore C$, then $I(P_n \wedge C) > I(P_n)$
(C2) $P_n \& P_m \therefore C$ and $P_n - P_m \therefore C$
(C3) $w(P_n) = R+$
(Ps) relevance

Inductive
(I1) If $P_n \therefore C$, then $I(P_n \wedge C) \geq I(P_n)$
(I2) $P_n \& P_m \therefore_{+/-} C$ and $P_n - - P_m \therefore_{+/-} C$
(I3) $w(P_n) =$ constant
(Ps) relevance, consistency

Deductive
(D1) If $P_n \therefore C$, then $I(P_n \wedge C) = I(P_n)$
(D2) $P_n \& P_m \therefore C$ and $P_n - P_m * \therefore C$
(D3) $w(P_n) =$ constant
(Ps) relevance, consistency

5. Discussion

If a unification of argument structures were to be achieved, then this unification would have come about because the weights (which arise in reconstructing conductive arguments) were "carried through" to the deductive and inductive structure (where they do not arise). Since these weights are set to a constant value in the inductive and the deductive case, they do not matter there. They are "hidden."

We lay no claim to the psychological reality of weights. The above is only a model, and needs to be developed. In particular, allowing weights from R+ appears to be too large a region. A smaller interval could suffice, though this should be left to the individual case under study. For the analyst, the choice might depend on her evaluative purposes; the same holds for a minimal weight requirement (see below).

On our proposal, the conductive structure can, but it need not be treated as a third top-level category. Rather, the three structures can be understood as variations along the dimensions "information content-difference between premise and conclusion" and "(premise conclusion) support behavior under premise change."

Taking the differential importance of premises seriously—by treating weights not as a *mere* metaphor—has useful implications for evaluating conductive arguments. As indicated above, if there is *no* weight difference between the summed weights of pro and con reasons, then—whatever the conclusion (C) may state—it cannot be more supported than its negation (*non* C). Hence, for any claim that a particular conclusion is, on balance, (significantly) *more* supported than another, there will be a weight assignment that makes it so.[25]

Any weight-update in response to new information can be traced. With respect to this update, then, additional normative constraints might be spelled out. Such constraints might include a *threshold* (the significance of a weight difference), *exhaustiveness* (all relevant considerations weighted), *homogeneity* (uniform weight-scales), *and ignorance* (absence of relevant considerations).[26]

Finally, provided the claim is raised—as it normally is when compromises between conflicting positions are supported—that counter-considerations are *respected* or *acknowledged* in a conclusion, then an evaluative condition consists in not allowing the assignment of the weight zero to any counter-consideration (*insincerity*). Content-wise, then, each counter-consideration must (somehow) be discernible in the conclusion (*differentiability*), unless the claim to having acknowledged it is simply false.

These constraints should be further developed and applied.

6. Conclusion

On two criteria, (i) the difference in information content between premises and conclusion and (ii) the dynamic behavior of the support for the conclusion upon premise change, the *deductive*, the *inductive* and the *conductive* structure may be distinguished. Allowing weights to be assigned to premises (which are variable in the conductive, yet constant in the deductive and the inductive structure), the three structures can be understood as variations on these criteria.

Should unification be achieved here, then this would have been made possible by taking the weight metaphor ("weighing pros against cons") seriously. Building on the assignments of weights, several evaluative conditions for conductive arguments were proposed. Perhaps most basic are the non-zero difference between summed weights and the non-zero weight for pro or con-reasons. The first addresses an *imbalance* between pro and con reasons, the second *falsely* claiming to acknowledge counter-considerations.

Further conditions may become available as the model is developed. Perhaps, the region R+ will be too large to be useful in evaluation. Future work should investigate overlap with

---

[25] Analysts may motivate aborting a case, when it becomes clear that participants apply such weights incorrectly or, perhaps, treat them as metaphors after all.

[26] The constraints discussed here partially overlap with those of Mann (1977). The ignorance and the exhaustiveness constraint might perhaps be drawn into one.

probabilistic modeling and importance measures, for example in risk assessment. Another task is to provide specifications of the on balance principle; one might investigate how a *proportionality principle* (or similar) differs from it (Zenker 2010). Finally, it might be possible to extend the "reduction" to abduction.[27]

---

[27] Earlier versions of this chapter were presented at the Symposium on Conductive Arguments hosted by the Centre for Research in Reasoning, Argumentation and Rhetoric, University of Windsor, ON, Canada, April 29–May 1, 2010; the Thirteenth Biannual Conference on Argumentation at Wake Forest University, Winston-Salem, NC, U.S.A., March 19–21, 2010; and the Higher Seminar in Theoretical Philosophy, University of Lund, Sweden, Dec 1, 2009. I am indebted to Ingar Brinck, Ingvar Johansson and Erik J. Olsson, as well as Anthony Blair, Thomas Fischer, Hans Hansen, David Hitchcock, Ralph Johnson, Fred Kauffeld, Robert Pinto, Christopher Tindale and Harald Wohlrapp for useful advice and comments. Research was conducted while funded by a postdoctoral grant from the Swedish Research Council.

PART III – EVALUATING CONDUCTIVE ARGUMENTS

Chapter 7

Weighing Considerations in Conductive Pro and Con Arguments

THOMAS FISCHER

1. Introduction: Wellman's "heft" and premise weight

Talk of "weighing" reasons pro and con is a common manner of speaking. "Premise weight" is an obviously metaphorical expression that some theorists view as an overstretched and faulty metaphor with respect to its application in theory of argument. For example, Harald Wohlrapp wrote in his *Der Begriff des Arguments*:

> The upshot of the discussion of conductive argument is the following: The conclusion reached with arguments presented is not the result of a weighing, whatever that may be. (Wohlrapp 2008, p. 333; trans. p. 21)

Trudy Govier is perhaps the only widely known theorist of argument who, in multiple publications, has endorsed and expanded upon Wellman's concept of premise weight. For Govier, premise weight is not literally measurable, which implies that premise weight must be non-numerical in some sense.

> It is important to note that "outweighing" is a metaphorical expression at this point. We cannot literally measure the strength of supporting reasons, the countervailing strength of opposing reasons, and subtract the one factor from the other. (Govier 1999, p. 171)

Carl Wellman, the originator of the concept of conductive argument, also seems to have understood premise weight to be non-numerical, as indicated in the following passage from his *Challenge and Response* (1971):

> Nor should we think of the weighing [of reasons] as being done on a balance scale in which one pan is filled with the pros and the other with cons. This suggests too mechanical a process as well as the possibility of everyone reading off the same result in the same way. Rather one should think of weighing in terms of the model of determining the weight of objects by hefting them in one's hands. This way of thinking about weighing brings out the comparative aspect and the conclusion that one is more than the other without suggesting any automatic procedure that would dispense with individual judgment or any introduction of units of weight. (Wellman 1971, pp. 57-58)

In this passage, Wellman distinguishes two concepts of weight, which we might conveniently call *scale-weight* and *heft-weight*. Scale-weight involves machinery, even if only a simple balance type of scale. The output of the scale-weight process is numerical. Even on a simple balance scale, the use of standard weights can provide numerical weight outcomes.

Scale-weight outcomes, being numerical, are precise and absolute rather than non-numerically comparative. Scale-weight is probably the current default meaning of "weight" in both theory of argument and in everyday contexts.

As Wellman, Govier and others have noted, scale-weight is not suitable as the literal basis for the premise weight metaphor. Per Wellman, heft-weight is the correct literal basis for this metaphor, and Govier would likely agree. To my knowledge, heft-weight has not received very much analytical attention in the literature on conductive argument, perhaps because heft-weight is viewed as uselessly vague and subjective. If this characterization is indeed suitable, then the concept of premise weight in theory of argument falls prey to a destructive dilemma. If scale-weight is the literal basis of the premise weight metaphor, then the metaphor is faulty and over-stretched. If heft-weight is the literal basis of the metaphor, then the metaphor is suitable, but premise weight is thereby uselessly vague and subjective. Perhaps the only way to save the concept of premise weight is to further recharacterize heft-weight. But how could this be done?

In contemplating heft-weight, we can imagine a person lifting several items one at a time and making a verbal pronouncement on each one. Initially the pronouncements will be comparative in nature, such as: *much heavier than, heavier than, same weight as, lighter than,* or *much lighter than.* A set of comparative, ranked, weight categories is thus progressively created. The objects ranked by comparative weight could then be divided into perhaps five or so categories of non-numerical, verbal weight quantities such as: *very heavy, heavy, medium, light,* and *very light.* We need not think of the objects as *individually* ranked *within* each weight category, however. The individual human being is here functioning as a comparative weighing machine. Due to the lack of precision of heft-weight, there would be blurred boundaries between categories, and some items would have disputable weight categories, even with just one individual doing the hefting.

The outcome of this individual weighing process is a series of judgments that is objective in the sense that the human body is typically a good, if only approximate, weighing machine that provides a non-numerical, comparative, quantitative output. If one object had a lot more heft than another but a mechanical scale reported the reverse, we would properly believe we had a broken scale. This individual judgment of heft-weight is thus not subjective in the sense of individual personal preferences such as 'chocolate tastes much better than vanilla'. But is heft-weight valid only for each individual weigher and thus non-objective in the sense of not intersubjective?

It seems to me that heft-weight should be understood as potentially intersubjective and thus objective, despite being non-numerical. As Aristotle noted, the solitary human being is either a beast or a God; so the standard case of Wellman's "hefting" individual is that he is a member of a group. Let's say this group has about forty or so people, like the pre-Neolithic human bands, and that there is a mixture of the young and the old, and the frail and the robust. While Wellman's individual lifter is doing his or her thing, the others are also picking up the same objects in the same way and classifying them into ranked weight categories.

It would soon be found that the mid-range of people in terms of physical ability generally find a group of objects heavy and another group of objects light in weight, approximately speaking. These objects would then be regarded as *intersubjectively* heavy, light, etc. The fact that the Milos of this group, the athletically trained weight lifters, found most of the common objects to be light in weight, and the small or frail of the group found most objects to be heavy would all be understood and adjusted for by members of the little group in the usual way. In effect, the mid-range of human strength becomes a kind of standard, much as color words are defined in the standard context of normal daylight. We do not think that red things turn black on a dark night, and we do not think that heavy things literally become light in Milo's hands.

According to the above account, heft-weight, properly understood is non-numerical, approximate, comparative, and objective (intersubjective). On this characterization, heft-weight has many of the virtues of scale-weight, the major exceptions being lack of numerical output and consequent precision. Instead of numerical output, heft-weight provides classification of objects into non-numerical, comparative quantity categories of an approximate nature. Understood in this way, heft-weight is a very plausible literal basis for the metaphor of premise weight.

It might be objected that approximate, non-numerical quantities are not really quantities at all because quantities are *by definition* expressed as *symbolic* numbers. Although such a stance may have numerous defenders, the science of cognitive psychology has recently produced some interesting, and I think relevant, findings about what has been called the *approximate number sense*. Perhaps the term "quantitative capacity" would have been a better choice here than "number sense", but the latter wording has taken hold. The distinction between two different quantitative 'senses' is more than just a conceptual one. While the *symbolic number sense* is processed in a spread-out fashion in the prefrontal cortex, the approximate number sense is embodied in another part of the brain called the *intraparietal sulcus* (Cantlon et al., 2009). The two number senses seem to be connected in interesting ways. Current research provides preliminary indications that math education can benefit by co-developing the approximate sense and the symbolic number sense (Halberda et al., 2008). Professional mathematicians are known to exercise their approximate number capacities when socializing at conferences. Classifying the approximate number sense as "mere intuition" is likely an inappropriate over-simplification, given recent findings in cognitive psychology.

A commonly used example of the approximate number sense is when someone views several supermarket lines and classifies them as "shortest, short, medium, long, and longest". Quantities are involved in this process, but typically no counting or symbols. Interestingly, other higher animals have this same ability, which provides obvious evolutionary advantages. The predator needs to choose which group of fleeing herbivores to chase; the fruit-eating animals need to pick which tree will provide the most fruit at the time. It seems quite plausible that this approximate number sense is involved in the process that produces heft-weight. The approximate number sense is comparative, non-numerical, and the product of individual judgment; and heft-weight is all of these things.

The correspondence between Wellman's verbal categories of heft weight, under my interpretation, and the commonly used categories of premise weight is straightforward:

heft-weight	very heavy	somewhat heavy	medium	light	very light
premise-weight	very strong	somewhat strong	medium strength	somewhat weak	very weak

Both heft weight and premise weight determinations are accomplished with the same general comparatives already mentioned: *much more, more, about the same, less,* and *much less.*' For both heft weight and premise weight, the number of categories is flexible and contextually and pragmatically determined. Such non-numerical quantity categories seem to be essential in human cognition and communication.

Trudy Govier has remarked that if the judgment is made to not use "weight" in theory of argument, then "one would have to figure out some other way of speaking. One might speak of deliberating, or comparatively considering, or making judgments of comparative significance" (Govier personal correspondence, 1/31/10). I think, and Govier might agree, that these potential substitutions for talk of premise weight would do less work overall than the premise weight concept, understood as heft-weight. We use comparative, non-numerical quantity categories in our reasoning all the time; so dismissing such reasoning as inherently faulty requires a high burden of proof which has not been met.

Non-numerical, comparative quantitative categories are frequently applied by speaking of *degrees of* this and that. For example, there are degrees of argument strength, degrees of importance, and so on in a great many areas of discourse. Govier has herself puzzled over the so-called "degrees" of argument strength: "What are these degrees anyway? There is no answer" (2009, p. 5). Perhaps the concept of "degrees" here is puzzling because symbolic numbers seem to intrude, so to speak, where they do not obviously belong. Perhaps the above account clarifies talk of non-numerical degrees.

Some theorists of argument do apply numbers to these categories of non-numerical quantitative classification. For example, "very strong" might be assigned a "5," "somewhat strong" a "4," etc. What are established in this process are *proportionalities*, e.g. one "very strong" premise is worth five "weak" ones, etc. This is a very common move in decision-making technologies. Any weight system which calls for an assignment of a rational number between zero and one inclusive is obviously also establishing proportionalities. For instance, if the above 5-scale system were applied to an argument with one strong reason pro and three weak reasons con, then the strong reason would be assigned $5/(5+1+1+1) = .625$, and each weak reason would be assigned 1/8 or .125. One can easily imagine a colored pie chart with eight pie sections, the size of each being proportional to the derived number. Perhaps the pro reasons could be colored green and the con reasons red. Some versions of such pie charts are likely used frequently in contexts of decision-making.

Just as having two or three or five or seven or more weight categories is contextually determined, so is the choice of number scale, e.g., 5-4-3-2-1 vs. 10-8-5-3-1. The number scale selection has a questionable rational basis in conductive argument evaluation for at least one major reason: The exact selection of the number scheme can actually *determine the evaluation* for some arguments. To provide just one example, choosing a number scheme of 3-2-1 vs. one of 10-5-2 for the three "strong/medium/weak" verbal categories *determines* the evaluation of an argument with the following premise weight classifications: four strong pro reasons, five moderate con reasons, and five weak con reasons. This type of argument supports its conclusion on a 3-2-1 assignment but not on a 10-5-2 assignment.

It seems to me that only legitimate use of numbers in premise weight contexts is to express the outcome of a very rough, quantitative, non-numerical process of comparison that has already been completed before numbers were applied. It is easy to see how premise weight determination has been rather often described as a purely subjective matter, since the application of numbers is problematic and in a sense occurs post-process. The fact that premise weight does not use numbers in the scientific way does not by itself imply that premise weight is only a subjective matter in the sense of making merely personal preferences and choices.

As previously mentioned, there is another and wider sense of 'objectivity', that of being able to make a rational argument, which obviously requires intersubjective contexts. Before further exploring issues of subjectivity and objectivity in a later section of the present paper, it would be best to first turn to a more detailed account of Govier's claims and some responses from some of her principal critics.

2. Govier's "exceptions" and issues of quantification

Govier's detailed account of weighing reasons is put forward in Chapter 10 of her *Philosophy of Argument* (1999) and in Chapter 12 of her textbook, *A Practical Study of Argument*, the current edition being the 7th (2010). In the first paragraph of her text's section on conductive argument evaluation, she writes of premises' "significance or weight for supporting the conclusion" (p. 359). She soon introduces the specifics of her concept of premise weight, as follows:

> While acknowledging that we are dealing here with judgment rather than demonstration, we will suggest a strategy for evaluating reasons put forward in conductive arguments. The premises state reasons put forward as separately relevant to the conclusion, and reasons have an element of generality. That generality provides opportunities for some degree of detachment in assessing the conclusion. Since this is the case, we can reflect on further cases when seeking to evaluate the argument. (2010, p. 361)

Govier's explication of premise weight uses as its principal example an argument for the legalization of voluntary euthanasia. Several of her major critics, including Harald Wohlrapp, have responded to her with further analyses of the same argument, so it is worth stating completely here:

> (1) Voluntary euthanasia, in which a terminally ill patient consciously chooses to die, should be made legal.
> (2) Responsible adult people should be able to choose whether to live or die.
> Also,
> (3) voluntary euthanasia would save many patients from unbearable pain.
> (4) It would cut social costs.
> (5) It would save relatives the agony of watching people they die an intolerable and undignified death.
> Even though
> (6) there is some danger of abuse,
> and despite the fact that
> (7) we do not know for certain that a cure for the patient's disease will not be found,
> (1) Voluntary euthanasia should be a legal option for the terminally ill patient. (Govier 2010, p. 360)

Govier identifies the associated generalizations for the pro reasons as follows, each with its *ceteris paribus* clause:

> 2a. Other things being equal, if a practice consists of *chosen* actions, it should be legalized.
> 3a. Other things being equal, if a practice would *save people from great pain*, it should be legalized.
> 4a. Other things being equal, if a practice would *cut social costs*, it should be legalized.
> 5a. Other things being equal, if a practice would *avoid suffering*, it should be legalized. (Govier 2010, p. 361)

Each generalization is seen to have exceptions, which are the subject matter of the *ceteris paribus* clause.

> For example, you could imagine social practices that would deny medical treatment to medically handicapped children, abolish schools for the blind, or eliminate pension benefits for all citizens over eighty. Such practices would save money, so in that sense they would cut social costs. But few would want to support such actions. Other things are not equal in such cases; the human lives of other people who are aided are regarded as having dignity and value, and the aid is seen as morally appropriate or required. (Govier 2010, p. 361)

The principle of cutting social costs has, in Govier's terms, a wide range of exceptions.

Perhaps Govier's most succinct statement about premise strength is in her *Philosophy of Argument* (1999, p. 171):

> A strong reason is one where the range of exceptions is narrow. A weak reason is one where the range of exceptions is large.

For Govier, and within the present paper, the following are treated as roughly synonymous expressions because all are quantitative in a similar way: premise *significance, weight, strength,* and *force*. At issue here is the quantitative force of reasons in the broadest sense, as least for Wellmanian "pattern 3" conductive pros and cons arguments.

Harald Wohlrapp challenges and rejects Govier's account of a quantifiable range of *ceteris paribus* exceptions:

> But why should the argument be weaker, because the associated if-then sentence has 'more exceptions'? Can I really compare the number of exceptions through enumeration? Must we not bear in mind that the general principles are situation-abstract and that, depending on how they are being situated, they can have arbitrarily many exceptions? Is there anything countable here? (2008, pp. 323-324; trans. p. 10)

I would like to address this important critique in two respects: (1) issues regarding the nature of these exceptions and in particular their quantifiability; and (2) the general role of the 'normal situation' and *ceteris paribus* in everyday argumentation vs. in scientific contexts. This second issue area will be addressed in Section III of the present paper. What sort of things are these so-called exceptions?

As quoted above, Govier states that the point of framing the generalization associated with a conductive argument consideration is to identify additional *cases* falling within that generalization. According to Govier, these cases are then to be *reflected on* in the appropriate process of evaluating premise weight in conductive arguments. Such cases would seemingly be of two kinds, (1) actual cases past or present, and (2) fictional *a priori,* "what if" cases, including potential future cases. It seems to me that the quantity of exceptions concerns not the number of items on a *list of exception categories,* which can be almost arbitrarily long. Rather, the quantity of exceptions must involve *cases,* actual or a priori as described above.

An illuminating question to ask at this point may be as follows: How does Govier come to reasonably believe that there are a great many exceptions to the generalization of cutting social costs? She obviously knows this from her experience living in a wide, but imprecisely delineated, moral community that one might call the developed democracies. She learned about the social values and behavior that create this "wide range of exceptions" by experiencing multiple cases of a normative nature. Two critical questions for Govier's account are: (1) How and in what sense are such cases counted or numerically assessed, and (2) How and in what sense are such cases relevant to the concerns of normative logic?

Any individual's knowledge of how many exceptions there are to the principle of reducing social costs is imprecise, which suggests the involvement of the approximate number capacity described above. Explicitly counting exceptions to the principle of reducing social costs is not commonly done. We simply do not go around stating, for example, that there were 794 exceptions to the principle of cutting social costs in the U.S. Congress from 2005 to 2009. Instead, we learn in living which types of cases are very common and which are rare in our moral, legal, and social communities. We do not have in mind the details of most cases and we do not typically count them. We know of a great many cases in which social costs are borne so that other objectives can be attained. We know of comparatively few cases in which unbearable human pain is knowingly tolerated in favor of controlling social costs. Comparative, non-numerical, and individual judgment is being exercised, and that judgment has some objective basis in the quantity of cases comprising the relevant evidence. We acquire knowledge of actual social values by experiencing a great many cases, both legal cases and cases the everyday sense or situations and decisions made. But how are these relevant cases evaluated and processed as evidence, and what concepts and issues within normative logic are involved?

A very fruitful distinction to apply here might be between case-based legal argument, emphasized in common law-oriented legal cultures, and rule-based legal argument found in civil-law-oriented legal cultures. If I am correct in interpreting Govier's exceptions-based understanding of conductive argument as a matter of supporting cases in the widest sense of "case," then the legal model of processing cases, rules and social values may provide insight into the normative aspects of everyday conductive reasoning.

A particularly interesting account of case-based and value-based legal reasoning has been provided by Trevor Bench-Capon and George Christie. A legal argument is a paradigm of an argued case. Of course legal arguments and reasoning have been foundational for normative logic since Toulmin. In comparing case-based, common law legal argument with rule-based, civil law legal argument, Christie very effectively highlighted the distinctive role of cases in the former:

> Under the approach to legal reasoning now to be described [case-based, common law], so-called rules or principles are merely rubrics that serve as the headings for classifying and grouping together the cases that constitute the body of the law in a case-law system. In such a system even statutes are no more than a set of cases, if any, that have construed the statute together with the set of what might be called the paradigm cases that are, in any point in time, believed to express the meaning of the statute. (2000, p. 147)

Arguing from a few precedent cases is of course a standard argument by analogy using the "argument from precedent" scheme. But the picture becomes more complex, and more interesting, once social values are brought in, as theorized by Bench-Capon. For Bench-Capon, a given case in law is appropriately decided within a key context of often many other cases—past, present and future:

> A given case is decided in the context both of relevant past cases, which can supply precedents which will inform the decision, and in the context of future cases to

which it will be relevant and possibly act as a precedent. A case is thus supposed to cohere with both past decisions and future decisions. This context is largely lost if we state the question as being whether one bundle of factors is more similar to the factors of a current case than another bundle, as in HYPO, or whether one rule is preferred to another, as in logical reconstructions of such systems. (2000, pp. 73-74)

The context of cases is key because, according to Bench-Capon,

> we see a case-based argument as being a complete theory, intended to explain a set of past cases in a way which is helpful in the current case, and intended to be applicable to future cases also. The two goals are closely linked. Values form an important part of our theories and they play a crucial rule in the explanations provided by our theories. (2000, p. 74)

Bench-Capon believes that "the 'meaning' of a case is often not apparent at the time the decision is made, and is often not fixed in terms of its impact on values and rules." He continues, "Rather, the interpretation of the case evolves and depends in part on how the case is used in subsequent cases" (2000, p. 74). Thus case-based argument in law it is commonly not about a small number of cases implying a value scheme but is rather about potentially many relevant cases that modify value schemes in ways not always understood until later interpretations. There is a "theory of cases" that new cases are constantly modifying earlier ones.

What is the theoretical relevance of these legal arguments, understood as above, to conductive argument evaluation? The *factors* of legal argument analysis seem to me to be fundamentally similar to the *considerations* of general pro and con conductive arguments concerned with evaluative issues:

> The picture we see is roughly as follows: factors provide a way of describing cases. A factor can be seen as grounding a defeasible rule. Preferences between factors are expressed in past decisions, which thus indicate priorities between these rules. From these priorities we can adduce certain preferences between values. Thus the body of case law as a whole can be seen as revealing an ordering on values. (Bench-Capon 2000, p. 76)

And further:

> In regard to legal theories cases play a role which is similar to the role of observations in scientific theories: they have a positive acceptability value, which they transfer to the theories which succeed in explaining them, or which can include them in their explanatory arguments. (p. 76)

Cases both express and develop value schemes, which consist of both lists of values and their prioritization in contexts of conflict. Henry Prakken has endorsed this approach as well: "As Bench-Capon [2] observes, many cases are not decided on the basis of already known values and value orderings, but instead the values and their ordering are revealed by the decisions. Thus one of the skills in arguing for a decision in a new case is to provide a convincing explanation for the decisions in the precedents" (Prakken 2000, pp. 8-9). The evaluation criteria for case theories for Bench-Capon are five: explanatory power, consistency, simplicity, non-arbitrariness of preference, and simplicity/safety. Although there are some numerical measurements within some criterion, e.g. explanatory power, the relative weighting of these criteria against each other does not involve numerical weights.

It seems very plausible to me that these points are applicable well beyond legal argumentation. Perhaps weight in conductive arguments, at least those focused on evaluational issues, might best be understood on the model of the above approach to legal case-based arguments. Our daily experience and decisions, both collective and individual, form a kind of case history that both expresses and continually forms and re-forms our values. Philosophers in recent decades have tended to understand moral issues (and sometimes practical issues) in terms of *rule-based models* rather than in terms of *case-based* models, but this long-term emphasis may have been overdone. It seems to me quite plausible that the case-based reasoning model would readily apply to non-moral, evaluative, conductive reasoning as well.

The idea of value schemes evolving with case decisions is entirely consonant with Stephen Toulmin's remarks in *The Abuse of Casuistry*: "Historically the moral understanding of peoples grows out of reflections on practical experience very like those that shape common law. Our present readings of past moral issues help us to resolve conflicts and ambiguities today" (1988, p. 316). Although Toulmin did not to my knowledge accept and apply the term "conductive argument", in his book on casuistry he frequently alludes to "weight" in argument evaluation, mentions a "network of considerations" (p. 34), and states the following in the closing pages of the last chapter: "Practical reasoning in ethics is not a matter of drawing formal deductions from invariable axioms, but of exercising judgment—that is, weighing considerations against one another" (p. 341). Toulmin pioneered the legal-based approach to general reasoning and argument. It seems to me that applying the developing case-based, value-based understanding of legal reasoning to everyday argumentation is a very promising direction indeed.

It is not presently clear to me the extent to which the above-proposed direction does or does not lead toward AI research in the sense of machine intelligence. But if AI in the full sense is involved, it seems to me that arguments might have to be understood as supporting as well as attacking, an idea put forward in a very different context of discussion by Cayrol and Lagasquie-Schiex (2009, pp. 65-84). Perhaps a very broad characterization of the type of reasoning in question might be what Robert C. Pinto and others have called "*support by logical analogy.*" In his (2001, p. 123), Pinto describes the method of logical analogy as "pre-eminently important." Pinto further notes in this passage: "Though it [argument from logical analogy] is fairly widely recognized as a method for justifying negative evaluation of arguments and inference, in my view it can also provide grounds for positive evaluations as well." Govier addresses refutation by logical analogy in her textbook's chapter on analogical reasoning. I am not aware of her addressing support by logical analogy elsewhere. David Hitchcock has written a very interesting paper (1994) on conductive argument validity which utilizes, according to my understanding of it, refutation by logical analogy; but I believe he does not address "premise weight" here specifically.

A point I would like to add is that support by logical analogy would seemingly involve analogous cases that might be argumentatively addressed in the mass, rather than in the substantial detail of a standard two-case argument by analogy. Toulmin's idea of case-based reasoning involving *pattern recognition* (1988, p. 40) might be key here. We think of a standard argument by analogy as involving a very small number of highly detailed cases, but pattern recognition operates typically over an indefinitely large number of cases through a kind of *inductive analogy*, at least with Wellmanian "pattern 3" arguments.

It might be objected that in focusing on Govier's talk of further cases to reflect on, I am hopelessly blurring the distinction between conductive and analogical argument. The claim that premise weight is commonly supported by, broadly speaking, analogical types of arguments does not imply that conductive arguments are types of analogical arguments. The main argument, the first tier of reasons above the conclusion (the main conclusion being at the bottom of the argument diagram), may be convergent but have analogical *subarguments* either in the dialectical tier or in corresponding evaluation arguments. It is interesting to note that analogical and conductive arguments are typologically "cousins" in a sense in that both are inherently *comparative* in nature.

Not all conductive arguments are about valuational matters. Some theorists' efforts regarding the "quantity of evidence" in conductive argument might best be seen as addressing conductive arguments with non-valuational conclusions rather than conductive arguments in general. For instance, in his *Cognitive Carpentry*, John L. Pollock proposed numerical quantitative assignments to premises for arguments that can be interpreted as statistical syllogisms. In his (2002), Alexander V. Tyaglo has applied probability theory to separate reasons in convergent arguments. The epistemic status of the probability numbers themselves makes this approach one of limited scope and value.

Ideas from Pollock and from Tyaglo may be applicable to *predictive* (or dispositional) conductive arguments, some of which seem to be arguments from sign. An example of such an argument appears early in Govier's textbook chapter on conductive argument: "She must be angry with John because she persistently refuses to talk to him and she goes out of her way to avoid him. Even though she used to be his best friend, and even though she still spends a lot of time with his mother, I think she is really annoyed with him right now" (2010, p. 366). Whether it is useful to identify two (or more?) basic subtypes of conductive argument, the empirical and the valuational, is an interesting question worth pursuing. The argument of the present paper concerns principally "valuational" conductive arguments. Premise weights are proportionalities, and probabilities are proportionalities, but their sharing this feature does not make them into identical properties.

A fairly controversial aspect of Govier's work on conductive argument evaluation has been her use of the important but difficult term *ceteris paribus*. This issue area is addressed in the next section.

3. *Ceteris paribus* and conductive evaluation

Regarding Govier's use of *ceteris paribus* in conductive argument evaluation, Wohlrapp and Zenker reach similar stances via distinct lines of argument. Wohlrapp believes that Govier's application of *ceteris paribus* is of no ultimate value because of, at least in part, an inherent vagueness regarding how to specify the "normal" situation:

> But in argumentative discourse, it [the *ceteris paribus* clause with generalization] carries meaning only if the proponent who wishes to place his thesis under the clause can name those conditions within the presumed normal situation that would have to be held "equal." (2008, p. 324; trans. p.10)

Wohlrapp describes the *ceteris paribus* clause as a "joker" (2008, p. 324; trans. p.10) because "it can always be pulled out in case the opponent shows that the thesis is not correct" (2008, p. 324; trans. p.10). After analyzing Govier's account at length, Frank Zenker concludes "cp[ceteris-paribus]-generalizations are irrelevant to evaluating conductive argumentation" (2007, p. 11). I would like to address both these critiques in some detail after first putting forward a broad thesis about some differences in using the *ceteris paribus* clause in scientific verses in everyday reasoning.

A useful view of *ceteris paribus* clauses is that they relate generalities and contexts, i.e., cases. In science, the context or case in question is standardly the *test case*. The purpose of the test case in science is to confirm or disconfirm the generality, a hypothesized natural law. In science the test case is thus a tool for addressing the generality. In non-scientific reasoning, I propose that this pragmatic ordering is inverted so that the generalities are tools for resolving the case in question, whether it be an actual or an *a priori* case. Let's see where this pragmatic distinction can take us. We shall begin by looking at scientific reasoning

The role of *ceteris paribus* in science has been controversial for decades and remains so. Only a brief sketch of a few aspects of the many issues and viewpoints can be made here. I will restrict the discussion to work in the philosophy of science by Frank Zenker and by Nancy Cartwright. The well-known views of Carl Hempel on the logic of scientific confirmation will also be applied.

In science, the *ceteris paribus* clause is most obviously applicable to contexts in which multiple factors or aspects are likely to be involved, which is the standard situation in scientific reasoning. The *ceteris paribus* clause is used to state a law according to which nature would behave, if there are no other causal factors involved. A standard example in the literature is Newton's laws of motion which specify the movement of bodies based entirely on gravitational force, mass and acceleration, as if there were no electromagnetic, strong nuclear, weak nuclear, or any other types of physical forces acting on motion of the bodies in the test case at hand. In order to analyze the phrase 'normal situation', we will need to briefly overview two viewpoints on laws and *ceteris paribu*s in the philosophy of science.

Philosopher of science Nancy Cartwright holds that we verify laws of nature by finding or constructing what she calls "nomological machines" (1999). A nomological machine can be put together for the purpose of running an experiment, for instance when special walls are constructed as an experimental chamber to literally shield out electromagnetic forces. Nomological machines are also sometimes found in nature, one example being our solar system. The great distances between the large bodies of our solar system naturally shield out electromagnetic and nuclear forces, thus restricting the effective forces on such bodies to those expressed in Newton's laws of motion. According to Cartwright, a nomological machine's functioning is determined by the (quasi-Aristotelian) *natures* of its component parts, whether those parts are assembled by a human experimenter or found in nature ready-made.

Cartwright controversially claims that regions of reality outside of such nomological machines cannot be known to be law-governed. For Cartwright, the universe is "dappled" with law-observing regions, which are the regions containing nomological machines—and that is all we can really know about the extent of applicability of these natural laws. The claim that confirmed natural laws obtain *outside* of identified nomological machines, natural or artificial, Cartwright calls unwarranted "fundamentalism" in the philosophy of science.

As I interpret Cartwright, "everything else is equal" only within these scarce nomological machines. The "normal situation" for Cartwright is thus the region of the nomological machines, natural or artificial, in which the putative law is revealed and confirmed. In Cartwright's terms, reality is "*ceteris paribus* all the way down" (in reference to the joke that in Hindu mythology the universe rests on turtles all the way down). I interpret this to mean that according to Cartwright, *ceteris paribus* applies both to laws and to the test cases, i.e., to experiments.

According to my understanding of Frank Zenker's dissertation, his position is opposed to Cartwright's with respect to *ceteris paribus* applying to natural laws. According to

Zenker, we should speak of *ceteris paribus* clauses as attached to test situations; but we should not speak of *ceteris paribus* laws. Zenker says, "nothing is gained by speaking of cp-laws to begin with" (2007, p. 112). According to Zenker, the *ceteris paribus* clause is properly viewed as containing any unidentified *antecedent test conditions*, in the sense of that phrase used in Carl Hempel's deductive nomological account of scientific confirmation and disconfirmation: "we can never do better than render the meaning of *ceteris paribus* by indexing the law instance's antecedent" (2007, p. 112). If it is believed in a scientific test that *all* of the relevant causal factors have been identified, then the *ceteris paribus* clause effectively disappears as vacuous, according to Zenker, there being no unidentified factors with which to 'stock' that clause, in my phrasing. Everything else is 'equal' in that context because all the multiple factors have been included as antecedent conditions rather than as exceptions. It therefore seems to me that, for Zenker, every situation is fundamentally a 'normal situation', i.e., that the normal situation is potentially everywhere in the sense that complete scientific knowledge, however elusive, is not *in principle* ruled out.

The third possibility, that the normal situation is found nowhere (rather than "everywhere" or in "dappled" patterns), has been expressed by famous mystery writer Raymond Chandler. In an essay on the craft of writing mysteries, Chandler quipped: "Other things being equal, which they never are..." (1934, p. 11). I think Chandler's sardonic humor may contain a serious point, at least as applied to non-scientific contexts. As previously stated, the case in question in a scientific context has as its purpose the confirmation of a generalization, or more typically of several of them as a conjunction. The case serves the generalization. But in much non-scientific reasoning, including practical reasoning, the contextual purpose is not assessing a *generality* but rather resolving the *case* at hand, with generalizations being tools for that projected case resolution, especially in practical reasoning.

This inherent pragmatic difference between scientific and non-scientific contexts for *ceteris paribus* might clarify the sense in which specifying the normal situation is not an applicable notion outside of science. In the standard example of the physics of motion, *all actual forces present* must be factored in together mathematically in order to create a useful test case prediction. But nothing corresponding to that can be done (or should be done) for *all possible considerations* (or values or frames/orientations) in a general, non-scientific context of conductive argument. The idea of specifying all possible considerations seems to me to be inappropriately borrowed from the scientific context. In fact, too many considerations tend make a conductive argument unwieldy and thus less useful and less resolvable. The inclusion of considerations thus has a pragmatic as well as an epistemic aspect. We do speak of all *relevant* considerations, which raises the issues as to how "relevance" here is to be understood in some non-arbitrary and non-subjective way. We shall address the 'subjectivity' issue shortly in another section, after working a bit more to develop interpretations and applications of the phrase *ceteris paribus* in everyday contexts.

I have long puzzled over what the "equal" means in the common translation of *ceteris paribus*. While archaic meanings and word roots do not determine contemporary meanings, historical references can still be helpful. According to William Whitaker's online Latin dictionary, the "par" in "paribus" means "equal" in the following senses, among others: *"a match for; of equal size/rank/age; fit/suitable/right/proper; comparable; commensurate (unlike qualities); adequate; reasonable."* A descriptive history of the usage of '*ceteris paribus*' might be of great interest, and it is true that "all else being equal" is the common English language version. Yet it still seems that other translations might be more in accord with actual usage. The following translations of *ceteris paribus* are interesting candidates as well: "All else being proper"; "all else being reasonable"; "all else being comparable." In this use of *ceteris paribus*, the phrase is a normative pointer, so to speak. The pointer suggests that there are other issues and cases to consider, that the generalization does not stand alone. This phrasing accords well with Govier's analysis of *ceteris paribus* in conductive argument.

Some of my above points may be useful in critiquing Frank Zenker's criticism of Govier on *ceteris paribus* in his (2007). Zenker claims there are two possible interpretations of Govier on *ceteris paribus*. With "CP" abbreviating '*ceteris paribus*' his first interpretation is that 'CP (x) (Fx → Gx),' "does sometimes warrant a transition to *particular* of its saturated instances" (2007, p. 5). According to his second interpretation, 'CP (x) (Fx → Gx)' "does never allow a transition to *any* of its saturated instances" (2007, p. 5). Zenker describes the first interpretation as "ultimately based on *frequency*. It assumes that past and future events are, in principle, subsumable under covering-laws or generalizations" (2007, p. 5, italics added). It seems to me that Zenker is here characterizing conductive reasoning as a kind of scientific inquiry involving covering laws. I question in several sections of the present paper whether Zenker's construal is the only plausible one and whether it is the best one.

Zenker argues that this first, *frequency* interpretation does provide Govier with the ranking of generalizations that are required for her concept of diverse premise weights, but he continues that it is not adequately applicable to real-life situations. This seems to be very similar to the one quoted above by Wohlrapp as to generalities being "situation-abstract," i.e., that there are no real-life "normal" situations, which is discussed above.

According to Zenker, the second interpretation does "more justice to cases of real life" by virtue of the fact that "the antecedent...is not sufficient for a transition to the consequent" (2007, p. 6). But this means, according to Zenker, that all *ceteris paribus* generalizations are on equal footing, so that Govier cannot use this interpretation to support diverse premise weights. Zenker concludes that both interpretations are to be rejected for different reasons, and thus that: "By now, it may be apparent that nothing is gained by ordering the above generalizations as *ceteris paribus* reasons" (2007, p. 8).

It seems to me that Zenker's critique, like Wohlrapp's, implicitly relies on the scientific, perhaps even *vector-based* applications of '*ceteris paribus*,' and perhaps somewhat on the formal logic that has been associated with natural science in the history of philosophy. I suggest that '*ceteris paribus*' is not as univocal and context-independent as Zenker seems to understand it. Although I argue that Zenker's counterargument against Govier is not successful, I am sympathetic with his general claim that conductive argument evaluation proceeds properly "only at the level of individual constants" (2007, p. 7), which I take to be the cases that are involved in evaluation of the argument at hand.

4. Cumulating independent reasons strands

Earlier sections of the present paper addressed the controversial concept of *individual* premise weights. In light of all of the above treatment, what can be usefully said about combining independent reason strands in a conductive argument evaluation? The origin of the term 'conductive' is apparently the Latin *conducere*, meaning "to bring together," like an orchestra conductor brings together many distinct musicians and instruments into a unitary performance. How are the various independent reason strands of a given conductive argument to be normatively "conducted" *together* as one argument subject to normative evaluation of the pro and con reasons?

In *The Philosophy of Argument*, Govier provides the following checklist for evaluating conductive arguments:

1. Are the premises rationally acceptable?
2. Is each premise, considered by itself, relevant to the conclusion?
3. How strongly a reason does each relevant premise provide for the conclusion?
4. Considering all the supporting premises together, how strong is the support provided for the conclusion?
5. What are the counter-considerations (strongly acknowledged by the arguer) that count against the conclusion?
6. What are the counter-considerations put forward by the evaluator or critic that count against the conclusion?
7. How strong is each of these counter-considerations as a reason against the conclusion?
8. How strongly do the counter-considerations, taken together, count against the conclusion?
9. Taking into account the deliberations at stages (4) and (7), how much support overall, or on balance, is provided for the conclusion by the premises? (Govier 1999a, p. 170)

Govier's model could be interpreted as involving a non-comparative weighing of each premise separately and then cumulating all the assigned weights in the pro group and then all the weights in the con group. As Wohlrapp and others have pointed out, the common, everyday practice of conductive argument evaluation does not very much resemble Govier's account above. Of course, a checklist is by no means a process description, but it is also true that a process and its associated quality controls must be related in discernible ways.

It seems to me that, descriptively, people commonly begin a conductive argument evaluation by viewing the whole argument and then classifying the various considerations on both sides as major or minor (strong or weak, or variations thereof) through a process of multiple comparisons. Ben Franklin famously crossed out opposing, equally (heft-) weighted considerations, and some argument theorists talk about balancing similar reasons pro and con. Descriptively, it seems to me that arguers commonly hold those considerations identified as "minor" in reserve, in case there is a perceived "tie" between the number of major considerations on each side. The principal aspect of evaluating pro and con arguments may typically lie mostly with individual premise weight determination, often by supporting arguments. Once individual premise weights are worked out, where they can be worked out, many pro and con arguments become intuitively decidable, e.g., deciding pro based on two strong pro reasons and one weak con reason. Other arguments with a closer balance of pro and con reason-weights may just be unresolvable, unless more considerations can be added and removed or individual premise evaluation differences resolved by the arguers.

The above common-sense observations and guidelines hardly constitute the kernel of a vigorous and effective theory of argument. It may very well turn out to be that normative logic ultimately has rather little to offer in terms of addressing premise cumulation in conductive argument. Harald Wohlrapp famously argues this point regarding Govier's approach, putting forward alternatively his dialectical *frame-integration* account of normative resolution. It seems to me that his approach rings true principally because it brings in values, a *frame* for Wohlrapp being a valuational perspective on a set of characterized (or re-characterized) facts. Addressing values directly is, as previously mentioned, also a feature of legal case-based, value-based reasoning. Values are very commonly brought into contexts of everyday conductive argument resolution as well. We will return to Wohlrapp's account in the next section.

It may be the case that any substantial contribution from informal logic on conductive argument evaluation would have to follow, and be based partly on, quite a bit more "dustbin empiricism." Understanding pro and con conductive argumentation practices in much more detail might suggest normative additions to what Robert C. Pinto calls *critical practice*, a checklist of questions as a guideline to normative argument evaluation, potentially expanding on and modifying Govier's list. Such developments would require joint work among cognitive psychologists, decisions theorists, and argumentation theorists. Values and preferences are brought in by several prominent critics of Govier's account, to which area we now turn.

5. Premise weight, subjectivity and objectivity

The theme of subjectivity verses objectivity has emerged several times in the above account. Harald Wohlrapp clearly holds that premise weight is subjective:

> You can cut the pie anyway you like, the opportunities of argumentative language use lie prior to calculation: namely in the how and why of a particular argument being assigned a particular weight-quantum. After all, the "weight" of arguments is primarily something subjective. (2008, p. 319; trans. pp. 4-5)

It is not clear to me to what extent the second sentence in the above quote is based on the scale-weight metaphor with its numerical weights—or of course whether Wohlrapp would accept the distinction between scale- and numerical-weight as I have drawn it. In any case, Wohlrapp's larger point is that the concept of premise weight is either uselessly vague or, where precise, uselessly subjective.

Christian Kock has also argued at length that premise weight assignments are subjective. One of his more prominent examples involves the preference of the rural Briton for keeping the pound as a symbol of British identity, whereas the cosmopolitan Briton who travels prefers an abandonment of the pound in favor of the Euro to eliminate the significant expense and bother of frequent currency conversions. Kock claims that these two preferences are both subjective and not reconcilable in any obvious way.

> What the example of the "national identity argument" demonstrates is, again, that in practical reasoning an argument may legitimately have different degrees of strength to different people; and it would demonstrate this no matter which absolute or relative definition of strength we might devise. (2007, p. 104)

With regard to establishing the objectivity of premise strength, Kock asks: "Will argumentation scholars tell voters just how much strength they *ought* to assign to the convenience argument, to the 'national identity' argument, and to the economic and political arguments [for Britain's converting from the Pound to the Euro] respectively?" For Kock, the subjectivity of premise weight is the cause or, perhaps better, a major cause, for some arguments being unresolvable. Wohlrapp also acknowledges that many pro and con conductive arguments are unresolvable:

> Finally, it should be clear that by far not every pro- and contra- debate, even under employment of this [frame-based] strategy, will lead to a clear conclusion. It is usually not easy for people to jump over their own shadows. (p. 331; trans. p. 18)

Wohlrapp's point here has some similarities to Kock's point about the rural, stay-at-home Brit and the traveling Brit, although Wohlrapp might use the term 'orientation' as he develops it. One aspect of Kock's argument can be summarized as an instance of denying the consequent, as follows: If premise weight is objective, then there would be relatively few premise weight disagreements; but there are countless such disagreements, so premise weight is subjective. Wohlrapp might endorse this argument as well, although he offers other arguments to this effect.

These arguments for the subjectivity of premise weight may be vulnerable with respect to the clarity and ultimate value of the concepts of subjectivity and objectivity that they employ. These concepts, members of one of Perelman's *philosophical pairs*, are notoriously slippery and yet apparently indispensable. The trio of terms, 'objectivity,' 'subjectivity' and 'argument,' are daunting ones to try to interrelate. Premise weight certainly does not have the "scientific" objectivity of numerical scale weight, and seemingly no theorist of argument claims that it does. Even though science is the quintessentially objective discipline, other philosophically legitimate meanings for 'objective' and 'subjective' do exist and may well be applicable here.

An interesting blend, so to speak, of the universal, the social, and the personal in value schemes is George Christie's concept of an ideal audience as each person's own construct. Christie's concept is modeled from Perelman's universal audience, but with some different emphases. Each person has her own views and preferences, but much of the time what is in play in argumentation is not so much one's own preferences as each person's own *construct* of the ideal audience. Along with an unavoidable personal origin, there is an intended universality of viewpoint, which is intrinsic to rational discussion. Christie's *The Notion of an Ideal Audience in Legal Argument* is reviewed by Bench-Capon in his (2001).

One alternative understanding of the terms "objectivity" and "subjectivity" in the present context can be developed form the following claim: Argument and argumentation constitute *par excellence* the process of moving from subjectivity to objectivity. Applying this formulation to Kock's concepts, I would say his points on subjectivity describe the *starting* point of arguments in general and the *ending* points of apparently unsuccessful arguments, of which there are course countless numbers in actuality. In a manner of speaking, the ultimately unsuccessful argument is the one that never starts, as happens often among groups or individuals with deep disagreements. What Kock calls the "subjective" might better be called the "personal," although Kock uses this term as well.

Frank Zenker has also addressed this issue of subjectivity and objectivity. In his (2007), Zenker discusses individual differences in strength of reasons and claims that "a communitarian may not [even see a reason to] care about the pain of *all* others." I understand this to be the problem of applying moral values only inside one's own moral community, which may exclude those of other races, religions, or even all those not of one's own extended family, as with the Mafiosi gangsters. As Richard Paul has indicated, critical thinking and good arguments are tools for reducing egocentricity and its familiar companion, sociocentricity. It seems to me that objectivity is a goal to strive for, like wisdom, and is likely an aspect of it. Only if all controversies are held up to the standards of objectivity of the settled physical sciences is the existence of disagreement an argument for subjectivity.

Zenker's point might interestingly be reframed in terms of Christie's concept of the ideal audience as a construct in each individual. For a single community, there will be as many perspectives on that community as there are members in it. One might ask what is a *single* community, given that modernity involves multiple overlapping community memberships for most individuals. In any case, community or social values are not monolithic in the sense of the settled sciences, e.g. physical chemistry. Rather social values are continually interacting with personal and ideal audience values in the space of argumentation. Social decisions alter social values, just as case-based decisions alter case law.

Even more generally, the everyday meaning of 'objective' can involve exactly the kind of realism that constructing a conductive argument can promote. In conductive argument, the bringing together of individual reason strands is commonly itself a process of becoming more objective in one's views. It seems to me proper to say that a person's ignoring relevant considerations in a conductive argument is not being objective about the matter at hand, which is the "fallacy" or cognitive error of *tunnel vision* mentioned by Govier in her textbook's chapter on conductive argument.

An illustration of the human tendency to ignore multiple factors, and thus keep multiple aspects of reality in separate tunnels or silos, is brought out in a passage from George Elliot's famous novel *Middlemarch*. In the story, Tertius Lydgate is a young and recently married physician whose expenditures are consistently well beyond his income. However, the young man continually fails to realize that he may be, through the accumulation of debts, in the process of becoming much like the poor people he attends to. The novel's narrator remarks of Mr. Lydgate:

> ... but, dear me! has it not by this time ceased to be remarkable—is it not rather what we expect in men, that they should have numerous strands of experience lying side-by-side and never compare them with each other? (*Middlemarch*, p. 558)

There is a strong sense in which objectivity is enhanced by bringing together independent strands of reasons and participating in conductive argument, whether the respondent is oneself or others.

Conductive argument is especially applicable in what Richard Paul calls '*multi-system*' thinking. For Paul, "*single-system*" thinking characterizes the settled sciences, e.g., chemistry; objectivity is therein at the maximum. "*No-system*" thinking characterizes preferences such as one's favorite ice cream flavor. "*Multi-system*" thinking occupies the great middle ground between full subjectivity and maximum objectivity. It seems to me that Koch, Wohlrapp, and Zenker may be working with a false dichotomy in terms of subjectivity and objectivity. What is excluded, for those who accept the overall account of the present paper, is the dichotomous view that premise weight is either entirely subjective or entirely objective. The present account instead supports a middle ground of intersubjectivity for at least many common types of premise weight determinations.

The issue of premise weight's subjectivity or objectivity is central in two at least two substantive differences between Govier and Wohlrapp: (1) the extent to which proper theory of argument should show how to resolve issues, and (2) the process-product distinction between the logic of single arguments on Govier's side and dialectical dynamics on Wohlrapp's side.

While these two areas of dispute are too wide in scope to address here, I would like to put forward what amounts to an intuition of possible value: Some (but not all) of the perceived differences between Wohlrapp and Govier may be due to their having different areas of primary focus rather than to their having substantive differences in theory of argument. I find suggestive evidence for this point in Wohlrapp's application of his frame-based strategy to Govier's textbook's example of an argument for the legalization of euthanasia, which is quoted earlier in the present paper. Using a frame shift, Wohlrapp concludes that "the arguments surveyed in the pro-compilation do in sum not speak for, but against a legalization of euthanasia" (p. 333; trans. p. 21). Wohlrapp concludes that Govier's "euthanasia" argument fails. His approach, he claims, has resolved the issue, whereas Govier's approach could not do so. A significant aspect of Wohlrapp's basis for his conclusion is as follows:

> Only in those few cases in which the terminally-ill patient would clearly want to die and could clearly not effectuate this himself, self-determination would increase. In all other cases, it would decrease. (p. 333; trans. p. 21)

What I find notable here is that the highly qualified nature of the above claim strongly resembles key aspects of the actual assisted suicide law approved and currently in effect in Oregon. As I read this public law, the availability of assisted suicide is granted only to those few parties characterized above, i.e., those few cases in which self-determination would increase through passing the law. The details are complex, but the relevant inference I draw here is that Wohlrapp's concepts and methods might be viewed as having to do with *normative issue resolution*, a concept that in some sense includes, but is broader than, *argument evaluation*.

On the broad topic of premise weight across theory of argument, Frank Zenker in his 2010 has put forward the very interesting proposal that deductive, inductive and conductive arguments all have premise weights but that the premise weights in deductive and inductive arguments are "equal" and thus in a sense tacit. The terms in italics below are proposed for adding to Zenker's account of normative argument evaluation typologies. The term 'inductive' would need more work here, in part because the status of analogical arguments is not clear enough. Obviously, the "comparative" characterization of conductive argument evaluation has good resonance with the "unequal-weight" feature.

- Deductive evaluation: *structural*, equal-weight reasons
- Inductive evaluation: *additive (or cumulative)*, equal-weight reasons
- Conductive evaluation: *comparative,* unequal-weight reasons

Further development of these ideas could be of considerable interest.

If the above directions for theory of conductive argument evaluation bear fruit, premise weight will turn out to be a varying combination of any or all of the following: (1) numerical quantities, (2) non-numerical quantities, and (3) values and goals related to rules by which they are promoted. Overall, the normative logic of conductive argument evaluation remains somewhat elusive, but perhaps we are collectively making some modest progress on these issues.

Chapter 8

Weighing Evidence in the Context of Conductive Reasoning

ROBERT C. PINTO

1. Introduction

The questions I am most interested in concern the procedures and the logical bases on which we must rely when confronted with the task of weighing evidence. Here I attempt to consider several aspects of that task that arise with respect to one particular type of reasoning or argument—what Wellman and Govier have called conductive reasoning or argument. I will be attempting to understand how we are to determine the relative *strength* and/or *weight* of pro considerations and counter-considerations when we are faced with the problem of evaluating conductive arguments.

2. Preliminary considerations

Before turning to questions concerning relative strength and/or weight, I will consider briefly (i) what is meant by the expression 'conductive arguments', (ii) the relationship between conductive reasoning and other types of defeasible reasoning, (iii) the relationship between pro and contra considerations on the one hand and what Pollock has called "defeaters" and diminishers on the other, and (iv) the question of what *makes* the considerations that come into play in conductive arguments positively or negatively relevant to the argument's conclusion.

2.1 What is conductive reasoning or argument?

Conductive arguments are *one* species of defeasible arguments. An argument is defeasible if and only if its conclusion and or its force can be called into question by considerations that are *consistent* with its premises and that do not call those premises into question. Arguments which are deductively valid are not defeasible in the sense just defined. If an argument, A, is deductively valid, then any consideration which calls A into question must either call one or more of its premises into question, or else call the conjunction of its premises into question (because it calls the conclusion entailed by the conjunction of those premises into question).

When he introduces the concept of conduction, Wellman (1971, p. 51) treats it as a kind of *reasoning* in which we find "the leading together of various [independently relevant] considerations" and he goes on to define it as follows (1971, p. 53):

> Conduction can be defined as that sort of reasoning in which 1) a conclusion is drawn about some individual case 2) is drawn nonconclusively 3) from one or more premises about that same case 4) without any appeal to other cases.

This definition makes it easy for Wellman to defend his claim that conduction differs from other types of defeasible reasoning: from induction (which on his account is defined [p. 32] as "the sort of reasoning by which a hypothesis is confirmed or disconfirmed by establishing the truth or falsity of its implications"), as well as from other types of argument that are neither deductive nor inductive in his sense: arguments from analogy (see p. 53), "explanatory reasoning" ("inference to the best explanation"), and some sorts statistical or probability inferences.

Although she is drawing the notion of conductive arguments from Wellman, Govier (1999b) gives an account of their nature which does not mention items (1), (3) and (4) in the Wellman definition just quoted. In addition to agreeing with Wellman that

> "[i]n a *conductive* argument, one or more premises are put forward as reasons supporting a conclusion. They are put forward as relevant to that conclusion, as counting in favor of it, but not as providing conclusive support for it" (Govier 1999b, p.155),

and that

> because they commonly acknowledge "counter-considerations" that "actually or apparently count against the conclusion" (*ibid.*) and are presented "so as to suggest openness to further reasons for support, and so as to suggest openness to counter-considerations," such arguments are offered "when we are in the domain of pro and con" (p. 157),

Govier stresses (p. 156) that

> [i]n conductive arguments in which there are several premises, those premises support, or are put forward as supporting, the conclusion convergently

and (p. 157) that

> the relevance of any given premise does not require that it be linked (conjoined) to another premise.[1]

In what follows, I will (with the caveat contained in note 1) follow Govier's less restrictive account of what a conductive argument is.

2.2 The relationship between conductive reasoning and other types of defeasible reasoning

Both Govier and Wellman want to insist that conductive arguments do not exhaust the category of non-conclusive (or defeasible) reasoning or argument, but constitute only one species of such reasoning or argument. Both, for example, want to insist that inductive argu-

---

[1] I am not sure that this last restriction fits *all* the examples of conductive arguments offered in Govier (1999b). For example, in the passages from Hurka she quotes on p. 160, Hurka's first "reason" seems to me to require 2 premises that are linked (*viz.*, that those who tell their children the Santa story know that what they're saying is false, but that "real myth-makers" believe their myths). See also the third reason offered in the passage she quotes from Trebbe Johnson on pp. 161-2 (that as a writer Johnson uses a great deal of paper, and that producing a great deal of paper requires the felling of many trees). The point I think Govier is trying to make might be better made if we distinguished between reasons and the propositions or premises that make up those reasons, and go on to say that if a conductive argument contains several *reasons* in support of its conclusion, each of those reasons provides nonconclusive support of the conclusion, and does so independently of the other *reasons*. One can make this point, while acknowledging that a single non-conclusive *reason* for a conclusion *can* require linking two or more "premises," no one of which supports the conclusion unless taken together with the other premises.

ments or reasoning don't count as conductive (though each means by "inductive" something different from what the other means[2]), nor do arguments based on analogy[3] nor reasoning to the best explanation.

Though it seems to me that Govier and Wellman are right to resist any attempt to *reduce* conductive reasoning to inductive, analogical or abductive reasoning, the relationship between conduction and these other sorts of reasoning may turn out to be more complicated than Wellman's or Govier's stories might lead us to suspect. Consider the following made-up example:

> Despite the fact that (1) Clark has only limited experience in management positions and (2) some of our employees may be uncomfortable with a woman in charge, I think (3) we ought to hire her as our executive director. For one thing, (4) she has recently earned an MBA from Harvard, and (5) the success rate for Harvard MBA's with problems like the problems we're facing right now has been fairly high. Moreover, (6) her management philosophy and her ideas about employee relations are very much like Wilson's, and (7) we all he agree he was an excellent manager before he retired. Finally, (8) placing a woman at the head of our organization at this time will project exactly the right sort of image to the community at large.

This passage purports to offer three reasons supporting the conclusion (3) that Clark ought to be hired as executive director, while acknowledging the two counter-considerations put forward in (1) and (2). None of the three reasons supporting (3) are "conclusive" reasons for accepting (3), and the case for (3) depends on the *convergence*, or cumulative effect, of those reasons. In terms of the *general* shape of Govier's account of conductive arguments,[4] these features of the argument would seem to qualify it as a conductive argument

But note that on the surface the first reason, (4) and (5), *appears to be* something Govier would recognize as an inductive argument for (3) and the second reason (6) *seems* to amount to an appeal to an inductive analogy. Of course, one might reconstruct the passage so that (4) and (5) "actually" constitute a subargument in support an unstated "real" first reason being advanced, namely that there's a reasonably good chance Clark will be successful in dealing with problems like the problems the organization currently faces. Analo-

---

[2] Thus Wellman (1971, p. 32) defines "induction" as "that kind of reasoning by which a hypothesis is confirmed or disconfirmed by establishing the truth or falsity of its implications", whereas Govier (1999b, p. 159) offers a different and much less restrictive account of "inductive" when she says, "Arguments that are in this traditional sense inductive have premises and conclusions that are empirical and are based on the rough assumption that experienced regularities provide a guide to unexperienced regularities."

[3] See Wellman (1971, p. 53) where he points out that arguments from analogy depend on the *experience* of analogous cases, whereas in conduction the link between premises and conclusion "is entirely a priori" and (in conformity to requirement 4 of his definition on p. 53) that conclusion is reached "without any appeal to other cases." See Govier, who distinguishes between a priori and inductive analogies (Govier 2001, chapter 10) and who presumably agrees with Wellman that arguments based on inductive analogies (which depend on experience) are distinct from conductive arguments, since she maintains (1999b, p. 157) that, "[i]n a conductive argument, each premise can provide support for the conclusion in the way that it does only if there is an appropriate *conceptual* or *normative* relationship between its content and the content of the conclusion [italics added]."

[4] The example does not conform to one particular requirement of Govier's account, namely that the reasons comprising a conductive argument consist of single premises that don't derive their force or relevance from being linked with other premises. But, as I pointed out in note 1 above, some of Govier's own examples seem to violate this requirement.

gously, we might interpret (6) and (7) as a subargument in support of another unstated "real" reason to the effect that Clark will, like Wilson, be an excellent manager.

But even if we choose to construe the pair consisting of (4) and (5) and the pair consisting of (6) and (7) as subarguments advanced to support unstated premises of the "root" argument, it will remain true that the force of the overall argument presented depends in part on the strength of the inductive inference on which the first reason depends and on the strength of the inductive analogy on which the second reason depends. Moreover, one of the things that will need to be explored in what follows is the *exact* role that assessing the strength such sub-arguments should play when we attempt to assess the overall strength of the pro considerations *taken together* and to balance them against the overall strength of the con considerations taken together.

Furthermore, recognizing the possibility that individual pro reasons and individual con reasons, considered by themselves, might turn out to be inductive arguments or arguments from analogy, etc., may help to bring into clearer relief what may be the two most important—and perhaps the defining—features of conductive reasoning, namely (1) that it involves the *convergence* of individual reasons of different kinds, and (2) that therefore the problem of "weighing" the pros and cons involves pitting the *combined* force of the pros against the *combined* force of the cons.

2.3 Pros and cons that occur "neatly in pairs"

One phenomenon comes into focus if we consider what Zenker (2010b, p, 9) says about a particular example of a conductive argument, which he sets out as follows:

(CC1) Aircraft travel leaves a large environmental footprint.
(CC2) Aircraft travel is physically exhausting.
(CC3) Aircraft travel is comparatively expensive.
(CC4) Airports do not always route baggage correctly.

(PR1) Aircraft travel is comparatively fast.
(PR2) I am overworked and likely able to sleep on the plane.
(PR3) My department reimburses travel expenses.
(PR4) Environmental footprint-differences can be compensated by purchase.

(OBP) PR1-PR4 outweigh/are on balance more important than (CC1-4)

(C) It is apt to travel to the conference by aircraft (rather than by train).

Commenting on this argument, Zenker says,

In this example, (PR2-PR4) counter (CC1-CC3), while (PR1) is not addressed by a counter-consideration ("is open"). It is difficult to discern how (PR1) could be addressed, other than by cancellation of a presupposition. Moreover, (CC4) remains unaddressed by any pro-reason.

Zenker *might* be taken to be suggesting that PR2 counters CC2, that PR3 counters CC2 and that PR4 counters CC1.[5]

---

[5] This impression might be reinforced by another comment he makes on the same page: "(PR3) could be retracted, e.g., upon coming to learn that the department cannot reimburse 100% of travel cost.

If this is what Zenker is actually suggesting (and I'm not completely sure that it is), we might be tempted to think that (OBP) is true in whole or in part because *individual* contra-considerations are outweighed by *individual* pro considerations. Wellman himself (1971, p. 68) says that "the factors [or considerations adduced in a conductive argument] do not *always* occur neatly in pairs, one pro balanced against one con" (italics added). In saying this he seems to be conceding that *sometimes* pro and con considerations do occur "neatly in pairs".

It is important to see that, even when pros and cons occur neatly in pairs, an individual pro does not "outweigh" the individual con by calling into question the truth or acceptability of the statement which comprises the con (or vice versa)—that my department reimburses travel expenses doesn't call into question the fact that air travel is more expensive than train travel. Rather, it "outweighs" the con by neutralizing or mollifying the strength or force which the counter-considerations can have to undermine the conclusion. For example, even though the price of a plane ticket is more than the price of a train ticket, that fact should not dissuade me from traveling by plane if I'm reimbursed by my department. Or the fact that I may be able to sleep on the plane doesn't change the fact that air travel is in many ways more exhausting than traveling by train– rather it calls attention to a fact that might make a plane trip in *this* case *less* exhausting than it otherwise might be and therefore a less compelling reason for avoiding it.

2.4 Defeaters and diminishers

Does this mean that, to the extent that pros and cons come "neatly in pairs", "weighing" them would come down to determining whether individual pros (or cons) are in some sense *defeaters* for individual cons (or pros)?

In answering that question it is worthwhile to locate the "effects" of this sort of "outweighing" in terms of John Pollock's account of *defeaters*. Pollock (2008, p. 4) has said: "Information that can mandate the retraction of the conclusion of a defeasible argument constitutes a *defeater* for the argument."

Pollock recognizes two and only two sorts of defeater – rebutting defeaters and undercutting defeaters. He writes (2008, pp. 4-5)

> The simplest are *rebutting defeaters*, which attack an argument by attacking its conclusion. …. For instance, I might be informed by Herbert, an ornithologist, that not all swans are white. People do not always speak truly, so the fact that he tells me this does not entail that it is true that not all swans are white. Nevertheless, because Herbert is an ornithologist, his telling me that gives me a defeasible reason for thinking that not all swans are white, so it is a rebutting defeater [for an inductive argument for the proposition that all swans are white].

He then (p. 5) introduces the second sort of defeater:

> Suppose Simon, whom I regard as very reliable, tells me, "Don't believe Herbert. He is incompetent." That Herbert told me that not all swans are white gives me a reason for believing that not all swans are white, but Simon's remarks about Herbert give me a reason for withdrawing my belief, and they do so without either (1) making me doubt that Herbert said what I took him to say or (2) giving me a reason for

---

This would constitute (CC5). Also (CC2) could be retracted and modified, e.g., upon coming to learn that one will fly first class or likely have an entire seat-row to oneself."

thinking it false that not all swans are white. Even if Herbert is incompetent, he might have accidentally gotten it right that not all swans are white. Thus Simon's remarks constitute a defeater, but not a rebutting defeater. This is an example of an *undercutting defeater*.

Pollock (2002, pp. 2-3) has argued that every defeater is either a rebutting defeater or an undercutting defeater.[6] Moreover, he insists (Pollock 2008, p.14) that an adequate account of defeaters requires us to introduce the idea of different "degrees of justification."

Not all reasons are equally good, and this should affect the adjudication of defeat statuses. For example, if I regard Jones as significantly more reliable than Smith, then if Jones tells me it is raining and Smith says it is not, it seems I should believe Jones. In other words, this case of collective defeat [roughly, cases where two inferences are so related that they appear to defeat each other] is resolved by taking account of the different strengths of the arguments for the conflicting conclusions. An adequate semantics for defeasible reasoning must take account of differences in degree of justification.[7]

According to Pollock (1995, pp. 103-104), differences in degree of justification necessarily come into play in determining whether a consideration *undercuts* an argument as well as in determining whether a consideration *rebuts* an argument.[8]

Pollock (1995, pp. 93-94 and 2002, esp. section 10 which builds on and modifies the earlier account) introduces methods which he thinks enable him to assign a *numeric* degree of strength or degree of justification to every argument. However, all that is actually required in order to take account of varying strength for purposes of determining whether a potential defeater *undercuts* or *rebuts* an argument from P to Q are judgments of *comparative* strength.

Now look back at Zenker's example, accepting the apparent suggestion that the role of the individual pro considerations in his example is to address individual counter-counterconsiderations. PR3 (my department will reimburse travel costs) can plausibly be taken to undermine any inference from CC3 (air travel is more expensive) to the negation of the conclusion C even though it does not imply the negation of the negation of the conclusion—it can therefore be seen as an *undercutting* defeater. (It is not a rebutting defeater because it is not a reason for preferring some *other* mode of travel to air travel.)

However, it is not clear that PR2 (I can probably sleep on the plane) either undercuts or rebuts an inference from CC2 (air travel is physically exhausting) to the negation of C. It is not a rebutting defeater, since it is not a reason for preferring some other mode of travel to air travel—obviously, I can probably sleep on the train as well. And it is not an undercutting defeater either: sleeping during the flight neither guarantees nor makes it probable that the "net exhaustion" is insignificant, so that fact doesn't deprive CC2 of its negative rele-

---

[6] In arguing this point, he is arguing against those who have maintained that "specificity" defeaters constitute a third type of defeater. Pollock (2002, p. 2) says about specificity defeaters that "...the general idea is that if two arguments lead to conflicting conclusions but one argument is based upon more information than the other then the 'more informed' argument defeats the 'less informed' one." Pollock (2002, p. 3) reconstructs specificity defeaters in such a way that they turn out to be a sub-type of undercutting defeater.
[7] Pollock 2005 (chapter 3, especially subsections 4 through 8) contains an earlier attempt to incorporate degrees of justification into the account of defeasible reasoning. The account there is superseded by a somewhat different account in Pollock 2002.
[8] A consideration D undercuts the argument from P to Q if from D we can infer that P does not support Q. Roughly, in order for D to undercut the argument from P to Q, the argument from D to "P does not support Q" must, according to Pollock, be at least as strong as the argument from P to Q.

vance. Despite this, PR2 is seems to have *some* effect on the force of CC2 as a counter consideration, since it suggests that the consideration highlighted by CC2 is *less compelling* than it would otherwise be.

Prior to 2002, Pollock (1995, pp. 102-103) had maintained that a potential defeater which is too weak to *defeat* an argument from P to Q does not diminish the strength of that argument or of the degree of justification of its conclusion. But subsequently Pollock (2002, second paragraph of the abstract) "argues that defeaters that are too weak to defeat an inference outright may still *diminish* the strength of the conclusion" (italics added)—a point that is elaborated on with considerable mathematical detail in sections 6 and 7 of that paper. Without committing myself to Pollock's account of the "mathematics" of what he calls *diminishers*, I want to suggest that PR2, considered in relation to CC2, is not a *defeater*, but rather plays the role of a *diminisher*—rendering an inference or argument "weaker" than it would otherwise be.[9]

2.5 What makes a consideration positively or negatively relevant in a conductive argument?

Pollock (2008, p. 3) writes,

> Defeasible reasoning is a form of reasoning. Reasoning proceeds by constructing arguments for conclusions and the individual inferences making up the arguments are licensed by what we might call *reason schemes*.

A page later he connects reason schemes with inference rules when he says,

> In deductive reasoning, the reason schemes employed are deductive inference rules.[10]

Even Wellman, who expressed (1971, pp. 59-70) very considerable skepticism about the possibility of any "logic" or set of criteria for judging the validity of conductive argument, admits (p. 65) the possibility of such reason schemes for conductive argument:

> Could there be principles of conductive reasoning? Since the validity of a conductive argument in no way depends upon the individual constants it contains, it should be possible in principle to formulate rules for conduction. Every valid argument belongs to a class of arguments which differ from it only in the individual constants used, and every member of this class is valid. Similarly, every invalid conductive argument is a member of a class of logically similar arguments all of which are invalid. Therefore, it should be possible to formulate a rule for each such class of conductive arguments declaring that all arguments of the specified kind are valid (or invalid).

And Govier (1999b, p. 171 and 2001, pp. 398-399) makes a similar point. Calling attention (1999b, p. 171) to the fact that "reasons must have a degree of generality," Govier identifies generalized "assumptions," which "underlie" the appeal to various considerations in conductive arguments. However, she insists on the further point that those generalized assumptions, such as

---

[9] It is perhaps worth noting that Wellman (1971, p. 57), when describing conductive arguments of the third kind (those that involve both pros and cons) speaks of the possibility of finding additional considerations that would "support or *weaken* the conclusion" (italics added).

[10] Also, compare Pollock (2002, p. 2): "The basic idea is that the agent constructs arguments using both deductive and defeasible reason schemes (inference-schemes)."

> Other things being equal, insofar as a practice would save people from great pain, it should be legalized

must always have *ceteribus paribus* clauses.

But where do such assumptions or reason schemas come from? What gives them the power to "license" individual arguments and inferences?

Wellman (1971, p. 66) suggests

> Such principles might be established in the same way that the principles of deductive logic are, by induction from clear cases of valid argument. Once established by clear cases, the rules of relevance might then come to be applied to arguments whose validity is in doubt.

Yet why are the "clear cases of valid argument" *clear* cases of validity? Perhaps in answer to such a question Wellman might fall back on something he said earlier (1971, p. 53), namely, that in conduction the link between premises and conclusion "is entirely a priori"—a note that is echoed in Govier's observation (1999b, p. 157) quoted above in note 3 that

> [i]n a conductive argument, each premise can provide support for the conclusion in the way that it does only if there is an appropriate *conceptual* or *normative* relationship between its content and the content of the conclusion [italics added].

Indeed, even Pollock (1995, p. 107) appears to suggest something similar when he says

> ... prima facie reasons are supposed to be logical relationships between concepts. It is a necessary feature of the concept *red* that something's looking red to me gives me a prima facie reason for thinking it is red. (To suppose we have to discover such connections inductively leads to an infinite regress, because we must rely upon perceptual judgments to collect the data for an inductive generalization).

Without developing the point in any detail, I note that Pollock's claim would turn out to be true on any conceptual role semantics, such as Brandom's, which recognizes "material inferences" which, though valid, are not formally valid. For on such a semantics, to recognize that an argument is valid but not formally valid is tantamount to recognizing that its validity is due to the nonlogical concepts occurring in its premises and conclusion. And given conceptual role semantics, that will be the case simply because the content of any concept *just is* a function of the "material" inferences involving that concept which are acknowledged or endorsed in the linguistic community in which the argument is put forth. In Brandom's account, "entitlement-preserving" inferences are defeasible,[11] and Brandom (2000, pp. 87-89) offers an explicit discussion of the nonmonotonic features of such inferences. It is also worth noting that although from one point of view Brandom takes material inferences to gain their force from the fact that they are acknowledged or recognized within a linguistic community, in the final analysis (1994, chapter 8, section 6) he wants to insist on the *objectivity* of the sort of "conceptual norms" implicit in such recognition and on the continuing

---

[11] The distinction between commitment preserving inferences (which are not defeasible) and entitlement preserving inferences which are defeasible is introduced in chapter 3 of Brandom 1994 (see esp. pp. 68-69).

possibility that the norms which are implicitly acknowledged or recognized by an entire community may turn out not to be correct. See also my comments in Pinto (2009, p. 286) about the relationship between the *implicit* norms involved when we *take* one thing to be a reason for another and the question of whether that thing *really is* a reason for the other:

> ... norms become *explicit* when such takings are challenged and discussion ensues about whether what has been taken to be a reason *ought* to be taken to be reason for this or that. When such discussion transpires, a space opens up in which the difference between our *taking* something to be or provide a reason and its *actually being* or providing a reason makes its presence felt.

3. The strength or weight of reasons that come into play in conductive arguments

Even where it is clear—perhaps on the sort of grounds alluded to in subsection *2.5*—that something is a reason for or against a possible conclusion, we encounter great difficulties in evaluating conductive arguments when we try to assess the *relative strength* of considerations pro and con. Indeed, after conceding (as we saw in *2.5* above) that there may in fact be principles or "reason schemes" we can appeal to for purposes of validating the legitimacy of various pro and con considerations, Wellman (1971, pp. 66-69) offers three reasons why the existence of such principles offers little prospect for what he calls (p. 69) a "logic of ethics in any interesting sense." The third reason (pp. 68-69), and to my mind most powerful of the three, is that

> ...even where these rules of relevance were applicable they would be insufficient to establish the validity or invalidity of a given argument. In any argument of the third pattern [i.e., one which mentions both pros and cons] it is not enough to know whether the premises are or are not relevant to the conclusion; one must know how much logical force the reasons for the conclusion have in comparison to the reasons against the conclusion. To determine the validity of any argument reasoning from both pros and cons, rules of relevance must be supplemented by rules of force. There is serious doubt whether this can be done.

3.1 Three types of question about the "logical force" to be attributed to a relevant consideration

There are at least three distinct types of question that can be raised about the strength, force or weight with which a consideration or set of considerations supports a conclusion.

(a) First, there are questions about whether—in the absence of counter-considerations—a single consideration, or a set of considerations, is *sufficient* to warrant adopting one or another propositional attitude toward a propositional content *P*. For example, does consideration *C* warrant *believing* that *P*? Or does it merely warrant *accepting* that *P* (where accepting that P is a matter of being prepared to *use it as a premise* in reasoning about the issue at hand, irrespective of whether we actually believe it)? Or again, does it warrant *suspecting* that *P*, or alternatively being *inclined to believe* that *P*? Does it warrant desiring that *P*? And so on. These sorts of questions do *not* involve explicit consideration of the *relative strength* of two considerations or of two sets of considerations. However, if we think of "positive" doxastic attitudes—e.g., suspecting that P, being inclined to believe that *P*, expecting that *P* will turn out to be the case (see Pinto 2007), being almost sure that *P*, and believing P without qualification—as forming a series of increasingly strong degrees of belief,[12] they may and often do concern "how strong a degree of belief" a consideration or set of considerations is sufficient to warrant.

(b) Second, there are questions about the *relative strength* of two or more considerations or sets of considerations which bear on the issue of whether to adopt a propositional attitude *A* toward a propositional content *P*. Among such questions, two sub-types are especially prominent. (i) Does a particular consideration or set of considerations which supports adopting a *positive attitude* (e.g., belief) toward *P* *outweigh* a particular counter-consideration or set of counterconsiderations which support adopting that positive attitude toward *not-P*? This is the sort of question we face in trying to determine whether counter-considerations *rebut* pro considerations (or vice-versa). (ii) Let *X* be a particular consideration or set of considerations which supports adopting a positive attitude toward *P*. Does the strength of *X* as a reason for adopting a positive attitude toward *P* outweigh a particular counter-consideration which threatens to *undercut* *X*'s support for adopting such an attitude toward *P*—i.e., a counter-considerations which threatens to bring it about that *X* no longer gives *any* support for adopting a positive attitude toward *P*.

(c) Finally, there is a third sort of question about force or weight that may arise. Let a consideration *C* support adopting a positive attitude toward *P*. Let *CC* be a counter-consideration which, in Pollock's language, neither rebuts nor undercuts *C*'s support for adopting a positive attitude toward *P*. A third type of question can then concern (i) whether *CC* *diminishes* *C*'s support for adopting such an attitude toward *P*, and (ii) whether, as a result of the diminished strength of *C*, the *overall* case for adopting some positive attitude toward *P* is no longer sufficient to warrant adopting that attitude toward *P*.

In what follows I will, for the most part, ignore questions of the first and third types, and concentrate rather on certain questions of the second type—questions about *relative strength* of two considerations or sets of considerations. And for the most part I shall be concerned with the questions about relative strength that must be answered in order to determine whether one consideration or set thereof *rebuts* or *undercuts* another.

3.2 A procedural proposal concerning the steps to be taken in answering questions about the relative strength of two or more considerations or sets of considerations

I suggest that the following is one way of making the process of assessing relative strength more manageable in cases in which there is more than one pro consideration and/or more than one con consideration.

(1) We first identify cases like those considered in section 2.3 above in which at least some pro and con considerations occur "neatly in pairs."
(2) For each such pair we determine whether one member of the pair either "defeats" or "diminishes" the other. We drop from further consideration any pro or con consideration which is defeated. (In cases of what Pollock calls "collective defeat" – i.e. cases where two consideration of equal strength defeat each other – we drop both the

---

[12] In Pinto (2006, pp. 270-271, and 2010, pp. 287, 300 and note 3 on p. 308) I have discussed what I call a *qualitative* version of evidence proportionalism, which can be enhancing on thinking of these doxastic attitudes as representing ascending degrees of belief.

pro and the con consideration.) And we explicitly mark as diminished any pro or con consideration which has been "diminished" but not defeated.[13]

(3) If, because of collective defeat, all pro and con considerations have been dropped, our verdict is that the result is simply a standoff and that as a result the argument for the overall conclusion simply fails.

(4) If only pro considerations or only con considerations remain standing, then no further task of determining relative strength remains. If only pro considerations remain standing, then the argument succeeds in supporting its conclusion. If only con considerations remain standing, then the argument fails.

(5) If we find that one or more pros and one or more cons remaining standing, then we proceed to the question of whether the set of remaining pros *taken together* outweigh the set of remaining cons *taken together,* or vice-versa. If neither set outweighs the other, or if the cons outweigh the pros, then the argument fails to support its conclusion, i.e., fails to support taking a positive attitude toward the conclusion. Otherwise the argument succeeds—that is to say, supports our taking a positive attitude toward the conclusion.[14]

3.3 Assigning numbers to the strength or weight of the considerations occurring in conductive arguments

In explaining what conductive arguments are, Frank Zenker (2010b, p. 2) has said that a feature of such arguments is that

> [p]ro-reasons and counter-considerations form (normally two) groups, the elements of which are partially ordered on some scale capturing the notion of comparative importance.

He suggests (p, 11-12) that in inductive arguments the importance of premises is constant,[15] whereas in conductive arguments it must be represented by an evaluative mark R+, which he says (p. 11) "can but need not be represented by a numeral." He adds:

> If it is [represented by a numeral], one speaks of a *weight*. Weights may be captured as a function assigning a real number to a premise.

Presumably, when he speaks of the weight of considerations, Zenker has in mind values other than purely epistemic values. He references (p. 11) Scriven's (1981) discussion of weight and sum methodology as it occurs in evaluation other than epistemic evaluation. But one ought not to forget the cautionary remark Scriven (1991, p. 380) later makes about that methodology:

---

[13] Where one consideration diminishes its counterpart, both considerations remain standing, though with the diminished consideration marked as such.

[14] Here again, as was pointed out above we may still want to raise a question about which *sort* of positive attitude is warranted by the argument—but this question is no longer a question about *relative strength* of support.

[15] Zenker 2010b is advancing the extremely intriguing idea that inductive arguments be viewed as a limiting case of conductive arguments. In explaining this idea he says (p. 12), "...to generate the inductive structure from the conductive one, the range of assignable weights is constrained from R+ to some constant value."

> Although this method is a very convenient process, approximately correct and nearly always clarifying, there are many traps in it.... The most intransigent problem arises from the fact that no selection of standard scales for rating weights and performances can avoid errors, because the number of criteria are not pre-assignable.... So, either a large number of trivia will swamp crucial factors, or they will have inadequate total influence, depending on how many factors there are.

More broadly speaking, many authors who are interested developing computational approaches to the evaluation of argument and inference—such as Pollock (1995, pp. 93-94 and 2002) and Thomas Gordon—have approached questions of the relative strength of arguments and inferences by devising ways to assign numerical values to the strength of *any* argument or inference.

Pollock's (1995 and 2002) attempts to assign real or cardinal numbers to strength of support and degree of justification is perhaps the most interesting, since he eschews the approach of what he calls "generic Bayesianism", by which he seems to mean any approach that makes support and justification depend *entirely* on probabilities,[16] and offers an account in which certain probabilities have an essential, but nevertheless severely *constrained* role in determining "degree of justification."[17]

Though I think that in special cases it is possible to assign real or cardinal numbers to strength of support, like Wellman (1971, p. 57)[18] and Govier (2001, p. 396) I find myself quite unpersuaded by the attempts to make such assignments across the board, as it were. Moreover, as I will point out shortly, I think there are be *at least* two distinct aspects to the weighing problem as it occurs in conductive arguments and that in many cases it is not easy to get clear about the interconnection or interaction between those aspects.

As a result, in what follows I will *not* assume that numeric quantification of strength of support is available to shed light on the problem of weighing evidence, and more generally that in most cases the best we can hope for is to make judgments about the *comparative* force or strength of individual considerations or sets of considerations.[19]

3.4 A suggestion by Govier about how to determine the strength of a consideration

There is an interesting suggestion in Govier (1999b, pp. 171-72 and 2001, pp. 399-400) about how we might determine the strength of the reasons that occur in conductive arguments. In Govier 1999b (p. 171), she begins by noting that when we put forward P1, P2 and P3 as reasons in a conductive argument for C, we are assuming something like

---

[16] Pollock (1995, p. 95) speaks of "a probabilistic model of reasoning according to which reasons make their conclusions probable to varying degrees, and the ultimate conclusion is justified only if it is made sufficiently probable by the cumulative reasoning. I will refer to this theory as *generic Bayesianism*."

[17] See my brief comment on Pollock's attempt in Pinto 2009 (p. 271 note 4).

[18] What Wellman says, though perhaps oversimplified, is nevertheless worth quoting: "The weighing should not be thought of as putting each reason on a scale, noting the amount of weight, and then calculating the difference between the weight of the reasons for and the reasons against. The degree of support is not measurable in this way because there is no unit of logical force in which to do the calculation."

[19] Of course, if we assume that the relevant notion of "stronger than" is transitive, we will usually be able to assign *ordinal* numbers to the considerations or arguments under consideration. I say "usually" rather than "always" because as Zenker (2010, p.2) seems to concede (in the passage quoted at the beginning of section 3.3 above) that the ordering may only be a partial ordering.

> 1. Other things being equal, insofar as P1 is true, C.
> 2. Other things being equal, insofar as P2 is true, C.
> 3. Other things being equal, insofar as P3 is true, C.

She then observes:

> By spelling out qualified universals, as in (1–3) above, we are able to move beyond the apparently irreducible claim that "P1 is *relevant* to C" (in just this sort of case). We therefore gain a broader perspective that enables us to evaluate the strength of the reasons. We have to ask ourselves *what other things would have to be equal* (or taken for granted) if we were to reason "If P1 then C," and so on.

And in the next paragraph she indicates how formulating these "qualified universals" will enable us to evaluate the strength of the reasons.

> A reason for hiring a manager or going on holiday is not a sufficient, compelling reason for doing so. It is a reason for doing so, *other things being equal*. To reflect on how strong a reason it is *in the case or context we are considering,* we have to reflect on how many other things would have to be "equal" and whether they are so in this case. A strong reason is one where the range of exceptions is narrow. A weak reason is one where the range of exceptions is large. (*Ibid.*)

The wording just quoted might seem to suggest that Govier takes the strength of such a reason to be a simple function of how many *kinds* of factor that constitute "exceptions" which would render the "qualified universal" inoperative. But that is not quite right, for in discussing another example she says (p. 172):

> That a person would want to see her mother before she died is a strong presumption, one that would be defeated only by a few and *rare* circumstances [italics added].

That is to say, the strength with which a consideration supports a conclusion depends on both the *kinds* of factors that constitute exceptions and the *frequency* with which those kinds of factors occur.

It might sound as though we're in the neighborhood of early versions of Reiter's default logic, in which we are supposed to have at our disposal a list of the exceptions which undercut the inference to the default conclusion.[20] However, in the slightly later presentation in Govier 2001 she makes it quite clear (p. 400) that

> [a] striking and important feature of *ceteris paribus* clauses is that such conditions [i.e., those that constitute exceptions to the qualified generalization] are not typically completely spelled out. In fact, to do this is usually not possible.

Despite the many aspects of this account that I find illuminating and appealing, I don't think that it can really shed light on how we can or should determine the *relative* strength of pro considerations and counter-considerations. That is because, as I see it, what Govier is calling an "exception" to a "qualified generalization" just *is* a counter-consideration which defeats—rebuts or undercuts—the "reason" put forward in a pro consideration. And I agree

---

[20] For a brief account of early default logic, see Walton (forthcoming).

with Pollock that to determine whether an alleged "exception" D *does* defeat the argument from a pro reason PR to a conclusion C we must *first* determine the strength of the argument from PR to C relative to the strength of another argument involving D. D will qualify as a defeater—will be a genuine exception to the "qualified generalization"—if and only if it is either a rebutting defeater or an undercutting defeater. D will qualify as a *rebutting defeater* only if the argument from D to the *negation* of C is at least as strong as the argument from PR to C. And D will qualify as *an undercutting defeater* only if the argument from D to the conclusion that in these circumstances PR does not support C is at least as strong as the argument from PR to C.

In short, we can identify "exceptions" to a qualified generalization only if we are *already* able to compare the strength of arguments licensed by that generalization to certain other arguments. Therefore our ability to compare the strength of arguments licensed by that generalization to other arguments cannot presuppose a prior ability to identify "exceptions."

Something like the point I'm trying to make emerges if we take seriously a somewhat similar suggestion made by Hitchcock (1994, p. 62), namely, that a conductive argument is valid if it is an instance of a certain sort of covering generalization. As he puts this point,

> A conductive argument "P(a), so c(a)" is non-conclusively valid if and only if it is not conclusively valid but, for any situation x, if P(x) then either c(x) or x has some overriding negatively relevant feature F which c(x) does not deductively imply.[21]

The rough idea in Hitchcock's suggestion is that the "consideration" mentioned in the premise of a conductive argument non-conclusively supports the conclusion of that argument if and only if whenever the premise-type is true of a situation then the conclusion-type will also be true that situation unless the feature mentioned in the premise-type is "*overridden*" by a negatively relevant feature present in that situation—that is to say, by an "exception" which constitutes something like a counterexample to the covering generalization.

If anything resembling Hitchcock's account is on the right track, then applying the very idea of the kind of support found in conductive arguments always presupposes that one has a way of determining whether one consideration overrides another. *Relative* "strength" of support may well turn out to be so basic to the concept of non-conclusive support that it can't be *explained* in terms of anything more basic.

3.5 The multidimensional character of our judgments about the relative strength of pro and con considerations

In subsection 2.2 above, I considered an argument which, although it might appear to be a "hybrid" argument, has an overall structure that would qualify it as a *conductive* argument. The example I used contained three reasons, one of which (call it reason 1) was or depended on an *inductive argument* (a variant on statistical or proportional syllogism) and another of which (call it reason 2) was or depended on an *inductive analogy*. An interesting feature of reason 1 and reason 2 is that—although the "reason schemes" which they (or the subarguments which support them) instantiate are *empirical* reasoning strategies that can be applied to a variety of different subject-matters—both reasons depend on and in a sense lead

---

[21] The final clause "which c(x) does not deductively imply" is present in order to avoid the consequence, which for certain technical reasons would obtain in the absence of that clause, that no conductive argument with a false conclusion could possibly be non-conclusively valid.

to something like value judgments (one concerned likelihood of *success*, the other concerned *how good a manager* someone would be).

Thus consider reason 1, as presented in the argument as originally formulated:

(4) She (Clark) has recently earned an MBA from Harvard,
(5) The success rate for Harvard MBA's with problems like the problems we're facing right now has been fairly high.

from which we might interpose the unstated conclusion:

(I) There's a reasonably good chance that Clark will be successful in dealing with problems like those we're facing right now.

In assessing the bearing of these consideration on the conclusion:

(C) We ought to hire Clark as our executive director

two types of question dealing with relative force of reason 1 into play.

(a) The first question concerns the *strength of the inference* from (4) and (5) to the conclusion that Clark will be successful in this regard, relative to the strength of the support for the various counter-considerations mentioned in the argument. For want of a better term for labeling such questions, I'll call them questions about *risk* we are taking in relying on the pro consideration relative to the risk we are taking on relying on the counter-considerations.
(b) The second question concerns how much "importance" or *weight* ought to be accorded to "success in dealing with just this set of problems with problems like those we're facing right now," relative to the "importance" or *weight* of factors mentioned in the counter-considerations. Because of the way the term 'importance' will be used in the following sections, I'll dub these simply questions about the *weight* to be accorded a premise or reason.

Analogous questions arise with respect to the second reason offered (which concerned how good a manager Clark will be): (a) how strong is the inference from (i) the similarity of certain of Clark's views to Wilson's views to the conclusion (ii) that Clark will an excellent manager and (b) how much weight should be accorded to "being an excellent manager," relative both to the other features mentioned in the pro considerations and to the features mentioned in the counter-considerations.

In short, in order to compare the strength or force of reasons 1 and 2 to the strength or force of the counter-considerations, we have to take account of both (a) the relative risk we take in relying on the "premises" on which those reasons depend and (b) the relative *weight* that should be accorded to the features cited in those "premises."

There is in this duality of dimension something *analogous* to the factors that are taken account of in certain applications of decision theory when one calculates the "expected utility" of the outcome of a course of action. One determines the expected utility of a course of action by listing its possible outcomes and then adding up the products of (a) the numeric *probabilities* of those outcomes and (b) numeric *utilities* of those outcomes. However, when comparing the weight or force of considerations and counter-considerations in a conductive argument we hardly ever have at our disposal either a numeric measure of the risks we're taking in relying on their various premises or numeric measure of the importance or "utility" of the feature or features with which those premise are concerned.

Nevertheless, it is crucial to remind ourselves that we often have good reasons for judging the reasons for one conclusion to be stronger (in the sense of involving less risk) than the reasons for another conclusion, even when we have no way to assign a number to the strength of either. Thus, for example, Wellman (1971 p. 63) reminds us that

> there are certain rules of thumb that serve as criteria for the strength of an argument from analogy. The greater the number of instances, the greater the variety within the known instances, etc., the more logical force the argument from analogy has.

And Hempel (1966, pp. 33-37) offers a more nuanced account the roles of quantity, variety and precision of supporting evidence in assessing the strength of the confirmation of a hypothesis by favorable test findings. The factors he discusses are presented as a basis for judging that the strength of supporting evidence in one case is greater than the strength of supporting evidence in another, even though those factors don't provide a basis for assigning a *numerical* assessment of the degree of support.

3.6 On assessing the relative strength of pro and con considerations: importance, weight, and force

For the most part the conductive arguments that Wellman (1971, chapter 3) discusses deal with ethical subject-matter. However, Wellman explicitly recognizes (p. 54) one exception to that generalization:

> Whenever some descriptive predicate is ascribed on the basis of a family resemblance conductive reasoning takes place. In all such cases there are several criteria for the application of the term and each of these criteria may be satisfied to a greater or lesser degree and they may vary in importance as well. The fact that one or more criteria are satisfied in a particular instance is a reason for applying the term, but the inference is non-conclusive and does not appeal to the fact that the criteria have been found empirically associated with the term in other cases.

We might say that descriptive predicates fitting this description exhibit *open texture*. If we examine the ten examples Govier (1999b, pp. 160-166) has assembled we will find, I think, that all but one them are arguments which turn on predicates that exhibit such open texture.[22]

The three characteristics Wellman ascribes to predicates exhibiting open texture, namely:

---

[22] The first example from Hurka turns on the concept of a "deeper truth in myths"; the second example from Hurka on the concept of "white lie"; the example from Trebbe Johnson on the concept of "environmentally conscious lifestyle"; the example from Griffin on the concept of "natural" psychological impulses; the example from Skinner on "needed changes in the human condition"; the first example from Schafer-Landau on the concept of what is "highly impractical"; the example in Schafer-Landau's account of Morris' arguments about punishment on the concept of being "morally insensitive"; the example from Solomon on the concept of a "vague incestuous aura"; and the example from Thomas Schelling on the concept of "beneficiaries" of programs to combat global warming. The one exception appears to be Wisdom's technical discussion of sense-perception—and I for one have trouble seeing the argument in this passage a being a conductive argument.

1) there are several criteria for the application of the term
2) the criteria can be satisfied to a greater or lesser degree
3) the criteria may vary in importance

also apply, I think, to the "good-making" or "right-making" characteristics on which we base our ethical or moral appraisals.

It is tempting to think, therefore, that what gives rise to the need to assess relative strength (in the sense of *weight*) of pro and con considerations in conductive arguments is rooted in the fact that the *conclusions* of such arguments involve the application of predicates (normative and/or descriptive[23]) whose applications are based on criteria or "features" exhibiting these three characteristics. In the case of normative predicates, the criteria on the basis of which we ascribe them are the non-normative "right-making" or "good-making" features on which the normative status ascribed in the conclusion "supervenes."

The first of the three characteristics listed above can explain why there can be both pro and con considerations for the application of the term to a particular situation—it is because each consideration will typically concern the application of the term to situations which exhibit *one but not all* of the criteria for its application. The second and third characteristics can explain why the *weight* of conflicting considerations can be compared. The *weight* of a consideration would be a function of (a) the extent or *degree* to which a criterion has been satisfied and (b) the importance of that criterion. And the overall *force* of any consideration would be a function of the *weight* of the consideration and the *risk* involved in relying on that consideration. Figure 1 presents a graphic representation of how the relationship of the force of a consideration is related to these factors.

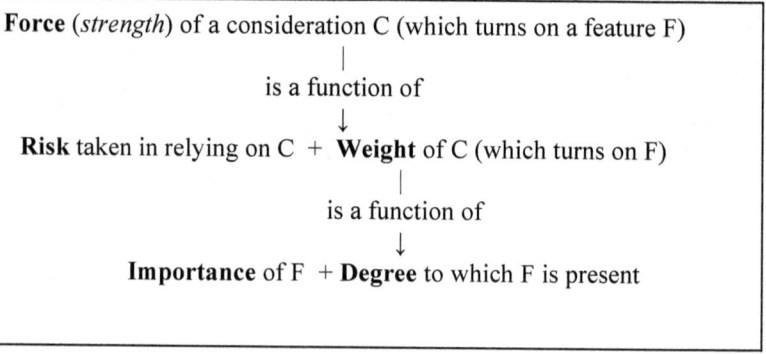

Figure 1

3.6.1 Assessing importance of criteria

What calls for further comment is the idea that criteria may vary in "importance." Here it may be useful to distinguish two types of issue:

---

[23] A few normative predicates appear to have little or no "descriptive" content—e.g., 'good,' 'bad', 'right', 'wrong', 'praiseworthy', 'blameworthy'. Many normative terms have both a normative and a descriptive dimension—e.g., 'murders', 'cheats', 'steals'. And of course many descriptive terms are often used in ways that exhibit no normative dimension at all—'white', 'purple', 'three inches long', 'French', etc.

(a) the relative importance of criteria for the application of predicates which have a *normative* dimension, and
(b) the relative importance of criteria for the application of *purely descriptive* predicates exhibiting open texture.

For each of these two types of issue, it *may* be possible to make at least some progress in understanding the basis on which we ascribe relative importance if we make particular assumptions about each of these types of issue.

(a) Assume that the *normative* assessments we make are tied to our *preferences*. Then (i) it is reasonable to suppose that two factors α and β will each be considered a ground for a positive evaluation of X's if other things being equal we prefer X's that exhibit factor α to X's that don't exhibit α and prefer X's that exhibit β to X's that don't. Moreover (ii) it is reasonable to suppose that α will be considered a "more important" factor than β if and only if, other things being equal, we prefer X's that exhibit α but not β to X's that exhibit β but not α. Approaching normative assessments in this way *need* not force us to view such assessments as "*purely* subjective." For we can distinguish, as I do, between (i) preferences which are grounded in good reasons all things considered and (ii) preferences which are not grounded in such reasons.
(b) Assume we learn to employ purely descriptive predicates exhibiting open texture at least in part from exposure to "prime examples" of items to which those predicates apply (as, presumably, we learn to apply color words). Then our application of such predicates to new cases can depend at least in part on our judgments about the relative similarity of new cases to those prime examples. Where we find ourselves judging that both A and B are Xs, but that A is more similar to a *prime* example of X than B, we can reflect on which differences between A and B are responsible for our similarity judgment concerning the case at hand. Reflection on such cases may lead us to realize that certain features should be treated as *irrelevant* to whether something is an X, and may also lead us to realize that among the features that *are* relevant some are responsible for our judging that one A is *more* similar to *prime* examples of X than B is. Features which account for judging new cases to be "more similar" to *prime* examples might then be deemed "more important" than relevant features which do not.

I do not offer these suggestions as *solutions* to the questions about the rational bases for judgments of comparative importance. But I offer them as avenues for further investigation and as indications that there may well be ways to uncover a *rational* basis for judgments of comparative importance.

3.7 On judging whether the pro considerations taken together *outweigh the con considerations* taken together

For starters, it is perhaps worth noting Pollock's (1995, pp. 101-102) discussion of "the accrual of reasons." Pollock says (p, 101):

> If we have two independent reasons for a conclusion, does that make the conclusion more justified than if we had just one? It is natural to suppose that it does, but on closer inspection that becomes unclear.

Pollock's arguments on this point trade on his idea that strength of support is often dependent to some degree on the probability of the conclusion given the premise. But it is easy to show that even where the probability of C given P1 is high and the probability of C given P2 is high it need not be the case that the probability of C given P1 & P2 is high. Accordingly, when we have two independent reasons P1 and P2 for a conclusion, what ought to matter is how "justified" the conclusion is on the *conjunction* of P1 and P2.

Wellman (1971, pp. 68-69) makes a similar point when, having conceded that there may indeed be "rules of relevance" to which we might appeal in evaluating conductive arguments, it is hard to see how we could have adequate "rules of force" that would enable us to settle questions about which *combinations* of pro (or con) considerations "take precedence" over *combinations* of con (or pro) considerations:

> ...the relevant factors do not always occur neatly in pairs. Any rules of logical force that will enable us to judge the validity of conductive arguments which incorporate all the relevant information must tell us which *combinations*, where the combination is a function of the degree of each factor as well as which factors are combined, *take precedence over which other combinations*. Each such *combination* has its *own* logical force and would require a separate rule of force. In the end, very little generalization is possible here. [Italics added.]

Govier (1999b, p. 170[24]) lists the "questions to be asked in evaluating conductive arguments," but she does not tell us how we are to go about *answering* those questions. And after listing the questions, she states:

> If we deem a conductive argument *cogent*, we commit ourselves to the judgment that the reasons in the premises, considered together, provide good grounds for the conclusion – even in light of the counter-considerations constituting reasons against the conclusion. That is, we commit ourselves to the judgment that, on balance, the pros *outweigh* the cons, and do so to a sufficient degree that they are good grounds for the conclusion.

A few sentences later, she comments, correctly in my view, that

> [t]his might all sound hopelessly difficult. But it cannot be so, because we do it all the time.

Granting that weighing pros and cons in these cases is something we do all the time, we can still ask,

(a) what *enables* us to do it, and
(b) what makes the answers we give to the questions Govier lists *reasonable* answers to those questions?

especially in light of the fact that we must typically compare the *combined* force of pro considerations to the *combined* force of con considerations. I want to suggest that the ob-

---

[24] See also Govier 2001 (pp. 401-02) where a similar, but shorter, list of steps is offered—but here the list is formulated as a list of things we must do in order to appraise a conductive argument.

servations in the preceding section (3.6) may enable us to *make a start* in answering questions (a) and (b). Since what follows is merely a tentative suggestion that might enable us to "make a start," I will make the simplifying assumption that the relative importance of pros and cons turns on criteria which warrant a normative conclusion (ignoring pros and cons that warrant the application of non-normative predicates exhibiting open texture).

3.7.1 Comparing the force of a single *pro consideration to a* single *counter-consideration*

In making such a comparison, we could begin by comparing the *importance* of the features. Let F1 be the feature on which one of those two considerations turns and F2 the feature on which the other consideration turns. If we prefer a situation which has F1 but not F2 to a situation to a situation that has F2 but not F1, then we judge the consideration which turns on F1 to be of greater importance than the consideration that turns on F2. Otherwise we judge the two considerations to be of equal importance. The greater the "degree to which we prefer one feature to the other" (e.g.," just a bit", "a fair amount", or "to a great extent"), the greater the relative importance we accord to the consideration on which that feature turns (e.g., slightly more, moderately more or a great deal more). Where neither feature F1 nor feature F2 comes in degrees, we may equate the relative weight of the considerations which turn on those features to be identical with their relative importance.

Where one or both of features F1 and F2 come in degrees, the relative *weight* of the considerations should depend not just on the relative *importance* we attribute to the considerations, but also on the *degree* to which we estimate the features on which the considerations turn are present in the situation with which the conductive argument is concerned. Here is a very preliminary proposal concerning how we might take such estimates into account. Let D1 be the degree to which feature F1 is present and D2 the degree to which F2 is present. In determining whether we prefer situations which have F1 but not F2, etc., we determine whether, other things being equal, we prefer F1 in degree D1 to F2 in degree D2. If we do, then we count the consideration that turns on F1 in degree D1 to have greater weight than the consideration which turns on F2 in degree D2. The greater the "extent to which we prefer one combination to the other" (e.g.," just a bit", "a fair amount", or "to a great extent"), the greater the *relative* weight we accord to that set of considerations in comparison with the other set of considerations ("slightly more weight," "moderately more weight," or "considerably more weight." If we don't prefer either combination to the other, we judge the two sets of considerations to be of approximately equal weight.

Where we estimate the risks taken in relying on competing considerations to be different, the estimated difference between them should be taken into consideration in judging the relative *force* of the two considerations (if no such difference obtains, then the relative force of the two considerations will have the same order of magnitude as their relative weight). Here again is a very preliminary proposal concerning how we might take such estimates of risk into account. For each consideration we roughly estimate the degree of risk incurred in relying on it as high, medium, low or nil—see the defense of such non-numeric estimates of the force of considerations in section 1 of Fischer (2010). We might then count a spread between high and low to be a marked difference in risk, and a spread between medium and either high or low to be a moderate difference in risk. Finally, we *might* adopt something like the following principles for estimating the comparative force of a single pro and single contra consideration on the basis of differences in risk and relative weight of those considerations:

(i) A marked difference in risk in favor of a *less* weighty consideration gives *slightly* more force to the *less* weighty consideration, but only if the latter had only *slightly* less weight than the weightier consideration.
(ii) A moderate difference in risk in favor of a *less weighty* consideration results in a 'standoff', but only if the less weighty consideration had only *slightly* less weight than the weightier consideration.
(iii) A moderate difference in risk in favor of *a slightly weightier* consideration gives *slightly* more force to the weightier consideration.
(iv) A moderate difference in risk in favor of a consideration which has moderately more weight gives *moderately* more force to the weightier consideration.
(v) A moderate difference in risk in favor of a consideration which has considerably more weight gives *considerably* more force to the weightier consideration.
(vi) A marked difference in risk in favor of a consideration which has moderately more weight gives it *considerably* more force to the weightier consideration.

If we accept anything along the lines of this sketch, we will be able to say that

(a) what *enables* us to compare the relative *force* of a single pro and a single con consideration is our ability (i) to estimate *the degree to which those features are present* in the situation with which those considerations are concerned, (ii) to determine our *preferences* with respect to the features on which those considerations turn, and (iii) to estimate the *degree of risk* we undertake in relying each of those considerations; and
(b) our comparisons of relative force based on these preferences and estimates will be *reasonable* if and only if both the preferences and the two sorts of estimates on which such comparisons depend are reasonable—i.e., are preferences and estimates *for which we have good reasons all things considered.*

3.7.2 Comparing the relative force of a set of pro considerations with a set of con considerations

Comparisons of the relative force of *sets* of pro and *sets* of con considerations is complicated by the fact that the relative force of a *combination* of two or more pro (or two or more contra) considerations doesn't follow in any straightforward way from the force of the *individual* considerations that comprise that combination. Thus I might have a very strong preference for the flavor of chocolate over most other flavors, and also a strong preference for the flavor of sour cream over most other flavors, but *abhor* the taste of anything that combined the flavor of chocolate with the flavor of sour cream. Because of this, when bringing our preferences into play, we must compare our preferences with respect to the *combinations* of features on which each set of considerations turn—that is to say, the combination of features on which the individual pro considerations turn (call it combination A) and the combination of features on which the individual con considerations turn (call it combination B). Moreover, in determining whether we prefer the conjunction of features on which the pro considerations turn, we ought to consider each feature to be present *in the degree to which the relevant consideration claims it to be present.*

An additional factor—which may in fact simplify our comparison—is that occasionally some one pro consideration or some one contra consideration may be an *overriding* consideration—"trumping," as it were, all the considerations on the other side (see Pinto and Blair, p. 207). For example, in deciding whether or not to purchase a particular vehicle, we might consider the fact that it is "unsafe at any speed" to be an overriding con consideration which cannot be outweighed by any combination of pro considerations—irrespective of how attractive we might consider that combination of those pro considerations to be. Or, consider the following example, suggested by Stephen Paterson. Suppose that my child has been bitten by a snake, and I think from my glimpse of it that the type of snake is not poisonous. I would be wise to consider even a small risk that my judgment about the type of snake is wrong sufficient to render the *possible* threat to my child's life an overriding reason to rush the child to a hospital immediately.

If, other things being equal, we prefer situations which exhibit one of the two combinations to situations which exhibit the other combination, then we judge the *set* of considerations which turns on the preferred combination to be of greater *weight* than the set of considerations which turns on the other combination. The greater the "extent to which we prefer one combination to the other" (e.g.," just a bit", "a fair amount", or "to a great extent"), the greater the *relative weight* we accord to that set of considerations in comparison with the other set of considerations. If we don't prefer either combination to the other, we judge the two sets of considerations to be of approximately *equal weight*.

But the relative *force* of a set of considerations can't be equated with their relative *weight*—as we saw in subsection 3.6 above, the force of a consideration is a function both of its weight and of the risk of error associated with that consideration. How then are we to take into consideration such relative risk of error when we are trying to estimate the relative *force* of the two sets of considerations? In cases, like the snakebite example above, where a small risk of error gives rise to an *overriding* consideration, taking risk of error into consideration is a fairly straightforward matter. But in situations where no single consideration is overriding, things are more complicated. At the present time, I see no alternative but to suggest that we must repeat the attempt to compare combinations of pro and con considerations, this time including in each component of a combination not just our estimate of the degree to which the relevant factor is present, but also the risk that our estimate of that degree is "off the mark". Though such a strategy strikes me as feasible for relatively small sets of considerations, I am not at all confident that it will prove feasible when *large* sets of considerations are at stake. For such larger sets, additional simplifying strategies will have to be considered—but that is a task which lies beyond on the scope of this paper.

3.8 Conclusion

If we accept anything along the lines of this sketch, we will be able to say that

(1) for *both* (a) comparisons of the relative force of a *single* pro and a *single* con considerations and (b) comparisons the relative force of a *set* of pro considerations and that of a *set* of con considerations, our ability to make such comparisons depends on our ability (i) to estimate *the degree to which the features on which those considerations turn are present* in the situation with which those considerations are concerned, (ii) to determine our *preferences* with respect to the combinations of features on which the considerations in those sets turn, and (iii) to estimate the *degree of risk* we undertake in relying on each of those considerations; and that
(2) our comparisons of relative force based on such preferences and estimates will be *reasonable* if and only if both the preferences involved and the two sorts of estimates on which such comparisons depend are reasonable—i.e., are preferences and estimates *for which we have good reasons all things considered.*

Finally, I would want to add a clarification to my claim that the preferences which guide our judgments about comparative weight are reasonable if they are preferences for which we have good reasons all things considered. When it comes to conductive arguments whose conclusion involves application of normative predicates (or involve decisions about what to do), that S has good reasons all things considered for preferring X to Y should *not* be taken to mean that the reasons which (potentially) ground S's preferences would be acknowledged by all, or even most, members of the discursive community S is addressing. What makes a preference an appropriate ground on which *S* might judge the relative force of considerations pro and con is that it is well-grounded within the context of *S*'s thought.

Chapter 9

Evaluating Conductive Arguments:
Critical Questions in Light of the Toulmin Model

JAMES B. FREEMAN

1. Introduction

Our aim is to present a constructive criticism of Wellman's characterization of conductive arguments in Chapter 3 of *Challenge and Response* (1971) and to advance the discussion of evaluating conductive arguments presented in (1971) and in Hitchcock (1994) and Govier (1999a). We believe Wellman's insights can be preserved and better appreciated through both a generalization of his notion of conductive argument and through asking how such arguments might be "laid out" on the Toulmin model. Since Toulmin's layout is motivated by evaluative concerns, it may direct our inquiry into evaluative issues.

2. Wellman's characterization of conductive arguments and their evaluation

According to Wellman, conductive arguments may exhibit one of three patterns: one reason is presented to support the conclusion; several independently relevant reasons are presented for the conclusion; negative considerations are entertained along with presenting independently relevant positive reasons. Since the third pattern clearly includes the second, and the second the first, we take it as paradigm for the class of conductive arguments. However, in the course of our discussion we may focus on the other types, especially the second. Besides these macrostructural considerations, Wellman also sees the premises, conclusion, and negative considerations constituting conductive arguments as subject to distinct constraints. The conclusion concerns an individual and is inferred from premises (and negative considerations) about that same case, which do not appeal to other cases as well (Wellman 1971, p. 52).[1]

3. Preliminary refinement of Wellman's notion of conductive argument

Wellman's speaking of individual cases already raises a question: Do only monadic predicates occur in the premises, conclusions (and negative considerations) of conductive arguments? A look at Wellman's first example shows otherwise: "You ought to take your son to the circus because you promised [to take your son to the circus]" (Wellman 1971, p. 51). Here both premise and conclusion assert a ternary relation. Both are singular statements.

How may we clarify the notion of the same individual case? Let us say that where $S_1, S_2, ..., S_m$ are statements, $S_1, S_2, ..., S_m$ concern the same individual case if and only if there is an n-tuple of denoting expressions $<d_1, d_2, ..., d_n>$ such that each of $S_1, S_2, ..., S_m$ asserts an n-ary relation of $<d_1, d_2, ..., d_n>$ and there is no k-tuple of denoting expressions $<d'_1, d'_2, ..., d'_k>$, where $<d_1, d_2, ..., d_n> \neq <d'_1, d'_2, ..., d'_k>$ such that $S_1, S_2, ..., S_m$ assert some k-ary predicate of the denotation of $<d'_1, d'_2, ..., d'_k>$. Hence, where $P^1 x_1, x_2, ..., x_n, P^2 x_1, x_2, ..., x_n, ..., P^j x_1, x_2, ..., x_n$ are n-ary predicates positively relevant to $Cx_1, x_2, ..., x_n, N^1 x_1,$

---

[1] By ruling out appeal to other cases, Wellman is excluding both quasi-syllogisms and arguments by analogy from the class of conductive arguments.

$x_2, ..., x_n, N^2 x_1, x_2, ..., x_n, ..., N^k x_1, x_2, ..., x_n$ are n-ary predicates negatively relevant to $Cx_1, x_2, ..., x_n$, and $d_1, d_2, ..., d_n$ are denoting expressions, the general form of a conductive argument may very well be expressed this way:

Since $\quad P^1 d_1, d_2, ..., d_n, P^2 d_1, d_2, ..., d_n, ..., P^j d_1, d_2, ..., d_n$
Even though $\quad N^1 d_1, d_2, ..., d_n, N^2 d_1, d_2, ..., d_n, ..., N^k d_1, d_2, ..., d_n$
Therefore $\quad C d_1, d_2, ..., d_n$

This account preserves Wellman's insistence that the component statements of a conductive argument be singular, which he regards as a salient characteristic for these arguments. "Perhaps the most striking feature of all the examples of conduction I have given is that they all deal with particular cases; each derives a conclusion about an individual act or object from information about that same act or object" (Wellman 1971, p. 52). Wellman's remark suggests that generalizations play no part in conductive arguments? But is this possible?

4. Conductive arguments, generalizations, and warrants

Many texts on elementary logic point out that to each argument there corresponds a conditional sentence: The conjunction of the premises constitutes the antecedent, the conclusion the consequent. As Hitchcock has pointed out in (1985), arguments properly judged on whether their premises conclusively establish their conclusions assume the truth of their associated conditionals. But as he has also taught us in (1985), such arguments assume more, namely the truth of a universal generalization of their associated conditionals "with respect to at least one repeated content expression" (Hitchcock 1985, p. 89).[2] This does not mean that the argument assumes the truth of the universal generalization over all the repeated content expressions. A concrete instance of our schema for conductive arguments above need not assume the truth of

$(\forall x_1)(\forall x_2)...(\forall x_n)[([P^1 x_1, x_2, ..., x_n \ \& \ P^2 x_1, x_2, ..., x_n \ \& \ ... \ \& \ P^j x_1, x_2, ..., x_n] \ \& \ [N^1 x_1, x_2, ..., x_n \ \& \ N^2 x_1, x_2, ..., x_n \ \& \ ... \ \& \ N^k x_1, x_2, ..., x_n]) \supset C x_1, x_2, ..., x_n]$

The generalization may be over only a proper subset of $\{d_1, d_2, ..., d_n\}$. We identify the subset on a case-by-case basis, making an intuitive judgment over the plausibility of the associated universal generalization. Intuitively, we generalize over the maximal number of content expressions without loss of plausibility.

Hitchcock has taught us something further about these universally generalized associated conditionals. Arguments assume them not as premises but as warrants in Toulmin's sense, specifically as "a rule of inference in virtue of which the conclusion follows from the premis(es)" (Hitchcock 1985, p. 94). I believe it will be perspicuous to distinguish the rule proper from the universally generalized associated conditional. An inference rule is of the form:

---

[2] A repeated content expression need not be a denoting expression. However, our discussion of conductive arguments does not require us to consider other types of repeated content expressions. Also, a repeated content expression need not have an occurrence in the conclusion of an argument if it occurs more than once in the premises.

From: $P_1, P_2, ..., P_n$
To infer: C

It is a license rather than a statement. As Hitchcock points out, such warrants are material inference rules, since they involve content expressions, here in particular the P^i's, N^j's, and C, as opposed to the purely formal rules of deductive logic. Although the inference rules are material, Hitchcock specifically says that the enthymematic arguments studied in (1985) *are not* non-deductive and may be evaluated for validity.[3] The criterion for connection adequacy is truth-preservation. By contrast, Wellman specifically says that conductive arguments *are* non-deductive when he specifies that the conclusion of a conductive argument "is drawn non-conclusively" (Wellman 1971, p. 52) from the premises. Clearly then truth-preservation is too strict a criterion for the ground adequacy of conductive arguments. Indeed, warrants for conductive arguments need to be qualified. We are not licensed to infer *simpliciter* but only *ceteris paribus*. So where 'x_i/d_i' indicates either 'x_i' if 'd_i' is a repeated content expression generalized over, and 'd_i' if otherwise, the general form of such warrants for conductive arguments is

From: $P^1 x_1/d_1, x_2/d_2, ..., x_n/d_n, P^2 x_1/d_1, x_2/d_2, ..., x_n/d_n, ..., P^j x_1/d_1, x_2/d_2, ..., x_n/d_n$
Even though: $N^1 x_1/d_1, x_2/d_2, ..., x_n/d_n, N^2 x_1/d_1, x_2/d_2, ..., x_n/d_n, ..., N^k x_1/d_1, x_2/d_2, ... x_n/d_n$
To infer *ceteris paribus*: $C x_1/d_1, x_2/d_2, ..., x_n/d_n$

However, that we are understanding the connection adequacy of enthymematic arguments through a condition on their warrants gives us a clue to developing a criterion for conductive arguments, when taken in conjunction with the Toulmin model. As Toulmin points out, warrants raise the question of backing, and their "authority and currency" (Toulmin 1958, p. 103) are certified by their backing. However, backing is field-dependent. Not all warrants will be backed in the same way. In (2005b), we argued for replacing Toulmin's problematic notion of a field with an epistemic systematization of warrants. That the notion of field may be problematic, then, does not affect our point here. A warrant which is sufficiently backed is reliable, at least *ceteris paribus*. Validity is a special limiting case of reliability. How then are the warrants of conductive arguments backed, and can we identify conditions under which that backing is sufficient to render the warrant reliable? Let us initially simplify our inquiry by setting aside questions of negative considerations, concentrating on the second pattern of conductive arguments which Wellman identifies. We shall integrate counterconsideration issues into our discussion in Sections 6 and 7. Also for simplification, where $x_1, x_2, ..., x_n$ are the variables replacing repeated content expressions, let us understand by

$\Phi x_1, x_2, ..., x_n$

the conjunction of the premises of the inference rule. Our question then is when

From: $\Phi x_1, x_2, ..., x_n$
To infer *ceteris paribus*: $C x_1, x_2, ..., x_n$

---

[3] For Hitchcock's account of enthymematic validity, see (Hitchcock 1985, p. 95).

is the warrant of a conductive argument, under what circumstances is that warrant properly backed to be reliable.

5. Warrants for conductive arguments and backing

Although Wellman in (1971) is principally concerned with ethical arguments, he specifically acknowledged that conductive arguments may appear in other contexts, in particular ascribing a predicate "on the basis of a family resemblance.... In all such cases there are several criteria for the application of the term.... The fact that one or more of the criteria are satisfied in a particular instance is a reason for applying the term..." (Wellman 1971, p. 54). Through a series of examples in (1999), Govier also points out that conductive arguments may occur in a number of fields besides ethics including the interpretive issue of whether a given story is properly a myth, a given lifestyle falls short of being totally environmentally friendly, a given behavior results from a learned response, and whether changes in human behavior are necessary causal conditions for realizing certain social ends. Overall, she find that conductive arguments "naturally occur in law, philosophy, interpretive studies–and in fact in any area, including science, in which there are reasons for and against, or 'pros and cons' which we must consider in order to make a judgment on an issue" (Govier 1999, p. 160).

Wellman presents three examples of conductive arguments from widely different fields:

(1) Bees have a language because they can communicate information about the location of flowers to one another.
(2) Hunting is a game because it is fun and involves a competition between the hunter and his prey.
(3) Although John can play only one instrument, and that not very well, he is still musical because he has a remarkable memory for music he has heard and composes on occasion. (Wellman 1971, p. 54)

Wellman makes a very significant statement about all such conductive arguments: The inference from premises which ascribe criteria for applying the property or relation ascribed in the conclusion "does not appeal to the fact that the criteria have been found empirically associated with the term in other cases" (Wellman 1971, p. 54). This statement needs to be unpacked in the light of our discussion. It contains both truth and a misleading suggestion. Each of these three arguments has a warrant.

(W1) From: Members of species X can communicate information about the location of flowers to other members of species X
To infer *ceteris paribus:* Members of species X have a language

(W2) From: Activity x is fun (for some participants) and x involves a competition between (certain) participants
To infer *ceteris paribus* : Activity x is a game

(W3) From: x has a remarkable memory for music x has heard and x composes music occasionally
To infer *ceteris paribus:* x is musical

As we developed in (Freeman 1991, pp. 81-84), warrants when properly understood as inference licenses are not properly parts of arguments, by contrast with premises and conclusions. Rather, arguments instance warrants. But this fact in no way gainsays that Toulmin's warrant introducing question "How do you get there [i.e., from data to claim]?" (Toulmin 1958, p. 98) is legitimate, especially when evaluating an argument for connection adequacy. Now if the warrant is not properly part of the argument, *a fortiori* neither is the backing. Should a warrant be backed by empirical evidence that the criteria in the premises have been associated with the term ascribed in the conclusion, Wellman is quite right that the conductive argument includes as a part or element no appeal to such evidence. However, this in no way gainsays the legitimacy of asking for such backing when evaluating the argument, as Wellman's remark might suggest. Again, Toulmin's question which a challenger might pose to a proponent who argues that Harry is a British subject because he was born in Bermuda—"You presume that a man born in Bermuda can be taken to be a British subject, ... but why do you think that?" (Toulmin, p. 103)—a request for backing, is as legitimate as ever.

Notice that Toulmin's question highlights further how Wellman's remark that conductive arguments do not appeal to empirical associations is right but nonetheless potentially misleading. That being born in Bermuda is a *prima facie* criterion for being a British subject is not a matter of empirical investigation but of British law. One would not verify that it is true by observing examples but by consulting reliable records of enacted statutes. A warrant need not be backed empirically, but this does not mean that the warrant is not backed (nor does it mean that the warrant is analytic) nor that asking for its backing is not a legitimate issue in argument evaluation. What is the implication of these considerations on warrants and backing for the issue of evaluating conductive arguments?

Some may wonder whether we are being too prodigal in the number of warrants we admit. This is understandable. After all, a formal deductive logic text will present a relatively small number of inference rules. Even if a set of primitive rules is supplemented by further derived rules, the entire set will still be relatively small. However, we do not find this reservation telling. Recall that human language is recursive. We are continually taking the words of a language and building new sentences from them that have never been constructed before. Sometimes these sentences are components of newly constructed arguments. So the class of arguments contains myriads of members. If a proponent is arguing sincerely, he will apprehend some relevance of the premises to the conclusion by virtue of recognizing some general connection between them. But since this is a general connection, it may be instantiated in a number of different arguments. There may be myriad inference rules, but there will be a one-many relation between them and the arguments which instantiate them, arguments whose ontological status we are willing to concede. If one allows these many arguments, one should not cavil at allowing their inference rules.

6. Backing and the evaluation of conductive arguments

We return to our question at the end of Section 4: Where

From: $\Phi x_1, x_2, ..., x_n$
To infer *ceteris paribus*: $Cx_1, x_2, ..., x_n$

is the warrant of a conductive argument, when is it properly backed? Our discussion in Section 5 has advanced our investigation by establishing this point: To attempt to answer this question in one fell swoop is wrongheaded. Different warrants may be backed in different ways. The question of proper backing should be considered separately for each type of warrant. But what types of warrants are there? In (2005b) we argued that we could distinguish four broad types of warrants corresponding to four distinct epistemic types of intuition: *a priori*, empirical, institutional, and evaluative.[4] *A priori* intuition grasps alethically necessary connections. Since conductive arguments are non-conclusive, we may set the class of corresponding warrants aside. Empirical, institutional, and evaluative warrants all grasp nomic connections, empirical on the basis of observing co-variation, institutional upon coming to understand the constitutive principles of some institution such as a branch of law, evaluative on recognizing how certain evaluative properties supervene upon certain evaluatively relevant (but not in general evaluative) properties.

How does making this distinction bear on backing warrants and thus on evaluating conductive arguments instancing those warrants? Let's consider in turn an example of an empirical, institutional, and evaluative warrant.

From: x is a light beam striking a reflecting surface at angle y
To infer *ceteris paribus*: x is refracted at angle y

Corresponding to the warrant is a well-known physical causal law, angle of incidence equals angle of refraction. The evidence for that law, ultimately the evidence of empirical observation, constitutes the backing of the warrant. Appraising such evidence involves questions of the extent and variety of observed evidence. But if the extent is sufficient and varied to take account of the potential effects of relevant variables, the causal law is confirmed and the warrant properly backed.

From: x kicked the soccer ball past the goalie into the opposing team's net
To infer *ceteris paribus*: x scored a goal

One who knows the constitutive rules of soccer, in particular what constitutes scoring a goal, knows that this warrant is reliable. No further evidence is necessary. If one has learned the rules through engaging in the practice, one could say that the warrant is self-backed, although in a dispute, an authoritative compendium of the rules of soccer should suffice for resolution.

From: x promised to take y to see movie z during time w and z is a good movie and x has nothing better to do during time w
To infer *ceteris paribus*: x ought to take y to see movie z during time w

(Compare Wellman 1971, p. 56.)
Ross (1930) would certainly regard the warrant

From: x promised to take y to see movie z during time w
To infer: x ought *prima facie* to take y to see movie z during time w

---

[4] In (Freeman 2005) we allowed that there can be further subdivisions of these types. That issue is beyond the scope of this chapter.

as self-evident. Ross holds that through recognizing particular cases of *prima facie* duty on the basis of recognizing some feature or property of the situation, we come to recognize that feature as a duty-making feature in general. From recognizing in several cases that our having made a promise gives someone the moral right to expect we shall keep that promise, we come to recognize the *prima facie* rightness of promise keeping in general. "What comes first in time is the apprehension of the self-evident *prima facie* rightness of an individual act of a particular type. From this we come by reflection to apprehend the self-evident general principle of *prima facie* duty" (Ross, p. 33). Should one accept that principles of *prima facie* duty are self-evident, construed as warrants they are also self-backed. We are not inductively generalizing from recognizing *prima facie* duties in particular cases, but are recognizing a general connection between certain deontically relevant properties and *prima facie* obligation. This self-evidence also backs our inferring *ceteris paribus* an actual duty from certain duty making properties, absent negatively relevant features also holding.

We can thus see that empirical, institutional, and moral warrants are all backed, but backed in very distinct ways. However, one can in each case appeal to the backing should a challenger question whether employing the warrant is justified. Invite the challenger to enter empathetically into certain conditions of promise making and she shall "see" the connection between making a promise and being obligated, *prima facie*, to keep it. Proffer an authoritative compendium of the rules of soccer, and one who can read this source with understanding will see that getting the ball into the opposing team's net constitutes scoring a goal. Present someone with observations confirming some physical generalization which satisfy criteria of extent and variety, and one recognizes that reasoning according to the warrant is justified, at least *ceteris paribus*. Recognizing that conductive arguments instance warrants and warrants can be backed advances our understanding of how conductive arguments may be evaluated beyond what Wellman thought possible. "By and large there is no way to judge the validity of these basic ethical arguments but by thinking them through and feeling their logical force" (Wellman 1971, p. 79). In none of these three cases need the proponent simply ask the challenger to reconsider the argument or its warrant again in the hope that through such reconsideration she will come to somehow intuit the warrant's justification.

However, up to this point, the warrants we have considered have authorized inferences just from positively relevant features, Wellman's second pattern of conductive argument. We have not yet addressed the third pattern which reasons from con as well as pro considerations. Wellman thought that the only way to appraise such arguments was to intuitively weigh the pro and con considerations against each other. Ross is in substantial agreement. He held that if one were to decide upon the actual as opposed to the *prima facie* rightness of an act, one might in general have to take account both of its *prima facie* right making and *prima facie* wrong making properties, weighing one against the other. "Right acts can be distinguished from wrong acts only as being those which, of all those possible for the agent in the circumstances, have the greatest balance of *prima facie* rightness, in those respects in which they are *prima facie* right, over their *prima facie* wrongness, in those respects in which they are *prima facie* wrong" (Ross, p. 41). Although some general principles may be available to discern the balance, in general Ross believes the judgment will be intuitive. Can we go beyond an intuitive weighing of positive over negative considerations and can the Toulmin model give us a way to make this advance? Let us first review the case Wellman makes for saying that reasoning with positive and negative considerations is a matter of intuitive weighing, and then suggestions of Hitchcock (1994) and Govier (1999) for getting beyond simple intuition.

7. The question of pro and con

Wellman believes that the metaphor of weighing, properly understood as analogous to hefting physical objects to determine intuitively which is heavier, is appropriate to discerning the balance of positive over negative considerations. An imprecise judgment as opposed to the precise reading of some scale is the best one can do. In addition, since there may be a number of positive and negative considerations, hefting each one by one (or two by two) may be necessary, as one might heft individually each rock in two piles to determine which pile has the greater weight. In discussing whether there can be a logic of conduction, specifically a logic of conductive ethical arguments, Wellman makes a remark which gets a special significance in light of our previous discussion:

> Conductive arguments are non-formal in the sense that their validity depends upon the predicate constants they contain as well as the logical terms they use. In no case, however, do the individual constants affect the validity of the argument. In this sense, validity remains universal even when it is not formal. (Wellman 1971, p. 61)

That is, the validity of conductive arguments is a matter of their warrants, as we have characterized warrant. In replacing the repeated content expressions by variables, we are constructing possibly complex predicate expressions, indicating that from one's holding, we may infer that the other holds, *ceteris paribus*. As Wellman further acknowledges, the warrants in conductive arguments are materially, not formally valid. "The validity of conductive arguments cannot be determined without considering their subject matter, for their validity is non-formal" (Wellman 1971, p. 62). Hence Wellman would substantially agree that conductive arguments involve material warrants and further agree on the nature of those warrants.

In line with Toulmin's conception, Wellman recognizes that warrants are principles of relevance. Also in line with Toulmin's conception, he agrees that warrants can confer different degrees of force. He is skeptical of whether comparative degree of force can be discerned in any general way apart from consideration of particular cases. Against the proposal for general rules of precedence for weighting one consideration or type of consideration over another, Wellman asks us to consider the principle that avoiding harm takes precedence over causing good. Acts that result in both harm and good would thus always be overall wrong. But is this correct? Amount of harm and amount of good caused can vary widely. Where an act would result in a small amount of harm and a great amount of good, is the act wrong simply because of this weak wrong-making property? To the proposal of constructing a comprehensive set of precedence rules to apply in particular cases, Wellman responds that "to be of any real help the rules of logical force would have to specify the priority for every degree of each factor for each possible pair of factors. Such a set of rules would be very complicated indeed" (Wellman 1971, p. 68).

Wellman points out that matters are even worse. Suppose one situation exhibits five positive factors and two negative factors, while another exhibits three positive factors against four negative considerations. Can there be a system of general principles of precedence that can be applied to these varying numbers of factors in all their varying degrees? Each combination of positive and negative factors of specific degrees "has its own logical force and would require a separate rule of force" (Wellman 1971, pp. 68-69). Wellman concludes that "to determine the validity of conductive arguments one would need a rule of inference for each set of predicates, where asserting a different amount of the same factor constitutes applying a different predicate" (Wellman 1971, p. 69). In short, to search for a relatively small number of general rules for the validity of conductive arguments, analogous to a complete set of rules for deductive arguments, is to seek for a will o' the wisp. The principles of validity for conductive arguments are the material warrants of the arguments themselves. To judge the connection adequacy of arguments instancing such warrants, one must weigh their positive against their negative factors.

We may agree with Wellman that the principles of conductive reasoning are the warrants of conductive arguments themselves, but we still question whether this limits evaluation of these arguments to an intuitive weighing of positive against negative considerations. Wellman denies that at least for ethical conductive arguments there can be objective criteria of validity against which we can check our intuitive judgments, as we may check our intuitive estimations of weight against an objective scale. Wellman believes that thinking the argument through again and again, if necessary, is the only way to judge an appraisal of conductive validity as correct or incorrect. In this way, we may be able to correct an intuitive judgment of validity, but we are left without a more objective criterion. Can we do better?

Hitchcock (1994) notes that if we may construct a counterexample to a deductive or more generally conclusive[5] warrant, we have shown the invalidity of an argument instancing that warrant. This procedure goes beyond thinking through the specific argument, for we are constructing a logical analog, employing the same warrant, which is manifestly invalid. Conductive arguments are not conclusive, but Hitchcock argues that the concept of conclusive validity can be widened to the non-conclusive case. Suppose a proponent has put forward a conductive argument with the warrant

From: $\Phi x_1, x_2, ..., x_n$
To infer *ceteris paribus*: $\Psi x_1, x_2, ..., x_n$

and the challenger has responded with a counterexample "Given $\Phi a_1, a_2, ...,a_n$, therefore $\Psi a_1, a_2, ..., a_n$," where "$\Phi a_1, a_2, ...,ax_n$" is true and "$\Psi a_1, a_2, ..., a_n$" is false. The proponent can counter that $<a_1, a_2, ..., a_n>$ has some further property χ which neutralizes or outweighs Φ. "Given $\Phi a_1, a_2, ...,ax_n$ & $\chi a_1, a_2, ..., a_n$, therefore $\sim\Psi a_1, a_2, ..., a_n$," All things are not equal.

Suppose, for example, the proponent argues that since there are strong reasons to build a new high school, we should proceed to build it in the municipal park. A challenger might respond that since there are strong reasons to build a new bridge, we should build it in the downtown historic area. The proponent replies that this counterexample is unfair, since the value of preserving the historic district outweighs the value of a new bridge. The warrant of both the proponent's original argument and the counterexample is

From: There are strong reasons to build y and A is an available site.
To infer *ceteris paribus*: Building y should take place at site A.

The proponent's response has as warrant

From: There are strong reasons to build y, A is an available site, but building y at site A destroys historic value.
To infer *ceteris paribus*: Building y should not take place at site A.

---

[5] See Hitchcock's discussion in (1994, pp. 59-60).

If the challenger could construct an example where it was true that there were reasons for building *y*, one should not build *y* at available site *A*, but there were no overriding reasons against building at *A* (all things were still equal), then she would have a counterexample to show the argument not valid. Hitchcock sums up his discussion of validity for conductive arguments this way:

> A conductive argument "P(a), so c(a)" is non-conclusively valid if and only if it is not conclusively valid, but for any situation x, if P(x) then either c(x) or x has an overriding negatively relevant feature F which not c(x) does not deductively imply. (Hitchcock 1994, p. 62)

The last clause, "which not c(x) does not deductively imply," Hitchcock adds for technical reasons. The overriding condition cannot be a deductive consequence of the falsity of the conclusion. Otherwise, one could not in principle ever find a counterexample, since any deductive consequence of the negation of the conclusion could serve as an overriding condition (Hitchcock 1994, p. 61).

We should note, what Hitchcock readily admits, that this criterion of validity for conductive arguments is a criterion for the relevance of the premises to the conclusion, not their ground adequacy. Unlike validity for deductive arguments, which establishes that the premises are adequate grounds for and *ipso facto* relevant to the conclusion, arguments may be non-conclusively valid "even when" Hitchcock points out, "the reason given for the conclusion provides very weak support for it" (Hitchcock 1994, p. 62). One may complain that the reasons may be so weak as to be virtually irrelevant. Our proponent's arguing from good general reasons to build a new high school to building it in the municipal park, a specific site, is a classic case of a *non-sequitur*. The issue is not whether to build a new high school but where.

Counting general reasons for building the high school as a relevant reason for building it at a specific site seems counterintuitive. Hitchcock's reply that there is more to evaluating a conductive argument than determining that its premises are acceptable and that the argument itself is non-conclusively valid, that "the evaluator must also look for other relevant features of the situation which might tip the judgment the other way" (Hitchcock 1994, p. 62) raises the question of whether evaluating conductive arguments for ground adequacy is still a matter of intuitively weighing positive versus negative considerations. If one can, at least frequently, intuitively judge premises as relevant, and Hitchcock's criterion may yield counterintuitive judgments of relevance on occasion, has his discussion of non-conclusive validity for conductive arguments advanced our discussion beyond what Wellman offers? Can Govier advance the discussion?

In addressing argument strength or ground adequacy for conductive arguments in (1999a), Govier proposes first assessing the strength of each relevant reason's support for the conclusion and then assessing their combined weight. One then identifies the counter-considerations acknowledged by the proponent and then those which a challenger would (or should) identify. One assesses the negative strength of each of these considerations individually and then their weight in combination. One then addresses the overall support for the conclusion, balancing positive against negative factors. So far, this elaborates how one might weigh positive and negative considerations, but does not seem to advance us beyond Wellman's conception. It is right here that Govier advances the discussion. The warrants corresponding to the individual positive and negative considerations are *ceteris paribus* warrants. "To reflect on how strong a reason is *in the case or context we are considering*, we have to reflect on how many other things would have to be 'equal' and whether they are so in this case. A strong reason is one where the range of exceptions is narrow. A weak reason is one where the range of exceptions is large" (Govier 1999a, p. 171).

Questions which are critical yet promise further advance immediately arise. Is the range of exceptions simply a function of the number of conceivable exceptions or is some further factor involved? Could we not contrast a situation where few exceptions to a positive reason are conceivable, but those few are very strong, with a situation where there may be many exceptions, even though each very weak? If this seems plausible, then the strength of a reason is not simply a function of the number of possible counterconsiderations to it. Counterconsiderations have a strength of their own. To assess their overall strength against one or more positive reasons, one has to take both this further dimension into account as well as the number of counterconsiderations.

Govier's discussion of two examples to illustrate her point indicates these two dimensions. "That a person would want to see her mother before she died is a strong presumption–one which could be defeated only by *few* and *rare* circumstances. That a painting is signed by a proven false signature is a strong reason to believe it is a forgery—because the *range of cases* in which an artist truly painted a piece and yet someone else signed it on his behalf will be *small*" (Govier 1999a, p. 172, italics added). In the first example, "few" refers to types or kinds of circumstances, but 'rare' refers to their relative frequency. Likewise, in the second example, saying that the range of cases is small refers not to the variety of cases encompassed by the range but to the low relative frequency of cases in that range among the cases of signed paintings by artists.

If we are to advance our understanding of weight or ground adequacy for conductive arguments, we must keep relative frequency and kind considerations distinct. As L.J. Cohen (1989) indicates, the first concerns enumerative induction while the latter concerns variative induction. Briefly put, enumerative induction concerns the number of instances examined to gain support for some hypothesis, while variative induction concerns the number of distinct kinds of relevant variables taken into account in a series of tests to confirm or refute the hypothesis. In conductive arguments, negative or counterconsiderations concern relevant variables. Taking account of negative considerations means subjecting a warrant to test. Should we entertain that

From: $\Phi x_1, x_2, ..., x_n$
To infer: $\Psi x_1, x_2, ..., x_n$

is a reliable warrant, by varying factors suspected of affecting whether $\Psi x_1, x_2, ..., x_n$ holds, we may test the warrant's reliability. Just what would it mean to say that the warrant survived that test and how might one go about ascertaining that it had? I believe that a satisfactory answer to these questions involves a theory of epistemic probability and a procedure of ascertaining epistemic probability in given cases. The negatively relevant features that Hitchcock considers, and the counterconsiderations that Govier considers, are instances of what Pollock calls rebutting defeaters, since they are negatively relevant to the conclusion. These he contrasts with undercutting defeaters. "Rebutting defeaters attack the conclusion of a defeasible inference, while undercutting defeaters attack the defeasible inference itself, without doing so by giving us a reason for thinking it has a false conclusion" (Pollock 2008, p. 453). A comprehensive account of connection adequacy for defeasible arguments in general must address both rebutting and undercutting defeaters. That is beyond our scope here. But discussing the weighing of pro against con considerations concerns premises versus rebutting defeaters.

As our discussion of epistemic types of warrant should suggest, we hold that the issue of epistemic probability should not be answered in one fell swoop but separately for each type of warrant. In (Freeman 2009), we argued that a purely enumerative account of epistemic probability was inadequate even for arguments with empirical warrants. Variative considerations are an essential factor. That negative considerations can play an indispensable role in evaluating conductive arguments indicates the indispensability of variative considerations in evaluating conductive arguments. Saying that such negative or variative considerations involve what Ralph Johnson calls the dialectical tier (see Johnson 2000, pp. 164-75.) seems straightforward. In the last section of this paper, I want to clarify the relation between positive and negative considerations and warrants, arguing that properly identifying the warrant of a conductive argument may very well take us to the dialectical tier.

8. Warrants and the dialectical tier for conductive arguments

Consider this simplification of an argument Govier presents in (Govier, pp. 161-62):

> (1) I travel 350 miles each week by car. Even though (2) in summer I pick fresh vegetables and fruits from my own garden, (3) in winter I buy them from health food stores that truck them east from organic farms in California. Again, even though (4) I write on both sides of the paper, (5) I use paper and a great deal of it. Hence, (6) I use waste making energy.

As Govier points out, this is a conductive argument presenting considerations both pro–(1), (3), (5) and con–(2) and (4). Diagramming just the positive core part of this argument is totally straightforward:

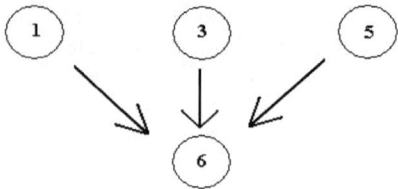

Although (1), (3), and (5) are independently relevant to (6), as our diagram shows, and assessing whether they in fact are relevant is a matter of determining the reliability of a separate warrant for each, *pace* Govier I believe it is a mistake in assessing the ground adequacy of these three premises to try to assess the weight of each separately and then try to add or otherwise arithmetically combine these weights together. This view was implicit in representing conductive arguments as having a conjunction of premises. Although we would expect that two premises might supplement each other's weight, in some cases they might cancel each other out. Hence, we should understand this argument as having not three warrants, but one licensing the move from the conjunction of (1), (3), and (5) to (6).[6] I suggest that we can more perspicuously represent the structure of the core argument this way:

---

[6] We deny that this entails that the argument has linked structure. We argue this point specifically in Chapter 6 of (Freeman 2011).

Evaluating Conductive Arguments: Critical Questions in Light of the Toulmin Model   139

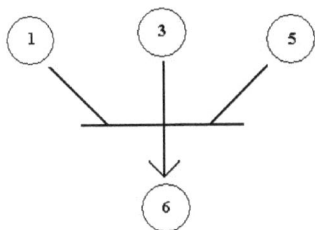

The warrant of just the core argument is

From: *x* travels 350 miles each week by car & in winter *x* buys
                    fruits and vegetables trucked east from California & *x* uses
                    a great deal of paper
To infer *ceteris paribus*: *x* uses waste making energy

We do not intend to deny that a proponent may present several completely independent arguments for the same conclusion. However, as long as taking several reasons, even though independently relevant, as constituting *one* argument for a given conclusion properly interprets the proponent's intentions, seeing the warrant of that argument as proceeding from the conjunction of the premises to the conclusion is appropriate.

Where do (2) and (4) as counterconsiderations fit into the argument? Govier suggests introducing wavy arrows pointing from their representations to the conclusion. I believe we can understand the function of these counterconsiderations more accurately and represent them more fully if we regard them as rebuttals. Here, we are taking a conception of rebuttal wider than Toulmin's in (1958), where he regards rebuttals as conditions of exception for the application of the warrant. In (Freeman 1991, pp. 152-55), we pointed out that Toulmin frequently speaks of rebuttals as being exceptional. We argued that this unduly restricts the class of rebuttals. We shall here understand a rebuttal to be any contra consideration. In the Toulmin model, the representation of the rebuttals appears below the representation of the modal qualifier. Although the argument we are considering does not have a modal qualifier, the horizontal line in our diagram indicates that the weights of (1), (3), and (5) are being combined in the case for (6). An explicit modality would appear in that position. Since our diagram in effect rotates the Toulmin model 90° clockwise, we represent rebuttals as attached to this horizontal line, enclosing them in a box:

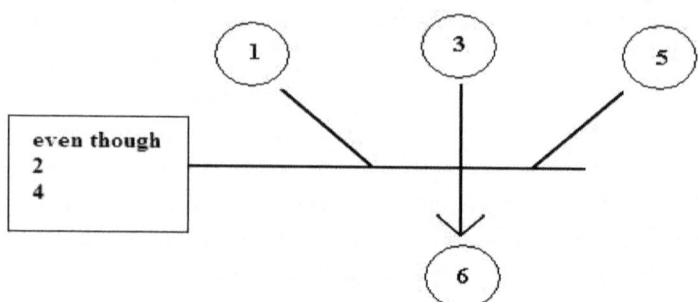

The diagram makes explicit that we regard counterconsiderations, even those which the proponent of an argument concedes as having so little weight as not to merit a reply or counterrebuttal, as part of the family of rebuttals. Below we shall see that a proponent may concede a rebuttal that calls for a response, in particular if he has a reason which undercuts the negative force of that rebuttal. Since the proponent simply concedes these counterconsiderations, the warrant of his argument as fully presented is

From: *x* travels 350 miles each week by car & *x* in summer picks fresh fruits and vegetables from *x*'s garden & in winter *x* buys fruits and vegetables trucked east from California & *x* writes on both sides of the paper & *x* uses a great deal of paper
To infer *ceteris paribus*: *x* uses waste making energy.

The question, then, of the ground adequacy of (1), (3), and (5), or more generally of how strongly the argument's premises support the conclusion, becomes a question of the epistemic probability of the full warrant.

The proponent did not reply to these counterconsiderations, but simply conceded them. Hence we include the counterconsiderations as conjunctions in the premise of the warrant. This should hold true whenever a conductive argument includes a rebuttal that has not been countered. But some rebuttals must be countered, on pain of in effect resigning the argument. Consider:

It will start raining in approximately three hours, since a cold front moving at 20 mph in our direction is now 60 miles away, even though the cold front will dissipate in one to two hours.

What type of argument is that! The rebuttal completely undercuts the force of the premise. Premise and rebuttal together give us good reason to believe that it will *not* start raining in three hours.

Rebuttals on the Toulmin model correspond to distinctions in formal disputation, as Rescher discusses in (1977). To the proponent's argument, a challenger could reply: It will not start raining in three hours, given that both a cold front is moving in our direction and the cold front dissipates. Please show that it will not dissipate. The challenger's distinction is called a weak distinction since she does not assert categorically that the cold front will dissipate in the next one to two hours but only asks to be shown that it will not. This accords with the challenger role in formal disputation, not to make assertions but to raise questions.[7]

As Rescher points out, the proponent has three countermoves available to reply to a weak distinction, and each is germane to the issue of evaluating conductive arguments. First, the proponent could assert categorically that the cold front will not dissipate in one to two hours. Second, the proponent could both categorically assert that the cold front will not dissipate and give a reason for why it will not, e.g., none of the meteorological factors which lead to a front's dissipation are present here. Third, the proponent could reply with a distinction of his own. I concede that the cold front will dissipate, but it will reform a half hour later.

In (1991), we called these countermoves to weak distinctions counterrebuttals. Although Toulmin does not make a place for counterrebuttals in his model, he does recognize that some assertions of fact have this function.

> The fact that Harry was born in Bermuda and the fact that his parents were not aliens are both of them directly relevant to the question of his present nationality; but they are relevant in different ways. The one fact is a datum, which by itself establishes a presumption of British nationality; the other fact, by setting aside one possible rebuttal, tends to confirm the presumption thereby created. (Toulmin 1958, p. 102)

In (1991), we indicated that we could include counterrebuttals in argument diagrams in a way which displayed their function of supporting the conclusion by setting aside a rebuttal. In general, we represent them through encircled numbers with arrows pointing from them to the rebuttal box. The arrow indicates support. Pointing to the rebuttal box indicates that the intended support comes through setting aside a rebuttal. To further indicate the countering function, we cross out the rebuttal countered if it is not conceded.

As Toulmin has indicated, our proponent may incorporate the challenger's weak distinction into his argument through an "unless" clause—

> (1) It will start raining in approximately three hours since (2) a cold front moving at 20 mph in our direction is now 60 miles away, unless (3) the cold front dissipates in one to two hours.

---

[7] The challenger is raising the issue of what Pollock would call a rebutting defeater, since it is negatively relevant to the conclusion. By contrast, an undercutting defeater would attack the warrant. To raise the question whether "When Q, so *ceteris paribus* P" (see Rescher 1977, p. 6) is not to claim one has a reason to deny P, but the step from Q to P. Rescher does not consider moves which would constitute undercutting defeaters in (1977), making the simplifying assertion that warrants licensing moves from premises to conclusions are always correct (p. 8). A complete account of the rebuttals that would appear in conductive arguments and how they could be countered would have to take into account such undercutting defeaters. That is beyond our scope here.

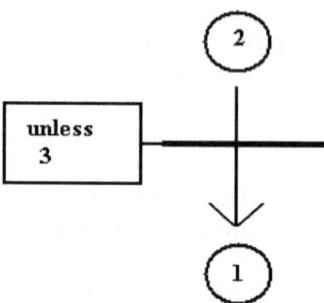

—should the proponent reply with a bald denial of the distinction. But (4) the cold front will not dissipate in one to two hours,

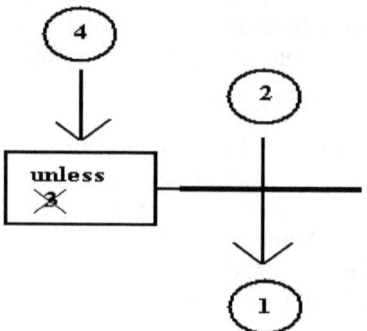

The above diagram includes representation of the counterrebuttal. Should the proponent argue for the counterrebuttal:

> because (5) none of the meteorological factors which lead to a front's dissipation are present here.

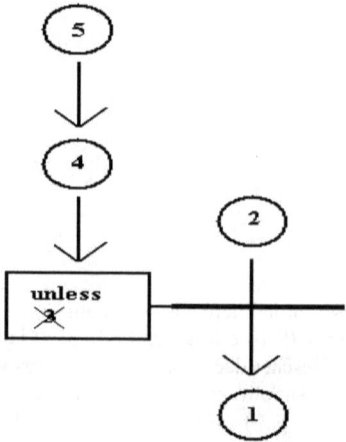

Evaluating Conductive Arguments: Critical Questions in Light of the Toulmin Model

The above diagram incorporates the subargument into the diagram, displaying its function.

Should the proponent respond to the challenger's distinction with a strong distinction of his own, he is conceding the rebuttal but replying that its force as evidence against the conclusion is undercut by the further distinction. Thus:

True, (3) the front will dissipate in one to two hours, but (4) it will reform one half hour later.

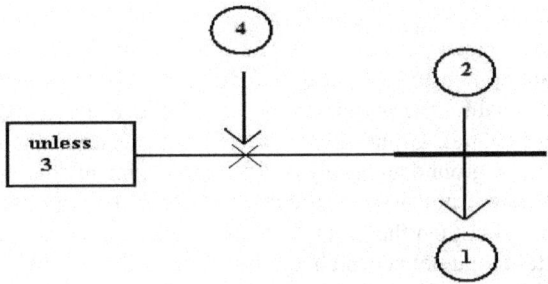

represents that the rebutting force of (3) is undercut and the presumption for (1) further confirmed.

What do these structural considerations have to do with discerning the warrants of conductive arguments? Let us consider each of the proponent's replies in turn. Should the proponent reply with a bald denial, that statement becomes a further premise. It is incumbent on the argument analyst to find a common content expression in the counterrebutting premise and the remainder of the argument developed thus far, replace that expression with a free variable, and add the resulting open sentence as a further conjunct to the warrant. This may involve a free hand rephrasing of the proponent's reply, if one wishes to speak loosely but nonetheless efficiently. In the example we have been reviewing, the common content expression–"here"–is implicit. Where the warrant of the original argument is:

From: A cold front moving at 20 mph in the direction of x is 60 miles from x
To infer *ceteris paribus*:   it will start raining at x in approximately three hours

the warrant of the expanded argument is:

From: A cold front moving at 20 mph in the direction of x is 60 miles from x & will not dissipate before it reaches x
To infer *ceteris paribus*:   it will start raining at x in approximately three hours

Notice that despite their functionally different roles, (2) and (4) converge on (1). In an overall evaluation of a convergent argument for logical cogency, the ground adequacy question concerns the sufficiency of the premises found acceptable and relevant to create a presumption for the conclusion. Obviously (2) and (4) are relevant to (1). Should premise (4) be acceptable, i.e. should there be a presumption for it from our point of view as critical challengers or evaluators of the argument, then the ground adequacy question becomes whether the expanded warrant has sufficient reliability to transfer the acceptability of the premises to the conclusion.

By contrast, should there be a presumption for the rebuttal (3) from our point of view, then we should treat (3) as we would treat a conceded counterconsideration. In assessing ground adequacy, the warrant to consider then becomes

From:	A cold front moving at 20 mph in the direction of x is 60 miles from x & will dissipate before it reaches x
To infer *ceteris paribus*:	it will start raining at x in approximately three hours

If there is neither a presumption for (3) or (4), then the warrant of the original argument suffices when assessing ground adequacy.

Should the proponent argue for the counterrebuttal, the warrant to be considered for the final step in his argument to the main conclusion would be identified just as if the counterrebuttal were simply asserted. Presumably, the proponent, at least, believes he must establish a presumption for the counterrebuttal. Granting this, should the subargument defending the counterrebuttal be cogent, the ground adequacy of the main argument again is a question of the reliability of the warrant from original premises and countererebuttal to conclusion. If the argument is unsuccessful, then the ground adequacy question is the same as for a merely asserted counterrebuttal found not acceptable.

Finally, should the proponent counter the rebuttal with a distinction, he is conceding the rebuttal but attempting to rebut its force. The warrant of the argument then incorporates two open sentences in connection with rebuttal and counterrebuttal, the variables replacing common content expressions shared with the remainder of the argument developed to this point.

From:	A cold front moving at 20 mph in the direction of x is 60 miles from x & will dissipate before it reaches x & will form again before it reaches x
To infer *ceteris paribus*:	it will start raining at x in approximately three hours

Assuming the acceptability of the premise that the front will reform, this expanded warrant serves as the warrant of the argument. If the premise is not acceptable, then, since the proponent has conceded that the front will dissipate, the situation is the same as where there is a presumption for the rebuttal.

As Govier has pointed out in (Govier 1999a, p. 170), in approaching an argument as critical challengers, we are not constrained to restrict our attention just to the rebuttals the proponent has considered in the course of his argument. Should we be able to frame rebuttals for which there is a presumption from our point of view, i.e. given our evidence, which have met no response in the argument, we should regard those rebuttals as conceded and frame the warrant of the argument accordingly. The proponent of the argument apparently has not anticipated these rebuttals, but we have. As critical challengers, it is incumbent on us to take them into account in evaluating the argument by adding them to the warrant.

Ground adequacy for conductive arguments then is a question of the reliability of the properly and comprehensively framed warrant of that argument, framed with respect to conceded rebuttals, including unanticipated rebuttals, and counterrebuttals. Ground adequacy amounts to the reliability of the warrant in transferring acceptability from premises to conclusion. The first issue in assessing the reliability of the warrant is determining its epistemic type. Once that is determined, reliability becomes a question of whether proper backing for that warrant is available in this case. If so–and we do not deny that there are plenty of open questions in explicating proper backing comprehensively–the premises of the conductive argument constitute grounds adequate for the conclusion.

Chapter 10

Guidelines for Reaching a Reasoned Judgment

MARK BATTERSBY & SHARON BAILIN

1. Introduction

When one begins to survey the work on conductive argument, two surprising facts emerge. One is that so little has been written on conductive arguments; the second is that much of what has been written has focused on establishing their existence. One would have thought that even a cursory observation of how arguments are conducted in all areas of life would bring to an observer's attention not only the existence of such arguments but their ubiquity. Making judgments based on both pro and con considerations is a common phenomenon in numerous domains, as Govier notes: "In my experience they [conductive arguments] naturally occur in law, philosophy, interpretive studies—and in fact in any area, including science, in which there are reasons for and against, or 'pros and cons' which we must consider in order to make a judgment on an issue" (Govier 1999b, p. 160).

That the ubiquity and importance of conductive reasoning has not been sufficiently recognized may be a function of its "messiness." Conductive arguments do not fit traditional argument patterns. The premises neither entail the conclusion nor do they support the conclusion in an unambiguous way as some of the 'premises' (or anti-premises, as some have called them) actually adduce reasons that count against the conclusion. Indeed, Johnson makes the point that conductive arguments are not easily identified as arguments by either Formal Deductive Logic or positivism (Johnson 2000a, p. 92).

Given their lack of conformity to traditional argument patterns, the appraisal of conductive arguments has becomes a central issue. As they are non-conclusive arguments, one cannot specify the criteria for their formal validity, as Wellman points out. And since they involve reasons against as well as for the conclusion, the problem arises as to how to weigh the various considerations and counter considerations, especially as such a weighing will be dependent on subject matter (Wellman 1971, pp. 61–62; Govier 1985, p. 261). For these reasons, some theorists have concluded that, "It is difficult to give any general guidelines about appraising conductive arguments" (Govier, p. 260). Wellman argues, in fact that, although it is meaningful to refer to the validity of conductive arguments, the only way to establish such validity or lack thereof is by thinking the argument through and feeling its logical force (Wellman 1971, p. 79).

It is our belief that there are, however, some general guidelines which can be offered with respect to doing conductive reasoning well and that these guidelines give rise to a set of criteria for identifying inadequate conductive arguments. It is such guidelines and criteria that we elucidate in the remainder of the paper.

2. What do we mean by conductive reasoning?

Before proceeding with that task, it is necessary to clarify how we are using various terms and to delineate the focus and scope of our project. Our focus is not on the structure or assessment of particular conductive arguments per se but rather on the enterprise of conductive reasoning. By conductive reasoning we are referring to the process of comparative evaluation of a variety of contending positions and arguments with the goal of reaching a reasoned judgment on an issue. We adopt this terminology and focus for a number of reasons.

The first is clarity. What are generally referred to as conductive arguments are most likely themselves constructed of competing arguments which may offer reasons in support of a particular claim, objections to and critiques of arguments offered, or responses to objections. We will call the collection of all arguments in a piece of conductive reasoning a *case*, and individual arguments, simply arguments. A case, then, is made up of a collection of arguments whose conclusion is intended to support a particular judgment on the issue in question. Let us illustrate with an example (taken from our textbook on inquiry). This dialogue takes place following an extensive evaluation by the two protagonists of the various arguments commonly offered for and against capital punishment.

> **Phil:** *You know, Sophia, we've looked at a lot of arguments and information on capital punishment. But I think that the conclusion is becoming obvious to me. The weight of arguments clearly points against capital punishment.*
> **Sophia:** *What made you come to that conclusion?*
> **Phil:** *Well—it's pretty clear that there's little evidence to support the deterrence argument.*
> **Sophia:** *Agreed.*
> **Phil:** *And the incapacitation argument is really 'overkill' (sorry about that) since the same result can be achieved by less drastic means.*
> **Sophia:** *Agreed again.*
> **Phil:** *The cost issue is a red herring since it's simply not true given the current system of appeals.*
> **Sophia:** *Right again.*
> **Phil:** *I think that there is something legitimate to the retribution argument in terms of the desire for justice. But you've convinced me that with capital punishment, we risk an even greater injustice, that of possibly executing an innocent person. Besides, retribution can be achieved with life imprisonment.*
> **Sophia:** *I'm with you.*
> **Phil:** *So what we're left with are all the moral problems of the state killing some of its citizens and, in particular, some of its citizens who are innocent. That's a very strong argument against.*
> **Sophia:** *Especially since there are alternatives.*
> **Phil:** *And especially given the worldwide trend toward abolition, supported by important organizations like the UN. The arguments for capital punishment would have to be very strong to counter that.*
> **Sophia:** *Which they're not.*
> **Phil:** *So all in all I have to agree with the abolitionists—we should not have the death penalty* (Bailin & Battersby 2010, pp. 174-175).

This dialogue may be seen as exemplifying a conductive argument in the usual sense, offering as it does a number of independent reasons in support of a conclusion as well as addressing objections and counter considerations. As noted above, however, this presentation of the case is preceded by considerable reasoning in the form of an evaluation of individual arguments and a comparative weighing of considerations that leads to the making of this conductive "argument." Cases are often presented in this way—as summaries of conductive reasoning, using primary claims to support a judgment without an explicit statement of the arguments that provide support for these claims. But good conductive reasoning involves a deeper process of inquiry in which the credibility of primary claims is based on an assessment of the arguments that provide support for these claims and in which competing considerations are explicitly weighed and balanced. This is the process in which Sophia and Phil have been engaged previous to this dialogue. It is this entire process of comparative evaluation and weighing which is the focus of our interest, and not simply the resulting "argument."

Conductive arguments, in the usual sense, can vary considerably in subject matter and complexity. Both the preceding argument regarding capital punishment and the argument: "I'm tired, but I should go to the store anyway because we need bread" have the structure of a conductive argument. Our focus, however, is on the former. We are interested in the pro and con reasoning which takes place in complex and controversial situations, the kind of comparative evaluation we make in actual contexts of disagreement and debate.

Another reason for focusing on conductive reasoning is our commitment to the view of argumentation as dialectical. According to Blair and Johnson, "To say that argumentation is dialectical ... is to identify it as a human practice, an exchange between two or more individuals in which the process of interaction shapes the product" (Blair & Johnson 1987, p. 46). Our primary focus is on what will make this process a successful one, thereby leading to an adequate product, i.e., a credible reasoned judgment.

3. Features of conductive reasoning

The guidelines and criteria we offer arise from the particular features of conductive reasoning.

The first characteristic of import here is that the appropriate goal of conductive reasoning is not the making of a conclusive argument but rather the making of a reasoned judgment. By a reasoned judgment we mean not simply a judgment for which one has reasons, but a judgment for which one has good reasons, reasons which meet relevant standards. A piece of conductive reasoning can, at best, offer good, but not decisive, reasons to support a conclusion over its competitors. Thus arriving at a reasoned judgment will require an examination and weighing of the reasons offered on different sides of an issue and the balancing of various considerations.

No survey of arguments will be exhaustive, however. The possibility always exists that additional reasons and arguments will be put forward which might affect the outcome of the reasoning. Thus the judgment that is the outcome of the conductive reasoning process is always provisional and open to further examination. In addition, because this type of reasoning takes place in complex contexts with dimensions of uncertainty, there may be more than one judgment that is defensible given the context. For these reasons, conductive reasoning needs to be seen in the context of an ongoing process of critical inquiry.

Conductive reasoning takes place in many domains (as mentioned above). It is common in practical reasoning (Hitchcock 2000, pp. 5–8) and in social theory and history (Govier 1985, p. 260), but can also take place in virtually any domain, including art interpretation and criticism, and scientific inquiry. In addition, reasoning about many contested issues will involve a range of types of considerations (for example, factual, ethical, practical). As a consequence, a variety of different types of considerations will often need to be taken into account in conductive reasoning and the criteria of specific domains of inquiry will often play an important role.

An important feature of conductive reasoning (of the kind which is of interest to us) is that it takes place in the context of a dialectic, of a historical and ongoing process of debate and critique, of competing views and the give-and-take among them. Reasons and arguments have been offered on various sides of the issue in question, objections have been raised to many of the arguments, responses have been offered to some of the objections, and alternative views have been put forth. This constellation of reasons, arguments, objections and responses constitutes what Johnson calls the dialectical environment (Johnson 2007). Having knowledge of the dialectical environment surrounding an issue is central to the enterprise of arriving at a reasoned judgment (Bailin & Battersby 2009). In addition, knowledge of the history of the debate can be of assistance in determining which arguments are salient and should be considered, which are considered strong, and which are considered defeated and why.

In addition to this dialectical context, we have identified several additional aspects of context that we believe are relevant to conductive reasoning by playing a role in the determination of both the significance and the weight of reasons. One is the state of practice, which refers to the current situation with respect to the issue at hand (e.g., is there currently capital punishment in the jurisdiction under discussion, and if not, when was it defeated and why). Knowing where the force of current practice and opinion lie can help us to understand what alternative views are up against and whether (and to what extent) any of these views bears the burden of proof. Knowledge about the intellectual, social, political and historical contexts that surround an issue can contribute to our understanding of the assumptions that lie behind various positions and why people might hold them. Hitchcock's observation that students' problems with conductive reasoning are due in part to a "lack of background knowledge to generate a full enough range and detail of competing considerations" (Hitchcock 2000, p. 7) points precisely to the centrality of this kind of contextual know-ledge.

The dialectical nature of conductive reasoning implies that the process will be dynamic. Particular arguments are often modified or reframed in response to criticism and objections, and these modifications may in turn result in a reframing of the objections, and so on. As Zenker points out, for example, "Typically, some premises appear only in response to and sometimes integrate an opponent's objections successfully" (Zenker 2007, p. 2). In this spirit, Wohlrapp argues against a view of (non-deductive) argumentation in terms of a sequence of isolated inference steps and for a view in which "premises and conclusions of an argumentation form a 'retroflexive' system of mutual support" (Wohlrapp 1998, p. 342). One implication of this dynamism is that weighing arguments cannot be simply a matter of placing competing arguments on a metaphorical balance scale because arguments will often change in the process of reasoning. Conductive reasoning will need to give attention to the modification, reframing, and synthesizing of arguments.

Because conductive reasoning involves the comparative weighing of reasons on various sides of an issue and because there will often be good reasons supporting different judgments, how strong the prevailing case is in comparison to the other cases will vary. Thus the strength of the judgments warranted by particular instances of conductive reasoning will vary as well. This feature of conductive reasoning points to the need to apportion the confidence of one's judgment to the strength of the reasons.

4. Guidelines for conductive reasoning

In what follows we offer guidelines for conducting conductive reasoning, and then use these guidelines to identify various fallacies in conductive reasoning that one might see either in the process of reasoning or in a case instantiating such reasoning. These guidelines arise from the dialectical and contextual nature of conductive reasoning reviewed above.

Guidelines for Reaching a Reasoned Judgment

(i) *Appropriately review the 'dialectical space', i.e., identify the relevant arguments and the history of the debate*

As noted above, in coming to a reasoned judgment, the first task is to conduct an appropriate inquiry into the relevant arguments, including a review of the history of the debate. In addition to providing information regarding the salience and strength of various arguments, the history of the debate provides a context without which it may be extremely difficult to understand some arguments. For example, the problematic nature of the debate in British Columbia and then across Canada about the wisdom of a carbon tax was largely the result of the fact that most citizens were unaware of the dialectical context of the debate. For many, it was just another "tax grab" by the government with the puzzling and suspicious feature that the money was being returned to the taxpayer. Most simply did not understand the economic argument about carbon being an externality (a cost that was not fed through the market) that needed to be woven into the price structure of goods if there was to be an economically rational revision of the use of carbon fuels. The context was not simply global warming, but an extensive debate that had occurred among policy theorists about how best to implement incentives for reduction of carbon use.

(ii) *Consider the full variety of objections to the various arguments and responses to the objections*

The arguments pro and con about an issue which are the substance of conductive reasoning need to be identified and evaluated along with their associated objections. It is worth noting that there are at least two kinds of objections to individual arguments that provide the support for the primary claims. We suggest using the following terminology. An *undercutter* is a critique of an argument offered in support of a primary claim. This critique could attack the premises of the argument or the inference to its conclusion. The goal of an under cutter is to show that the conclusion of the argument is poorly supported so that the argument's conclusion cannot serve as a credible primary claim in support of the case's judgment. For example, an under cutter for the argument that capital punishment deters would be evidence showing that jurisdictions which eliminated capital punishment did not experience an increase in murder. Another kind of objection to an argument in a case is a *specific counter*—a countervailing argument or claim meant to provide a countervailing consideration to a particular primary claim. The claim that capital punishment will inevitably result in the execution of people who are innocent is directly countered by the argument that all socially useful practices have downsides which must be accepted; on this view the execution of innocents is just something that society needs to accept in order to have appropriate punishments for first degree murders. These two kinds of objections directed at particular primary claims differ from general counter arguments or *con arguments*. *Con arguments* provide a different kind of objection. For example, the argument that capital punishment is a barbaric practice inappropriate to civilized countries is not an argument directed at any particular argument for capital punishment. Rather, it is a general countervailing consideration or *con argument*.

(iii) *Evaluate individual arguments according to relevant criteria*

Since the very concept of conductive reasoning involves marshalling both pro and con arguments and relevant objections, one of the primary requirements for reaching a reasoned judgment is that relevant pro and con arguments must be evaluated (just as one would do with any argument). This is not an assessment of the "weight" to be given to a certain claim in the case, but rather an assessment of credibility of the primary claim given the review of the supportive arguments and objections. For example, one could evaluate the arguments for the claim that capital punishment does not deter using the usual criteria for causal claims in the social sciences. Alternatively, one could point out that the appeal to a police chief's opinion is a fallacious appeal to authority. One could evaluate the evidence for the claim that historically, innocent individuals have been executed and for the claim that it is unlikely that this problem could be eliminated (the latter by appealing to historical evidence, legal scholars, etc.). Finally one could evaluate the moral argument that capital punishment is the only appropriate punishment for certain kinds of murder—this would require a largely philosophical inquiry.

(iv) *Establish the burden of proof and standard of proof required*

One role that the consideration of context plays is to help identify, where appropriate, which side bears the burden of proof and the relevant standard of proof required. In scientific inquiry, the burden of proof bears on any novel theory or on claims counter to well established views. Science is inherently conservative in this way. In the political situation, those who argue for change in statutes or other political arrangements inevitably bear the burden of proof. But the standard here can clearly and reasonably evolve. After fifty years of widespread usage of marijuana and at least some scientific studies, the claim that it is relatively harmless (not harmless, but compared to alcohol...) is widely accepted and therefore claims of relative harmlessness would not bear the same burden of proof as they might have in 1960. Even more decisively, the argument that prohibition would not stop usage seems so obvious that it could almost be assumed in the argument. Returning to the capital punishment debate, the claim that capital punishment is not an effective deterrent against murder is now the accepted view of criminologists and anyone arguing for a deterrence effect would bear the burden of proof.

(v) *Assess possibilities in light of alternatives*

Part of the assessment of particular arguments should involve consideration of whether there are better alternatives to the position being advocated. For example, with respect to the claims that capital punishment is necessary for both incapacitation and retribution, the existence of the less morally troubling alternative of life imprisonment provides an alternative that weakens the force of those claims. In addition, since the goal of conductive reasoning is reasoned judgment, an inquirer should not be restricted to only considering alternatives that have been put forward in the past. Part of the resolution of a longstanding controversy may well be to consider totally different alternatives rather than trying to decide which of given alternatives is worthy of support. On the question of the legalization of marijuana, for example, there is a wide range of alternatives to consider. While California contemplates legalization of marijuana, many other jurisdictions are considering just decriminalization for possession, or as in The Netherlands, its sale in only certain "coffee bistros."

(vi) *Take into account the relevant range of considerations*

Because reasoning about many contested issues will involve a range of types of considerations (for example, factual, ethical, practical), it is important to ensure that one has taken into account the appropriate range of considerations when attempting to make a reasoned judgment. So, for example, in examining the issue of whether we should eat meat that comes from factory farms, it would be important to take into account both factual considerations about the conditions of animals kept on these farms and ethical considerations regarding whether humans have a moral obligation to animals. In inquiring into the debate over the raising of the minimum wage, it would be important to consider not only statistical information, but also the differing assumptions about equity and merit which are inherent in different positions in the debate. In dealing with public policy issues, it would be important to consider ethical as well as instrumental considerations, ends as well as means, costs as well as benefits, and long term as well as short term consequences.

(vii) *Take into account and consider a variety of perspectives*

The goal of reasoned judgment involves the attempt to make a decision or assessment from an ideal observer's or 'objective' point of view, striving for the "view from nowhere" as the regulative ideal. Striving for this ideal involves attempting to look at an issue from many relevant perspectives—e.g., in a moral dilemma trying to see the perspective of both the moral actor and those who are the victims or beneficiaries of the action. One might consider, for example, the controversy surrounding Peter Singer's advocacy of the euthanasia of disabled babies (McBryde Johnson 2003). Many disabled groups argued that he had failed to consider their perspective.

(viii) *Consider differences in how issues, arguments, and reasons are framed*

Opposing arguments are frequently characterized by different ways of framing or setting up the issue. Particular ways of framing may slant an inquiry in a particular direction and reframing may affect the outcome of the reasoning. Kahneman and Tversky (1982) have shown, for example, that the question of whether a decision is framed in terms of losing lives versus saving lives has significant impact on the way most people make the decision. As another example, a deontological approach to moral issues would frame a moral dispute quite differently than would a consequentialist perspective. The debate over carbon tax provides yet another illustration of the significance of framing. After the public outrage in British Columbia about the carbon tax, a PR person suggested that what the government should have done was to reframe the issue from a proposal for a tax increase to a proposal for "tax shifting"—i.e., shifting taxes from income tax to carbon producing activities. The carbon tax would not be a tax increase but a tax shift, which would be more acceptable and intelligible to the average citizen, a claim supported by poll results (Barrett 2008). Recognizing differences in framing can often help one to understand the assumptions underlying opposing arguments and thus to be in a better position to comparatively evaluate them. It also opens up the possibility for a mediation of frames that may lead to a judgment that incorporates the strong points of the opposing views.

(ix) *Recognize and attempt to incorporate/synthesize strong points from different positions*

Good reasons often do not reside entirely in one or other of the conflicting views. Thus it is important, in arriving at a reasoned judgment, to recognize the valid points in each view. The best-justified judgment is often one that incorporates the strong points in opposing views. In the dialogue, for example, our participants acknowledge that the need for deterrence, incapacitation and retribution are legitimate concerns, but they argue that they can all be addressed through life imprisonment.

(x) *Appropriately weigh and balance different considerations, values, and arguments*

A central aspect of arriving at a reasoned judgment involves weighing the various reasons pro and con. Although there will likely be some differences in views about comparative weight, it is possible to justify one's assignment of weight and to criticize reasoning for inappropriate weighting (see below for a detailed discussion of weighing).

(xi) *Consider whether one's own personal convictions and experiences may be coloring one's judgment*

Since we are focused on the process of arriving at a reasoned judgment, there is a requirement for the participant(s) in this process to be aware of their own biases and prejudices. Increasingly convincing research has demonstrated the difficulty people have in making reliably rational judgments. Efforts, including the sharing of discussion with others, identifying one's perspectives and biases, and avoiding the more common generic biases such as representativeness (thinking individual events or experiences are representative of what generally happens) and confirmation bias (seeking only instances that provide support for one's view) can all serve to make it more likely that one comes to judgment which is truly reasoned. One key strategy to avoid bias in one's judgment is to give due attention to evidence and arguments that counter one's own point of view. As noted above, we have built such considerations into the process of inquiry, so there is already an important check on confirmation bias, although other biases may need to be addressed with different strategies. An awareness of the historical basis of one's views and those of others can also help to undermine an inappropriate confidence in one's views.

(xii) *Make a judgment at the appropriate level of confidence—apportion one's judgment to the strength of the reasons*

Part of rational self-awareness involves assessing how much confidence one should have in one's judgments given the arguments that one has reviewed. It may be that one can conclude with considerable confidence that capital punishment should not be used by a state, but as current debate about global warming or the debate about the causes of obesity show, not all judgments can be made with the same degree of confidence, even though there may be an urgent need to act on such judgments. Judgments of the likelihood of descriptive factual claims present one sort of problem, but any judgment about what to do must also take into account future states of affairs that are usually less certain than judgments about current states of affairs. And finally, while there are some accepted general moral principles, their application in particular cases, especially ones where accepted principles conflict, inevitably creates significant uncertainty. The unpredictability of the future means that almost all significant actions need to be based on judgments that are at best less than fully confident. In our text we suggest the following table as a guide.

Judgment and Confidence

- A *very confident judgment* is warranted when the weight of reasons clearly supports the judgment and the issue is considered settled.
- A *reasonably confident judgment* is warranted when the weight of reasons strongly supports the judgment but the issue is still controversial.
- A *tentative judgment* is warranted when the weight of reasons is not overwhelming but is supportive of one position, and we can make a judgment *on balance*.
- A *suspended judgment* is warranted when the reasons for different positions are closely balanced or when there is insufficient evidence to make a judgment.

5. Fallacies of judgment

Our focus to this point has been on offering guidelines for reaching reasoned judgments. We also believe that these guidelines can furnish the basis for identifying certain kinds of

Guidelines for Reaching a Reasoned Judgment

problems in particular pieces of conductive reasoning, or cases. A given case can be evaluated in terms of the extent to which it deals with, or fails to deal with, the relevant considerations for reaching a reasoned judgment. We have termed the failures 'fallacies of judgment.' As is the case with traditional informal fallacies, fallacies of judgment are most useful in identifying bad arguments rather than in specifying good ones. We propose that proffered cases are inadequate to the degree to which they fail to take into account the various relevant considerations. The following is a description of the fallacies of judgment which we have identified.

i) Failure to undertake a comprehensive examination of the various competing arguments
Since reaching a reasoned judgment involves a comparative evaluation of the various reasons and arguments on an issue, the failure to take into account any of the significant arguments on the issue constitutes a serious defect in a case.

ii) Failure to consider objections
Because argumentation is dialectical, any reasoned case, in addition to offering arguments, must also respond to any known and important objections. Failure to do so significantly weakens the case.

iii) Failure to consider implications
Many cases concern decisions about what to do. However correct an action may appear on the basis of the arguments provided, failure to consider consequences (typically unintended consequences) significantly weakens the case.

iv) Failure to give appropriate consideration to the burden of proof
Failing to determine where the burden of proof lies or misplacing the burden of proof may result in an inappropriate determination of how much evidence is needed to make a case or of when a case has been made successfully.

v) Failure to consider a range of considerations
Judgments which fail to take into account relevant considerations are faulty for that reason.

vi) Failure to consider alternative solutions or possibilities
The strength of a case can only be evaluated in light of the alternatives available. Ignoring possible and plausible alternatives would be a ground for criticism of a given case.

vii) Failure to consider the uncertainty of claims
Taking claims as certain where the evidence in support of the claim is not, in fact, compelling or taking a claim as more certain than the evidence warrants may result in making an unjustified judgment or making a judgment with a greater degree of confidence than is warranted.

viii) Biased framing
Too narrow framing of an issue or argument, or framing in a way that slants the discussion toward a particular perspective may exclude the consideration of other possibilities and thus bias the judgment.

ix) "Either/Or" fallacy
Given that many issues have more than two sides, and that there are often intermediate possibilities between two opposing positions, viewing all issues in terms of 'either-or' – as a choice between two opposing positions, can oversimplify issues and result in a failure to recognize other, possibly more reasonable possibilities.

x) Inappropriate weighting
This fallacy consists in giving undue weight to certain aspects of an issue when making a judgment.

xi) Making a judgment at an inappropriate level of confidence
Asserting a judgment with more or less confidence than warranted by the strength of the reasons constitutes another fallacy of judgment.

6. Weighing and balancing considerations

A central notion in discussions of the evaluation of conductive reasoning, including our own, is that of weighing. Whatever guidelines may be offered, in the final analysis, reasons pro and con must be weighed in order to reach a reasoned judgment. Yet weighing is a metaphor that is difficult to cash out in the context of arguments, as numerous theorists have pointed out. Is it possible to quantify the weight or strength of various reasons or arguments? And if it is not, then does the notion become so vague as to be of little use or so subjective as to be devoid of evaluative purchase (Kock 2007c)?

It is our view that weighing is a meaningful, if imperfect, metaphor, and that although weights are not quantifiable and will sometimes be the object of disagreement, they are nonetheless not (or not primarily) subjective. Weightings can be justified (or criticized) by appeal to objective factors and considerations, for example by appeal to certain widely shared values and principles. Moreover, arguments can be evaluated in terms of both the likelihood that they are true and the support or weight that they give to the judgment. An argument which, if its conclusion is credible, gives considerable weight to a judgment will add little or no weight if it is doubtful. In the court context, for example, an argument that shows that the accused had a good alibi will largely exclude a conviction, whereas if the alibi is in question, the weight it provides is greatly diminished. On the other hand, the fact that an individual has a credible motive adds relatively little weight given that many people may have motives for committing a certain crime.

The excerpt of the dialogue on capital punishment quoted earlier can be used to illustrate some of these aspects of weighing. It is important to bear in mind, however, that a considerable amount of discussion regarding the relative weight of various arguments has already taken place before this dialogue occurs (e.g., **Phil:** *But you've convinced me that with capital punishment, we risk an even greater injustice ...*) and that this discussion process has been a dynamic one, with some of the arguments being modified or reframed in the course of the reasoning that has led to the presentation of the case that we see in the dialogue excerpt.

When reviewing their previous evaluation of individual arguments, Phil and Sophia agree that two of the pro capital punishment arguments, the deterrence and cost arguments, do not hold up—their conclusions are not justified. They are refuted by under cutter arguments and thus are given no weight. However, in addition to the likelihood that the conclusion is true or credible, the arguments can also be assessed with respect to the amount of support (positive or negative) they provide for the case for capital punishment.

And each of the deterrence and cost arguments, if they had been credible, would have added different amounts of weight to the case for capital punishment. If capital punishment really did serve as a significant deterrent to murder, that would be a strong argument in its favor, grounded as it is in the widely shared value of saving the lives of innocent people. Even if it were true, however, that the costs are greater to incarcerate for life than to execute, that would not constitute a strong argument in light of the moral objections to capital punishment because of the *prima facie* presumption that moral issues should generally trump instrumental issues such as cost.

Another of the pro capital punishment arguments, the incapacitation argument, is recognized as sound in the sense that it is true that dead murderers cannot murder again. Nonetheless it is seen as a rather drastic way of removing murderers from circulation given there are other possibilities and so is not a very strong argument for capital punishment. Thus this argument is weakened by a specific counterargument that there is a less morally troubling alternative—life imprisonment—that can achieve the same goal. The retribution argument, on the other hand, is seen as based on strong grounds—an appeal to justice, which is a widely shared value and one that is inherent to any legal system. Nonetheless, although the legitimacy of the appeal to justice is recognized, the weight of the argument as a justification for capital punishment is lessened because life imprisonment can be seen as an alternative which also meets the demand for justice. For both the incapacitation and retribution arguments, then, their weight in the debate is reduced because of the existence of less problematic alternatives.

The likelihood of executing innocent people is viewed by our two inquirers as a very strong argument against capital punishment, indeed as a consideration which overrides most other considerations, appealing as it does to a very strongly held value (not to kill innocent people) and a basic principle of the law (not to punish the innocent). It is true that any system of punishment will have errors no matter how good a job the system does in trying to avoid them. It is, however, crucial to the strength of the argument that some executions (and other long-term incarcerations) have been shown to have been erroneous. So the execution of innocent people is not just a theoretical possibility or an exceedingly rare occurrence. The frequency of such occurrences and the racial bias evident in many cases, in at least some locations, add to the strength of the argument. The weight given to this argument must still be seen as comparative, however, in that, if it could be shown that capital punishment were a significant deterrent and that it would thereby prevent many more innocents from being murdered than would be victims of system error, a much stronger case could be made for the practice. Because of the comparative nature of these evaluations, numbers, if credible and appropriate, may be significant.

We can also see how an appeal to the question of burden of proof is used to help determine how strong the arguments on various sides would need to be in order to prevail. In this case, the worldwide trend toward abolition sets up a burden of proof on the retentionist side. The determination of burden of proof is less pivotal in this case as the anti capital punishment arguments have been judged to be considerably stronger, but it can be decisive with respect to issues where the reasons on each side are judged to be more evenly balanced. Consider the criminal trial situation where the burden of proof is clearly on the prosecution. The failure of the defense to decisively undermine the prosecutor's argument should not result in the defendant being convicted since all the defense needs to do is show that there is a reasonable doubt about the guilt of the accused.

One aspect of weighing that is illustrated in the proceeding is that an important ground for justifying assigned weights is an appeal to widely shared values and principles. The extent of agreement in this regard should not be underestimated. There would, for example, be widespread agreement that the legal system should instantiate principles of justice; that moral considerations should generally take priority over cost considerations; that the state executing innocent people is extremely ethically problematic. Some of these values and principles are built into various domains and related to the 'point of the practice.' It is, for example, a basic principle in law not to convict or punish an innocent person. The alleviation of suffering is a foundational value in medicine. Education is grounded in the learning of the child. Assigned weights can be legitimately justified in terms of such values and principles, and judgments can be rationally criticized which exhibit inappropriate weights. We would, for example, be justified in criticizing an educational policy if it was seen to value administrative efficiency over the learning of the child.

An excellent example of this aspect of weighing is provided by Allen in his paper discussing Canada's Rape Shield decision (Allen 1993) where he cites an excerpt from the opinion of one of the judges regarding the exclusion of possibly prejudicial evidence in rape cases:

> When, however, prejudicial evidence is for the defence, the prejudicial effect it would have if admitted must *substantially* outweigh its probative value before a judge can exclude it. This is because a free and democratic society attaches great importance to the principle that an innocent person must not be convicted. (p. 106)

Here we have both an explicit statement of a central principle that ought to be appealed to in legal decisions and a judgment about the appropriate weighing of considerations in a particular case based on this principle.

There can, of course, be disagreement, even at times deep disagreement, about the relevant or primary considerations, as seems to be the case, for example, in the abortion debate. It is often the case, however, that there will be agreement on the considerations but disagreement over how to prioritize them or how they play out in particular instances. In the rape shield decision cited by Allen, for example, a dissenting opinion by another of the judges argued that the excluded sexual history evidence "is either irrelevant or so prejudicial that its minimal probative value is overwhelmed by its distorting effect" (Allen 1993, p. 107). In this case there is agreement regarding the principles that are relevant, i.e., prejudicial effect vs. probative value, but disagreement about their relative weights in this particular context. As another example, amongst people toward the left of the political spectrum, there are those who support a carbon tax because they believe that it would have a positive impact on the environment while there are others who oppose it because they believe that it would have a negative impact on economically disadvantaged individuals. Although both groups value both the environment and economic equality, they prioritize these values differently with respect to this particular issue. These differences in judgment may be based to some extent on differences in how the likelihood or the severity of the various possible outcomes is assessed or how the short term versus the long term costs and benefits of the different policies are calculated. But these are differences for which one can offer justifications and about which one can reason.

Another example of an explicit discussion of weighing can be seen in a groundbreaking paper by Cornfield (1959) in the context of the early debate about whether smoking caused lung cancer. Cornfield argued that despite the fact that researchers could not provide a good biological model (i.e., animal experiments) to demonstrate the link between smoking and lung cancer, in this case that criterion should not be given the weight it usually receives in epidemiological reasoning. His argument was that, since smoking exhibited very strong correlations and a strong "dose relationship" with lung cancer, these facts and the fact of the lack of credible alternative explanations for the data should be taken as adequate to establish a causal link between smoking and lung cancer. This was one of the first successful arguments in epidemiology since the late 19th century to subordinate the biological account to the results of large-scale statistical results.

We take these examples to show that there is a role for a rational examination of the considerations that lie behind how weights are assigned. In this regard, the two opinions cited in the rape shield case (or the argument by Cornfield) can be seen as models for the role of the justification of assigned weights. Such explicit justifications puts them forwardfor scrutiny in the arena of public reason where they can be the basis for deliberation by others and for ongoing inquiry. Since weighing is a dynamic process, there is always the possibility that arguments and even issues may be reframed, resulting in the dissolution of a disagreement over how values or considerations have been weighed. An example would be a public policy debate, initially framed in terms of the competing rights of various parties being reframed in terms of the welfare of the community. Such a process will not necessarily lead to agreement among the interlocutors, however. But unless and until the issue is considered settled, any evaluation made can be seen as a moment in and contribution to on ongoing public process of reasoning about the issue by others as well as ourselves.

PART IV – CASE STUDIES AND SPECIAL TOPICS

Chapter 11

Ranking Considerations and Aligning Probative Obligations in Balance of Consideration Arguments

FRED J. KAUFFELD

1. Introduction

Following Wellman, it is broadly agreed that some conductive arguments (reasoning) explicitly involves consideration of matters supporting their conclusions in relationship to contrary matters; moreover, such contrariety is conceptually potential in all conductive arguments/reasoning (Wellman, 1971). From a logical perspective (I have learned) this raises a question of how these pro and contra considerations figure into the argument (reasoning) which leads to the conclusion. Govier puts the question this way:

> If we deem a conductive argument *cogent*, we commit ourselves to the judgment that the reason in the premises, considered together, provide good grounds for the conclusion—even in the light of counter-considerations constituting reasons against that conclusion. That is, we commit ourselves to the judgment that, on balance, the pros *outweigh* the cons, and do so to a sufficient degree that there are good grounds for the conclusion. (Govier 1999, p. 170)

She goes on to observe:

> It is important to note that "outweighing" is a metaphorical expression at this point. We cannot literally measure the strength of supporting reasons, the countervailing strength of opposing reasons, and subtract the one factor from the other. We have to think these matters through. ... This might all sound hopelessly difficult. But it cannot be so, because we do it all the time. (*Ibid.*)

Hans Hansen carries this line of thought a step further, analyzing this species of conductive arguments as *balance-of considerations arguments* which have this structure:

> A set of statements consisting of (i) at least one reason for a conclusion, *k*, that does not entail *k*, but commonly two or more such independent reasons that do not entail *k*, and (ii) at least one counter-consideration that does not entail *not-k*, but not uncommonly two or more such independent counter considerations none of which entail *not-k*, and (iii) an *on-balance* premiss with the content that the combined force of all the stated reasons for *k* outweigh the combined force of all the stated counter-considerations against *k*." It would seem that the on-balance premiss in this structure would require support of a kind which assigns some rank to considerations. (Hansen 2010, pp. 9-10.)

This analysis supposes that we have some rational means for fixing the acceptability of *on-balance* premises. But how do we do that? For as Govier observes, we do it all the time.

Harold Wohlrapp presents what he regards as a contrasting account of these matters, arguing that the picture presented by Govier (and elaborated by Hansen) misses the dynamics of this kind of reasoning/argument (Wohlrapp 1995, 1997). I confess to finding myself somewhat in sympathy with Wohlrapp's rather more "rhetorical" account, but my aim here is to shed some light on how we do "all the time deal with such matters."

To that end, I invite reflection on what goes on and into consideration of pro and contra arguments in conductive reasoning/arguments.

2. Managing considerations

Reflection on and discussion of conductive arguments broadly uses the term 'considerations' to refer to the rational "components" leading to the argument's conclusion. This terminological choice is apt. 'Considerations' does refer to factors bearing on a conclusion, which have some potentially good claim for thought and attention. We rely on our ordinary concepts of considering and consideration to marks out the process and the components, which in our ordinary understanding of conduction lead to a "considered" conclusion.

One way to get a handle on how we ordinarily reach conclusions that involve "balancing" or otherwise handling of considerations is to engage in a somewhat preliminary exercise of what J.L. Austin refers to as "linguistic phenomenology" (Austin, 1961). We more or less share a well-established concept of considering and consideration, concepts which enable us to truthfully describe what we are doing when we "consider things" and to identify the properties we look for when we do such things as "weigh considerations." So, by a preliminary analysis, albeit here a rather rough and ready one, of our concepts of "considering" and "consideration," we may bring into view how we manage considerations in conductive reasoning/arguments. What, then, in our ordinary understanding and practice of conduction is a consideration?

Of the various senses of 'consideration,' we can roughly identify three relevant to our inquiry. The first and primary sense refers to the *activity of considering*. Consideration is what we give to matters when we consider them, as when we devote careful thought and attention to a proposal. The second sense refers to matters which can be introduced, taken up, and acted upon in the course of considering something, *matters which merit or fail to merit consideration*. And third, we have a sense that refers to the *product of considering something*, a considered conclusion or, more briefly, a "consideration."[1] Let us take these up in turn.

The activity of considering something involves: (i) the introduction of considerations (how they raised, intrude themselves, etc.), (ii) the activity of reckoning with considerations and, thereby, taking the considerations into account or dismissing them or setting it aside in arriving at a conclusion, and (iii) reaching a considered conclusion, known as a "consideration."

As regards the first sense, the activity, we should notice that matters introduced as considerations or raised as consideration must show themselves to be or be shown to merit consideration, or they expire, i.e., cease to qualify as considerations. Petty considerations are properly dismissed; trivial considerations do not make it into the game. Matters which

---

[1] Abstracted from: *The American Heritage Dictionary of the English Language, Third Edition* Copyright © 1992 by Houghton Mifflin Company. Electronic version licensed from Lernout & Hauspie Speech Products N.V.

merit consideration are to be *taken into account* in various ways; they can be *set aside*; they can be *outranked*; they *weighed*, handled carefully or mishandled, they can make (or fail to make) a significant impression, and they can seem to merit corresponding responses.

The activity of considering a matter can be assessed in various ways. The consideration (in the activities sense) given to a matter can be shallow or deep, hasty or thorough, prolonged or brief, balanced or one-sided, misguided or careful.

Turning to the second sense of the term, considerations, the matters we take up for careful thought and attention, can be ranked relative to each other and to the responses they merit and evoke.

(1) Rank in relationship to other considerations:

Overriding considerations (concerns)
Decisive considerations (may belong under 2 below)
Controversial considerations
Paramount considerations
*Insignificant considerations—fails to qualify as a consideration
*Trivial consideration—fails to qualify as a consideration

(2) Rank in relationship to the conclusion (or the question):

Relevant considerations—considerations as candidates for thought and attention; relevant ones qualify, but not irrelevant ones
*Irrelevant considerations—fails to qualify as a consideration

(3) Rank in relationship to the response merited:

Noteworthy considerations
Weighty considerations
Sobering considerations
Tiresome considerations
Serious considerations (subject to qualification by degree)
Compelling considerations
Powerful considerations
Persuasive considerations
Disturbing considerations
Reassuring considerations
Interesting considerations

When we consider a matter we look to the reasons for a conclusion, and we try to take into account those reasons that argue against that conclusion. Or we look to the reasons against a conclusion and try to take into account the reasons that argue for it.

Consideration is said to be detached, objective, it takes into account other points of view, etc. It has answers for them.

3. A case study in the management of disparate considerations: The debates over the ratification of the U. S. constitution

How do these conceptual resources work in cases involving arguments for and against a proposition? This, of course, is a very large question. But we can get a glimpse of answer by reviewing a case of competent pro and contra argumentation. Elsewhere I have discussed at some length the management of issues in the Debates over Ratification of the U. S. Constitution (Kauffeld 2002). By revisiting that case study, viewing the contest as a body of competing considerations, we can form some idea of complexity of competent conductive arguments in a historically significant context.

Debates over ratification of the United States Constitution commenced with the proposal of new plan for national government by the Philadelphia Convention in September of 1787 and continued through ratification of the Constitution in Virginia on June 27, 1788, approval in New York on July 26 and North Carolina on August 4. These debates were conducted in the press, via pamphlets, at public meetings and at ratification conventions held in each of the States.

At the outset of the ratification process, proponents of the new Constitution, the Federalist Party, called for a quick and favourable decision based on the authority and reputation of the leaders who had framed the Constitution while meeting at Philadelphia (Hamilton, 1993, pp. 9-11; "A Revolution Effected by Good Sense and Deliberation," Anonymous, 1993). The fact that the distinguished company of gentlemen meeting in Philadelphia (which included George Washington, Benjamin Franklin, Alexander Hamilton, and many other leading figures from all parts of the country) could agree on this document constituted, the Federalist maintained, *a decisive consideration* favouring its ratification by the states.

Federalist demands for speedy adoption were quickly countered by angry objections raised by their Anti-Federalist opponents. While generally conceding the need for stronger national government, the Anti-Federalists maintained that the proposed Constitution was simply too dangerous to adopt. The proposed change, the Anti-Federalists warned, would create a national government with a structure and powers that posed the gravest threats to the liberty of ordinary citizens. They claimed that a consolidated national government would be too large in extent to survive as a republic in which the rights of men were respected. Its principles of representation would leave plain citizens with no real voice in the affairs of the nation, while it consolidated unlimited powers of purse and sword in the hands of national leadership. Its division of powers between the judicial, executive, and legislative branches would not conform to principles known to be essential to the preservation of liberty. And the proposed Constitution did not even contain a Bill of Rights to protect rights of citizens. The Anti-Federalists maintained these and other threats to liberty as *overriding considerations* each of which sufficed to warrant rejection of the Constitution or to necessitate its amendment prior to ratification. And they angrily condemned the whole proposal as an aristocratic plot to usurp power and destroy the liberties won by the Revolution (Kenyon 1966, pp. xxxix-ixxiv).

In response to this onslaught, the Federalist initially granted that the Constitution contained some defects, but they maintained that strengthening the national government was critically important and *that on the whole the merits of the constitution outweighed its defects* (Wilson 1993, pp. 63-69). The Federalists' position at this stage in these debates framed the issues as counter-balancing considerations capable of summation.

Thus the Anti-Federalists and the Federalists differed in the rankings they assigned to the considerations each thought relevant to the decision regarding adoption of the proposed

Constitution. The Anti-Federalists urged rejection on the grounds of over-riding considerations; the Federalist urged adoption on the basis a summative consideration of its merits and defects, the former outweighing the latter. From the standpoint of the Anti-Federalists, the Federalists' response simply failed to take their objections into account, i.e., it failed to recognize that their objections to the proposed Constitution were based on over-riding considerations. Such consideration could not be weighed in a balancing act with the consideration of mere merits. From the Anti-Federalist perspective, the Federalist position claimed to counterbalance the dangers inherent in the Constitution with considerations that could not conceivably outweigh those evils. The Federalist simply did not take into account the perilous nature of the possibilities inherent in the proposed Constitution. Accordingly, the Anti-Federalist regarded the Federalists' argumentation as irrelevant. These contending parties initially occupied positions that were incommensurable. Their debate started as between ships passing in the night.

In an extended series of essays written under the pseudonym of Publius for publication in New York newspapers and widely circulated in other states, Alexander Hamilton, James Madison, and John Jay radically reconfigured the positions previously adopted by parties engaged in the ratification contest (Hamilton, *et al.* 1961). As noted above, the Anti-Federalists and Federalists assigned disparate rankings to the considerations they respectively regarded as relevant. The *Federalist Papers* radically altered this configuration of the issues. They articulated a comprehensive principle for ranking the need for the proposed Constitution in relation to the dangers that might attend its adoption. And they established this principle as the pivot on which the probative responsibilities of the contending parties turned.

Responding to Anti-Federalist claims that the potential abuses of power proposed for the new government provided over-riding reason to reject the Constitution, Publius strategically altered the way in which the Federalists framed the issues under consideration. Where his colleagues' answers left the two parties occupying disparate positions, Publius constructed his probative responsibilities in terms which rendered the Federalist and Anti-Federalist positions commensurable. He first maintained that a competent national government was in the interest of all, and he articulated a broad conception of its responsibilities (*ibid.*, pp. 37-98, and see summation at p. 99). Then, given these suppositions, Publius responded to Anti-Federalist charges by arguing that *when considering any of the powers granted the national government under the new Constitution, it is not enough to ask whether granting such a power is dangerous; rather it should first be asked whether this power is necessary and, then, whether adequate safeguards have been provided to protect against its abuse* (*ibid.*, p. 256).

This construction of the considerations at hand afforded Publius a platform that recognized the alarms raised by the Anti-Federalist as paramount consideration and which took them into account as matters subject to safeguards built into the proposed Constitution. At the same time, this platform enabled Publius to present the powers granted by the Constitution as necessary to the paramount consideration of establishing a satisfactory national government. Where a power was arguably necessary, Publius's frame denied the status of over-riding concern to potential dangers arising from the exercise of that power. Rather the dangers that might arise from the exercise of any essential power were to be considered in terms of whether the Constitution provided adequate safeguards against abuse of that power. Publius's position, in short, reconfigured these considerations so as to take into account the Anti-Federalist objections within a framework that allowed him to present the risks inherent in adopting the Constitution as commensurable with the necessity for a competent national government, while minimizing the former and magnifying the latter.

The argumentation that Publius provided in defence of the Constitution had the power to make his ranking of relevant considerations the crux upon which deliberation about the Constitution would turn. The vehicle for moving Publius's construction of the issues to this central position was the burden of proof. Hamilton introduced this famous series of essays by proposing the Constitution for consideration by his countrymen in terms which openly accepted a probative obligation to (a) show that adoption of the Constitution is in his countrymen's interests—is the safest course for their liberty, dignity, and happiness—and (b) to give a satisfactory answer to all the objections which shall have made their appearance that may seem to have any claim to their attention (*ibid.*, pp. 35-36). Recognizing that angry objections raised by his Anti-Federalist opponents were creating a climate ill-suited to candid and judicious consideration of the Constitution, Hamilton openly undertook a proposer's burden of proof in order to induce calm and careful consideration of the matter.

Following his design for the issues, the *Federalist Papers* systematically examined the powers to be granted the proposed national government and conspicuously provided answers to the challenges raised by anti-Federalists. At the conclusion of the *Papers*, Publius claimed to have discharged his burden of proof; i.e., to have shown that adopting the proposed Constitution was in his countrymen's interest and to have answered all doubts and objections worth considering. Given the dire national emergency growing out of the imbecility of government under the older Articles of Confederation, Publius maintained, (i) that his readers now had an obligation to carefully consider his arguments and (ii) that the Anti-Federalists had an obligation to justify the time and risk involved in further consideration by addressing with reason and evidence the considerations as configured and ranked by the *Federalist* (Hamilton 1961, pp. 552-553). The apparent force of the argumentation in the *Federalist Papers*, as construed by Publius, was to shift the burden of proof to the Anti-Federalists and demand that they justify continued debate over the Constitution by speaking to the considerations as he framed them. Were that force acknowledged, his configuration of the paramount considerations would become the pivot on which the probative responsibilities of the advocates turned. Within that frame, Publius could claim to have taken into account and answered the seemingly ominous considerations raised by the Anti-Federalists.

It might now be wondered whether Publius's frame for considering the issues and attendant probative burdens carried any force beyond the pages of his essays. The debates over the Constitution at the Virginia Ratification Convention provide an especially interesting and convenient site for investigating this question. Virginia was a key state in the ratification contest. Had she failed to approve the Constitution, the ratification process could have stalled and reform might well have been thrown into a second Constitutional Convention. Moreover, the contest in Virginia was very close; at the outset of the Virginia Ratification Convention, neither Federalists nor Anti-Federalists were confident of victory (Banning 1989, p. 262). More importantly, from our point of view, as the debates in Virginia unfolded the probative responsibilities of the advocates came to turn on Publius's construction of the construction of impending paramount considerations.

The considerations as initially framed and ranked by the contending parties at the Virginia convention correspond closely to the disparate positions articulated by each side prior to the publication of the *Federalist Papers*. At the start and continuing through much of the Convention, the Virginia Anti-Federalists claimed that the powers vested in the national government by the Constitution were so dangerous as to constitute overriding reason for its rejection. The Virginia Federalists initially argued that "though some small defects may appear" in the Constitution, "yet its merits ... will amply cover those defects" (Kaminski & Saladino 1988, p. 918). These positions exhibit the incongruity which Publius's argumentation managed to overcome.

Madison's participation in the Virginia Convention was delayed by illness, but on June 6, he introduced the demand that Anti-Federalists accept a burden of proof apportioned along the lines propounded by Publius at the conclusion of the *Federalist Papers*. As a matter of the delegates' duty to deliberate and decide, Madison demanded that the Anti-Federalists accept a burden of proof corresponding to the Federalists acknowledged probative responsibilities:

> . . . we ought not to address our arguments to the feelings and passions, but to those understandings and judgments which were selected by the people of this country, to decide this great question, by a calm and rational investigation. I hope that Gentlemen, in displaying their abilities, on this occasion, instead of giving opinions and making assertions, will condescend to prove and demonstrate, by a fair and regular discussion. (Kaminski & Saladino 1988, p. 989.)

Then turning to Patrick Henry's complaints, Madison responded as follows.

> He told us, that this Constitution ought to be rejected, because it endangered the public liberty, in his opinion, in many instances. Give me leave to make one answer to that observation--Let the dangers which this system is supposed to be replete with, be clearly pointed out. If any dangerous and unnecessary powers be given to the general legislature, let them be plainly demonstrated, and let us not rest satisfied with general assertions of dangers, without examination. If power be necessary, apparent danger is not a sufficient reason against conceding them. (*Ibid.*, p. 989.)

Here and in subsequent argumentation Madison relied upon Publius's principle for framing the paramount considerations in the ratification controversy: ask first whether a power was necessary and, then, whether it was well-guarded against abuse. And, following Publius's strategy, Madison coupled this principle with the demand that as Federalist discharged their probative obligations, the Anti-Federalist were to accept the burden of substantively addressing the considerations as framed and ranked by the Federalists.

Madison's construction of the issues was promptly adopted by his colleagues as the core of the Federalist position at the Virginia Convention.[2] And as the Federalists, responding to Anti-Federalist charges, mounted arguments designed to show that the powers allocated to the national government under the proposed Constitution were both necessary and well guarded, they sought to impose upon their opponents the burden of substantiating objections to the Constitution. On June 14, in a statement representative of the tenor of Federalist argumentation, Henry Lee pointedly criticized the Anti-Federalist reliance on suspi-

---

[2] Instances of Federalist argumentation which framed the issues in Madison's mode abound in the record of the Virginia debates. The following are good examples. On June 7, Francis Corbin discussing the power of laying direct taxes, argued that this power is indispensable, not liable to abuse, and guarded by the suffrage (Kaminski & Saladino, pp. 1011-1012). Regarding the same power, Edmond Randoph maintained that it would be "utmost folly to say that a Government could be carried on without this great agent of human affairs" (*ibid.*, p. 1016, repeated at p. 1023), and later in the same address he maintained that within the Constitution's system of representation direct taxation was protected from abuse and would be "neither inconvenient or oppressive" (*ibid.*, p. 1022, parallel arguments at p. 1027). Still discussing the power of direct taxation, John Marshall applied Publius' basic principle, "Our enquiry here must be, whether the power of taxation be necessary to perform the object of the Constitution, and whether it be safe and as well guarded as human wisdom can do it" (*ibid.*, p. 1119).

cion of the mere possibility of harm and their propensity to speculate about dangers without regard for the consistency of their arguments:

> I am anxious to know the truth on this great occasion. I was in hopes of receiving true information, but have been disappointed. I have heard suspicions against possibility, and not against probability. As to the distinction that lies between the gentlemen for and against the Constitution: In the first place most of the arguments the latter use, pay no regard to the necessity of the Union, which is our object. In the next place they use contradictory arguments. ... Ought we to adduce arguments like these, which imply a palpable contradiction? We ought to use arguments capable of discussion. (Kaminski & Saladino, pp.1292-1293.)

As the Anti-Federalists persisted in speculations about the possible dangers posed by the Constitution, the Federalist repeatedly criticized their opponents for failure to shoulder the probative obligations presumably incumbent on them and for wasting time by raising matters not worth considering, and, hence, for violating their duty to deliberate and decide in a timely fashion. Eventually, the Federalist refused further response, claiming that the Anti-Federalist objections had sufficiently answered (*ibid.*, pp. 1287 & 1293).

The Anti-Federalists did not immediately capitulate to their opponents' demands. To the bitter end, Patrick Henry stood fast in his role as a "centinel," insisting that possibilities for abuse warranted the conclusion that the proposed "change is dangerous and ought not be made" (*ibid.*, p. 1317). His ally, George Mason, refused to abandon the principle that, since "what may be done, will be done," the mere possibility of abuse sufficed as cause for alarm (*ibid.*, p. 1291). In these and other avowals, the leadership of the Anti-Federalist party clung tenaciously to the position that since the possibility of grave abuse had not been refuted, their continued opposition to the Constitution was warranted.

It is, however, apparent from the record that Henry's colleagues were moved to address the considerations as framed and ranked by Madison. On June 10, Anti-Federalist James Monroe opened his consideration of the powers granted the Federal Government, not by claiming the powers granted under the Constitution were so dangerous as to comprise overriding objection to its adoption, but by asking "What are the powers the Federal Government ought to have?" While Monroe's answers to this question argued that various powers provided by the new Constitution were unnecessary, it joined the debate within the framework of considerations laid out by Madison (*ibid.*, pp. 1109-1110). On June 14, George Mason's arguments implicitly accepted Madison's ordering of paramount considerations. Admitting "that the nature of the country rendered a full representation impracticable," he urged that "this impracticality constituted a conclusive reason for granting no powers to the Government, but such as were absolutely indispensable, and these to be most cautiously guarded" (*ibid.*, p. 1290). In the sessions that followed, Mason repeatedly argued within Madison's construction of paramount considerations (for examples, see *ibid.*, pp. 1317, 1363). His consideration of the treaty making powers to be vested in the national government illustrates Mason's drift into the structure established by Madison:

> I acknowledge such a power must rest somewhere. It is so in all Governments. ... For my part I have never heard it denied that such power must be vested in the Government. —Our complaint is, that it is not sufficiently guarded, and that it requires more solemnity and caution than is provided in that system. (*Ibid.*, p. 1390.)

In the face of Federalist demands that they live up to their probative responsibilities, the Anti-Federalist leadership at the Virginia Convention reluctantly and fitfully came to argue within construction of paramount considerations originally delineated by Publius and introduced into the Convention by Madison.

Eventually the Convention settled down to the clause-by-clause consideration of the Constitution to which it had initially committed itself, and as the end of that consideration approached, the Anti-Federalists did little to resist the Federalist claim that their responses to objections raised against the Constitution warranted termination of the debate. On June 25, Nicholas called for an end to the deliberations. "I do not mean enter into any further debate. The friends of the Constitution wish to take up no more time, the matter being fully discussed. They are convinced that further time will answer no end but to serve the cause of those who wish to destroy the Constitution. We wish it to be ratified, and such amendments as may be thought necessary to be subsequently considered by a Committee, in order to be recommended to Congress, to be acted upon according to the amendatory mode presented in itself" (*ibid.*, p. 1516). The final vote, approving the Constitution by a narrow but significant ten-vote margin, reflected the fact that wavering delegates were in the final analysis not moved by the Anti-Federalist position.

4. Concluding thoughts

What does this brief effort to parse the debates over ratification of the U.S. Constitution in terms of our ordinary concept of "considerations" suggest about pro and contra conductive arguments? It seems apparent that one way in which we manage considerations involves assigning weights to the various considerations and weighing them; that is basically the second strategy adopted by the Federalists in responding to Anti-Federalist attacks on the proposed Constitution. However, this seems to be only one of several ways in which we manage pro and contra conductive arguments in attempting to reach a well reasoned conclusion. More basic reasoning/argument strategies involve ranking consideration and taking opposing considerations into account. By weight seems to be only one of several ways in which considerations can be ranked. It does not seem that, e.g., overriding or paramount considerations simply outweigh other considerations; rather, they do not seem to fit on the same scale with lesser considerations. The Federalist's claim that the merits of the proposed Constitution outweighed its defects seems to have made little headway against the Ant-Federalist claims that the proposal was fraught with overriding dangers. The stronger Federalist response required some parity of ranking among the matters under consideration; Madison treats both the need for each power to be granted the national government and the danger of abuse posed by each as paramount concerns. However, this strategy would seem to require more than merely weighing contending concerns. If a potential for abuse (or other danger) is a paramount concern, then it somehow needs to be taken into account. Paramount concerns, by their very nature, dominate other considerations. I do not offer these tentative observations as conclusions; they are merely suggestions that may merit consideration as students of argumentation grapple with the complexity of conductive arguments.

Chapter 12

Conductive Arguments and the Toulmin Model: A Case Study

DEREK ALLEN

1. Introduction

I examine a legal case concerning the constitutional validity under the *Canadian Charter of Rights and Freedoms* of a provision of the *Criminal Code* of Canada prohibiting hate propaganda directed in public at certain identifiable groups. My focus will be on the reasons of two judges on the Supreme Court of Canada, which heard the case (*R. v. Keegstra*) on appeal in 1990. Both judges (Chief Justice Brian Dickson, as he then was, and Madam Justice Beverley McLachlin, now Chief Justice) employ conductive arguments. In section 8 I reconstruct some of these arguments, and for each but one of the reconstructed arguments I provide a warrant and a backing. In section 9 (the final section of the paper) I examine several related matters, one of which bears on a question James Freeman asks: "Can we go beyond an intuitive weighing of positive and negative considerations and can the Toulmin model give us a way to make this advance?" (Freeman 2010, p. 12). Another of the related matters is whether Toulmin methodology is compatible with the methodology the Supreme Court of Canada has developed for conducting an analysis under section 1 of the *Charter*. Sections 8 and 9 require stage-setting, which I provide in sections 2-7.

2. The *Canadian Charter of Rights and Freedoms*

The *Canadian Charter of Rights and Freedoms* was enacted in 1982 and is part of the Constitution of Canada. (To be more precise, it is Part 1, Schedule B, of the Constitution Act of 1982.) As its name suggests, it sets out a list of rights and freedoms; some of these belong to "everyone" while others belong to "every citizen of Canada." They are divided into the following categories: Fundamental Freedoms; Democratic Rights; Mobility Rights; Legal Rights; Equality Rights; Minority Language Educational Rights.

The rights and freedoms set out in the *Charter* are not absolute. This is made clear in section 1 of the *Charter*:

> The *Canadian Charter of Rights and Freedoms* guarantees the rights and freedoms set out in it subject only to such reasonable limits prescribed by law as can be demonstrably justified in a free and democratic society.

In a *Charter* case concerning the constitutional validity of a particular statute, the court must first decide whether the statute imposes a limit on a *Charter* right or freedom. If it does, the limit it imposes is "prescribed by law," and the law that prescribes it is the statute itself. Whether the statute is nevertheless constitutionally valid will depend on whether the limit it imposes on the right or freedom in question is a reasonable limit that can be demonstrably justified in a free and democratic society. If it is, the statute is constitutionally valid, despite the fact that it limits a *Charter* right or freedom; if it isn't, then the statute is not constitutionally valid.

A statute that is found in a *Charter* case to be constitutionally valid despite limiting a *Charter* right or freedom is said to be "saved" under s. 1 (section 1) of the *Charter*. In order to decide whether a law that limits a *Charter* right or freedom can be saved under s. 1, the

Supreme Court of Canada has developed a test. The test is called the *Oakes* test, after the case in which it was first proposed (*R. v. Oakes*, 1986).

3. The *Oakes* test

The test has two main parts. The first part is concerned with the *objective* of the impugned measure. The second part is concerned with the impugned measure considered as a *means* of achieving its objective.

Part 1: The objective of the impugned measure must be "sufficiently important to warrant overriding a constitutionally protected right or freedom" (*R. v. Oakes* 1986, p. 5). At a minimum, it "must relate to societal concerns which are pressing and substantial in a free and democratic society" (p. 5). In deciding whether this requirement is met, a court "must be guided by the values and principles essential to a free and democratic society" (p. 5), for these "are the genesis of the rights and freedoms guaranteed by the *Charter*" (p. 40). In *Oakes* they were said to embody, among other values/principles, "respect for the inherent dignity of the human person, commitment to social justice and equality, accommodation of a wide variety of beliefs, and faith in social and political institutions which enhance the participation of individuals and groups in society" (p. 40).

Part 2: This part of the test "is a form of proportionality test" (p. 43) with three requirements. (a) The impugned measure "must be rationally connected to [its] objective" (p. 43). This matter may be viewed in two ways. The first is whether the measure is carefully designed to achieve its objective. For this to be the case, the measure "must not be arbitrary, unfair, or based on irrational considerations" (p. 43). The second is whether, given the actual *effect* of the measure, there exists a rational connection between it and its objective. (b) The second requirement is that the impugned measure must impair the *Charter* right or freedom in question as little as reasonably possible—that is, no more than is reasonably necessary to achieve its objective. Here the court may consider whether there is some reasonable alternative means by which the state could achieve its objective with fewer detrimental effects on the freedom or right in question. (c) The third requirement is that there must be a proportionality between the effects of the measure and its objective.

> Even if an objective is of sufficient importance, and the first two elements of the proportionality test are satisfied, it is still possible that, because of the severity of the deleterious effects of a measure on individuals or groups, the measure will not be justified by the purposes it is intended to serve. The more severe the deleterious effects of a measure, the more important the objective must be if the measure is to be reasonable and demonstrably justified in a free and democratic society (p. 44).

For an impugned measure to pass the *Oakes* test (and thus be saved under s. 1 of the *Charter*), it is necessary and sufficient that it satisfy all the requirements of the test. That is to say:

(1) the measure must serve an objective that is pressing and substantial in a free and democratic society;
(2) it must be rationally connected to its objective;
(3) its impairment of the *Charter* right or freedom that it limits must be no greater than is necessary for it to achieve its objective;
(4) its effects must be proportional to its objective: the more severe its deleterious effects, the more important its objective must be.

If the impugned measure fails to satisfy any one of these requirements, it fails the *Oakes* test and so cannot be saved under s. 1 of the *Charter*.

Finally,

> [t]he standard of proof under s. 1 is the civil standard, namely, proof by a preponderance of probability. The alternative criminal standard, proof beyond reasonable doubt, would ... be unduly onerous on the party seeking to limit. Concepts such as "reasonableness", "justifiability" and "free and democratic society" are simply not amenable to such a standard. Nevertheless, the preponderance of probability test must be applied rigorously.... Within the broad category of the civil standard, there exist different degrees of probability depending on the nature of the case.... Having regard to the fact that s. 1 is being invoked for the purpose of justifying a violation of the constitutional rights and freedoms the *Charter* was designed to protect, a very high degree of probability will be, in the words of Lord Denning, "commensurate with the occasion" (pp. 41-2).

4. The *Irwin Toy* test

Section 2(b) of the *Charter* guarantees various freedoms, among them freedom of expression. In *Attorney General of Quebec v. Irwin Toy Inc.* (1989), the Supreme Court had to decide whether commercial advertising directed at children ("persons under thirteen years of age" (*Irwin Toy*, p. 3)) was within the scope of freedom of expression. In that case the Court developed a test for deciding whether a government measure (action) that is alleged to violate the *Charter*'s guarantee of freedom of expression actually does violate it. The test is known as the *Irwin Toy* test, and has two steps:

Step 1 is concerned with the *activity* that is the subject of the impugned measure and consists in deciding whether it is protected by s. 2(b)'s guarantee of freedom of expression. This depends on its *content* and *form*. In order for the activity to be protected by s. 2(b) its content must be *expressive*. Its content is expressive if and only if the activity conveys or attempts to convey a *meaning*, regardless of what that meaning is. If the content of the activity *is* expressive, then the activity is *prima facie* protected by s. 2(b). Whether it is protected not just *prima facie* but all things considered depends on its form. If the activity is *violent* in form, then it is not protected by s. 2(b); if, however, it is not violent in form, then, provided that its content is expressive, it *is* protected by s. 2(b).

Step 2 is concerned with whether the impugned measure infringes s. 2(b)'s guarantee of freedom of expression. It does, "[i]f the government's purpose is to restrict the content of expression by singling out particular meanings that are not to be conveyed" (p. 51). But suppose this is not the government's purpose. Still, the impugned measure infringes s. 2(b)'s guarantee of freedom of expression if its *effect* is to restrict freedom of expression. A government measure has this effect (according to the *Irwin Toy* test) if and only if the activity that is the subject of the measure promotes one or more of the values underlying the freedom of expression guarantee in the *Charter*. Those values (as stated in *Irwin Toy*) are the following: (1) the pursuit of truth; (2) participation in the community (or, more specifically, participation in social and political decision-making); (3) individual self-fulfilment and human flourishing (p. 7; see also p. 53). (The values underlying s. 2 (b) are sometimes stated differently. For example, in *Keegstra*, Dickson speaks of the attainment of truth and the common good (p. 69), and McLachlin says that "the values upon which s. 2(*b*) of the *Charter* rests [are] the value of fostering a vibrant and creative society through the marketplace of ideas; the value of the vigourous and open debate essential to democratic government and preservation of our rights and freedoms; and the value of a society which fosters the self-actualization and freedom of its members" (p. 171).)

Summary: A government measure violates s. 2(b)'s guarantee of freedom of expression if and only if (1) the activity that is the subject of the measure is protected by s. 2(b), and (2) the purpose or the effect of the measure is to restrict freedom of expression.

5. *R. v. Keegstra*

(i) *Facts:* The following summary is from the majority opinion (*R. v. Keegstra*, pp. 21-2).

Mr. James Keegstra was a high school teacher in Eckville, Alberta from the early 1970s until his dismissal in 1982. In 1984 Mr. Keegstra was charged under s. 319(2) (then s. 281.2(2)) of the *Criminal Code* with unlawfully promoting hatred against an identifiable group by communicating anti-semitic statements to his students. He was convicted by a jury in a trial before McKenzie J. of the Alberta Court of Queen's Bench.

Mr. Keegstra's teachings attributed various evil qualities to Jews. He thus described Jews to his pupils as "treacherous," "subversive," "sadistic," "money-loving," "power hungry" and "child killers." He taught his classes that Jewish people seek to destroy Christianity and are responsible for depressions, anarchy, chaos, wars and revolution. According to Mr. Keegstra, Jews "created the Holocaust to gain sympathy" and, in contrast to the open and honest Christians, were said to be deceptive, secretive and inherently evil. Mr. Keegstra expected his students to reproduce his teachings in class and on exams. If they failed to do so, their marks suffered.

Prior to his trial, Mr. Keegstra applied to the Court of Queen's Bench in Alberta for an order quashing the charge on a number of grounds, the primary one being that s. 319(2) of the *Criminal Code* unjustifiably infringed his freedom of expression as guaranteed by s. 2(*b*) of the *Charter*..... The application was dismissed..., and Mr. Keegstra was thereafter tried and convicted. He then appealed his conviction to the Alberta Court of Appeal, raising the same *Charter* issues. The Court of Appeal unanimously accepted his argument, and it is from this judgment that the Crown appeals.

(ii) *Criminal Code* (*Keegstra*, pp. 23-4)

> s. 319....
> (2) Every one who, by communicating statements, other than in private conversation, wilfully promotes hatred against any identifiable group is guilty of (*a*) an indictable offence and is liable to imprisonment for a term not exceeding two years; or (*b*) an offence punishable on summary conviction.
> (3) No person shall be convicted of an offence under subsection (2)
> (*a*) if he establishes that the statements communicated were true;
> (*b*) if, in good faith, he expressed or attempted to establish by argument an opinion on a religious subject;
> (*c*) if the statements were relevant to any subject of public interest, the discussion of which was for the public benefit, and if on reasonable grounds he believed them to be true; or
> (*d*) if, in good faith, he intended to point out, for the purpose of removal, matters producing or tending to produce feelings of hatred towards an identifiable group in Canada....
> (7) In this section,
> "communicating" includes communicating by telephone, broadcasting or other audible or visible means;
> "identifiable group" has the same meaning as in section 318;

"public place" includes any place to which the public have access as of right or by invitation, express or implied;
"statements" includes words spoken or written or recorded electronically or electromagnetically or otherwise, and gestures, signs or other visible representations.

s. 318. . . .
(4) In this section, "identifiable group" means any section of the public distinguished by colour, race, religion or ethnic origin.

(iii) *Issues*

The main issue in *Keegstra* was whether s. 319(2) of the *Criminal Code* of Canada (the hate law, as I shall call it) is constitutionally valid. (As McLachlin puts it: "It is not the statements of Mr. Keegstra which are at issue in this case, but rather the constitutionality of s. 319(2) of the *Criminal Code*" (*Keegstra*, p. 157).) The subsidiary issues included: (1) Does s. 319(2) infringe freedom of expression as guaranteed by s. 2(b) of the *Charter*? (2) If it does, can it nevertheless be saved under s. 1 of the *Charter*? What follows is a summary of the main elements of the reasoning of Dickson and McLachlin on these issues.

(iv) *Dickson's s. 2(b) analysis*

Dickson's s. 2(b) analysis consists in using the *Irwin Toy* test to determine whether the hate law infringes the *Charter*'s guarantee of freedom of expression.

Step 1: The first question Dickson considers is whether the type of activity prohibited by the hate law is *expressive*. It consists in communications, other than in private conversation, that wilfully promote hatred "towards any section of the public distinguished by colour, race, religion, or ethnic origin." Whether activity of this type is expressive depends on whether such communications convey or attempt to convey a meaning. Clearly they do convey a meaning. Hence they count as expressive activity. But are they violent in form? Dickson does not consider this question; he evidently assumes that the wilful promotion of hatred need not be violent in form. Accordingly, he moves on to the second step in the *Irwin Toy* test.

Step 2: Here Dickson considers what the purpose of the hate law is. Its purpose (as he expresses it in his s. 2(b) analysis) is "to restrict the content of expression by singling out particular meanings that are not to be conveyed" (*Keegstra*, p. 38).

From steps 1 and 2 Dickson concludes that the hate law infringes the *Charter*'s s. 2(b) guarantee of freedom of expression.

(v) *Dickson's s. 1 analysis*

Since Dickson has found that the hate law infringes s. 2(b) of the *Charter*, he must conduct an s. 1 analysis to determine whether the hate law can be saved. His s.1 analysis consists in a methodical, step-by-step application of the *Oakes* test.

The objective of the hate law:

The first part of the *Oakes* test requires him to determine what the objective of the hate law is and whether that objective "relates to concerns which are pressing and substantial in a free and democratic society" (p. 52).

In his s. 2(b) analysis Dickson characterizes the purpose of the hate law as being "to restrict the content of expression by singling out particular meanings that are not to be conveyed" (p. 38). But in his s. 1 analysis, he says that Parliament's purpose in enacting the hate law "was to prevent the harm ... caused by hate-promoting expression" (p. 56). This is a different purpose from the one he identifies in his s. 2(b) analysis. Is he being inconsistent? Not necessarily. The purpose he identifies in his s. 1 analysis can be considered the *ultimate* objective of the hate law, while the purpose he identifies in his s. 2(b) analysis can be considered one that is also a means of promoting that ultimate objective.

According to Dickson, hate propaganda has two harmful effects. First, it does "emotional damage" (p. 53) to the members of the target group(s). Second, it is capable of creating "serious discord between various cultural groups in society" (p. 55). Both of these harmful effects are "of pressing and substantial concern." Hence the objective of the hate law "is of the utmost importance" (p. 65). Thus Dickson finds that the first part of the *Oakes* test is satisfied.

Proportionality:

Dickson begins by asking how close a connection there is between the expression prohibited by the hate law and the free expression values that underlie s. 2(b) of the *Charter*. He argues that hate propaganda does little or nothing to promote these values. "There is very little chance that statements intended to promote hatred against an identifiable group are true, or that their vision of society will lead to a better world" (p. 70). Nor does hate propaganda promote participation in social and political decision-making. This is because it fosters a society in which "the democratic process is subverted and individuals are denied respect and dignity simply because of racial or religious characteristics" (p. 71). As for individual self-fulfilment and human flourishing, hate propaganda "represents a most extreme opposition to the idea that members of identifiable groups should enjoy this aspect of the s. 2(b) benefit" (p. 70). In sum: hate propaganda is "only tenuously connected with the values underlying the guarantee of freedom of speech" (p. 93). Having concluded his preliminary comments, Dickson turns to the three segments of the proportionality branch of the *Oakes* test.

Rational connection:

The hate law prohibits the wilful promotion of hatred, other than in private conversation, towards any section of the public distinguished by colour, race, religion or ethnic origin. The (ultimate) objective of the hate law is to prevent the harm caused by hate-promoting expression. It seems obvious that there is a rational connection between the hate law and its (ultimate) objective—that the prohibition contained in the hate law is well-designed to promote that objective. But it has been argued (Dickson notes) that *the actual effect* of the hate law may prevent it from being rationally connected to its (ultimate) objective. There are three worries here. The first is that the hate law may promote the cause of hate-mongers by gaining them excessive media attention, and may also generate sympathy for them as underdogs doing battle against the powers of the state. The second worry is that the public may think that there must be an element of truth to hate propaganda, or the state wouldn't bother to suppress it. The third worry is that hate laws are ineffective; after all, Germany of the 1920s and 1930s had hate propaganda laws, but those laws "did nothing to stop the triumph of a racist philosophy under the Nazis" (p. 75).

Dickson acknowledges that it is impossible to define the effect of the hate law with precision, but he is unconvinced by the view "that there is no strong and evident connection between the criminalization of hate propaganda and its suppression" (p. 75). It is true that the prosecution of hate-mongers will gain media attention; but it is also true that it will send out the message that hate propaganda is harmful and that society will not tolerate it. As to whether government suppression of hate propaganda will gain sympathy for hate-mongers, Dickson doubts that this is so. Nor, in his view, will government suppression of hate propaganda make the expression attractive. He does not explicitly deal with the second worry listed above, that suppression of hate propaganda may lead people to think that there must be truth in such expression, but he may be thinking of this worry when he denies that government suppression of hate propaganda will make the expression attractive. As for the final worry, that hate laws are ineffective, Dickson does not claim that *by themselves* they are sufficient to prevent the spread of racism, but he does think that they are *one aspect* of a democratic society's fight against racism.

On the basis of these considerations, Dickson concludes that the hate law is rationally connected to its objective.

Minimal impairment:

The question Dickson has to consider next under the *Oakes* test is whether the hate law is "carefully tailored so as to minimize impairment of the freedom of expression" (p. 78). He notes two reasons given in earlier argument for saying that it is not. The first was that "the legislation is overbroad, its terms so wide as to include expression which does not relate to Parliament's objective" (p. 78) in enacting the hate law. The second was that the hate law is "unduly vague, in that a lack of clarity and precision in its words prevents individuals from discerning its meaning with any accuracy" (p. 78). If the hate law is overbroad, then it prohibits expression that does not count as hate propaganda, as well as expression that does count as hate propaganda. If it is vague, then people will be unsure what counts as the wilful promotion of hatred, and this could have "a chilling effect" on public discourse and debate.

In order to determine whether the hate law is overbroad or vague, Dickson examines its terms. In particular, he considers the phrase "promotes hatred against an identifiable group," and offers explanations of the meaning of the terms "promotes," "identifiable group" and "hatred." I will not reproduce his explanations here. Instead, I will simply report his conclusion, which is that the hate law "suffers from neither overbreadth nor vagueness" (p. 92).

In earlier argument, a further possible reason for thinking that the hate law does not satisfy the minimal impairment requirement was given, namely that "a criminal sanction is not necessary to meet Parliament's objective" (p. 90) in enacting the hate law. Non-criminal responses, such as information and education programs and the use of human rights statutes, would be more effective in fighting the harm caused by hate propaganda than the criminal law, or so it was argued. Dickson replies that it is open to the government to use a number of different means to promote its objective of fighting the harm caused by hate propaganda and that one of these means may be the criminal law; by using the criminal law, the government can "send out a strong message of condemnation" (p. 92) of hate propaganda.

This completes Dickson's examination of the reasons given in earlier argument for the view that the hate law does not satisfy the minimal impairment requirement. He finds that they do not establish the truth of that view. On the basis of his criticism of them, he concludes that the hate law "does not unduly impair the freedom of expression" (p. 93), hence that the minimal impairment requirement of the *Oakes* test is satisfied.

Effects of the limitation:

Here Dickson begins by saying that "[t]he third branch of the proportionality test entails a weighing of the importance of the state objective against the effect of limits imposed upon a *Charter* right or guarantee" (p. 93). Recall that in the comments he made before turning to the second part of the *Oakes* test, Dickson argued that hate propaganda is only tenuously connected to the values underlying the guarantee of freedom of speech. This being so, he concludes that the suppression of hate propaganda that results from the hate law "represents an impairment of the individual's freedom of expression which is not of a most serious nature" (p. 93). On the other hand, the (ultimate) objective of the hate law is of "enormous importance," for "[f]ew concerns can be as central to the concept of a free and democratic society as the dissipation of racism" (p. 94). On the basis of these considerations, Dickson concludes that the importance of the (ultimate) objective of the hate law outweighs the effect of the limit that the hate law imposes on freedom of expression. In his view, then, the hate law satisfies the final requirement of the *Oakes* test.

(vi) *McLachlin's s. 1 analysis*

McLachlin agrees with Dickson that the hate law infringes s. 2(b) of the *Charter*. I will not summarize the reasoning in her s. 2(b) analysis. Instead, I will summarize her s. 1 analysis.

The objective of the hate law:

According to McLachlin, the objective of the hate law is "to prevent the promotion of hatred towards identifiable groups within our society" (p. 154). Is this objective "of a pressing and substantial nature"? McLachlin thinks it is, "[g]iven the problem of racial and religious prejudice in this country" (p. 156). Indeed, she thinks that "the objective of the legislation is of sufficient gravity to be capable of justifying limitations on constitutionally protected rights and freedoms" (p. 156). Thus, in her view the hate law satisfies the first requirement of the *Oakes* test.

Proportionality:

On the other hand, she does not think that the hate law satisfies any of the three requirements in the proportionality branch of the test: rational connection, minimal impairment, "importance of the right versus benefit conferred" (p. 170).

Rational connection:

Here there are two questions to consider. "The first is whether Parliament carefully designed s. 319(2) to meet the objectives it is enacted to promote" (p. 159). The second is whether "given the actual effect of the legislation, a rational connection exists between it and its objectives" (p. 159). In response to the first question McLachlin concedes that the hate law does, at least at one level, further Parliament's objectives, for prosecuting hate-mongers may well affirm certain values of a pressing and substantial nature. But in response to the second question, she argues that the actual effect of the hate law is such that there is not a rational connection between it and its objectives. She thinks that the hate law may promote the cause of hate-mongers because prosecutions under the hate law will attract intense media coverage. Further, the criminal process may bring the hate-monger sympathy. And it may lead people to believe "that there must be some truth in the racist expression because the government is trying to suppress it" (p. 161). Finally, historical evidence (mainly the case of pre-Hitler Germany) suggests that hate propaganda laws may not be effective in promoting the cause of multiculturalism and equality. McLachlin concludes that "[v]iewed from the point of view of actual effect, the rational connection between s. 319(2) and the goals it promotes may be argued to be tenuous. Certainly it cannot be said that there is a strong and evident connection between the criminalization of hate propaganda and its suppression" (p. 162). Accordingly, the hate law does not satisfy the rational connection requirement of the *Oakes* test.

Minimal impairment:

Here there are again two questions to consider. The first is whether the hate law is overbroad. "The second is whether criminalization of hate mongering may in itself be an excessive response to the problem, given the alternatives" (p. 163).

McLachlin argues that the hate law *is* overbroad. Part of the problem lies in the different interpretations that may be given of the word 'hatred': "'hatred' is a broad term capable of catching a wide variety of emotion" (p. 164). Consequently, the hate law may have a chilling effect on public discourse, leading people to confine their expression to non-controversial matters.

Turning to her second question, McLachlin says that "the very fact of criminalization itself may be argued to represent an excessive response to the problem of hate propagation" (p. 168). Remedies other than the criminal law "are perhaps more appropriate and more effective" (p. 169)—for example, human rights legislation. "Under the human rights process a tribunal has considerable discretion in determining what messages or conduct should be banned" (p. 170).

McLachlin concludes from these considerations that the hate law does not satisfy the minimal impairment requirement of the *Oakes* test.

Importance of the right versus benefit conferred:
McLachlin first considers the significance of the hate law's infringement of the guarantee of freedom of expression. She argues that, viewed from the perspective of our society as a whole, the hate law's infringement of the freedom of expression guarantee is a serious one that "invokes all of the values" (p. 171) that underlie the guarantee. This is so partly on account of the hate law's overbreadth: "[i]t is capable of catching ... works of art and the intemperate statement made in the heat of social controversy" (p. 171). Further, a prosecution under the hate law may result in imprisonment. "These considerations establish an infringement of the guarantee of freedom of expression of the most serious nature" (p. 171).

What about the benefit to be gained by the hate law? McLachlin is doubtful that the hate law really does achieve its goal of discouraging the spread of hate propaganda; instead, it may promote the cause of hate-mongering extremists.

McLachlin concludes that any benefit that may be achieved by the hate law is outweighed by its significant infringement of the constitutional guarantee of freedom of expression. Thus, the hate law does not satisfy the final requirement of the *Oakes* test.

(vii) *Decision*

The Court held, in a 4-3 decision, that the hate law was constitutionally valid.

We now have in place the information we need about the *Canadian Charter of Rights and Freedoms*, the *Oakes* test, the *Irwin Toy* test, and the *Keegstra* case. In the next two stage-setting sections we will be mainly concerned with conductive arguments and the Toulmin model (section 6) and with some remarks by James Freeman in (2010) on warrants and backings (section 7).

6. Conductive arguments and the Toulmin model

Wellman distinguishes three patterns of conductive argument. (1) "[A] single reason is given for the conclusion" (1971, p. 55). (2) "[S]everal considerations, each of which may be independently relevant, are brought together into a unified argument from which a single conclusion is drawn" (p. 56). (3) "[S]ome conclusion is drawn from both positive and negative considerations. In this pattern reasons against the conclusion are included as well as reasons for it" (p. 57). In the case of a conductive argument fitting any of these three patterns, the conclusion "is drawn non-conclusively" (52). It was Wellman's view that the conclusion drawn is "about some individual case" (52); I will follow Govier in dropping this restriction (1987a, p. 69).

In the abstract for (2010), Freeman says:

> The Toulmin model throws distinct light on the issue of evaluating conductive arguments, allowing us to refine and extend Wellman's account in *Challenge and Response*. Implicit in Wellman's discussion is the notion of warrant, when understood as an inference rule. Making this notion explicit links the issue of evaluating conductive arguments with Toulmin's notion of backing. A properly backed warrant is a necessary condition for a *prima facie* cogent conductive argument....

An inference rule, Freeman explains, is of the form

From: $P_1, P_2,...P_n$.
To infer: C.

"As Hitchcock points out, such warrants are material inference rules, since they involve content expressions...as opposed to the purely formal rules of deductive logic." (2010, p. 4). Since the conclusion of a conductive argument is "'drawn non-conclusively' from the premises ... truth-preservation is too strict a criterion for the ground adequacy of conductive arguments. Indeed, warrants for conductive arguments need to be qualified. We are not licensed to infer simpliciter but only *ceteris paribus*" (p. 5). That is,

From: $P_1, P_2...P_n$.
To infer *ceteris paribus*: C.

"As Toulmin points out, warrants raise the question of backing" (p. 5). For Toulmin, "backing is field dependent" (p. 5), but in (2005b) Freeman argues for "replacing Toulmin's problematic notion of a field with an epistemic systematization of warrants" (p. 5). In (2010) he says that "[a] warrant which is sufficiently backed is reliable, at least *ceteris paribus*" (p. 5). In the case of a conductive argument, ground adequacy is a question of the reliability of the argument's warrant "in transferring acceptability from premises to conclusion" (pp. 30-1). Freeman continues:

> The first issue in assessing the reliability of the warrant is determining its epistemic type. Once that is determined, reliability becomes a question of whether proper backing for that type of warrant is available. If so—and we do not deny that there are plenty of open questions in explicating proper backing comprehensively—the premises of the conductive argument constitute grounds adequate for the conclusion. (p. 31)

Earlier Freeman says that "[i]n an overall evaluation of a convergent argument for logical cogency, the ground adequacy question concerns the sufficiency of the premises found acceptable and relevant to create a presumption for the conclusion" (p. 29). The same must be true, then, of pattern-2 conductive arguments and of pattern-3 conductive arguments with two or more premises, since such arguments are convergent. Thus Freeman must mean that if proper backing is available for the warrant of a conductive argument, the premises of the argument *if found acceptable* "constitute grounds adequate for the conclusion." For a premise to be acceptable, Freeman holds, is for there to be "a presumption for it *from our point of view as critical challengers or evaluators of the argument*" (p. 29, italics added). Thus if the premises of a conductive argument are adequate grounds for the conclusion only

Conductive Arguments and the Toulmin Model: A Case Study 177

if found acceptable, then ground adequacy for conductive arguments is adequacy from the point of view of a critical challenger/evaluator of the argument.

7. Five transitional matters

(a) In the following section, I will present reconstructions of three arguments made by Dickson, and of three arguments made by McLachlin, in their respective s. 1 analyses in *Keegstra* of the constitutionality of Canada's hate law. Two of the Dickson reconstructions will be pattern-3 conductive arguments; the third will be an argument with a pattern-2 conductive subargument. Two of the McLachlin reconstructions will be conductive arguments (one pattern 2, the other pattern 3); the third will not be a conductive argument. For each but one of the conductive arguments, I will construct a warrant for the argument and a backing for the warrant partly with a view to showing how this might be done for (reconstructions) of some (real) conductive arguments made in a context that calls for (as McLachlin puts it in *Keegstra)* the "weighing and balancing" (p. 152) of different considerations. This exercise will also prepare the ground for remarks in section 9 on four related matters: Dickson vs. McLachlin on the seriousness of the hate law's infringement of the *Charter*'s freedom of expression guarantee; intuitive weighings; "outweighing" arguments; Toulmin methodology and the methodology of a s. 1 analysis.

(b) Freeman speaks of assessing the reliability of a warrant. He also says, in connection with some examples he gives of warrants and backings for them, that "one can in each case appeal to the backing should a challenger question whether *employing the warrant is justified*" (2010, p. 11; italics added). One of his examples is of an empirical warrant, and in connection with it he says: "Present someone with observations confirming some physical generalization which satisfy criteria of extent and variety, and one recognizes that *reasoning according to the warrant is justified, at least ceteris paribus*" (pp. 11-12; italics added except for "*ceteris paribus*"). The backings I shall construct below will be ones that I think the judges concerned might have given had they wished to show that reasoning according to the warrants in question is justified, at least *ceteris paribus*.

(c) As noted above, Freeman tells us that the first step in assessing the reliability of a warrant is to determine its epistemic type. He distinguishes "four broad types of warrant corresponding to four distinct epistemic types of intuition: *a priori*, empirical, institutional, and evaluative" (2010, p. 9). Warrants of all but the first of these types "grasp nomic connections, empirical on the basis of observing co-variation, institutional upon coming to understand the constitutive principles of some institution such as a branch of law, evaluative on recognizing how certain evaluative properties supervene upon certain evaluatively relevant (but not in general evaluative) properties" (p. 9). The warrants I shall be constructing will have evaluative conclusions (of different kinds) and so by this measure may be classified as evaluative; but their premises will not all be of any single one of Freeman's epistemic types. Rather, they will be a heterogeneous lot, involving, for example, empirical, institutional, evaluative, and interpretive considerations.

(d) As explained by Freeman, the construction of a warrant (understood as a material inference rule) for a conductive argument requires the replacement of at least one repeated content expression in the argument by a variable. By way of illustration, Freeman provides warrants for three examples of conductive arguments given by Wellman, including these two (2010, p. 7):

(1) Bees have a language because they can communicate information about the location of flowers to one another.

(2) Hunting is a game because it is fun and involves a competition between the hunter and his prey.

Freeman's warrants for these arguments are the following (p. 7):

(W1) From: Members of species X can communicate information about the location of flowers to other members of species X.
To infer *ceteris paribus*: Members of species X have a language.

(W2) From: Activity x is fun (for some participants) and x involves a competition between (certain) participants.
To infer *ceteris paribus*: Activity x is a game.

Later, Freeman considers in turn an example of an empirical, institutional, and evaluative warrant. The empirical and institutional warrants are these (p. 10):

(F1) From: x is a light beam striking a reflecting surface at angle y.
To infer *ceteris paribus*: x is refracted at angle y.

(F2) From: x kicked the soccer ball past the goalie into the opposing team's net.
To infer *ceteris paribus*: x scored a goal.

In (F1) and (F2) each variable replaces a repeated content expression referring to a particular thing (F1) or person (F2). In (W1) and (W2), by contrast, each variable replaces a repeated categorial content expression ('bees,' 'hunting'; not an expression referring to a particular bee or to a particular instance of hunting). Further, the replacement assumes a (more general) classification of the referent of the categorial expression (bees as members of a species, hunting as an activity). The warrants I construct below resemble (W1) and (W2) in these respects, rather than (F1) or (F2). Collectively, they employ two variable content expressions. One is "provision p of the *Criminal Code* of Canada," which I shall abbreviate as "provision p." (Why not a more general expression, such as 'law p'? The reason is that the impugned legislation in *Keegstra* is a *criminal* law, and this is a key consideration in the s. 1 analyses in the decision.) The second variable content expression is "expressive activity x." (Why not the more general expression 'activity x'? The reason is that in *Keegstra* the impugned legislation prohibits certain *expressive* activity, hence activity that, unless it takes a physically violent form, is protected by s. 2(b) of the *Charter*.) Why call it (expressive) *activity*? The reason is that this term is used in the *Irwin Toy* analysis of the term 'expression' in s. 2(b) of the *Charter*, which analysis includes the following point: "Activity is expressive if it attempts to convey meaning" (*Irwin Toy*, p. 45).

(e) Freeman tells us what would count as backing for warrants (F1) and (F2). For (F1) it would be the evidence for the "physical causal law, angle of incidence equals angle of refraction" (2010, p. 10). For (F2) it would be "an authoritative compendium of the rules of soccer" (p. 11), although Freeman also says that "[i]f one has learned the rules through engaging in the practice, one could say that the warrant is self-backed" (p. 10). As these examples indicate, the backing for a warrant will not (or at any rate need not) employ the warrant's variable content expression(s); more generally, it will not (or need not) contain a variable replacing a repeated content expression in the argument instancing the warrant.

8. Dickson and McLachlin: Arguments, warrants and backings

Dickson begins the proportionality part of his s. 1 analysis by considering whether the expression prohibited by the hate law is closely linked to the values underlying the *Charter* guarantee of freedom of expression. In his opinion it is not. One of those values is participation in social and political decision-making. Dickson comments: "The connection between freedom of expression and the political process is perhaps the linchpin of the s. 2(b) guarantee, and the nature of this connection is largely derived from the Canadian commitment to democracy" (*Keegstra*, p. 70).

Dickson reconstruction 1 (DR1): pattern-3 conductive (*Keegstra*, p. 71)

Even though (1) the use of strong language in political and social debate—indeed, perhaps even language intended to promote hatred—is an unavoidable part of the democratic process, and even though (2) hate propaganda is putatively of a category (the "political") that places it at the very heart of the principle extolling freedom of expression as vital to the democratic process, nonetheless (3) hate propaganda works to undermine our commitment to democracy by arguing for a society in which the democratic process is subverted and individuals are denied respect and dignity simply because of racial or religious characteristics. Thus (4) this brand of expressive activity is wholly inimical to the democratic aspirations of the free expression guarantee.

In DR1 counterconsiderations (1) and (2) are conceded, as indicated by the use of the phrase "even though". Accordingly, following Freeman (2010, p. 24), I include them as conjuncts in the premise of the following warrant (and similarly below in WDR2 and WMR2).

A warrant for DR1(WDR1):

> From: The use of strong language in political and social debate—indeed, perhaps even expressive activity x—is an unavoidable part of the democratic process & expressive activity x is putatively of a category (the "political") that places it at the very heart of the principle extolling freedom of expression as vital to the democratic process & expressive activity x works to undermine our commitment to democracy by arguing for a society in which the democratic process is subverted and individuals are denied respect and dignity simply because of racial and religious characteristics.
> To infer *ceteris paribus*: Expressive activity x is wholly inimical to the democratic aspirations of the free expression guarantee.

A backing for WDR1:

> If an expressive activity argues for a society in which the democratic process is subverted and individuals are denied respect and dignity simply because of racial and religious characteristics, then, *ceteris paribus*, the activity is wholly inimical to the democratic aspirations of the free expression guarantee of the *Charter*, because the Canadian commitment to democracy is in part a commitment to ensuring that "participation in the political process is open to all persons," and "[s]uch open participation must involve to a substantial degree the notion that all persons are equally deserving of respect and dignity" (Dickson in *Keegstra*, pp. 70-1). Further, even if the expressive activity concerned is an unavoidable part of the democratic process and is putatively of a category (the "political") that places it at the very heart of the principle extolling freedom of expression as vital to the democratic process, this does not prevent other things from being equal if the activity does not further democratic principles/values or is not supportive of democ-

racy itself, as is the case if it argues for a society in which the democratic process is subverted and individuals are denied respect and dignity simply because of racial and religious characteristics.

Dickson reconstruction 2 (DR2): pattern-3 conductive (Keegstra, pp. 69-71, 93)

Dickson argues that the expressive activity at which the hate law aims is of a category "only tenuously connected with the values underlying the guarantee of freedom of speech" (*Keegstra*, p. 93). The following is a pattern-3 conductive reconstruction of (elements of) his argument. It includes a counterconsideration from DR1 and, as a premise, DR1's conclusion.

(1) S. 319(2) of the *Criminal Code* of Canada prohibits the willful promotion of hatred, other than in private conversation, towards any section of the public distinguished by col'r, race, religion or ethnic origin. (2) The values underlying the *Charter*'s free expression guarantee are: the attainment of truth and the common good; individual self-fulfilment and human flourishing; participation in social and political decision-making. It is true that (3) freedom of expression is necessary to ensure that truth and the common good are attained, whether in scientific and artistic endeavors or in the process of determining the best course to take in our political affairs, but (4) there is very little chance that statements intended to promote hatred against an identifiable group are true, or that their vision of society will lead to a better world. It is also true that (5) the public purveying of hate propaganda contributes to the purveyors' ability to gain self-fulfillment by developing and articulating thoughts and ideas as they see fit, but (6) their message represents a most extreme opposition to the idea that members of identifiable groups should enjoy the self-fulfillment aspect of the free expression guarantee. (7) Hate propaganda is putatively of a category (the "political") that places it at the very heart of the principle extolling freedom of expression as vital to the democratic process, but (8) this brand of expressive activity is wholly inimical to the democratic aspirations of the free expression guarantee. Thus, (9) the expressive activity at which s. 319(2) aims is of a category only tenuously connected with the values underlying the *Charter*'s guarantee of freedom of expression.

A warrant for DR2 (WDR2):

From: Provision p of the *Criminal Code* of Canada (hereafter "provision p") prohibits expressive activity x, other than in private conversation, directed towards any section of the public distinguished by color, race, religion or ethnic origin & the values underlying the *Charter*'s free expression guarantee are: the attainment of truth and the common good; individual self-fulfilment and human flourishing; participation in social and political decision-making; & freedom of expression is necessary to ensure that truth and the common good are attained, whether in scientific and artistic endeavors or in the process of determining the best course to take in our political affairs & there is very little chance that statements communicated in expressive activity x are true, or that their vision of society will lead to a better world; & publicly engaging in expressive activity x contributes to the agents' ability to gain self-fulfillment by developing and articulating thoughts and ideas as they see fit & their message represents a most extreme opposition to the idea that members of identifiable groups should enjoy the self-fulfillment aspect of the free expression guarantee; & expressive activity x is putatively of a category (the "political") that places it at the very heart of the principle extolling freedom of expression as vital to the democratic process & expressive activity x is wholly inimical to the democratic aspirations of the free expression guarantee.

To infer *ceteris paribus*: The expressive activity at which provision *p* aims is of a category only tenuously connected with the values underlying the *Charter*'s guarantee of freedom of speech.

A backing for WDR2:

It is self-evident that, *ceteris paribus*, there is at best a very weak connection between an expressive activity prohibited by the *Criminal Code* of Canada and the free expression values of (i) the attainment of truth and the common good and (ii) individual self-fulfillment and human flourishing if there is very little chance that the activity furthers the attainment of truth and the common good and is antithetical to the idea that members of identifiable groups should attain self-fulfillment, even if freedom of expression is necessary for the attainment of truth and the common good and even if publicly engaging in the prohibited expressive activity contributes to the agents' ability to gain self-fulfillment by developing and articulating thoughts and ideas as they see fit. Further, even if the activity is putatively "political" and thus at the very heart of the principle extolling freedom of expression as vital to the democratic process, if it is wholly inimical to the democratic aspirations of the *Charter*'s free expression guarantee, then the connection between it and the free expression value of (iii) participation in social and political decision-making is, in the Canadian context, weak at best, given that in Canada participation in social and political decision-making is intended to be a democratic process open to all persons. Given these considerations, it is reasonable to infer, *ceteris paribus*, that the prohibited activity is of a category only tenuously connected with the values underlying the *Charter*'s free expression guarantee (viz., values (i)-(iii) above).

Dickson reconstruction 3 (DR3) (*Keegstra*, pp. 93-4)

The final stage of Dickson's s. 1 analysis is an argument in which he weighs the cost of the hate law (its infringement of the *Charter* guarantee of free expression) against the importance of its objective. The following is a reconstruction of his argument. It includes as a premise the conclusion of DR2.

(1) The expressive activity at which s. 319(2) of the *Criminal Code* aims is of a category only tenuously connected with the values underlying the *Charter*'s guarantee of freedom of speech.

Moreover,

(2) the narrowly drawn terms of s. 319(2) and its defenses prevent the prohibition of expression lying outside this narrow category.

Consequently,

(3) the suppression of hate propaganda effected by s. 319(2) represents an impairment of the individual's freedom of expression which is not of a most serious nature.

On the other side of the scale,

(4) the objective fueling s. 319(2) is of enormous importance and of such magnitude as to support even the severe response of criminal prohibition.

I conclude that

(5) the effects of s. 319(2) are not of such a deleterious nature as to outweigh any advantage gleaned from the limitation of the guarantee of freedom of speech.

The subargument for (3) from (1) and (2) is pattern-2 conductive.

A warrant for the subargument in DR3 (WSubDR3):

> From: The expressive activity at which provision p aims is of a category only tenuously connected with the values underlying the *Charter*'s guarantee of freedom of speech & the narrowly drawn terms of provision p and its defenses prevent the prohibition of expression lying outside this narrow category.
>
> To infer *ceteris paribus*: The suppression of expressive activity effected by provision p represents an impairment of the individual's freedom of expression which is not of a most serious nature.

A backing for WSubDR3

> For the suppression of expressive activity prohibited by the *Criminal Code* of Canada to represent an impairment of the individual's freedom of expression that *was* of a most serious nature it would be sufficient for the following conditions to be satisfied: (1) The suppressed activity is strongly connected to the freedom of expression values: it is useful for the attainment of truth and the common good; it is conducive to individual self-fulfillment (and not antithetical to the self-fulfillment of the members of any identifiable group), and it plays a constructive role in social and political decision-making in a democratic society. (2) The terms of the prohibiting provision of the *Criminal Code* are broadly drawn and the provision contains no defenses against a charge laid under it, and these facts create a substantial risk that it will catch expression that ought not to be prohibited.
>
> Neither of these conditions is satisfied if (i) the suppressed activity is of a category only tenuously connected with the values underlying the *Charter*'s guarantee of freedom of speech, and (ii) the prohibiting provision's terms and defenses are such as to prevent the prohibition of expression lying outside the category covered by its terms. Consequently, if conditions (i) and (ii) are satisfied it is reasonable to infer, *ceteris paribus*, that the suppression of the prohibited activity represents an infringement of the individual's freedom of expression which is not of a most serious nature.
>
> Next, McLachlin. The final part of her s. 1 analysis is titled "Importance of the Right versus Benefit Conferred". Here, she says, "[t]he analysis is essentially a cost-benefit analysis" (*Keegstra*, p. 170):

> On the one hand, how significant is the infringement of the fundamental right or freedom in question? On the other hand, how significant is the benefit conferred by the impugned legislation? Weighing these countervailing considerations, has the state met the burden upon it of establishing that the limit on the constitutionally guaranteed freedom or right is reasonable and demonstrably justified in a free and democratic society? (p. 170)

McLachlin's *Keegstra* reasoning on these questions includes a "cost" argument and a "benefit" argument, the (main) conclusions of which can interpreted as premises of what I shall call her "synthesis cost-benefit argument." I begin with a reconstruction of her "cost" argument.

McLachin reconstruction 1 (MR1): "cost" argument (*Keegstra*, p. 171)

From the perspective of Canadian society as a whole:

> (1) S. 319(2) does not merely regulate the form or tone of expression – it strikes at its content and at the viewpoints of individuals.

(2) It strikes at viewpoints in widely diverse domains, whether artistic, social or political.
(3) It is capable of catching works of art and the intemperate statement made in the heat of social controversy.
(4) Many individuals fall within the shadow of its broad prohibition.
(5) It applies to all public expression.

Thus[1],

(6) the limitation on freedom of expression created by s. 319(2) invokes all of the values upon which s. 2(b) of the *Charter* rests – the value of fostering a vibrant and creative society through the marketplace of ideas; the value of the vigorous and open debate essential to democratic government and preservation of our rights and freedoms; and the value of a society which fosters the self-actualization and freedom of its members.

From the viewpoint of the individual caught within the net of s. 319(2):

(7) The exercise of the right of free speech contrary to the provisions of s. 319(2) may result in a criminal record and imprisonment of up to two years.
(8) No warning, other than the description in s. 319(2) itself (which necessarily includes subjective elements) is given as to what speech is liable to result in prosecution.
(9) Those individuals not caught within the net of s. 319(2) may find their expression restricted by the fear of running afoul of a vague and subjective law.

These considerations establish that

(10) The infringement of the guarantee of freedom of expression effected by s. 319(2) is of the most serious nature.

This is a pattern-2 conductive argument (for 10 from 6-9) with a pattern-2 conductive subargument (for 6 from 1-5). I shall not provide a warrant for it (or for its subargument).

McLachlin reconstruction 2 (MR2): "benefit" argument (pattern-3 conductive) (Keegstra, p. 172)

(11) There is no question but that the objectives which underlie this legislation are of a most worthy nature.

But

(12) it is far from clear that the legislation does not promote the cause of hate-mongering extremists and hinder the possibility of voluntary amendment of conduct more than it discourages the spread of hate propaganda.

Therefore,

(13) the claims of gains to be achieved at the cost of the infringement of free speech represented by s. 319(2) are tenuous.

A warrant for MR2 (WMR2):

From: The objectives which underlie provision p (which prohibits certain expressive activity) are of a most worthy nature & it is far from clear that provision p does not promote the cause of extremists purveying the messages it prohibits and hinder the possibility of voluntary amendment of conduct more than it discourages the spread of the messages it prohibits.

To infer *ceteris paribus*: The claims of gains to be achieved at the cost of the infringement of free speech represented by provision p are tenuous.

---

[1] "Thus" here replaces the phrase "[i]n short," which McLachlin uses to introduce (6).

WMR2 is self-backing. Should this not be immediately evident, it can perhaps be made evident as follows. If it is far from clear that a provision of the *Criminal Code* of Canada that prohibits a certain expressive activity does not promote the cause of extremists purveying messages of the kind that the provision prohibits and hinder the possibility of voluntary amendment of conduct more than it discourages the spread of such messages, then it is far from clear that the provision is not self-defeating, in which case, even if its objectives are of a most worthy nature, it is reasonable to infer, *ceteris paribus*, that the claims of gains to be achieved at the cost of the infringement of free speech represented by the provision are tenuous.

McLachlin reconstruction 3 (MR3): "synthesis cost-benefit" argument
- (10) The infringement of the guarantee of freedom of expression effected by s. 319(2) is of the most serious nature.
- (13) The claims of gains to be achieved at the cost of the infringement of free speech represented by s. 319(2) are tenuous.

Therefore,
- (14) any questionable benefit of the legislation is outweighed by the significant infringement on the constitutional guarantee of free expression effected by s. 319(2) of the *Criminal Code*.

This argument is linked, hence not conductive.

9. Four related matters

9.1 Dickson vs. McLachlin on the seriousness of the hate law's infringement of the Charter's freedom of espression guarantee (subDR3 & MR1)

Dickson and McLachlin disagree as to whether the hate law's infringement of the *Charter*'s guarantee of freedom of expression is "of the most serious nature." The subargument in DR3 reconstructs Dickson's argument on the point; MR1 reconstructs McLachlin's argument (her "cost" argument). The conclusion of the subargument in MR1 says in part:

(MR1:6) The limitation on freedom of expression created by s. 319(2) invokes all of the values upon which s. 2(b) of the *Charter* rests ... [The balance of (MR1:6) lists those values.]

Premise 1 of the subargument in DR 3 says:

(DR3:1) The expressive activity at which s. 319(2) of the *Criminal Code* aims is of a category only tenuously connected with the values underlying the *Charter*'s guarantee of freedom of speech.

(MR1:6) and (DR3:1) are mutually consistent. (MR1:6) is a claim about the hate law—more specifically, about the limitation it creates on freedom of expression; (DR3:1) is a claim not about the hate law but about the expressive activity at which the hate law aims. Thus neither claim challenges the other. But McLachlin would consider (MR1:6) to be a counterconsideration to the conclusion of the subargument in DR3:

(DR3:3) The suppression of hate propaganda effected by s. 319(2) represents an impairment of the individual's freedom of expression which is not of a most serious nature.

and Dickson would consider (DR3:1) to be a counterconsideration to the (main) conclusion of MR1:

(MR1:10) The infringement of the guarantee of freedom of expression effected by s. 319(2) is of the most serious nature.

Further, he would claim that (DR3:1) and

(DR3:2) The narrowly drawn terms of s. 319(2) and its defenses prevent the prohibition of expression lying outside this narrow category

(jointly) outweigh the premises of MR1. McLachlin, for her part, would claim that the premises of MR1 outweigh (DR3:1).

What would she say about (DR3:2)? Would she say that it is false or that it is outweighed by other considerations? According to (DR3:2), the terms of s. 319(2) are "narrowly drawn." One of its terms is 'hatred.' According to Dickson, this word must be defined "according to the context in which it is found" (*Keegstra*, p. 83)—that is, in the context of s. 319(2) itself. McLachlin, by contrast, reports that the *Shorter Oxford English Dictionary* defines 'hatred' as "[t]he condition or state of relations in which one person hates another; the emotion of hate; active dislike, detestation; enmity, ill-will, malevolence" (*Keegstra*, p. 163), and she remarks that "[t]he wide range of diverse emotions which the word 'hatred' is capable of denoting is evident from this definition" (p. 163). Dickson (who has read McLachlin's opinion) rejoins by saying that "[a] dictionary definition may be of limited aid [in defining 'hatred' as used in s. 319(2)], for by its nature a dictionary seeks to offer a panoply of possible usages, rather than *the correct meaning of a word as contemplated by Parliament*" (p. 84, italics added). He continues: "Noting the purpose of s. 319(2), in my opinion the term 'hatred' connotes emotion of an intense and extreme nature that is clearly associated with vilification and detestation" (p. 84). McLachlin need not disagree that this is the meaning of the word as contemplated by Parliament. But she would say that this may not be how the word is interpreted by the authorities (e.g., customs officers faced with deciding whether a work of fiction is hate literature) or by political activists or writers, who may agree with her that "'hatred' is a broad term capable of catching a wide range of emotion" and curb their speech accordingly for "fear of running afoul" (p. 171) of the hate law. McLachlin has a further worry: "'Hatred' is proved by inference—the inference of the jury or the judge who sits as trier of fact—and inferences are most likely to be drawn when the speech is unpopular" (p. 164). The gist of (DR3:2) is that the terms and defenses of the hate law are such as to "prevent the prohibition of expression lying outside" the narrow category covered by its terms. McLachlin, on the other hand, says that "many fall within the shadow of its broad prohibition" (MR1:4). She does not find its prohibition to be "narrow," and so she would say that (DR3:2) is false. Yet she admits that "few may actually be prosecuted to conviction" (p. 171) under the hate law. And so she might entertain a two-prong strategy: first argue that (DR3:2) is false, then argue that even if it is true, it is outweighed by other considerations. These would include the concern that "the chilling effect of the law may be substantial" (p. 167) and the worry that hatred may be inferred "when the speech is unpopular" (p. 164). I said above that McLachlin would claim that the premises of MR1 outweigh (DR3:1). Here I would add that the second prong of the envisaged strategy would enable her to argue that the premises of the subargument of DR3 are (jointly) outweighed by other considerations, among them the premises of MR1.

What might she say about the above warrant for the subargument of DR3 and the backing for it? About the warrant she might say that other things are not equal if the limitation on freedom of expression effected by provision p invokes all of the values underlying the *Charter*'s guarantee of freedom of expression. As to the proffered backing, she might say that an alternative set of conditions under which the suppression of expressive activity prohibited by the *Criminal Code* of Canada would represent an impairment of the individual's freedom of expression that was of a most serious nature would be the following: (a) the prohibition invokes all of the values underlying the *Charter*'s guarantee of freedom of expression; (b) it is vague and subjective, and so (c) individuals not caught within its net may find their expression restricted by the fear of running afoul of it. She might continue: If the suppressed activity is of a category only tenuously connected with the values underlying the *Charter*'s guarantee of freedom of speech, this consideration is outweighed by condition (a), if (a) is satisfied. And if conditions (b) and (c) are satisfied, then it is not the case that the prohibiting provision's terms and defenses are such as to prevent the prohibition of expression lying outside the category covered by its terms.

9.2 Intuitive weighings

The subargument of DR3 offers two (independent) reasons in support of the claim that the suppression of hate propaganda effected by s. 319(2) represents an impairment of the individual's freedom of expression which is not of a most serious nature. The backing for the subargument's warrant states two conditions under which the suppression of expressive activity prohibited by the *Criminal Code* of Canada would represent an impairment of the individual's freedom of expression that *was* of a most serious nature, and the comment on that backing which I have just said McLachlin might make states a set of alternative conditions under which (she might say) this would be the case. In the first of these contexts (the subargument of DR3), the reasons given are thought to be of sufficient weight to establish that the freedom-of-expression impairment is not of a most serious nature, while in each of the other two contexts (the backing for WsubDR3 and the comment on that backing) it is thought that were certain indicated conditions satisfied, this would be a consideration of sufficient weight to establish the opposite in respect of the suppression of expressive activity prohibited by the *Criminal Code* of Canada.[2]

Each of these three weightings is intuitive. I note this because at the heart of Freeman (2010) are the questions "Can we go beyond an intuitive weighing of positive and negative considerations and can the Toulmin model give us a way to make this advance?" (p. 12). Freeman thinks we can and that it does. We will advance our understanding of weight for conductive arguments by advancing, with the aid of the Toulmin model, our understanding of ground adequacy for such arguments. As we know, Freeman holds that ground adequacy for conductive arguments is a question of the reliability of their warrants and that their reliability is a question of whether proper backing for them is available. But does this procedure necessarily take us beyond an intuitive weighing of positive and negative considerations? The DR3 contexts just described, though they instance only positive considerations, would seem to show that it does not. I say "would seem to show" because one can perhaps

---

[2] The subargument of DR3 is pattern-2 conductive. Wellman thinks that "the model of weighing" fits pattern-1 and pattern-2 conductive arguments "less well" than it fits the pattern-3 variety. "Although one can think of one or several reasons as giving weight to or weighing for a conclusion, to do so seems to clarify very little" (1971, p. 59). For my present purposes, the point Wellman makes in his "although" clause is sufficient.

imagine an expansion of the backing for WsubDR3 (and similarly for the envisaged comment) that would offer support for the claim that were the conditions stated in the backing satisfied, this would be a consideration of sufficient weight, etc. And perhaps one can imagine a further expansion offering support for the claim that the reasons given in the first expansion are of sufficient weight, etc. But at some point the expansions, and so the argument, must stop, on pain of infinite regress. At that point (if not earlier) the sufficiency of the weighting concerned must be grasped intuitively (or not at all).

I think Freeman would not deny this. In (2005b) he notes Toulmin's point that to avoid an infinite regress "'[s]ome warrants must be accepted provisionally without further challenge,' taking for granted 'the existence of considerations such as would establish the acceptability of the most reliable warrants'" (Freeman 2005b, p. 334). As Freeman observes, this claim "raises some significant epistemological questions. Do we simply provisionally accept certain warrants or are some warrants accept*able* in a basic way, analogous to acceptable basic premises? If the acceptable warrants are those most reliable, how do we recognize these warrants?" (p. 334). In Freeman's view, corresponding to each of the four types of warrants he distinguishes "is a distinct type or mode of intuition" (p. 337), for which "we may identify conditions under which it grasps warrants in a presumptively reliable way, certifying these warrants as presumptively reliable" (p. 337). He adds that "in certain cases, although intuition may grasp a suggested connection, one may also recognize that this intuitive grasping is not in itself sufficient to presume the reliability of the warrant and thus defense or argumentation for the warrant is required" (p. 337). Consider WsubDR3:

> From: The expressive activity at which provision *p* aims is of a category only tenuously connected with the values underlying the *Charter*'s guarantee of freedom of speech & the narrowly drawn terms of provision *p* and its defenses prevent the prohibition of expression lying outside this narrow category.
> To infer *ceteris paribus*: The suppression of expressive activity effected by provision *p* represents an impairment of the individual's freedom of expression which is not of a most serious nature.

Do we grasp this warrant intuitively "in a presumptively reliable way," with the result that it is certified as presumptively reliable? If so, then backing for it is not needed. We see intuitively, and in a presumptively reliable way, that the considerations (conjuncts) in the premise are of sufficient weight it make it reasonable to infer the conclusion *ceteris paribus*. Or is this a case in which intuition grasps the suggested connection but defense or argumentation for the warrant is nevertheless required? If so, such defense or argumentation (or an expansion of it) might itself depend on an intuitive grasping; indeed, this seems likely given that the issue is whether the premise considerations are of sufficient weight to make it reasonable to infer, *ceteris paribus*, the evaluative claim that a certain infringement of an individual's freedom of expression effected by a provision of the *Criminal Code* of Canada "is not of a most serious nature."

9.3 "Outweighing" arguments

Govier writes:

> [C]onductive argumentation is a favored context for 'pros' and 'cons' in arguing. We may allow that there are factors relevant to the conclusion that count against it, mention these in the argument, and then cite supportive factors for the conclusion.

We judge, and ask our audience to judge, that the supportive factors outweigh the counterconsiderations. (1987a, p. 68)

Such an argument is of the form (F1) "C even though $(N_1, N_2....N_n,)$ because $(P_1, P_2...P_n)$." From this argument form we may distinguish the argument form (F2): "$(P_1, P_2...P_n)$ therefore consideration (factor) X outweighs (is outweighed by) consideration (factor) Y." An instance of (F2) is MR3:

(10) The infringement of the guarantee of freedom of expression effected by s. 319(2) is of the most serious nature.
(13) The claims of gains to be achieved at the cost of the infringement of free speech represented by s. 319(2) are tenuous.
Therefore,
(14) any questionable benefit of the legislation is outweighed by the significant infringement on the constitutional guarantee of free expression effected by s. 319(2) of the *Criminal Code*.

(F1) and (F2) are both forms of "outweighing" arguments. There is this difference: in an (F2) argument an "outweighing" claim is explicitly made and supported, whereas in an (F1) argument there is no explicit "outweighing" claim, though such a claim is implicit and is signaled by the fact that the conclusion is drawn from the premises despite the counterconsiderations.

An (F1) argument is pattern-3 conductive. An (F2) argument need not be conductive—MR3 is a case in point. Thus an "outweighing" argument need not be conductive; *a fortiori*, it need not be pattern-3 conductive. Wellman would not disagree: he says that "weighing of the evidence does not occur only in conductive reasoning" (1971, p. 58). Nor need Govier disagree: her claim that "conductive argumentation is a favored context for 'pros' and 'cons' in arguing" (1987a, p. 68) does not commit her to denying that "outweighing" arguments can be made in other contexts.

9.4 Toulmin methodology and the methodology of a s. 1 analysis

In (2010) Freeman proposes a methodology for evaluating ground adequacy for a conductive argument: determine whether proper backing is available for the argument's properly framed warrant, having first determined the warrant's epistemic type. I shall call this a Toulmin methodology. (It is not quite *Toulmin's* methodology because for Toulmin "backing is field dependent," and Freeman replaces "Toulmin's problematic notion of a field with an epistemic systematization of warrants" (2010, p. 5).) Here I have provided warrants and backings for reconstructions of several conductive arguments made in a Supreme Court of Canada case involving the Canadian *Charter of Rights and Freedoms*. It is obvious that each proffered backing is open to assessment in respect, for example, of the weight it attaches to considerations bearing on whether, *ceteris paribus*, it is reasonable to infer the warrant's conclusion from the warrant's premise, and in respect of the truth or falsity of such factual assertions as it may contain. (The comment that I said McLachlin might make on the proffered backing for WsubDR3 demonstrates the possibility of such assessments.) There is no reason to doubt, then, that the ground adequacy of the reconstructed arguments can be assessed according to Freeman's Toulmin methodology. This is not a surprising finding—why would it be otherwise? On the other hand, however, there is a striking difference between a Toulmin methodology and the methodology that the Supreme Court of Canada has developed for conducting a s. 1 analysis in a *Charter* case. A Toulmin methodology requires the construction of a warrant and a backing for it, and this involves abstracting from one or more particularities of the argument concerned (by generalizing over at least one repeated content expression in the argument). By contrast, the methodology of a s. 1 analysis requires judges to remain rooted in the particularities of the case at hand. Whether or not a *Charter* right or freedom prevails over the countervailing objective(s) of a law that limits it will depend on the facts of the case—on the interests and values at stake therein. In *Keegstra* McLachlin gives a clear account of the matter:

> The task which judges are required to perform under s.1 is essentially one of balancing [a violation or limitation of a fundamental right or freedom against the importance of a conflicting legislative objective].... This exercise is one of great difficulty, requiring the judge to make value judgments. In this task, logic and precedent are but of limited assistance. What must be determinative in the end is the court's judgment, based on an understanding of the values our society is built on and *the interests at stake in the particular case*.... [T]his judgment cannot be made in the abstract. Rather than speak of values as though they were Platonic ideals, *the judge must situate the analysis in the facts of the particular case, weighing the different values represented in that context*. Thus it cannot be said that freedom of expression will always prevail over the objective of individual dignity and social harmony, or vice versa. The result in a particular case will depend on weighing the significance of the infringement on freedom of expression *represented by the law in question*, against the importance of the countervailing objectives, the likelihood *the law [in question]* will achieve those objectives, and the proportionality of the scope of *the law [in question]* to those objectives (pp. 152-3; italics added).

The methodology of a s. 1 analysis would not lead Dickson or McLachlin, in an assessment of the ground adequacy of one another's conductive arguments, to frame generalizing warrants for the arguments and consider whether proper backing for them is available. Rather it would (and does) lead each of them to ask such questions as whether the other's approach to interpreting the terms of the hate law is a reasonable one and whether the other has established that the hate law does, or does not, invoke all of the values underlying the *Charter*'s freedom of expression guarantee.

In the abstract for (2010) Freeman says that "[a] properly backed warrant is a necessary condition for a *prima facie* cogent conductive argument." Pretty clearly, it doesn't follow that forming a reasoned judgment as to whether the premises of a particular conductive argument constitute, at least *prima facie*, grounds adequate for the conclusion requires constructing a warrant for the argument and deciding whether a proper backing for it is available. (I here assume that the ground adequacy question concerns what Freeman says it concerns: "the sufficiency of the premises found acceptable and relevant to create a presumption for the conclusion" (2010, p. 29).) Recall our discussion of what McLachlin would say about the (pattern-2 conductive) subargument in DR3,

(1) The expressive activity at which s. 319(2) of the *Criminal Code* aims is of a category only tenuously connected with the values underlying the *Charter*'s guarantee of freedom of speech.
Moreover,
(2) the narrowly drawn terms of s. 319(2) and its defences prevent the prohibition of expression lying outside this narrow category.
Consequently,

(3) the suppression of hate propaganda effected by s. 319(2) represents an impairment of the individual's freedom of expression which is not of a most serious nature.

She would say that premise (1) is outweighed by other considerations (namely the premises of MR1, the reconstruction of her "cost" argument) and that premise (2) is false, hence unacceptable (from her point of view), and that even if it were true it would be outweighed by other considerations. She would conclude (I now add) that the premises are not adequate grounds for the conclusion. This would be a reasoned judgment on her part, but she would not have arrived at it by framing a warrant for the argument and deciding that proper backing for it is not available.

Similarly, a reasoned judgment may be made that, *prima facie,* the premises of a particular conductive argument *are* adequate grounds for the conclusion: they are found to be acceptable and relevant and to outweigh a set of counterconsiderations. The evaluator therefore concludes that the argument is *prima facie* cogent. *Ex hypothesi*, this judgment is arrived at without the Toulmin apparatus, but it may nevertheless be the case that the judgment is not correct unless a properly backed warrant for the argument is available. However, an evaluator of conductive arguments who assessed them otherwise than by means of the Toulmin apparatus but held that a conductive argument is *prima facie* cogent only if a properly backed warrant for it is available would be guilty of a pragmatic inconsistency: her *de facto* criteria for assessing a conductive argument would not include a criterion which she holds must be satisfied if the argument is to be *prima facie* cogent. But a judge on the Supreme Court of Canada who subscribes to and practises the Court's methodology for a s. 1 analysis will not find herself in this position, for she will not hold that a conductive argument is *prima facie* cogent only if a properly backed warrant for it is available; or rather, to be more precise, it will not be the case that she holds (*ex officio*) that a conductive argument made in a s.1 analysis (by herself or another judge) is *prima facie* cogent only on this condition. In the case of an external evaluator of a conductive argument made by a judge in a s. 1 analysis (that is, an evaluator who is not a judge on the Supreme Court of Canada—an academic, for example) the situation will be different; he should (if Freeman is correct) take the view that a conductive argument made in any context (including that of a s. 1 analysis) is *prima facie* cogent only if a properly backed warrant for it is available.

Chapter 13

Conductive Arguments in Ethical Deliberation

DOUGLAS WALTON

1. Introduction

The term 'conductive reasoning' is not used much in current work in argumentation studies, and it is not easy to see at first how it is different from case-based defeasible reasoning. One difference is that the "even-if" characteristic of conductive reasoning takes into account the arguments on both sides of a disputed issue, the pro and the contra. Another is that conductive reasoning, on Wellman's definition, is drawn without appeal to other cases, thereby excluding analogical reasoning. In this paper, argumentation tools are applied to one of Wellman's examples of conductive reasoning. Argument mapping tools are devices used to visualize the premises and conclusions of arguments in a tree structure, and display a sequence of connected arguments chained together to support an ultimate conclusion. More than forty such tools are described by Scheuer et al. (2009). Any of them could be used, but in this paper we use diagrams made up of leaves (text boxes) that represent statements that act as premises and conclusions of arguments, and nodes that represent arguments. This way of visualizing arguments inserts information about the argument, including its argumentation scheme, in the node, following the Carneades model of argumentation (Gordon and Walton, 2009).

The study of argumentation schemes, or forms of argument that capture stereotypical patterns of human reasoning, has also been a main working tool of argumentation research (Walton and Krabbe 1995; Walton 1996). Argumentation schemes have been put forward as a helpful way of characterizing structures of human reasoning that have proved troublesome to view deductively. Appealing to an authority during an argument, for example, may be reasonable, if expressed and supported properly, or may be fallacious. A systematic analysis of many common schemes, and a compendium of 68 schemes, are given in (Walton, Reed and Macagno 2008). In this paper, the schemes for practical reasoning and argument from positive and negative values will be shown to be helpful for learning about conductive argumentation.

Wellman defines conductive reasoning as meeting four requirements (1971, p. 52). First it is about a conclusion in some individual case. Second it is drawn inconclusively. Third it is drawn from one or more premises about the same case. And fourth, it is drawn without appeal to other cases. He tells us as well that the most striking feature of all the examples of conductive reasoning he has given is that they all deal with particular cases. He adds that all the examples of conductive reasoning he has given have been ethical arguments that conclude to an ethical statement about a particular case from factual premises (1971, pp. 53-54). In addition he tells us that there are three patterns of conductive reasoning. The first is one where a single reason is given for the conclusion, like "You ought to help him for he has been very kind to you" (1971, p. 55). In the second type, several reasons are given to support the conclusion, for example "You ought to take your son to the movie because you promised, and you have nothing better to do this afternoon" (1971, p. 56). In the third type, the conclusion is drawn from both positive and negative considerations. The example he gives here is this one: "Although your lawn needs cutting, you ought to take your son to the movies because the picture is ideal for children and will be gone by tomorrow" (1971, p. 57). The third type brings out the nature of conductive reasoning most revealingly, because it has the pro-contra feature. In this paper, we will work on an example of this sort as our case study.

2. The Professor example

This paper started out to try to deal with several of Wellman's examples of conductive argument, but in the end dealt only with one. It is a bit frustrating reading the part of Wellman's book *Challenge and Response* (1971, pp. 51-83) on conductive reasoning that he gives only brief examples like those above. These brief example have their place, but it would have been more helpful if he could have given some case studies, some longer examples showing how conductive reasoning works and how it should be dealt with. Generally, ethical philosophers, and analytical philosophers of that time did not believe in case studies or detailed treatment of examples, as casuistry was highly unfashionable. However, Wellman actually did give us some examples of this sort in his later textbook *Morals and Ethics* (1975). In this book he examines arguments on both sides of ethical disputes that were highly controversial at the time, including civil disobedience, premarital sex, and capital punishment. It is through his handling of these ethical problems what we see better what conductive reasoning is all about, in my opinion.

On the other hand, trying to deal with an extensive example of this sort, with many pro and contra arguments that need to be taken into account, is too much of a lengthy exercise for this short paper to tackle. However, Wellman did give one mid-size example, short but not a one-liner, that is more useful for this purpose. The mid-size example that Wellman gave in *Morals and Ethics* is quoted below (Wellman 1975, p. 308). We will call it the Professor example.

> Suppose, for example, that a professor is trying to decide whether to cheat on his income tax. Although his regular salary is reported to the Internal Revenue Service, he also has a modest amount of unreported income from giving lectures and acting as a consultant. It would be easy enough to refrain from listing this marginal income and pay a tax on the regular salary only. How does the professor know whether it would be right for him to cheat on his income tax? He must weigh the reasons for cheating against the reasons for not cheating. He really needs the money he would pay in extra taxes in order to keep up his payments on his large mortgage; it is unlikely that he would be detected and punished for his act; and he really does believe that the military spending for which much of his tax money would be used is wrong. On the other hand, if he were detected, the result would be disgrace and punishment; he does receive many benefits from his government, benefits made possible by the taxes of the general public; and he strongly approves of many welfare programs that are supported by tax funds.

This example has some pro and contra arguments on both sides of an issue that has the format of an ethical deliberation. A professor is trying to decide whether to report some income on his tax return. If he fails to report it, that would be "cheating" in Wellman's terms, and if he does report it, that would be not cheating. Hence the framework of the deliberation can be determined by specifying three factors.

> Participants: There is just a single agent, a professor who is considering the argument on both sides by reasoning with himself.
> Choice to Make: The professor is trying to decide whether to cheat on his income tax.

Conductive Arguments in Ethical Deliberation

Circumstances: Although his regular salary is reported to the Internal Revenue Service, he also has a modest amount of unreported income from giving lectures and acting as a consultant. It would be easy enough to refrain from listing this marginal income and pay a tax on the regular salary only.

The professor considers several arguments, stated by Wellman, but we are not told anything about how strong the arguments are, or what the professor's values are that might play a role in determining how he should make the decision. Also, we are not told about any further arguments that might be used to justify or attack any of these given arguments. As the deliberation framework states, there are two conclusions, "The professor should cheat" and "The professor should not cheat." Let us say that the pro arguments are for cheating and the contra arguments are for not cheating. Let us start by making a key list of these explicit premises on each side.

Key List of Explicit Premises for Pro Argumentation:
   P1. He really needs the money he would pay in extra taxes in order to keep up his payments on his large mortgage.
   P2. It is unlikely that he would be detected and punished for his act.
   P3. He really does believe that the military spending for which much of his tax money would be used is wrong.

Key List of Explicit Premises for Con Argumentation"
   C1. If he were detected, the result would be disgrace and punishment.
   C2. He does receive many benefits from his government, made possible by the taxes of the general public.
   C3. He strongly approves of many welfare programs that are supported by tax funds.

In Figure 1, it is shown that the arguments can be divided into two sides, the pro arguments on the left and the con arguments on the right. The node in the middle, labeled "cheating," represents the statement that it is right for the professor to cheat on his income tax. Pro arguments are indicated by a closed (darkened) arrowhead, while contra arguments are indicated by an open arrowhead.

To take the first steps toward structuring this argumentation a bit better, let us see how we could represent it with an argument map that brings out its conductive aspect by showing how the arguments on one side are weighed against the arguments on the other side. Figure 1 seems to represent conductive argumentation in an intuitive way. The three arguments on the left side are counterbalanced by the three on the right side.

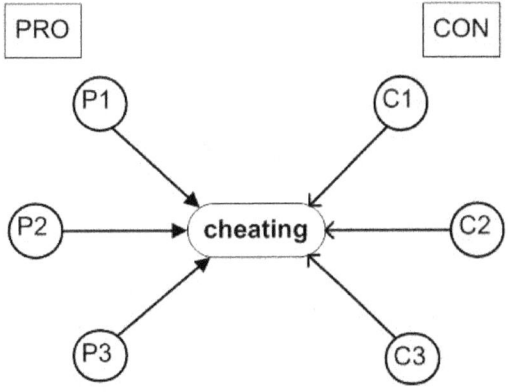

Figure 1. First representation of the Cheating example

This map is not quite right, however. One rebuttal of another argument is involved. P2 rebuts C1, rather than supporting "cheating" directly. By undercutting C1, P2, indirectly provides support for "cheating." To insert this chain argument, and better represent the argumentation in the case, we can picture it as shown in Figure 2.

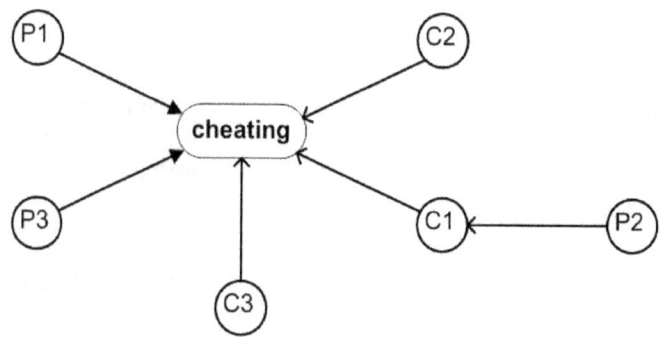

Figure 2: Second representation of the Cheating example

In Figure 2, we still have the three pro argument and the three con arguments. But it is not so obvious that that they are evenly balanced, three against three. It is three against two, with one of the two having an argument to back it up. P2 on the right is merely backing up one of the other con arguments. In Figure 1, P2 was represented as a positive pro argument for cheating in its own right.

3. Analyzing practical reasoning in the example

So far we have only examined the statements put forward by Wellman as explicit premises or conclusions in the pair of opposed arguments. We now take the next step of looking around for implicit elements that can be conjectured. We can carry out such a reconstruction by using the argumentation scheme for practical reasoning. As the analysis proceeds in this section, we will have to bring in an analysis of some implicit premises and conclusions in Wellman's example, thus confronting the problem of enthymemes. This problem is dealt with by building on current argumentation methods by giving some account of where the missing assumptions in the argument should come from.

There are simpler and more complex versions of the argumentation scheme for practical reasoning presented in the current literature, but here we begin with the simplest one below from (Walton, Reed and Macagno, 2008, p. 323). In this version of the scheme, the first-person pronoun 'I' represents a rational agent, an entity that has goals, some knowledge of its circumstances, and the capability of acting to alter those circumstances

> MAJOR PREMISE: I have a goal G.
> MINOR PREMISE: Carrying out this action A is a means to realize G.
> CONCLUSION: Therefore, I ought (practically speaking) to carry out this action A.

The premise P1, the statement that the professor really needs the money he would pay in extra taxes in order to keep up his payments on his large mortgage, is connected with the rest of the argument, we now claim, based on practical reasoning. The reasons behind this claim can be explained as follows. One of the professor's goals is presumably to keep up his payments on his large mortgage. In order to accomplish this goal, he really needs the

Conductive Arguments in Ethical Deliberation

money he would pay in extra taxes, we are told by P1. According to the circumstances, it would be easy enough to refrain from listing this marginal income and pay a tax on the regular salary only. The implied conclusion, based on practical reasoning, is that these premises provide a reason for refraining from listing this marginal income and for paying tax on the regular salary only.

This part of the argument is based on practical reasoning, as shown in Figure 3.

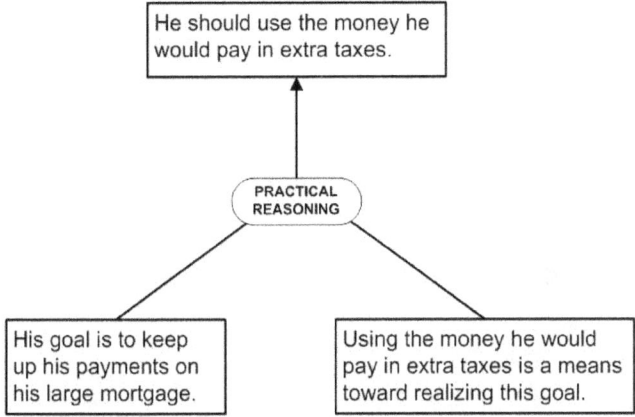

Figure 3: First use of practical reasoning in the Professor example

How did we get this argument out of P1, the explicit premise that he really needs the money he would pay in extra taxes in order to keep up his payments on his large mortgage? The answer is that P1 expresses a means-end relation. So it can be broken down into two components, a statement of a goal and a statement expressing a means towards realizing the goal. Using the scheme for practical reasoning, these two statements can be fitted together and onto the implicit conclusion that he should use the money he would pay in extra taxes. This statement is shown as the conclusion in Figure 3.

Having gone this far, we can see that the dots need to be connected in the chain of practical reasoning required to get to the ultimate conclusion. The professor's problem is now a practical one, once he has made the steps of reasoning shown in Figure 3. His subtask is now to use the money in order to keep up the payments on his mortgage. Thus he has a subgoal that needs to be postulated. He now has the goal of using the money. But he can't do that directly. He has to get the money first. These implicit goal and means statements can be put in as implicit premises in a chain of practical reasoning connecting them to the ultimate conclusion of "cheating" as shown in Figure 4.

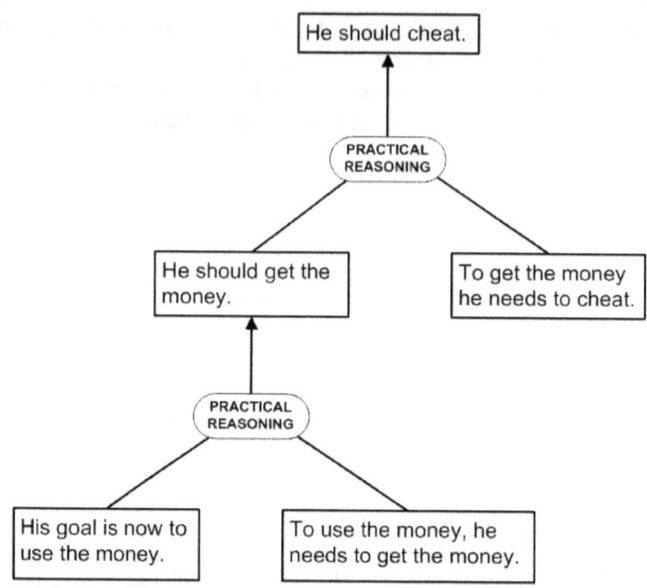

Figure 4: Implicit chain of practical reasoning to the ultimate conclusion

We can now link up the chain of reasoning with that in Figure 4 as follows. The conclusion shown in Figure 3 leads to the premise at the bottom left of Figure 4, the statement that his goal is now to use the money. The reason is another implicit premise that in order to use something like money for some ultimate end, you first of all have to get the money, or at least obtain control over how to use it. Once we have connected up the argument maps in Figure 3 and Figure 4 together, we have displayed the longer chain of reasoning leading from P1 to the ultimate conclusion that the professor should cheat on his income tax. However, this is only part of the story. We still need to look at other supporting reasons on this side of the issue, and as well at the chain of reasoning on the opposing side. But before we can do that we need to ask a question. The question is where the last implicit premise, as well as the other implicit premises came from. This last one was the premise in order to use something like money for some ultimate end, you first of all have to get the money, or at least obtain control over how to use it. To answer this question we have bring in case-based reasoning, and learn a little about how it uses common knowledge to fill in gaps in a chain of reasoning.

According to the theory of enthymemes presented in (Walton, 2008), enthymemes are sometimes based on an arguer's commitment in a dialogue, and sometimes based on common knowledge. The assumption that in order to use something like money for some ultimate end, you first of all have to get the money, or at least obtain control over how to use it, is an item of common knowledge. Govier (1992, p. 120), designated common knowledge as consisting of statements known by virtually everyone. She gave the examples, "Human beings have hearts" and "Many millions of civilians have been killed in twentieth-century wars" (p. 120). Freeman (1995, p. 269) designated common knowledge as a set of statements that many, most or all people accept.

A different kind of common knowledge has also been recognized as important in artificial intelligence. The open mind common sense system (OMCS)[1] included such statements as "If you hold a knife by its blade then it may cut you" and "People pay taxi drivers to

---

[1] http://commonsense.media.mit.edu/cgi-bin/search.cgi

drive them places" (Singh, Lin, Mueller, Lim, Perkins and Zhu, 2002, p. 3). Common knowledge of this kind represents knowledge about action sequences that are connected into familiar and normal routine ways of doing things in everyday life. We all know how knives are normally used to cut things, and we are so familiar with this common procedure that we know that if you try to do it by grasping the blade of the knife, it is very easy to cut your finger. And we are familiar with the sequence of actions in taking a taxi to get somewhere, and we know that taxi drivers normally have to be paid (subject to exceptions). According to Schank and Abelson (1977), this kind of common knowledge is based on what they call a *script,* a body of knowledge shared by language users concerning what typically happens in certain kinds of stereotypical situations, and which enables a language user to fill in gaps in inferences not explicitly stated in a text of discourse. They used the famous restaurant example. We are told explicitly that John went to a restaurant, the hostess seated John and gave him a menu, and John ordered lobster. Later, we're told, John left a tip, and left the restaurant. Given this explicit text, we can infer other implicit statements that fill in gaps in the account. The whole sequence of events and actions in the standard restaurant routine is called a script.

To answer the question of where the implicit premise in the Professor example came from, we need to see how we can fill in implicit elements from the explicit text of the Professor example given by Wellman. The example above was the premise that in order to use something like money for some ultimate end, you first of all have to get the money, or at least obtain control over how to use it. Adding in this premise makes the reasoning used in the example hang together much better, because it makes explicit how the argumentation is based on practical reasoning. But what basis do we have for justifying the claim that we can reconstruct the argumentation in the example by plugging in this assumption as an implicit premise? The answer is that the process of getting money to use it to some end is a highly familiar script, a routine sequence of actions in everyday life. Nobody would be likely to dispute the general principle that in order to use something like money for some ultimate end, you first of all have to get the money, or at least obtain control over how to use it. They might, in some cases, but this general principle is not part of the issue in the Professor example, so far as we know yet, at any rate. Therefore it is reasonable to accept it as an implicit premise on the one side of the argument in the Professor example.

4. Schemes for instrumental and value-based practical reasoning

Now we have seen how practical reasoning is involved in the Professor example, we need to continue analyzing some of the other parts of the argumentation. One of the arguments put forward on the contra side is this one: "[O]n the other hand, if he were detected, the result would be a disgrace and punishment." The type of argument involved here is called argument from negative consequences (Walton 1996, p. 75).

> PREMISE: If A is brought about, negative consequences will plausibly occur.
> CONCLUSION: A should not be brought about.

Argument from negative consequences is a form of counter-argument that cites the negative consequences of a proposed course of action as a reason for not taking the course of action. There can also be argument from positive consequences, which has the same form, except that positive consequences are cited as reasons for carrying out the contemplated action (Walton 1996, p. 75).

PREMISE: If A is brought about, positive consequences will plausibly occur.
CONCLUSION: A should be brought about.

There are three critical questions matching argumentation from consequences (Walton, 1996, 76-77).

CQ_1: How strong is the probability or plausibility that these cited consequences will (may, might, must) occur?
CQ_2: What evidence, if any, supported the claim that these consequences will (may, might, must) occur if A is brought about?
CQ_3: Are there consequences of the opposite value that ought to be taken into account?

These forms of argument the argument are defeasible, meaning that each of them is cast into doubt if there is a failure to answer any critical question adequately. Both schemes are built on the use of values in argumentation and are associated with schemes for argument from positive values and negative values.

The argument from negative consequences is a separate type of argument from practical reasoning in its own right, but it is very often used as a way of rebutting or questioning arguments based on practical reasoning. This relationship is shown when one examines the set of critical questions matching the scheme for practical reasoning (Walton, Reed and Macagno 2008, p. 323).

CQ_1: What other goals do I have that should be considered that might conflict with G?
CQ_2: What alternative actions to my bringing about A that would also bring about G should be considered?
CQ_3: Among bringing about A and these alternative actions, which is arguably the most efficient?
CQ_4: What grounds are there for arguing that it is practically possible for me to bring about A?
CQ_5: What consequences of my bringing about A should also be taken into account?

Critical question CQ_5 often called side effects question, is closely related to argument from negative consequences. The difference is that the side effects question is merely a question, while argument from negative consequences is a counterargument that has a burden of proof attached to it. This means that when an opponent puts forward a counter-argument that has the form of argument from negative consequences, he needs to justify that argument by citing some specific negative consequences in order to make is argument effective as an attack against the opposed viewpoint.

Both arguments from positive consequences and negative consequences are based on assignments of values. Consequences following from the contemplated course of action are being evaluated as positive (good) or negative (bad), according to some set of values presumably shared by the participants in the argument. The argument that if the professor's act of cheating were to be detected the result would be a disgrace and punishment, is an instance of argument from negative consequences. The reason is that disgrace and punishment are taken to represent negative values, and therefore the argument is that the contemplated course of action that would have these consequences is one that should not be undertaken.

For these reasons, we can see that arguments from positive and negative consequences are closely related to an even more fundamental type of argument called argument from values. This type of argument also has two forms, argument from negative value and argument from positive value. The scheme for argument from negative value is from (Walton, Reed and Macagno 2008, p. 321).

MAJOR PREMISE: If value V is negative, it goes against commitment to goal G.
MINOR PREMISE: Value V is negative.
CONCLUSION: V is a reason for retracting commitment to goal G.

The scheme for argument from positive value is the same, except that 'positive' is substituted for 'negative' in both premises. To illustrate the argumentation scheme for argument from values, Bench-Capon (2003) presented the example of Hal and Carla. Diabetic Hal needs insulin to survive, but cannot get any in time to save his life except by taking some from Carla's house without her permission. The argument from positive value for preserving life is pitted against the negative value is weighed against the argument from negative value of taking someone's property without his or her permission. As shown by the case of Carla and Hal, arguments from values are typically combined with practical reasoning. On value-based reasoning generally, see (Bench-Capon, 2003; Bench-Capon and Atkinson, 2009).

Finally, we need to see how argumentation from values is connected to practical reasoning, which is very often based on positive or negative values. The simplest form of practical reasoning shown above is instrumental in nature. It makes no reference to values. A more complex form of practical reasoning is called value-based practical reasoning (Atkinson *et al.* 2006). The following argumentation scheme for value-based practical reasoning is quoted from (Atkinson, Bench-Capon and McBurney 2006, p. 160).

> In the current circumstances R
> we should perform action A
> to achieve new circumstances S
> which will realize some goal G
> which will promote some value V.

According to this way of defining the scheme, goals promote values, and values can be reasons that can support goals. Classifying consequences as good or bad, positive or negative, depends on some prior assignment of values.

The scheme for value-based reasoning has sixteen critical questions (Atkinson *et al.* 2006). The following three are significant in the Professor example.

CQ$_1$: Will the action achieve the new circumstances?
CQ$_2$: Will the action demote some other value?
CQ$_3$: Is there another action which will promote the value?

The formal framework for the scheme for value-based practical reasoning above is different from the framework used to formulate the scheme for instrumental practical reasoning given above. To help make the two compatible, there is following scheme for value-based practical reasoning (Walton, Reed and Macagno 2008, p. 324).

MAJOR PREMISE: I have a goal G.
MINOR PREMISE 1: G is supported by my set of values, V.
MINOR PREMISE 2: Bringing about A is necessary (or sufficient) for me to bring about G.
CONCLUSION: Therefore, I should bring about A.

Framed in this way, value-based practical reasoning can be classified as a hybrid scheme that combines argument from values with practical reasoning.

One of the premises, C1 (If he were detected, the result would be disgrace and punishment) is about negative consequences of one of the courses of action being contemplated.

The argument that if he were detected, the result would be disgrace and punishment, is an argument from negative values used by the con side to oppose the practical reasoning argumentation put forward by the pro side on the issue of cheating. This opposing argument only works if the original argument from practical reasoning is value-based. Values have to be taken into account. One way to do this is to see values as supporting goals. An agent's values give reasons for supporting or questioning his goals.

5. Applying schemes to the example

It needs to be recalled from figure 2 that there is a prior argument on the pro side rebutting the rebuttal based on argument from negative consequences. This is the argument that it is unlikely that he would be detected and punished for his act, expressed in explicit statement P2. In Wellman's example, this argument is stated prior to the argument from negative consequences, and the statement can be classified as a proleptic argument put forward to rebut the potential argument from negative consequences even before it has been raised by the opposing side. When reconstructed more fully, the argument can be expressed as follows: it may be true that if he were detected, the result would be disgrace and punishment, but if it is unlikely that he would be detected, it is also unlikely that the result would be disgrace and punishment. The structure of this argument would not be straightforward to represent using formal logic, because it combines counterfactual conditionals and probability. But it can be represented by argumentation schemes. The argument from negative consequences is being attacked by raising the critical question about how likely the consequences are. It is being argued that if they are not very likely, there is a good chance of avoiding the negative consequences. This kind of argument is centrally a practical one. It is not disputing that the negative consequences are bad, or represent negative values. It is merely suggesting that if they're not likely to occur, from a practical point of view they may be avoided.

On the other hand, argument from values is very important to understanding the structure of the conductive argumentation in the Professor example. The terms 'disgrace' and 'punishment' express negative values, and even the term 'cheating' that occurs in Wellman's statement of the ultimate issue to be decided, incorporate negative values.

The argument from values fits in with argument from negative consequences and value-based practical reasoning in the example, but it is not clear how these three schemes fit together in a way that can yield an overall understanding of how the conductive chain of argumentation works in the example. There are some problems with how this task should be carried out that can be expressed in a helpful way using Figure 5.

The first problem is that the use of argument from values shown at the top left of Figure 5 does not perfectly fit the scheme for argument from negative value. In the versions of the schemes for arguments from positive and negative value given above, a value supports or goes against commitment to a goal. In the Professor case, there is no explicit statement of a

Conductive Arguments in Ethical Deliberation

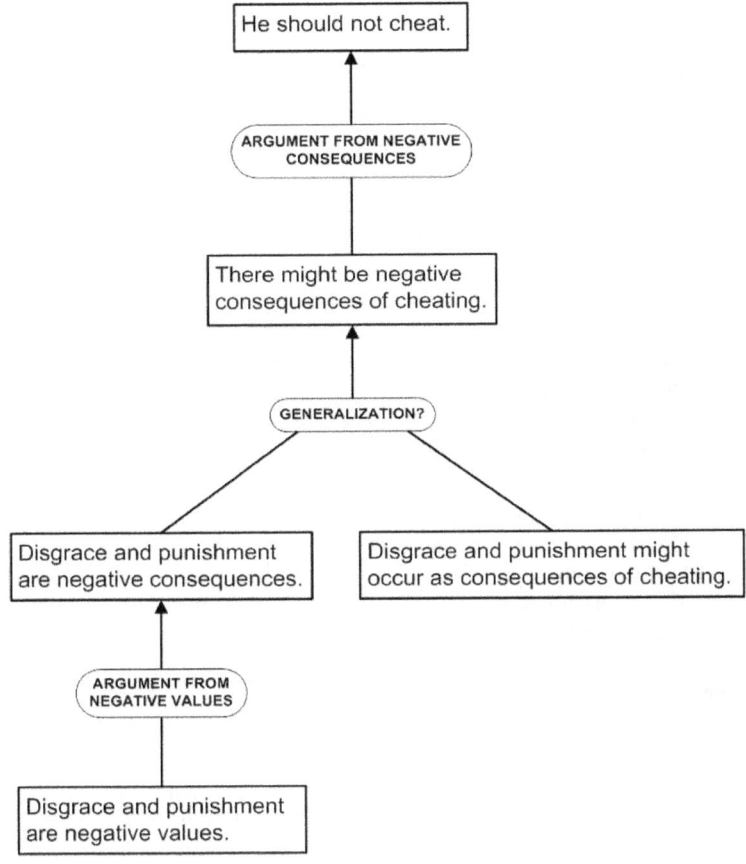

Figure 5: Attempt to fit values schemes together

goal that would fit this scheme in the right way to structure this part of the argument using the scheme. What we have done in reconstructing the argument while trying to use argument from negative values is to draw in a step from the premise that disgrace and punishment are negative values to the conclusion that disgrace and punishment are negative consequences. The assumption is that because disgrace and punishment are negative values, these values can be attached to consequences that can be described using the words 'disgrace' and 'punishment.' This is a kind of stopgap measure however. It suggests that reconfiguring the scheme for argument from negative values may be required to do a good job of reconstructing the argumentation in the example.

The next problem occurs in the middle section of the argument visualized in figure 5. Once we have arrived at the conclusion that disgrace and punishment are negative consequences, in order to use the current version of argument from negative consequences to get the premise that there might be negative consequences of cheating, we need the additional premise that disgrace and punishment might occur as consequences of cheating. So this is how we have built the argument map. Notice that we have used several implicit premises. In fact, all the premises except the ones saying that disgrace and punishment might occur as consequence of cheating are implicit. This kind of result is expected when dealing with argument from values, because the use of this type of argument is typically hidden. For example in this instance, disgrace and punishment are not explicitly said to be negative values. It is because of the negative emotive connotations of these terms, as they are often called, that it can be implicitly assumed in the argument they are taken to represent negative values.

This way of representing the conduct of argumentation in the Professor case is not entirely satisfactory. What is suggested by the example is that some of the schemes need to be reconfigured so that they can fit together better in typical cases of ethical reasoning using conduct of argumentation like this one. These are very commonly used kinds of arguments, and the way the schemes for practical reasoning, argument from consequences and argument from negative values should fit together in reconstructing such arguments should be more natural.

Another unsatisfactory aspect of the example is the way Wellman set up the decision to be made. He began the example by asking us to suppose that a professor is trying to decide whether to cheat on his income tax. Of course, "cheating" is a negative term that refers to something that is morally wrong. It expresses, or is based on, a negative value. Hence the decision to be made is one-sided. From the beginning, there is a conductive weight in place on one side of the decision as opposed to the other. Cheating is wrong, and so there is already an implicit argument against the option not to disclose the income in place on one side. This aspect is concealed, however, for as noted above, arguments from values are typically embedded in positive or negative emotive language, and are therefore implicit. Wellman could have set up the issue more fairly if he had posed the decision to be made in the deliberation as a choice between disclosing the unreported income or not. That way it would be much easier to set up the conductive argumentation on both sides using argumentation from positive and negative values and displaying these types of arguments as factors to be weighed against each other on either side.

Finally, something remains to be said about the premises P3 and C3 in the argument. These are the arguments concerned with the professor's approval of spending for welfare programs and disapproval for military spending. These could be classified as arguments from positive and negative values. For example the military spending argument could be reconstructed by postulating the professor's implicit acceptance of some value like the value of peaceful coexistence with one's fellow human beings, which could be called the value of peace. The other value could perhaps be called the value of looking after one's fellow human beings who are in less fortunate circumstances. This could be called the value of charity, or something of that sort. Another way of reconstructing the arguments could be to view them as instances of argument from commitment. On this view, statement C3 expresses the professor's commitment to welfare programs, while the statement P3 expresses his commitment against military spending. Use of the word 'approves' in C3 suggests the use of argument from values.

6. Arguments from classification and values

The use of terms, like 'cheating' and 'disgrace,' that express and are based on negative values, is an important aspect of the conductive argumentation used in the Professor example. By classifying the professor's contemplated actions under these terms, the example is using an ethically significant argument that can be represented by the scheme for argument from verbal classification (Walton 1996, p. 54).

> MAJOR PREMISE: If some particular thing a can be classified as falling under verbal category C, then a has property F (in virtue of such a classification).
> MINOR PREMISE: a can be classified as falling under verbal category C.
> CONCLUSION: a has property F.

The following example, based on a comparable example in (Hastings 1963, p. 36) can be used. 2% can be classified as a poor return rate on a bond. This bond has a 2% return rate. This bond has a poor return rate. The major premise is: if a bond can be classified as falling under category of having a 2% return rate, then it has the property of having a poor return rate. The minor premise is: this bond can be classified as having a return rate of 2%. The conclusion is: this bond has a poor return rate. The major premise represents a defeasible generalization in typical instances of ethical argumentation. If there is a dispute about the classification, it can be questioned, and the argument may be weakened or even defeated.

Contra argumentation can be carried out by questioning the major premise generalization or by questioning whether it fits the particular action or event at issue. There are two critical questions (Walton 1976, p. 54) for this scheme:

CQ_1: Does *a* definitely have *F*, or there is room for doubt?
CQ_2: Can the verbal classification (in the major premise) be said to hold strongly, or is it one of those weak classifications that is subject to doubt?

However, the classification premise itself can also be challenged by asking whether 2% really is a poor return for bonds. In many instances, the argument would not be plausible unless the property *F* had an argumentative value based on a commonly accepted meaning of a term, like 'poor return rate', which can vary with time and circumstances. Thus argument from classification is very often questioned by raising questions about definitions. Hence argument from classification is often linked to the scheme for argument from definition to classification.

Arguments from classification are typically used in a way that conceals an implicit premise. For example, if an action is classified as cheating, an implicit premise is that cheating is wrong, stemming from the accepted meaning of the word 'cheating'. Hence a particular event or action at issue, like 'what Bob did', once classified under the term 'cheating', leads to the conclusion, via argument from verbal classification and argument from negative values, that what Bob did was wrong.

Use of terms that express values in ethical reasoning is often associated with Stevenson's theory of emotive ethics (Stevenson, 1944). Stevenson's theory sees such use of emotive language in ethics as expressing subjective personal preferences, as in the statement "I like chocolate ice cream." This approach to value-based ethical reasoning has turned out to be misleading, however, as values of the kind supporting practical reasoning can often be widely shared and can be supported by reasons. As Stevenson argued, such verbal categorization may be based on a speaker's individual emotive reaction in some instances, but it may also be backed by shared knowledge of commonly accepted values. For example, we don't need to argue that cheating is wrong, because it is generally accepted that if something can be classified as cheating, that is a reason to think it is wrong. However, such arguments are defeasible. There may be contra arguments showing that even though it can be reasonably argued the action at issue be classified as cheating, there may also be opposing arguments to show that the action was not wrong in exceptional circumstances. The problem is that using language that expresses values often conceals argumentation. The reasons are hidden in the wording.

Another issue that looms large here is the perennial one of whether, if something can be classified as cheating or lying, it is always wrong. Can there be circumstances, for example, in which lying is justified because it prevents a greater harm? The main problem, however, is the more technical one of how argument from value is connected to argument from classification. The Professor example can be used to show these how these two forms of argument are connected in conductive reasoning used in ethical deliberation, but we leave this as an exercise for the reader.

It is somewhat surprising that Wellman would configure the example by using the loaded term 'cheat' in the conclusion, and even more surprising that he does not even take the illegality of tax evasion into account as a serious reason for not cheating. However, our aim in this paper has not been to improve on Wellman's example, but only to study the example as Wellman presented it. However, it is not easy to resist the temptation of thinking up our own moral judgments on what the professor should do by adding new pro or contra arguments to the example. Such matters as how to frame the methods and conclusions of the investigation of the paper are taken up in Section 9.

7. The method of challenge and response

Asking whether there could be any testing procedure for ethical arguments, Wellman (1971, p. 62) wrote, "I am not sure, but I doubt it." But actually he does have a kind of testing procedure. Later in his book (1971, Chapter 5), he put forward his challenge-response method of ethical justification. Maybe his reservations were about whether the challenge-response method was exact enough to qualify as a testing procedure. The cost-benefit method of decision-making weighs the expected costs of a set of alternative course of action costs against its expected benefits, and decides the outcome by selecting the alternative with the highest expected utility. This paper has suggested an alternative approach based on argumentation schemes helping us to identify and analyze the pro and contra arguments in a case. However, we said at the beginning that the framework of the deliberation can be determined by citing three factors: participants, choice to make, and circumstances. But is the framework one of deliberation or persuasion?

The type of dialogue that has been most intensively studied in argumentation is that of persuasion dialogue (Prakken 2006). In this type of dialogue, there are two parties, there is some central statement at issue, and the goal of one side is prove the statement, while the goal of the other side is to disprove or doubt it. Deliberation has a different kind of goal. It is to solve a problem about what course of action to take. The problem statement is not a proposition, but a question, called a governing question by McBurney, Hitchcock and Parsons (2007). Examples of these are: "Where should we go to dinner?" and "How can we provide all Americans with health care insurance?" The goal of a deliberation is to find a solution to common problems.

There are several key differences between persuasion and deliberation frameworks. Persuasion is more adversarial, while deliberation requires more cooperation. In persuasion, each side has its own set of commitments, and each argues to persuade the other using the commitments of the other as premises. In deliberation, they get their common data on the circumstances as information they are all privy to (Walton *et al.* 2010). In contrast to the case of a persuasion dialogue, the problem is the need to make a choice between courses of action. Deliberation dialogue is not centrally an attempt by one participant to persuade another to become committed to a particular course of action, although it is quite common for there to be a shift to persuasion dialogue as arguments for or against a proposed action are justified and criticized. In deliberation dialogue a choice of action that is optimal for all those affected, may not be optimal for the deliberating participant (McBurney, Hitchcock and Parsons 2007, p. 98). In a deliberation dialogue, a participant must be willing to share his/her preferences and information.

As Aristotle emphasized (*Nicomachean Ethics*, $1112^b 10$), we deliberate about things that are inherently subject to change. Thus deliberation is a type of dialogue that is inherently different from scientific demonstration. Deliberation is employed in practical matters where the generalizations that function as important parts of the reasoning used to arrive at a conclusion are defeasible. In deliberation, the particular circumstances tend to be constantly changing. For this reason deliberation is inherently subject to revision, and even retraction of commitments, as new information comes in. An important property of intelligent deliberation is being open to new information that may be coming in quickly, and being flexible in changing one's plan in response to this new information.

It needs to be added that both persuasion and deliberation can be about which action is best, but persuasion is more typically about whether a statement is true or not. Both often use the same kinds of arguments, but the illocutionary force of the speech acts used in them is different. Although the participants can perform similar speech acts, the way they react to them is different. In persuasion there is more attacking whereas in deliberation there is more trying to work together to find a common solution to a problem.

It is interesting to quote Wellman's remarks (1975, p. 309) on how the arguments should be weighed in a case of ethical decision-making like the Professor example:

> How do we weigh the relevant considerations in making moral judgments? We cannot put arguments on any scale and read off their weight from the pointer, nor can we literally heft the arguments in our hands to feel their relative weights. What we can and must do is to think through the various arguments and feel their logical force, or lack of it. What we feel is the persuasiveness of the argument, its psychological force. The logical force of an argument is its psychological force after criticism. In weighing an argument, it is not the strength of its first impact upon the mind that counts, but the persuasion it continues to exert after one has reflected on the argument, formulated it as clearly as possible and considered objections to it, discussed its point and its merit with other rational persons, and then reflected some more. The logically valid argument is the one that retains its persuasiveness throughout this critical process of reflection and discussion. We come to know which act is right by subjecting all the pro and con arguments to this sort of criticism and then feeling which seem the more persuasive.

Wellman does talk about persuasiveness but links it to psychological force, contrasting that with logical force. What matters is not the first impact on the mind, but the persuasiveness that remains after another process has taken place. He describes this process as one in which the decision-maker has followed this five-point sequence: (1) he has reflected on the argument, (2) formulated it as clearly as possible, (3) considered objections to it, (4) discussed its point and its merit with other rational persons, and (5) reflected some more. This process could be modeled as a three-stage dialogue. There is an opening stage where the problem is formulated, an argumentation stage where a group of rational persons has considered objections to the arguments pro and contra, and discussed the "point and merit" of the arguments, and a closing stage, where further reflections take place. I think this structure is a good description of the testing procedure that comprises Wellman's method of challenge in response in outline.

The challenge-response process fits the deliberation model better than the persuasion model, as do the other examples of conductive reasoning quoted from Wellman in the introduction. They are all examples of what somebody ought to do in a particular set of circumstances where a choice needs to be made between two opposed courses of action. The professor is not trying to persuade himself on whether to cheat or not, given that he has a conflict of opinions about which course of action is the better one. He is trying to choose which course of action is the better one based on all the facts and circumstances of his situation, on defeasible generalizations on what can normally be expected to happen as the results of his possible actions, on his values, and on how all these factors relate to the values and circumstances of others who may be involved in the decision-making and its consequences. Very often deliberation is a form of group decision-making, but in this instance the agent is weighing the arguments by himself.

8. Problems to be solved

Two specific problems with the example remain to be solved. The first problem we confronted in analyzing the conductive argumentation in the Professor example was the one about how argument from values is connected to argument from consequences in typical cases of ethical deliberation like this one. One way to solve the problem would be to change the argumentation schemes for arguments from consequences by adding a new premise. Argument from negative consequences would now look like this.

> MAJOR PREMISE: If A is brought about, consequences will plausibly occur.
> MINOR PREMISE: These consequences are negative.
> CONCLUSION: A should not be brought about.

Argument from positive consequences will be comparable.

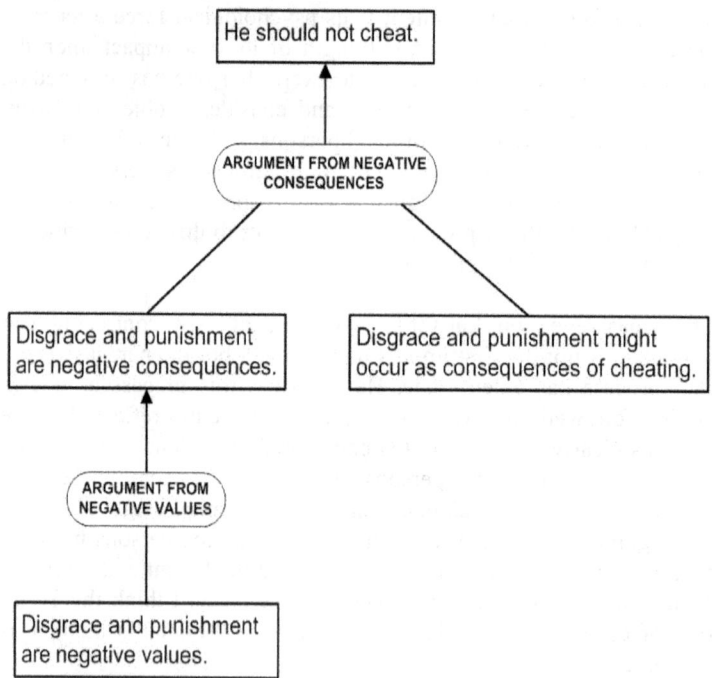

Figure 6: Reconfiguration of argument from consequences in Professor example

> MAJOR PREMISE: If A is brought about, consequences will plausibly occur.
> MINOR PREMISE: These consequences are positive.
> CONCLUSION: A should be brought about.

Using this new version of the scheme for argument from negative consequences, the chain of reasoning in Figure 4 can be reconfigured as shown in Figure 6.

Conductive Arguments in Ethical Deliberation 207

This reconfiguration of the schemes for arguments from consequences makes it simpler to visually represent the conductive argumentation in the Professor example. It also seems better generally as a way of representing common cases where arguments from values are chained to arguments from consequences. This is the recommended solution.

The second problem is to see how argument from verbal classification is connected to argument from negative values in the Professor example.

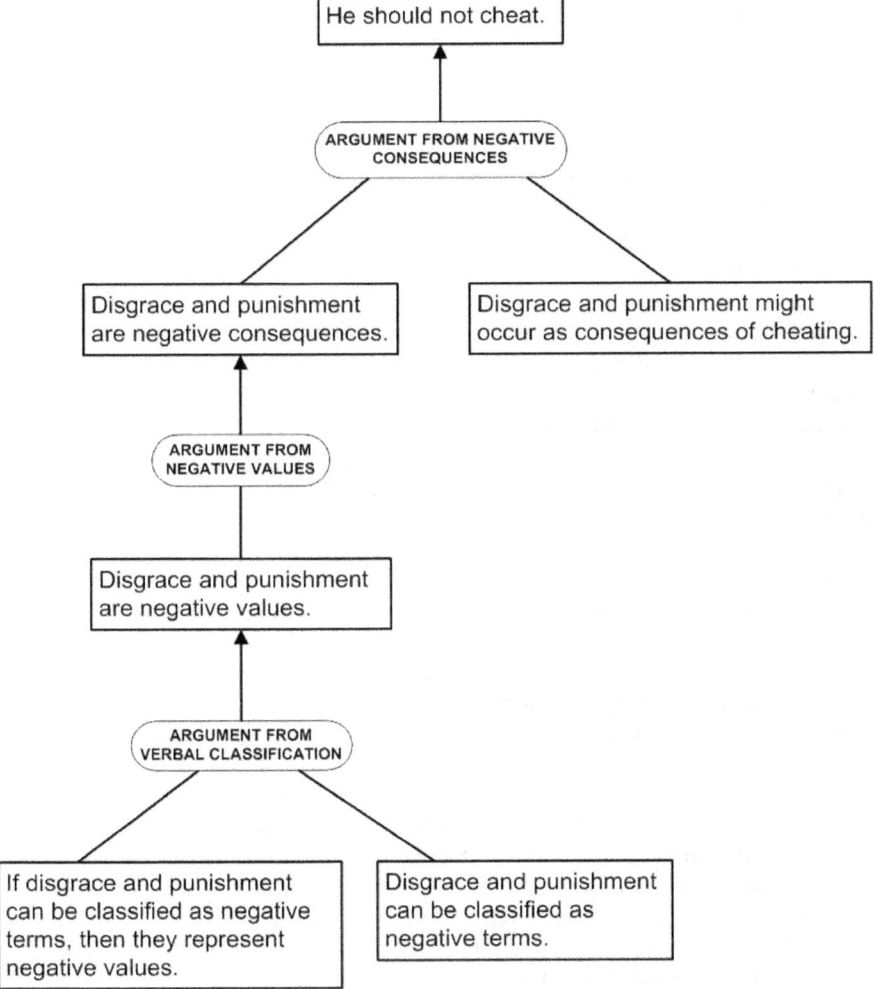

Figure 7: Incorporating argument from verbal classification

This is not an easy problem to solve, because the argument from values is based on an implicit classification through the use of the negative terms 'disgrace' and 'punishment' (not to mention the use of the term 'cheating' again). Nevertheless, in figure 7, we can summarize a large part of the sequence of conductive argumentation by showing how argument from negative consequences is based on argument from negative values, which is in turn based on argument from verbal classification.

Finally now this much has been done, we have to show how the whole network of argumentation is truly conductive by taking all the arguments from figure 3 through to figure 7, and showing how they can be divided into two argument networks, one on the pro side and one on the contra side, as shown in figure 1. We will not attempt this task here, but the reader can imagine roughly how it should be done. Once this much of the structure of the argumentation on both sides in the Professor example has been exposed, it is not hard to see generally how Wellman's five point process of conductive argument evaluation could work. Even though we cannot apply this process to the Professor example, because it is incomplete, we can see how it is to be done, on Wellman's vision, by weighing the one argument against the other.

9. Conclusions

An important fault to try to avoid in weighing the arguments used in deliberation is sometimes called Monday morning quarterbacking, meaning that some time after that the decision has been made, it may be very easy to see that it was the right decision or the wrong one, and therefore it is tempting to criticize the decision in light of this later information. Once the actual consequences of the decision are known, it may be very clear that a mistake was made, and this was the wrong decision, or that things turned out extremely well, and it was the right decision. Monday morning quarterbacking is, however, often a kind of fallacious or defective reasoning, precisely because such decisions need to be judged in light of the circumstances that were actually known to the decision maker at the time the decision had to be made. Even though the decision turned out badly, for example because of unanticipated developments that could not have been reasonably foreseen, it may have been absolutely the right decision in light of the circumstances that were known at that point the decision was made.

Some people, when exposed to the exercise of analyzing an example like this one by identifying the reasons that can be given on both sides of the issue, think that this procedure should come to a definite right answer. In other words, the expectation is that this procedure should solve the problem by telling the professor that he should either cheat on his income taxes or not by showing that the argument on the one side is stronger than the argument on the other. This outcome might actually happen in some cases, but generally in the kinds of cases we are interested in ethics, it is not to be expected. Ethical deliberation software, for example, might be useful to help users identify and consider pro and contra arguments, and weigh them against each other, rather than to make ethical decisions for the user. The task selected in this paper was not to make the right decision. As we must keep in mind, it was to study Wellman's example as he set it up, in order to use it to reveal more about the structure of conductive reasoning.

It is surprising that Wellman left out the illegality of tax evasion as a reason to be taken into account. Many respondents might feel indeed that this is the decisive reason why the professor should not cheat on his income tax. Perhaps one reason for this omission was that at the time this example was used in an ethics textbook, civil disobedience was a prominent subject for discussion in ethical writings, and there was a climate of opinion supporting the notion that disobeying the law for ethical reasons can be acceptable. Of course, the time of writing of Wellman's book was during the Vietnam War era. Still, if you or I were trying to weigh the arguments in the case (which we are not, for the purpose of this paper), we should take the illegality of tax evasion into account as a weighty argument, or even as outweighing the other arguments.

Analyzing the Professor example has given us a fairly good idea on how Wellman's method of ethical decision-making uses conductive reasoning to weigh the pros and cons of the argumentation on each side of an ethical issue to be decided. In the quotation in section 7, Wellman has given us a general overview of how his challenge and response method of weighing the arguments on both sides works. To frame it more precisely using concepts of argumentation developed after Wellman's books, we have modeled the process as a dialogue structure in which the two sides probe into the arguments on each side critically, going through a five-point sequence in a dialogue with three stages. Is it a persuasion dialogue or a deliberation dialogue? The answer shown by the analysis in the paper is that the argumentation in the Professor example is part of a deliberation dialogue. The example is a good one to illustrate the main features of conductive argument and show how the pro and con arguments can be tested using Wellman's method of challenge and response. The example has proved to be fertile as well, in that in that it does fit very well with argumentation tools developed more recently, including defeasible argumentation schemes and formal models of dialogue.

Our aim was to use this example to learn more about the structure of this pro and contra weighing process that Wellman identifies with conductive argument. The objective of this paper was not to criticize or improve Wellman's way of posing and structuring his example. It was to study his way of analyzing the argumentation in the example by looking at the reasons that could be given on both sides to weigh those on the one side against those on the other in a challenge and response format. How, in the Professor example, should we weigh up the arguments on both sides to tell the professor what is his best choice, or to tell us what he should have done? These are the key questions that, no doubt, many readers will have. The answer is that there is no answer, because Wellman merely described the main arguments on each side, essentially comprising the explicit premises P1-P3 and C1-C3. So we are not in position to carry out the weighing procedure yet. In order to do this, we need to have more dialogue in which the arguments on each side are shown to interact with those on the other side. We did this up to a point by analyzing some of the support and attack relations in these arguments and identifying some implicit assumptions needed to better analyze them. But that is as far as we can go in the Professor example, because Wellman only gave us a summary of the main arguments on each side. We might have been able to carry out an argument evaluation using conductive argumentation if he had told us, for example, which values the professor holds more strongly than others. But he didn't do that either. It would be an interesting project to extend the example by adding new factors to it, or bringing it more into line with current ethical concerns, based on what we have found out about conductive arguments and the method of challenge and response in this paper.[2]

---

[2] The research on this chapter was supported by a research grant from the Social Sciences and Humanities Research Council of Canada. Among those who made comments I would especially like to thank Hans Hansen, David Hitchcock, Christian Kock and Steven Patterson.

Chapter 14

Conductive Argument: A Misleading Model for the Analysis of Pro- and Contra- Argumentation

HARALD WOHLRAPP

1. Introduction

1.1 The question

The question I want to treat in my contribution is the following: What are the terms and principles that may be adequate for description, analysis and evaluation of a "PCTC-setting"? The acronym PCTC stands here for an argumentative setting in which Pro- and Contra- Arguments for and/or against a thesis and/or a counter-thesis (T) appear, and in which a conclusion (C) is sought, which takes the pro-arguments as well as the contra-arguments into consideration. The special focus of the present paper will be the question of how far the "conductive argument" scheme, invented in the 1970s by Carl Wellman (Wellman 1971, 1975) and elaborated subsequently by Trudy Govier (Govier 1987, 1997) can be helpful. My answer to the question will be that the conductive argument is a bold but half-done idea, which is mainly misleading. An adequate treatment of PCTC-settings needs more complex analytical tools, which have to cover the (widely ignored) procedural and subjective aspects of argumentation.

1.2 Historical background

PCTC-settings are nothing new. They have been practiced and theorized in ancient and medieval rhetoric and dialectic within philosophy, theology and sciences; apparently there was even a term established: "*argumentatio in utramque partem*" (Kienpointner 1992, p. 162).

Since the Age of Enlightenment they have been present especially in academic debate training, practicing and evaluation. Debate is, however, a special kind of PCTC. It requires a jury with a granted potential of impartial judgement. In consequence there is no conclusion developed out of the thesis and the exchange of arguments, but the jury has to decide which party's thesis has been defended more accurately. Therefore procedure tends to become mainly competitive, with victory as its aim; and theory is specially concerned with strategies to "beat" the other party respectively, to "win over" the jury.

In the 1970s the new wave of informal logic and argumentation theory arose. It was, however, triggered by the works of Toulmin (1958) and Perelman and Olbrechts-Tyteca (1958), where the focus laid upon single units of arguments or argumentative figures. This focus coined research that followed and motivated among other things a special interest in non-deductive inferences (inductive, analogical, abductive, etc.). Therefore, Wellman's idea of conductive argument (as being somehow parallel to deductive and inductive argument) could appear as a pertinent suggestion to enclose the manifold occurrences of the PCTC-Setting into a single, nice and unifying inference pattern. Wellman himself was not shy about extensively musing about its "logical force" (Wellman 1971, e.g. p. 29) and when Govier came up with a method to diagram it (Govier 1997), conductive argument quickly became welcomed in the modern hall of informal logic as a new and promising non-deductive argument scheme.[1]

Since then scholars who investigate PCTC-Settings seem to be equipped with a line of thinking which allows them to grasp the rather competitive and heterogeneous process of pro- and contra- argumentation in a simple one-dimensional and structural way. The figure looked solid and clear and therefore the conductive argument pattern was established not as a problem but as a solution that at most would deserve some clarification here and there (Hitchcock 1994).

It was in 2009 that a cooperative research project between the Universities of Windsor and Hamburg proved that the question of how to describe, analyse and evaluate the pro- and contra- arguments—which appeared in the subject of our joint research: the discussions about human embryonic stem cells—is a controversial issue. The participants found themselves in disagreement about ways of analysing arguments, especially PCTC-settings. Soon it came out that, for some, the conductive argument scheme was too unclear to serve as a way of thinking. Partly in response, the present symposium was planned and papers were called for to display the state of the art thinking about the conductive argument.

2. Some examples

In my contribution I will, when necessary to elucidate details of the proposed view and of my critique, refer to examples. (It is good to have more than one, and not only ethical ones.) None of these examples is precisely analysed here. Therefore it is enough to let them have (mostly) just one pro-argument and one contra-argument. Below I display three normative and three descriptive examples. Four of them are taken from Govier's work (Govier 1987a, 1997) and one from Finocchiaro's (Finocchiaro 1980); the first one is my own.

2.1 Normative examples

2.1.1

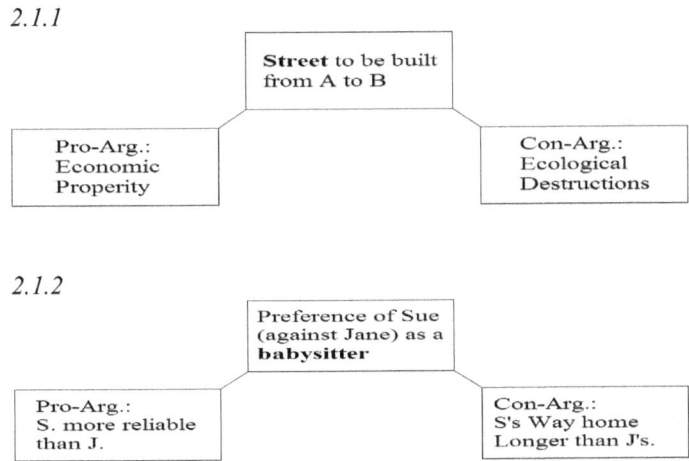

2.1.2

---

[1] Some details were criticised by D. Allen (Allen 1990, 1993). Another criticism was Wohlrapp 1995.

2.1.3

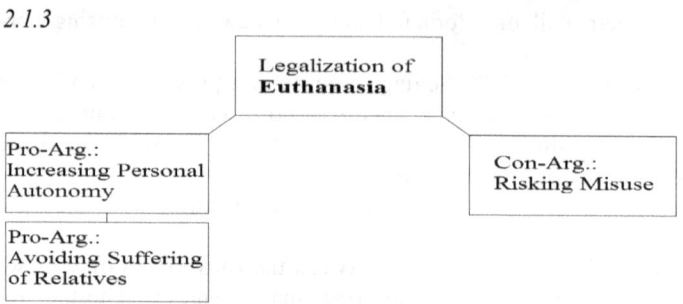

2.2 Descriptive examples

2.2.1

2.2.2

2.2.3

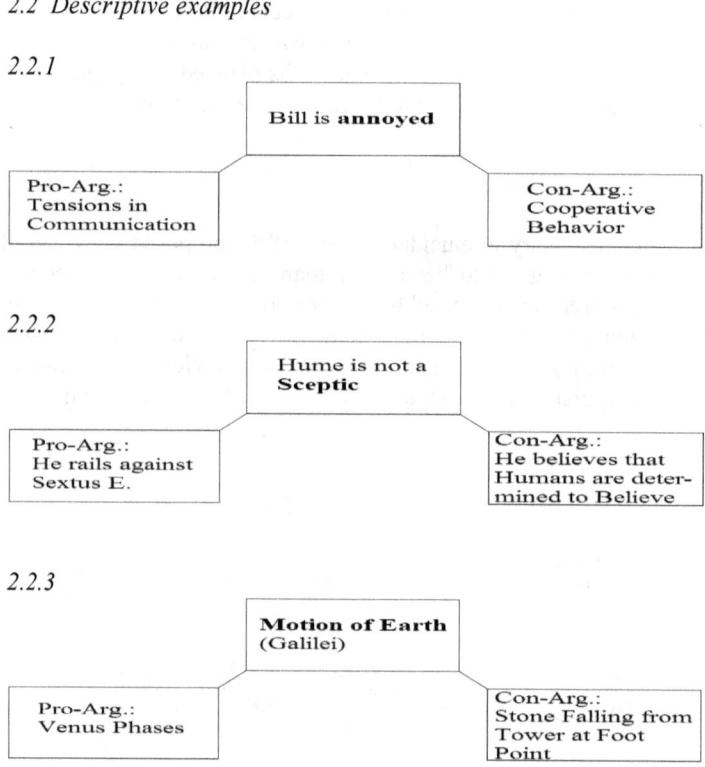

3. The square of dimensions

Let me make a few general remarks at the beginning of this section. Mankind is obviously able to use arguments. Difficulties that arise within this usage have provoked the development of theory—in Europe at least since ancient Greek culture. The question is: How to build (good) theory about argumentative praxis? In the course of history some overriding distinctions for kinds of theories have been widely established: logic, rhetoric, topics, dialectic, the product approach, the process approach, or the procedure approach, etc. These

Conductive Arguments: A Misleading Model

distinctions, however, have meanwhile become more or less sharp dichotomies and have led to unfruitful separations and obstacles.[2]

Therefore I propose a fresh start (see the "pragmatic approach" in Wohlrapp 2009) with a general overriding description of argumentative praxis in which these dichotomies are dissolved into "dimensions" (aspects, perspectives) of the activity. I have found it useful to work with two pairs of dimensions, which can be diagrammed as a kind of square:

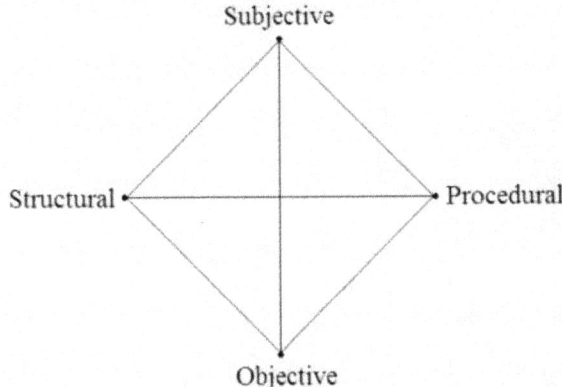

I will now try to describe this square of dimensions. The problem is that the basic underlying ideas seem to be not very familiar to the usual North-American reader, so that their full explanation would need quite a few words; however, I am aware that I should be brief here.

3.1 Structural and procedural dimension

There is a well known and broad stream of thinking about arguments (beginning with Aristotelian syllogistics) in what I call "the structural dimension." This means that we are used to identifying units in the argumentative praxis and relationships between those units. The units (of various kinds, like syntactical, semantical, functional) that are established are, for example: concepts, propositions, rules, theses, arguments and conclusions. Relationships between units are, for example: conjunction, adjunction, subjunction and entailment. The most important feature of the structural dimension is a special relationship between two sentences. It could be called "the inference pattern":

$P \Rightarrow Q$ (if P is given then a transition to Q is viable)

For illustration, I would like to refer to the table of examples in Section 2. There we can identify a lot of concepts—such as "economic prosperity," "reliability" (of a babysitter), "personal autonomy" and "sceptic"—which would have to be properly defined if the respective arguments were to be seriously investigated. Also we can recognise some (underlying) inference patterns, such as, "If a street is built, there will be economic prosperity"

---

[2] One result is, that some people seem to select an analytical approach in the way they chose a necktie in a department store, see e.g. Jin, this volume. Postmodernism may be good in arts and architecture. If argumentation theory is supposed to be theory, one has, however, to consider the arguments that have been given for and against certain approaches and thus show that one's decision is not purely arbitrary.

and "A philosopher who believes that humans are determined to believe is not a sceptic," etc.

On the other side, there is the "procedural dimension." It is traditionally understated. Certainly people are aware that arguing is a process, but this is usually not taken as an essential feature because the results of this process seem to depend again on "structures" (concepts, rules, entailment-relationships, etc.). Even if their appearance may have a temporal aspect, the structures themselves are static; they are not "flowing." One could put it this way: in theory we are used to following Parmenides and Plato and not Heraclitus and Hegel. I think, however, for an adequate analysis of arguments we need both views. The procedural dimension comes in not so much because the process takes time, but because the units usually undergo changes as they function in arguing—especially arguing in PCTC-settings.

Let me draw your attention to some of those changes.

(a) Change of *strength*. Arguments can, when investigated, be sharpened and pointed, but as well they can be weakened. (Quite common is the case that an argument makes use of a generalisation that turns out to be hasty and is then modified. Also a more precise definition of a concept can change the strength, see example *2.1.3*: Depending on how "personal autonomy" is understood, the argument can be sharpened or weakened.)
(b) Change of *number*. Arguments can be put together by abstraction, so that several arguments come out as one, or an argument can get analysed and becomes two or more. (See again *2.1.3*: avoiding unnecessary suffering can be one argument, or can be split into avoid the suffering of patients, of relatives, or even of doctors or nurses.) Arguments can completely disappear (they can be refuted or recognised as irrelevant; see once more *2.1.3*: avoiding the suffering of relatives can be refuted with the statement that such suffering is part of a humane living[3]) or new arguments can emerge (see my treatment of the case in Wohlrapp 2008 where my discussion concentrates on the frame structures and brings out the new argument: that through the legalization of euthanasia, the whole frame of suffering for terminally ill patients would be transformed.)
(c) Change of *function*. These are the most striking changes. Pro-arguments can become (when reframed) con-arguments (see example *2.1.1* where the pro could be transformed into a con by a reply like: "Don't you realise what a nasty company it is that would mainly profit by the new road?") and vice-versa (see example *2.1.2* where the con could be transformed into a pro, if the reply were: "Sure, her way home is longer, but I like to talk with her and I have no other opportunity…").
(d) Change of *reflective depth*. On the occasion of questions like, "Is this a suitable concept, claim, argument, etc.?" an argumentative meta-level can be opened.

The underestimation of the procedural dimension is notorious in contemporary argumentation theory. Most scholars who care about it work with some dialogue model. Yet these dialogues are usually games, defined by rules and therefore they keep a static character instead of representing real argumentative exchanges. This goes as well for the very popular "pragma-dialectic" dialogue model (van Eemeren & Grootendoorst 1992), and also for the rather sophisticated model of Krabbe and Walton which provides a whole bunch of dialogue types that can merge into each other (Walton & Krabbe 1995, Ch. 3). Certainly

---

[3] Russell in his *Autobiography* recalls the death agony of Mrs. Whitehead, his friend's wife, and he states that the sharing of her agony changed his life from an unripe intellectual existence into a humane being (Russell 1967, p. 146).

this latter model shows some of the features of real conversation, but these changes are not conceived as changes required by the pursuit of the argumentation around a thesis.

3.2 Subjective and objective dimensions

The second pair of dimensions contains again one dimension which is common and one which is not adequately recognised. The "objective dimension" seems to be simple and obvious. It has to do with everything concerning the issue, the matter, the facts, etc. that are referred to in the argumentation. Obviously these (issue, matter, fact…) appear in our arguments in the shape of verbal theoretical constructions. Of course, the best of these would be in "knowledge," viz., in true propositions about the issue. But of course our knowledge is limited and therefore we operate also with assumptions, suppositions that we hope will come out as reliable theory about the issue. To sum up: in argumentation the objective dimension is apparent in the "theoretical basis," that is, in all the "theories" which are at hand about an issue. Working in the objective dimension means questioning the theoretical basis with respect to its reliability; i.e., checking its stability, especially the stability of the inference patterns that we use.

Illustrations of such checking:

> Example 2.1.1 How safe are the inferences from the street's having been built, to economic growth, and to ecological damages, respectively?

> Example 2.2.3 Are the Venus phases (observed through the telescope) real; and if so how do they cohere with the motion of the earth?

By the way, the typical "convergent argument" relies upon the fact that the theory that is available about an issue may not represent it completely and definitely but just cover some aspects where we have pertinent experiences and plausible explanations for them. This kind of theory is used in collections of "criteria"; e.g. what a "good manager" is or (example 2.2.1) what counts as an "annoyed colleague." (The next case may already demand changes.)

Opposite to the objective dimension we have the "subjective dimension." It enters the stage because the arguers are subjects, that is, persons or collectives with specific knowledge, needs, beliefs, preferences, wishes, idiosyncrasies. Whether or not a claim or an argument is relevant, important, valid, sufficient, useful, etc., always has a subjective side: it is so or it is not so "for someone." The subjects for whom things are important or useful etc., are different. Therefore this subjective dimension has to be taken into account in argument analysis and evaluation.

(By the way, in formal systems—logic, mathematics, probability theory, etc.—this subjectivity plays a role only in the context of discovery; but when some formal element is applied in argumentation praxis or analysis, then subjectivity is certainly present.)

Theory (mostly technical theory) about subjective differences and their role in argumentation has been constructed in rhetoric (already in pre-Socratic times). With regard to truth, rightness, validity, etc., the (rhetorical) theory that is aware of the multitude of subjective views tends towards relativism. Since this is not really satisfying, a demand for universal characteristics (such as education or impartiality) in the audience was raised. Yet the real arguer with his/her specific system is never an ideally universal being (Perelman's "universal audience" does not exist). Subjectivity has to be taken as an indispensable condition in argumentation praxis and theory.[4] Therefore I have proposed to establish it as one of its basic "dimensions."

The normal appearance of subjectivity in argumentation is the frame structure of theses and arguments (see Section 4). Observing frame structures and having tools to treat them is, however, not enough. The arguers must be prepared to distance themselves from their subjective furnishings (see Section 7: "The Principle of Transsubjectivity").

4. Frame structures

Frame theory (main sources: Edmund Husserl[5], Ludwig Wittgenstein[6] and Erving Goffman[7]) is meanwhile accepted in social sciences, especially political sciences, but the theoretical penetration of frame structure is generally low (for a thorough elucidation, see Wohrapp 2009, Ch. 5[8]). The rhetorical relevance of frames can be seen quite easily. They have, however, an epistemological relevance too—this latter being far more important for argumentation theory.[9] Let me mention three points:

(a) A frame is the structure of the *(latent) classification* in which an issue is conceived.
(b) It is a generic term which fits for the issue as it appears for a *specific subject*.
(c) It imposes a *restriction of the features* which are considered to be about the issue.

To recognize the frame(s) in which you focus an issue you can ask yourself: "*In what way, as what,* do I see the issue?" Thus the frame structure would be:

I seen as X by S (issue I seen in frame X by subject S)

Illustration (taken from Wittgenstein 1969, p. 504)—the duck-hare head:

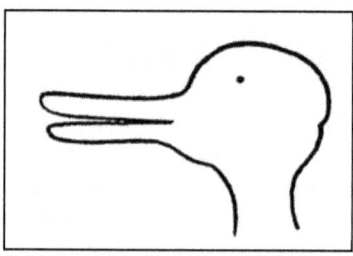

---

[4] One of the scholars who seriously envisages the subjectivity of arguers is Christian Kock (Kock 2010). Yet I cannot help myself: I find his subjectivist view goes too far and risks eliminating the merits of argumentation at all. Of course he is right in stressing that with deep (frame) differences we have no tools to safely derive a conclusion. But the characteristic power of a frame touching argument lies in its chance to loosen the "cage" of the subjective frame structures in which the issue is perceived. If, however, reasonable argument does not bring about insight, and we need to decide the issue, we have to leave argument and look for a formal procedure like a vote.
[5] Husserl's term for what I call a frame was "Noema" (Husserl 1976, §§ 87-96 and 128-135).
[6] Wittgenstein mused about frames (yet restricted to visual perception) under the title of "seeing as" (Wittgenstein 1969, Part II, § XI).
[7] Goffman 1974.
[8] See my first plea to integrate a concept of frame into argumentation theory in Wohlrapp 1995.
[9] A rhetorician who does recognise the epistemological impact of frames is Fred Kauffeld, (see Kauffeld, this volume).

Conductive Arguments: A Misleading Model 217

You can see this figure as a hare; or as a duck. You might at first see it as a hare without realizing that you could also see it as a duck; and vice versa. Important for argumentation: in the duck frame the "fingers" on the left are the beak, whereas in the hare frame they are a pair of ears. Obviously a beak is not a pair of ears. This is the shape of most of the contradictions that confuse our discussions. For illustration see the table of examples in section 2.

>   2.1.1 Some see the street (primarily) as a simplification for the traffic.
>   Some see the street (primarily) as a gash in the forest.
>
>   2.1.3 Some see euthanasia (primarily) as a matter of personal freedom.
>   Some see euthanasia (primarily) as a matter of social costs.

In PCTC-settings arguments can be "independent" from each other because the issue appears in different frames. Take again example *2.1.1*: Shall we build a street from A to B through the forest? Yes, because it simplifies traffic and thus will cause economic growth. No, because it harms the wildlife. How shall we compare these arguments? Is this a problem of our "weighing" the economic argument against the ecological one? Who in this case would be "we"?[10]

For an arguer who likes living on a simple economical level, surrounded by nature, ecology weighs more than for someone who has no developed feelings about nature at all. What can be done to achieve the necessary standardisation here?

When argumentation praxis hits frame differences it may be useful to provide some tools for frame treatment. I have proposed the following strategies to tackle the problems with divergent frames (Wohlrapp 2009, p. 330f), namely:

- Frame criticism
- Frame ranking
- Frame harmonizing
- Frame synthesizing

Here are some very short characterisations.

Frame *criticism* means showing that the frame (of a thesis or argument) is not adequate. See example *2.2.3*: In the debates about the motion of the Earth, the concept of "motion" had been treated (tacitly) as "operative" motion, until finally Galileo criticised that frame as being too narrow and invented a more general concept of "motion."[11]

Frame *ranking* means to resolve a competition between frames by ranking one above the other. Take example *2.1.1*. For most people believing in globalisation, the ranking of economy over ecology is the right option (until a giant tsunami-wave washes their homes away...).

Frame *harmonizing* means resolving a frame competition by modifying one or both so that they can co-exist. This is the usual task in intercultural connections.

Frame *synthesising* means resolving a frame competition by loosening the restrictions implied by the frames so that one can, but is not required to, be ranked over the other and vice versa. A very amusing example of frame synthesis is Mark Twain's Episode of Tom

---

[10] Before we can think about a "weighing" procedure or resume the result of such a procedure as an "on balance considerations," we have to solve two problems, which I have called the "comparison problem" and the "common ground problem" (see Wohlrapp 1998).
[11] By the way, frame revision via detecting a latent frame, criticising it as being too narrow and enlarging it, is the secret of most of scientific paradigm shifts.

Sawyer's painting the fence on a Sunday afternoon. The activity was started as stupid labor and was finally executed as a pleasant play.

In order to avoid misunderstandings, I should add here that these strategies are no more than possibilities for treating problems with different and incompatible framing in argument. None of them offers a way to a granted, or even a cogent, conclusion. If this is seen as a defect, that is because one continues to believe that an argument should be cogent. Cogency is, however, too narrow a standard for argument evaluation. Enlightening and enriching the understanding and insight into the issue may often be more adequate.

Finally, arguers must certainly be aware that very often frame differences cannot be overcome and that the argumentative effort may come to an end without having achieved a conclusion. This may be regrettable but has to be accepted. If, however, the issue *needs* to be decided, then something different is necessary: namely a decision according to some formal procedure such as majority vote or authoritative intervention.

5. Critique of Wellman's "conductive argument"

Carl Wellman's "Conductive Argument" is a PCT-setting of a very special kind. Its main characteristics, as described in Wellman 1971, were the following:

> (a) The conclusion is about an individual case, (b) it is drawn "inconclusively", (c) it is drawn from one or more premises which (d) can even be negatively relevant.

These characteristics seem to be rather enigmatic.[12] (a) is generally not understood at all, and has therefore mostly been dropped.[13] (b) has drawn a lot of attention (see e.g. Hitchcock 1994; and has meanwhile been replaced by the view that a special "on-balance-premise" should be added, see, e.g., Hansen this volume). (c) is mostly interpreted as the "convergent" argument form (see Govier 1997) and (d) raises irritating questions about the differences between a "premise" and a "counter-consideration."

For a general assessment of the model one should at first resist the suggestive parallelism of conduction with deduction, induction, abduction, etc. Deductive entailment is something far more basic than inductive or even conductive and abductive inferences. Whereas the latter three are (at least meant as) inferences which lead to "new" conclusions ("new" with regard to their content), the deductive inference is merely a formal (truth-preserving) rebuilding of propositions and has nothing to do with any content.[14] The bogus parallelism

---

[12] See Blair's symposium paper (Blair, this volume), offering an impressive bunch of problems. Readers should, however, be aware, that some of them are not simply due to Wellman's half-done idea, but also to the defects of (seemingly) well-established concepts like "convergent arguments," "premise" (as giving support to a conclusion), the "strength" of an argument and finally even the concept of "argument" itself.

[13] The "individual case clause" becomes understandable if one deepens Wellman's "process" and admits a "procedural dimension" of the whole argumentative activity. Then the issue (and the arguers) is an open source of possible information out of which new arguments (and reformulations of arguments and of theses) can always spring. Yet the necessary differentiations will need the *individual case*—otherwise one may notoriously end up in stating: Whether this or that consideration is relevant and what it contributes to a thesis or an argument depends on the case.

[14] I am grateful to David Hitchcock for an extensive discussion about this topic. I now realize that we can construct a purely formal (extensional) way of talking about "content" (as the "logical space" which is excluded by what we are saying). Yet this means to be confined to classical logic, viz., the

of conduction with induction or deduction has led scholars to the bizarre idea of comparing those inference forms with respect to quantities of "informational content." In deductive inference, this informational content would not increase from premises to conclusion, whereas in inductive and conductive inference it would do so. One must be on a modest level of understanding formal deductive logic to accept this (prima facie) intuitive wording. How can we count or measure the "informational content" of a proposition? Some theorists obviously believe that this is not a problem because the informational content could simply be identified with the propositional truth-value (for example Zenker, this volume). This is not a very good idea.

For example, take the proposition: "Sue Miller is ill." It seems easy to accept its informational content being equal to the one in: "Dick Jones is ill." But what about "Barack Obama is ill"? Is the informational content still equal, despite the fact, that the illness of the U.S. President is far more important than that of some citizen? You think, this is not grave? Well, then look at this example: Any proposition p entails logically the disjunctive proposition $p \vee q$. Therefore we can, without changing the truth value, go from p to $p \vee q$. Is this also possible without changing the informational content? Let p be the proposition "The remains of the space capsule will go down over the Pacific." In a News Agency which receives this information, there is an employee who has learned some logic. Maybe he has heard that in a valid deductive inference, the informational content cannot increase from premises to the conclusion. Therefore he might be inclined to transmit that information as: "The remains of the space capsule will go down over the Pacific or over Los Angeles." Would we really believe that he has not increased the informational content of the original news? I will not continue this line of thought here. I will not try to clarify the pragmatic differences between the concepts "propositional truth" and "information." I will only state once more that we should be very careful with Wellman's suggestion, that conduction is something parallel to deduction and induction.

Concerning Wellman's own description and evaluation of the conductive argument, there is a remarkable shift in his writings. Whereas in the book of 1971 he seems to be rather proud of his developing a new inference form, whose essential operation consisted in "weighing" the pro-arguments against the contra-arguments, he published in 1975 a second book on normative argumentation where he discusses at length several important moral issues: civil disobedience, abortion, premarital sex, marijuana, capital punishment etc. There he writes:

> We cannot put arguments on any scale and read off their weight from the pointer, nor can we literally heft the arguments in our hands to feel their relative weight. What we can and must do is to think through the various arguments and feel their logical force or lack of it. ... The logical force of an argument is its psychological force after criticism. In weighing an argument, it is not the strength of its first impact upon the mind that counts, but the persuasion it continues to exert after on has reflected on the argument, formulated it as clearly as possible and considered objections to it, discussed its point and its merit with other rational persons, and then reflected some more. The logically valid argument is the one that retains its persuasiveness throughout this critical process of reflection and discussion. We come to know which act is right by subjecting all the pro and con arguments to this sort of

---

set of truth-definite propositions—which is too small a basis for argumentation theory; also the irritations of my space capsule example (see below) cannot be overcome on this line of thought.

criticism and then feeling which seem to be more persuasive. (Wellman 1975b, pp. 291-292)

Let me stress the most remarkable points. The metaphor of "weighing" seems now to be dissolved into the idea of an argumentative *process* which:

- involves *others*,
- considers *objections*,
- is *reflective* (i.e., in distance, involving a meta-level).

This is very similar to the setting I use in my theoretical approach (Wohlrapp 2009); and it is apparently something very different from applying some nice argumentation scheme that then would somehow deliver an output conclusion. If we take the demands about the "critical process" into account we will surely make a better use of Wellman's ideas. And if we go into studying the exemplary discussions in his second book, we will find that, in what he *does* when he argues, he is much better than what his *description* would suggest. Yet even in the second book—an interesting and inspiring set of arguments—he appears (in my eyes) to be fenced in a cage of logical-, objective- and product-thinking. I might sum up my criticism in two main objections.

5.1. The procedural dimension is underestimated

It is a striking fact that Wellman, even if he insists in a PCT-setting being a process of thinking and rethinking arguments, seems to be quite unaware of the changes that the arguments undergo: about how and why they appear. Take, for example, his discussion of premarital sex. There he considers the argument that it could be done out of love and would then be good because loving acts are good (Wellman 1975b, p. 110). When he rethinks this argument, he adds the observation that love can be responsible or irresponsible and that, if premarital sex is an act of irresponsible love, it has to be judged as morally evil (Wellman 1975b, p. 123).

What happens here is that a differentiation is introduced in the concept of love, so that we can now distinguish two kinds of love. With regard to that distinction the pro-argument undergoes a change and becomes a con-argument. Therefore the model of listing the pros and listing the cons in order to weigh them against each other seems to be no more than the final step of a process in which a bunch of pros and cons have to be collected, generated, checked, confirmed, criticised, replaced and thus transformed into a group which represent the "essential" arguments. Please note that this process is not just a prelude to, but is crucial for, the argumentation about the issue. And it will usually not be enough to justify a final balancing and weight-comparing operation, which might be necessary. Also this final operation can have rather different shapes, some of which may be quite obvious while others may need very extensive justifications.

5.2. The subjective dimension is underestimated

Wellman produces his conclusions mainly in two steps. At first he distinguishes types of cases whose evaluation (as "wicked" or "virtuous" cases) seems to be obvious or can easily made plausible via adding new aspects in the rethinking. Then he looks at whether the wicked cases are more frequent or more normal than the virtuous cases. If this can be stated, his respective conclusion is already won. Thus he devaluates premarital sex because he finds very few virtuous cases compared to a lot of wicked cases. (Among the virtuous cases is the following melodramatic story: an attractive young spy manages to squeeze some important secret out of the chief spy of the enemy, an evil state, by having intercourse with him, of course reluctantly, and thus serving her country (Wellman 1975b, p. 127).) If, however, there is no extra weight to be added due to the frequency or usualness of the good or the bad types of case, then he himself performs a ranking, i.e., he states that something is more important than some other thing. For instance, about abortion he finds that the benefits of abortion for mothers with problems and (would-be) children with handicaps outweigh the loss of beings that could become persons (Wellman 1975b, p. 168[15]). And about marijuana, he believes that the benefits of peaceful and appreciative consumption are outweighed by the evils of the criminal environment and the health risks (Wellman 1975b, p. 74).

Although his conclusions are rather cautious and hesitant, they come along not as subjective judgements but as assessments of the "logical force" of the considered arguments. We are told that the "logical force" of an argument should be seen as its "psychological force after criticism." Yet it remains doubtful how something like a universal way of feeling with regard to the persuasive force of arguments can be admitted. Wellman seems not to acknowledge at all that such a ranking or weight comparison will usually be relative to a subject system. It is the arguer (or the group of arguers who have come to an agreement) who states that "for me/for us" some things are more important than some other things. This "weight-comparison consideration" can and should be justified (if it is not only a momentary decision without any general impact) with the help of the norms, uses, preferences of the subject—and if the subject is a society, then with the help of the moral or legal norms of that society.

Subject systems, however, tend to be different. (In Germany, for example, we have come to quite the contrary conclusions about the issues of marijuana and abortion.) These subject differences should not be ignored; they should be taken into account and have, in case of conflict, to be worked out. What can be done via argumentation here is what I have sketched above in Section 5 (see the reframing strategies). Yet this will only help if it is done in the spirit of "transsubjectivity" (see Section 7).

6. The Retroflexive Structure

How can a dialogue with pros and cons be analysed, if the model of Wellmann's Conductive Argument is put aside as misleading and the above-sketched square of dimensions is taken up as a guideline? This question will certainly arise here, but I am afraid I am not able to answer it sufficiently in this paper. What I will do is to give just a rough overview of the "retroflexive structure"; namely, the structure of the dynamic process that emerges out of a pro and contra argumentation when it is performed and/or analysed in the light of the four dimensions.

Whenever an argumentative dialogue is opened, a thesis is claimed. This expresses the fact that there is at least some intuition about how a gap or an unclear spot in our understanding (our belief- or orientation system) could be filled. The thesis will be the theoretical articulation of that intuition.

In order to see whether we can accept the thesis as a new orientation for praxis and living (that is, whether or not the thesis is "valid" [gültig]) we then look for arguments to justify the thesis. Justifying it means connecting it to an established theoretical basis (what is best: connecting it to some knowledge, see above, Section 3.2. "objective dimension").

---

[15] The final conclusion (Wellman 1975b, p181) shows a slightly different accentuation.

The task of justifying a thesis is pursued by producing a sequence of pro-arguments for it. Sometimes, however, we face objections (contra-arguments) which shows that we have done our justification:

- wrongly,
- loosely, or
- one-sidedly.

Objections that arise can articulate criticism towards every part of the argumentation: against theses, sub-theses, inference-patterns, concepts; but also against whole arguments, and here as well against pro- as against contra- arguments. If an objection appears, it is usually not simply accepted as a contra-argument, but it is firstly discussed (as Wellman has put it: It has to be "thought through").

Generally the argumentative activities move in the following scenario: Arguments make use of theoretical bases in order to justify or criticize a thesis or any argument. The argumentative process does not progress in a linear way, but works forwards and backwards, reformulating on one side the arguments and the thesis and on the other side rearranging and/or correcting the basis. When the process eventually comes to a successful end, then it has produced not only the adequate conclusion, but also the essential arguments (i.e., those which are suitable for the production of that conclusion) and finally an appropriate theoretical basis on which the conclusion as well as the arguments rely.

Diagram:

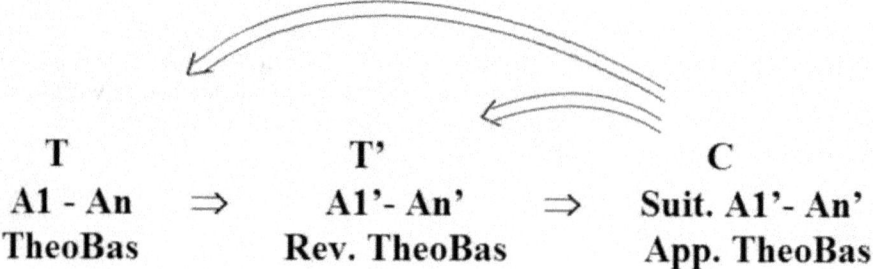

T   **T'**   **C**
A1 - An ⇒ **A1'- An'** ⇒ **Suit. A1'- An'**
TheoBas   **Rev. TheoBas**   **App. TheoBas**

Legend: T stands for 'Thesis', T' for 'revised or modified thesis', C stands for 'conclusion'. A1-An stands for the Arguments A1-An, A1'-An' stands for that same row of arguments but which now includes at least one argument that has undergone a change. Suit. A1'-An' stands for the row of those arguments which have been selected to be "the essential arguments"; they are suitable to produce the conclusion.

In search of a name for this character of the argumentative process I have christened it "the retroflexive structure".[16] With regard to Wellman's bold sketch, I dare say that the retroflexive structure is the very truth of the conductive argument scheme. Please be aware that when this structure is acknowledged there is no longer a one-sided linear, but a mutual sup-

---

[16] This structure did not come to my mind just recently. I have tried to explain it for the first time in Wohlrapp 1990, in English in Wohlrapp 1997. It has even been integrated—apparently with at least some useful effect—into an approach for the formalisation of deliberation dialogues (see McBurney, Hitchcock & Parsons 2007).

port relationship between the selection of "premises" (i.e., the arguments which have been found to be suitable premises) and the selection of the conclusion.

For those readers who find this view strange, it could be helpful to consider as an analogue the famous "reflective equilibrium" in John Rawls' *Theory of Justice* (Rawls 1971, pp. 48-51). This figure is supposed to explain the development of (a) general principles out of (b) the common sense of justice, applied to (c) a judgement of a specific case. For the forming of a verdict the jury has to activate its sense of justice which itself has to be articulated in principles. Principles, however, are strictly general sentences. They must fit not only the actual case but others too, cases which are not yet known. Rawls is well aware that none of the three elements of the process is ready and clear in advance and that in order to produce a more or less stable result one has to work from both ends—forwards and backwards—until an "equilibrium" is achieved (in general argumentative terms: until no relevant objection is open any more).

7. The Principle of Transsubjectivity

In a last section I will very briefly try to shed some light upon what I consider the most important and at the same time the most underestimated element of the argumentative praxis and theory. Argumentation is not only instrumental but it requires a special attitude and education in the personality of the arguer: The orientation towards truth and rightness, the conviction that one's certainties (not only our vested interests and prejudices but even our knowledge) have to be subordinated to the aim of truly understanding and shaping the human world. This intention is the secret spirit of the argumentative praxis. It is only partly externalisable and therefore can hardly be safeguarded by prescribing rules or procedures of argumentation. The best articulation of this spirit that I know of is Paul Lorenzen's "Principle of Transsubjectivity".

Lorenzen was the founder of Operative Mathematics and Dialogue Logic in Germany during the 1950s and 1960s. This is well known. Less known is, that in his late work he engaged in constructing a framework of concepts and principles for reasonable ethics and politics. Very soon he realised that all the specific norms that could be considered had to be based upon the willingness to work upon one's subjectivity. This willingness he proposed to articulate in a general principle, "Transsubjectivity":

> Transsubjectivity is not a fact, but it is not a postulate either. Transsubjectivity is simply a term characterizing that activity in which we are always already involved if we begin to reason at all... Transsubjectivity ... is still subjectivity, but a subjectivity which is aware of its own limits—and tries to overcome them.... No person can do more than try to overcome his/her subjectivity. (Lorenzen 1969, pp 82f)

Please note that here we envisage something like a middle course between the sheer acknowledgement of subjectivity and a complete self-surrender. I will not go into further considerations about a more conscious implantation of this principle into argumentation. I would only like to finally state: Without a commitment to the principle of transsubjectivity (of course not necessarily under this name), all arguing will be no more than sophistry.

Chapter 15

Conductive Arguments: A Meta-argumentation Approach

MAURICE A. FINOCCHIARO

1. Introduction: An historical-textual approach to conductive meta-arguments

In 1971, Carl Wellman coined the terms conduction, conductive argument, and conductive reasoning to characterize a type of argument or reasoning intended to be a distinct alternative to deduction, induction, and even abduction. He thought this new concept of conduction was needed in order to make sense of an important type of argument that is especially prevalent in ethics, but also common in many other fields. The problems dealt with under this label involved issues such as the accumulation of evidence, the convergence of multiple reasons, the balance of pros and cons, and the possibility of good but nonconclusive inference. Wellman's account generated a considerable body of literature dealing with such problems and using his terminology.[1] This literature and these problems are sufficiently important to deserve continued attention, and my primary aim here is to undertake a critical examination of it.

I believe this is worth doing despite the fact that the topics and theoretical problems just mentioned have been fruitfully studied also by many other scholars without referring to Wellman or using the conductive terminology. An example of such studies is John Stuart Mill's essay *On Liberty*, but he is only a classic case.[2] This fact might lead some to regard the notion of conduction as simply a different way of talking about such problems, and thus to dismiss the views of Wellman and his followers. However, the fact of the existence of this other literature leads me to want to explore the relationship between the two. Thus, after my critical examination of the literature on Wellman and conduction, I also plan to provide some perspective by briefly discussing the views of other scholars who have dealt with the same problems under different terminology. Such a perspective is a secondary aim of this chapter.

A third aim is to analyze some important actual or real cases of conductive argumentation, and relate them to the views of both Wellman and the other explicit conductive theorists on the one hand, and Mill and the other implicit conductive theorists on the other. One of these cases is an opinion published in 2009 in the *New York Times* by columnist David Brooks about the U.S. heath-care reform law. The other case is the argument in favor of the Copernican theory of the earth's motion advanced by Galileo Galilei in his book *Dialogue on the Two Chief World Systems, Ptolemaic and Copernican* (1632).

The approach I am going to follow is a further instantiation of the historical-textual approach I have used and reflected upon before (see Finocchiaro 1980, pp. 293-431; 2005a, pp. 21-91). In this approach, one studies reasoning and argumentation found in actual, real, or realistic texts that have some historical importance, with the aim of deriving, testing, or refining general concepts and principles that may be normative or evaluative, as well as

---

[1] It is useful to have a complete list of these works, dealing *explicitly* with conduction: Allen 1990, 1993; Bickenbach and Davies 1997; Ennis 2004; Govier 1980a, 1980b, 1980c, 1987b, 1999b, 2001 (pp. 392-412), 2010 (pp. 352-377); Hitchcock 1981, 1983, 1994; Johnson 2000a (pp. 84-88, 92-95); Johnson and Blair 2000; Wohlrapp 1995, 1998, 2008; Zenker 2009b.

[2] Other works, to be cited or summarized below, are: Eisend 2006; Finocchiaro 2010; Jacquette 2007; Johnson 2000a; Kock 2003, 2007b, 2007c, 2007d; O'Keefe 1999; Scriven 1981.

descriptive or explanatory. In the present investigation, the real arguments on which I am going to focus are those found in the theoretical literature dealing explicitly with conductive arguments, as well as in the two just-mentioned important actual examples of conductive argumentation dealing with concrete issues. The former focus represents a leap onto the meta-level and into meta-analysis. In a sense, such a leap is an obvious and natural thing to do for a theorist of argument who follows the historical-textual approach. But I have another motivation for doing so here.

That is, for the past several years I have been studying a special class of arguments which I call meta-arguments (cf. Finocchiaro 2007a, 2007b, 2007c, 2009, 2010a, 2010b). I define a meta-argument as an argument about one or more arguments. A meta-argument is contrasted to a ground-level argument, which is typically about such topics as natural phenomena, human actions, or historical events. Meta-arguments are special in at least two ways. First, as just defined, they are a particular case of argumentation, and so their study is or ought to be a particular branch of the theory of argument. Secondly, they are crucially important because the theory of argument consists, or ought to consist, essentially of meta-argumentation. From this point of view, the literature on conductive arguments provides good material for a case study in meta-argumentation, or to be more precise for the historical-textual study of meta-argumentation.

In the present case, however, this literature has an additional relevance. For besides containing important actual arguments and thus being amenable to the historical-textual approach, and besides containing meta-arguments and thus being amenable to the meta-argumentation focus, this literature contains many arguments that are themselves conductive, as some of the relevant authors have pointed out. In other words, the material we are dealing with consists not only of actual arguments (at least if that material is properly so analyzed), and not only of meta-arguments (given its theoretical nature), but also of conductive meta-arguments (at least in large measure).

A final procedural or methodological point is worth making. It turns out that the meta-argumentation approach is worth pursuing in this case also because conductive arguments themselves happen to have a significant meta-argumentative aspect; or at least, this is a *working hypothesis* which I would like to explore or test in this investigation. My theoretical assumption is that an essential characteristic of conductive arguments is a *balance-of-considerations claim* that must be implicitly made, explicitly formulated, or critically justified for the construction, interpretation, or evaluation of conductive arguments; and such a balance-of-considerations claim is an irreducible meta-argumentative aspect of conductive arguments. I stress that this assumption is a working hypothesis in the sense that it provides a substantive theoretical guide in this investigation. Whether it is true, or to what extent it is true, is something to be determined at the end, or as a result, of this investigation. The presence of this working hypothesis should also clarify that although my historical-textual approach is a type of empirical approach, it is not empiricist in the sense of pretending to study the empirical material with a *tabula rasa*.

The implementation of this approach requires that the arguments contained in the conductive-argument literature be reconstructed with the care, explicitness, and regimentation which argumentation theorists usually practice or preach for the reconstruction of arguments that are *the subject* of their reflections. A common way of doing this involves utilizing a methodical numbering system for keeping track of various claims in argumentation, and for indicating their place in the network that makes up the propositional macrostructure of arguments. In what follows, I use a version of this method which I have adapted from

Angell (1964, pp. 369-93).[3] In my exposition below, the numbers are given in brackets at the beginning of the sentences or clauses that express the various claims. Although this will add considerable visual encumbrance to parts of the exposition, I find it an efficient way, in the course of long and complex arguments, of indicating explicitly what propositions relate to what and how, and hence of enhancing logical clarity and acuity. Here such numbers are usually inserted without comment and intended to be an aid in the reconstruction; but this is not meant to exclude more analysis later.

The full details of this numbering system cannot be elaborated here and must be largely presupposed. Suffice it to say that the key idea is that if a given claim is labeled [n], then the premises that directly support it are labeled [n1], [n2], [n3], etc.; and if claim [nm] is part of some argument, then the premises directly supporting it are labeled [nm1], [nm2], [nm3], etc. Such numbering is also associated with the visual representation of complex arguments by means of structure diagrams in the shape of either tree roots or tree branches. Following Angell, I use the tree-root pattern. In any case, here such diagrams will normally *not* be drawn, since their construction is a mechanical procedure entailed by the numbers. However, a few examples will be given.

The main complication worth elaborating here relates to the difference between independent and interdependent (or linked) support provided by two or more premises for a conclusion. When [n] is supported *independently* by two or more sets of premises, then letters should be used to distinguish one set from another, e.g., [na1], [na2], [na3], ..., [nb1], [nb2], [nb3], ..., [nc1], [nc2], [nc3], etc. Such labeling of independent support is crucial for expressing and understanding the logical structure of an argument when there are sets of premises that provide independent support and sets that provide interdependent (linked) support. For example, suppose some conclusion C is supported by proposition P and by propositions Q and R in such a way that P supports C independently of Q and R, but Q and R support C interdependently with each other, rather than independently of each other; then to reflect this structure properly, the systematic labeling would be: P = Ca1; Q = Cb1; and R = Cb2.

However, sometimes some simplifications are possible. For example, suppose that a conclusion C is supported by three propositions, P, Q, and R, and that all three provide independent support, or all three provide interdependent support. Then the strict systematic labeling would be Ca1, Cb1, and Cc1 if they are all independently supportive; and it would be C1, C2, and C3 if they are all interdependently supportive. But there is no loss of clarity if in the former case we drop the 'a', 'b', and 'c' and use only sequential numerals; that is, if the three premises are labeled C1, C2, and C3 even when they are all independently supportive. In short, the different labeling of independently and interdependently supportive premises will be implemented only when necessary, which happens when a given step or subargument contains both independent and interdependent support.

Similarly, suppose conclusion C is independently supported by premises Ca1 and Cb1. Then, in a context where there are other propositions interdependent with these, say Ca2 and Cb2, it is important and necessary to keep both the letters and the numerals modifying the 'C'. However, in a context where there are no other propositions interdependent with Ca1 and Cb1, their independent support for C can be represented equally well by dropping the numerals and labeling them more simply Ca and Cb. In short, when a conclusion C is supported independently by a sequence of single premises, Ca1, Cb1, Cc1, etc., we can drop either each occurrence of the numeral 1 (resulting in the labels Ca, Cb, Cc, etc.), or we

---

[3] See also: Scriven 1976, pp. 41-43; Finocchiaro (1980, pp. 311-31; 2005a, pp. 39-41); Eemeren and Grootendorst 1984, pp. 87-93; Eemeren, Grootendorst, and Kruiger 1984, pp. 17-36; Freeman 1991; Snoeck Henkemans 1992.

can drop the lower-case letters and use different numerals in sequence (resulting in the labels C1, C2, C3, etc.).

2. Wellman's invention of conduction

Wellman's main argument can be interpreted as an attempt to justify the claim that [W1] there is an important special type of argument called conductive argument. Its details can be reconstructed as follows.

[W11] Conductive arguments are arguments "in which 1) a conclusion about some individual case 2) is drawn nonconclusively 3) from one or more premises about the same case 4) without any appeal to other cases" (52).[4] [W12] Such arguments are common in ethics, but also in law, politics, and philosophy, and indeed in all fields where evaluations, recommendations, classifications, or interpretations are common.

However, [W13] conductive arguments are not deductive, since [W131] the nonconclusive clause (no. 2) of the definition implies that they neither are nor are claimed to be deductively valid, and [W132] deductive arguments are those that claim to be deductively valid (4).

[W14] Nor are conductive arguments reducible to deductive form (83), for several reasons. One is that [W14a1] conductive arguments usually involve the weighing of pros and cons, [W14a2] which has no place in deduction (25-28). To see why [W14a2] "deductivism ... leaves no room for the weighing of pros and cons" (25), [W14a21] consider a typical conductive argument of what Wellman calls "the third pattern ... that form of argument in which some conclusion is drawn from both positive and negative considerations" (57). [W14a22a1] We could reconstruct it as a deductively valid argument whose premises would include all the pros and all the cons, as well as an additional premise that the pros outweigh the cons (or vice versa); [W1422a2] but such an additional premise would have to be justified by actually weighing the pros and cons, and not by deductive reasoning; "therefore, [W14a22] the difficulty has simply been pushed back one stage in the process of justification" (26). [W14a22b1] Or we could reconstruct the conductive argument as a deductively valid argument whose premises would again include all the pros and cons, but with the additional premise being a generalization covering and connecting all the premises and the conclusion; but [W14a22b2] such a generalization would have to be justified by means of an induction by enumeration based on particular cases; and [W14a22b3] to justify each of these cases we would need to engage in weighing the pros and cons for that particular case; therefore, again [W14a22] the nondeductive weighing of pros and cons has to be done at another stage of the process of justification.

Another reason why [W14] conductive arguments are not reducible to deductive form is that [W14b1] such arguments are characterized by a convergence of evidence, [W14b2] which deductive arguments do not exhibit (28). [W14b3] Convergence of evidence is the phenomenon of the accumulation of weight, i.e., the increase of the logical force, i.e., the strengthening of the "implicative link" (29) resulting from different premises. Now, [W14b21] there is no accumulation of evidence within a single deductively valid argument with multiple premises, because [W14b211] no individual premise by itself lends any support to the conclusion, whereas [W14b212] all together they provide perfect support. [W14b22] For the case of a given conclusion supported by several deductively valid arguments, there is still no accumulation of evidence or convergence, because [W14b2211] each

---

[4] In this section, references to Wellman 1971 will be given by just citing the page number(s) in parenthesis, as done here.

argument provides conclusive support for the conclusion, and so [W14b221] the sum total does not exceed the support of any one argument. [W14b23] The point of multiple deductively valid arguments is to increase the "probative force" of the whole set. On the other hand, [W14b24] "where there is genuine convergence of evidence it is the logical force, not the probative force, of the argument that is increased with the addition of each new premise" (29).

[W15] Conductive arguments are not inductive either, since [W151] induction means "that sort of reasoning by which a hypothesis is confirmed or disconfirmed by establishing the truth or falsity of its implications" (32), and [W152] conductive arguments are not instances of the testing of hypotheses based on the testing of their consequences.

However, [W16] conductive arguments are capable of being "valid" or "invalid," in a general sense of these terms meaning good or bad. For [W16a1] "to say that an argument is valid is to claim that, when subjected to an indefinite amount of criticism, it is persuasive ..." (110);[5] and [W16a2] "to say that an argument is persuasive is to say that it usually persuades one who accepts ... its premises, who rejected or doubted its conclusion just before being subjected to the argument, and who thinks through the argument" (91); and [W16a3] "by criticism I mean a process of thinking about and discussion of the argument" (92), such that "the process ... does not so much discover which arguments are antecedently persuasive or unpersuasive as make them persuasive or unpersuasive" (95).

Moreover, [W16b1] there is a practical guideline for checking the "validity" of conductive arguments, at least those of the "third pattern." [W16b11] The basic principle is that "one decides whether an argument is valid [i.e., good] by weighing the pros and the cons" (57). But [W16b12] this principle does not amount to a quantitative method: "the weighing should not be thought of as putting each reason on a scale, noting the amount of weight, and then calculating the difference between the weight of the reasons for and the reasons against" (57). And [W16b13] the principle does not amount to a mechanical process: "nor should one think of the weighing as being done on a balance scale in which one pan is filled with the pros and the other with the cons" (57). Instead [W16b14] the principle requires an exercise in judgment: "rather one should think of the weighing in terms of the model of determining the weight of objects by hefting them in one's hands" (58). But we need one more refinement, i.e., "thinking through the arguments" (80): [W16b15] "suppose that I must estimate the relative weight of two piles of stones. In this case I am only strong enough to take one or two stones in a hand at a time. Hence I must lift the stones in each pile one after the other in order to estimate their total weight. Similarly ... it is usually necessary to turn over the pros and cons successively in one's mind" (58).

Any elaborate analysis and evaluation of Wellman's account is best postponed until we have examined the relevant views of other scholars who have already examined it. However, a few comments are relatively obvious and can be stated immediately. Wellman's definition of 'conductive argument' (proposition W11) is largely stipulative, since the term 'conduction' is relatively, if not absolutely, new. The common occurrence of conductive arguments (proposition W12) is an empirical claim, but it is an extremely important one and grounds the importance of this class of arguments. The account is assuming a definition of 'deductive argument' (proposition W132) that is relatively common but highly controversial. Similarly, Wellman is assuming a definition of 'inductive argument' (proposition W151) that is highly idiosyncratic and highly questionable. Furthermore, he is using the

---

[5] Here Wellman's sentence continues by saying "... for everyone who thinks in the normal way" (110), which is an important qualification in his full account (see Wellman 1971, pp. 96-98), but which I am overlooking in this discussion for simplicity's sake (and hopefully without oversimplification).

Conductive Arguments: A Meta-argumentation Approach

term *valid* argument in the ordinary-language sense meaning *good* argument, but this contravention is best avoided since it contradicts standard technical logical terminology, and since several other ordinary terms are easily available and avoid confusion (such as good, cogent, strong, inferentially adequate, etc.). On the other hand, the content of his conception of good ("valid") argument, proposition W16a, is extremely interesting and suggestive insofar as it is involves the notion of ability to withstand criticism. Finally, his normative notion of "thinking through an argument" to weigh the pros and cons (proposition W16b14) is not completely opaque or empty, since it is elaborated in terms of an enlightening analogy with estimating the weight of physical objects by lifting them with one's hands.

Before proceeding, it will be useful to draw the structure diagram for Wellman's argument, in order to provide a visual illustration of its propositional macrostructure corresponding to the numbering system I am using in these reconstructions. Drawing this particular diagram will also suggest that for the other arguments here such diagrams will not be really necessary and can be dispensed with.

This diagram will be drawn in two parts because subargument W14 is by itself so large and complex that the whole diagram for the whole argument would require more space than a normal printed page or computer screen. Thus the first part of the diagram represents the reconstructed argument minus the W14 subargument, although it contains proposition W14 as unsupported. The second part of the diagram represents the structure of the subargument supporting W14, and contains proposition W14 as the final conclusion. The two parts are, respectively, the following:

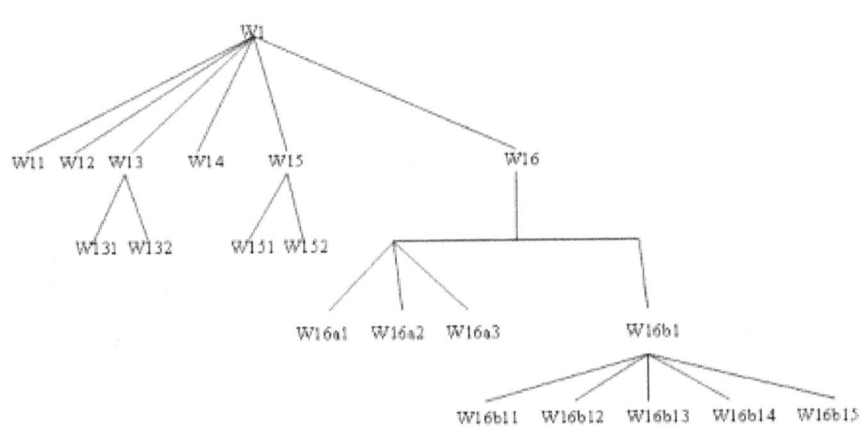

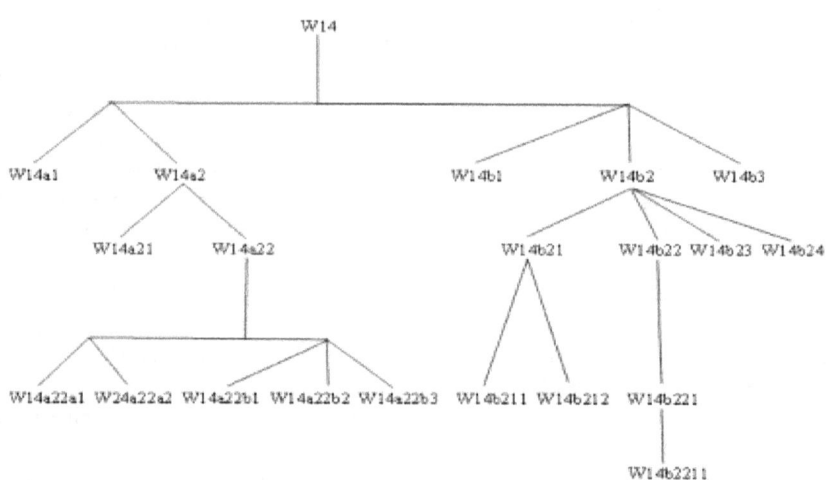

3. Hitchcock on conductive adequacy

In a number of works, David Hitchcock (1980, 1981, 1983, 1994) has elaborated a constructive interpretation of Wellman's account which I would reconstruct as follows.

Hitchcock's main conclusion may be taken to be the claim that [H1] there is an important and distinctive standard of appraisal of arguments that is called conductive adequacy.

[H11] An argument is *conductively adequate* (1983, p. 105) if and only if the premises when true provide reasons for accepting the conclusion that are [H11a] nonconclusive, jointly as well as separately (1983, p. 106), [H11b] separately relevant to the conclusion, and [H11c] mutually enhancing (1983, p. 51), i.e., cumulatively weighty (1983, p. 52), i.e., jointly supportive, i.e., jointly cumulative; and that [H11d] outweigh the considerations opposing it (1983, pp. 105, 132; 1994).

[H12] Conductive adequacy is a very useful standard of appraisal because [H121] it is the most relevant one for arguments supporting evaluations, recommendations, interpretations, and classifications, and [H122] such arguments are ubiquitous (1983, pp. 105-6, 130-34).

[H13] Conductive adequacy cannot be reduced to deductive validity because [H131] the needed extra premises would not be true or independently justifiable (1983, p. 131), or the conclusion could not be usefully qualified (1981).

[H14] Conductive adequacy is partly similar to, and partly different from, inductive probability. [H141] It is partly similar because [H1411] they are both special cases of deductive invalidity, and because [H1412] both conductively adequate and inductively probable arguments are nonmonotonic in the sense that "new information independent of the truth value of the premises but relevant to the conclusion should lead us to re-examine our acceptance of the conclusion" (1981, p. 15). And [H142] they are partly different because [H1421] inductive probability is often quantifiable but conductive adequacy (by definition) never is, and because [H1422] the tacit premises added to make an argument more explicit often involve *ceteris paribus* clauses for conductive adequacy, but not for inductive probability (1981).

Note that in the way I have reconstructed Hitchcock's account of conduction, it has striking structural parallelisms with Wellman's account. Both accounts are meta-arguments whose main conclusions are existential generalizations; and in each case, the key premises are, in turn, a definition, an empirical claim, an anti-deductivist claim, and an anti-inductivist claim. And to Wellman's nuanced and complex anti-deductivist subargument, there corresponds Hitchcock's nuanced and complex anti-inductivist subargument. Moreover, it should be noted that the respective main conclusions, besides being existential claims, are from another point of view importance claims. This feature is itself important because at this point students of conduction will sense that arguments justifying claims of importance are typical cases of conductive arguments and/or arguments for which questions of conductive adequacy are especially relevant. This feature may be worth elaborating later, as our discussion proceeds.

The main substantive difference is that the focus for Wellman is conductive arguments and for Hitchcock conductive adequacy. That is, Wellman's conductive argument is an interpretive category that defines a particular type of arguments in terms of a number of properties specifying features of the argument's premises and conclusion, and such that some conductive arguments are good and some bad. However, Hitchcock's conductive adequacy is an evaluative category that defines a particular standard of appraisal, which may be compared and contrasted with other standards, and which may be applied in principle to all arguments, with the result that some arguments are conductively adequate and some conductively inadequate.

On the other hand, Wellman does explicitly articulate an evaluative guideline for conductive arguments, namely the weighing of pros and cons (proposition W16b11). And this corresponds to the main element of Hitchcock's standard, namely that the favorable reasons outweigh the opposing considerations (proposition H11d). Conversely, Hitchcock does not define a particular type of argument called conductive argument, but he does define (1983, pp. 130-34) at least three particular classes of arguments for which the standard of conductive adequacy is especially relevant and appropriate, namely arguments that justify recommendations, evaluations, or classifications. And these three classes correspond to the prototypical cases of Wellman's conductive arguments. Moreover, in Hitchcock's definition of 'conductive adequacy,' the first three clauses are essentially equivalent to a notion of conductive argument as a type of argument. In fact, we can preview immediately that they corresponds to Trudy Govier's definition of the conductive type of argument.

In any case, this (H) account is a good example of Hitchcock's usually insightful work. Those familiar with it, in particular his views on the distinction between deduction and induction, will recognize the familiar theme. That is, Hitchcock has argued plausibly and convincingly that deduction and induction are not interpretive but evaluative categories. They do not represent two distinct types of arguments defined in terms of discernible properties, but rather two distinct standards of appraisal that can be applied to all arguments, although the conditions and relevance of applicability depend on the context, and on the type of argument we are dealing with, where distinct argument types are defined independently of deduction and induction. Hitchcock recognizes that this approach is not totally original with him, but rather that it can be traced to philosophers such as Brian Skyrms (1966, pp. 6-16; 1975), and I might add Robert Ennis (2001, p. 98). However, no one has stressed and exploited the evaluative approach to deduction and induction as Hitchcock has. In fact, his account of conduction may be regarded as an extension of that approach.

However, I think that the evaluative approach is much more feasible and viable for deduction and induction than it is for conduction. For in the former two cases, one can take as one's starting point the relatively clear and uncontroversial definitions of deductive validity and inductive probability; then the application of these definitions to any argument whatever is a feasible and highly valuable enterprise; furthermore, one can give relatively clear and uncontroversial definitions of various particular subtypes of arguments in ways that are completely independent of the notions of deductive validity and inductive probability; and finally, one can formulate rough guidelines for deciding which one of the two general standards to apply for which particular subtypes of arguments. However, in the case of conduction, this is not equally viable because the definition of conductive adequacy is not completely independent of the definition of the conductive type of argument. This difficulty I propose as an open problem for further investigation.

Moreover, even for the cases of deduction and induction, the evaluative approach may be deemed too self-limiting insofar as it fails to take seriously and exploit the possibility of formulating what might be called a conductive definition. A conductive definition of deductive argument and of inductive argument as types of argument would be a set of conditions whose application would yield an interpretive claim that a given argument is a deductive type of argument (or inductive, as the case may be) based on a *conductive* meta-argument. On the other hand, Hitchcock's criticism of the distinction between a deductive type and an inductive type of argument, and the usual critiques by other scholars (e.g., Ennis 2001), seems to presuppose that the interpretation or classification of an argument as deductive or inductive should be based on a deductive or deductively valid meta-argument.[6]

Such a conductive definition of deductive and inductive arguments has been provided by James Freeman, whose insight I am here adapting. His conductive definition is this: "An argument is to be judged deductive (inductive) as the balance of deductive indicators outweighs the balance of inductive indicators (the balance of inductive indicators outweighs deductive indicators). In particular, all things being equal, when an argument specifically claims that its premises guarantee the truth of its conclusion or when it belongs to a deductive family, it should be judged deductive. Similarly, when it claims that its premises only give evidence for its conclusion, or when it belongs to an inductive family, it should be judged inductive" (Freeman 1983, p. 9; see Freeman 1988, pp. 225-29). Deductive indicators are, of course, words such as necessarily, entails, and proves; whereas inductive indicators are words such as probably, likely, and supports. And the deductive family includes argument types such as *modus ponens*, *modus tollens*, and categorical syllogism; whereas the inductive family includes induction by enumeration, statistical syllogism, and inference to the best explanation. Then Freeman insightfully asks: "What is the status of an argument, A, pray tell, which argues that a certain argument, B, is either deductive or inductive? Is A inductive or deductive?" (1983, p. 10). And he answers: "by taking account of various factors each of which is a relevant mark for the argument's being deductive or inductive ... such an argument, or much of the reasoning in it, is conductive" (1983, p. 10). I believe this is correct, at least in the usual case. But if and when we can apply the clauses "when it belongs to a deductive family" and "when it belongs to an inductive family," then the meta-argument will be deductive.

Now, if conductive definitions have some viability for defining the interpretive notions of deductive argument and inductive argument, then surely the possibility of a conductive definition of conductive argument deserves serious consideration. This would be a definition of a type of argument called conductive such that its application to determine whether a given argument is or is not a conductive would involve a conductive meta-argument. Wellman's own definition of conductive argument (proposition W11) appears to be not

---

[6] For the case of induction, I have elsewhere elaborated a criticism of the deductivist definition of inductive argument and proposed what might be called an inductive definition of inductive argument; see Finocchiaro 1980, pp. 295-96.

conductive but rather deductive because it consists of four individually necessary and jointly sufficient conditions, and so its application to a given argument would consist of a deductive meta-argument. As regards Hitchcock's account, he does not really advance a definition of conductive argument, but the one buried within his definition of conductive adequacy (namely propositions H11a, H11b, H11c, which as stated earlier correspond to Govier's definition) also looks like a deductive definition. In constructing a conductive definition of conductive argument, one would have to exploit notions such as conductive family and conductive indicators: the conductive family would include argument types such as balance-of-considerations arguments and pro-and-con arguments; and conductive indicators would be phrases such as *ceteris paribus*, other things being equal, and notwithstanding.

Finally, it should be noted that in this reconstruction of Hitchcock's account of conductive adequacy, I have reluctantly but deliberatively disregarded the more formal notion of conductive "validity" which he elaborates elsewhere (Hitchcock 1994). For it is difficult to disagree with Govier's (1995, p. 411) judgment that one remains "not convinced that the 'formalization' contributes significantly to our understanding. The need for intuitive notions such as negative relevance and positive relevance has not disappeared. Nor has the need to make judgments." Indeed, Hitchcock himself (1994, p. 62) points out that "on this conception it is difficult to show that a conductive argument is invalid ... conductive arguments will turn out to be valid even when the reason given for the conclusion provides very weak support for it. Even worse, they will turn out to be valid even when there are unstated overriding reasons why the conclusion is false." Hitchcock does attempt to defuse this devastating implication, but the attempt only reinforces Govier's point about judgment.

4. Govier's synthesis

Trudy Govier's main conclusion can be stated as essentially identical to Wellman's: [G1] there is an important, special class of arguments called conductive arguments. However, the details of her argument are different because she rejects some of his claims and makes a number of modifications, while retaining the substance, as well as his general tone and flavor. Thus, it will be useful to begin with some of her critical arguments.

First of all, she rejects the individual-case clauses of Wellman's definition, namely propositions W11(1) and W11(3). Her argument here could be stated by saying that [G2] the individual-case clauses of Wellman's definition of conductive argument should be dropped because [G21] some arguments have all the essential features of conductive arguments, but have conclusions and premises that are generalizations. And she gives some examples (1987b, p. 69). I find this argument cogent and essentially correct.

Another one of Govier's cogent critical arguments is the one that questions Wellman's definition of induction. This argument could be reconstructed as follows: [G3] Wellman's definition of induction is both too narrow and too broad. For [G31] by induction he means, as we have seen, confirmation or disconfirmation of hypotheses based on establishing the truth of falsity of their consequences. But [G32] this definition excludes many types of argument generally recognized as inductive, such as inductions by enumeration and causal inferences; and [G33] it includes such obviously deductive arguments as refutations of hypotheses by *modus tollens* (1987b, p. 67).

Going back to Govier's main argument, the first important element is her modified definition of conductive argument: [G11] a conductive argument is best defined as an argument that has the following features. *First*, [G111] the premises support the conclusion *nonconclusively* (1999b, p. 155); that is, the premises do not deductively entail the conclusion, nor support it with the kind of evidence provided in strong inductive arguments, such as induction by enumeration, inference to the best explanation, or causal inference (2010, p. 352); I would rephrase this condition by saying that a conductive argument is one that is *neither deductively valid nor inductively probable* (or *strong*). *Second*, [G112] the premises support the conclusion *convergently* (1999b, pp. 156-57; 2010, pp. 352-54, 375); that is, [G112a1] the premises are *separately relevant* to the conclusion (1999b, p. 155; 2010, pp. 38, 352-54), but [G112a2] they support the conclusion *cumulatively* (2010b, pp. 55, 353). *Next*, [G113] there are *counterconsiderations*, namely "claims negatively relevant to the conclusion" (1999b, p. 155); and they are explicitly acknowledged or implicitly presupposed by the arguer (2010, p. 375). *Finally*, on several occasions Govier stipulates another condition, namely that [G114] the relevance of the premises to the conclusion is *a priori* or non-empirical (1987b, pp. 66, 69), and presumably non-inductive; also conceptual, normative, or criterial (1987b, p. 70; 1999b, p. 157); and nondeductive (1999b, p. 157).

Regarding this last condition, the motivation and import are relatively unclear. It seems[7] that they involve the desire to distinguish conductive arguments from inductive arguments and not just from inductively probable arguments, together with the assumption that inductive arguments have an irreducibly empirical element. However, this assumption could be questioned by adapting L. Jonathan Cohen's plausible argument that analyses of concepts in analytical philosophy involve essentially inductive arguments whose conclusions are generalizations and whose premises are particular statements embodying particular linguistic intuitions (see Cohen 1986; see also Finocchiaro 2005a, pp. 193-206).

Having defined conductive arguments in this manner, Govier is keen to show that [G12] "there really are such things as conductive arguments" (1999b, p. 166), that indeed [G12a] such arguments are common in everyday life, [G12b] as well as in such fields as ethics, politics, law, philosophy, and literary criticism. We have seen that this thesis was also advocated by Wellman and Hitchcock, although they did not stress it and they were not as explicit. In particular, Govier deserves credit for having stressed and disseminated one particular strand of this subargument, involving a subthesis which is both little known and extremely important: that [G12c] conductive arguments are common in science, including the physical and biological sciences, and not just the social sciences (1987b, p. 77; 2010, pp. 298-302, 354). The argument for this claim is as follows (see Finocchiaro 1981, 1986; Laudan 1983; Pera 1994).

On many occasions scientists want to argue and need to argue that one theory is better than, or preferable to, or more acceptable than, another. They typically do so by appealing to a number of methodological principles, which formulate various desirable features, such as: empirical accuracy, explanatory power, predictive power, research fruitfulness or fertility, problem-solving effectiveness, simplicity, systemic coherence, mathematical elegance, and conceptual intelligibility. The usual situation is one in which one theory ranks higher than another with respect to some of these criteria, and the other theory does so with respect to other criteria. Moreover, normally these criteria are not weighted equally, but there are frequently individual differences in the weight or importance attached to these criteria. Thus the choice of one theory over another requires balancing the relative merits of the two theories. It follows that the justification of a particular choice consists of an argument that is nonconclusive, convergent, and mindful of counterconsiderations.

The conductive nature of such arguments for theory choice should not be surprising if we reflect on the fact that theory choice in science is really a special case of evaluation or recommendation, and we have already seen that conductive arguments are the norm in the justification of evaluations and recommendations in general. In fact, a similar kind of eval-

---

[7] Private communication from Trudy Govier.

uation occurs in another common type of scientific argument, namely inference to the best explanation. For to show that a particular hypothesis is the best explanation of some data, one has to show both that it explains the data and that it explains them better than the available alterative(s). The latter claim (or series of claims) would have to be justified by some subargument(s) comparing the relative merits of the hypotheses, and such subargument(s) would normally be conductive. It follows that inferences to the best explanation have a component that is conductive.[8]

Continuing to echo, but also to clarify and amplify Wellman (his subargument W14), next Govier argues that [G13] conductive arguments should not be interpreted or assessed as enthymematic deductive arguments. For [G13a11] "possible additional premises are either false, unverifiable independently of a judgment about the individual case, or impossible to formulate in advance" (1987b, p. 73), and so [G13a1] "the enthymeme approach makes an inference watertight at the cost of introducing an unknowable premise" (1987b, p. 73). Moreover, [G13b1] such premises "may distort the original argument, which is typically not put forward as being conclusive" (1987b, p. 73). Finally, [G13c1] the deductivist reconstruction is such that "one argument is turned into several" (1987b, p. 73); and there are three reasons why [G13c2] one should not break down a conductive argument into several smaller ones. They are: "First, [G13c2a11] the diverse considerations in conductive arguments are characteristically put forward together ... [and so] [G13c2a1] their collective bearing on the conclusion should be taken into account when we are deciding whether to accept the conclusion. The second reason is that [G13c2b1] were we to break such a conductive argument into separate arguments, we would have to consider the various premises together when we arrived at the point of deciding how well the premises support the conclusion. ... A third reason for marking conductive arguments as a distinct type is that [G13c2c1] a number of credible authors on normative reasoning and critical thinking (including Michael Scriven, James Freeman, Kurt Baier, and Stephen Thomas) have acknowledged their existence" (2010, pp. 353-54).

Here it is worth noting that Govier herself characterizes this last subargument, in support of proposition G13c2, as a conductive argument (2010, p. 353). This note may serve as a second reminder that a relevant research project would be to analyze all these philosophical meta-arguments being reconstructed here from the point of view of conduction; this project would not be aimed at showing that all these arguments are conductive, but rather at determining which are and which are not. But note also that, since this point applies to all the constituent subarguments, this research project is an indefinitely long one.

As far as I can tell, Govier does not incorporate into her account an anti-inductivist thesis, analogous to that of Wellman, proposition W15 (which she criticizes as misconceived), nor one analogous to Hitchcock's more nuanced and sophisticated claim that there are both differences and similarities, proposition H14. This should not be surprising since she does not need such an anti-inductivist thesis; in fact, she makes conductive arguments non-inductive by definition, when she elaborates the first definitional clause, stipulating non-conclusiveness, by saying that conductive arguments are not only not deductively valid, but

---

[8] Thus it is not surprising that in the fifth edition of her textbook, in a new chapter on causal inductive arguments, in the context of a discussion of inference to the best explanation, Govier (2010, p. 302, p. 317n20) explicitly notes this connection between explanation and conduction. Nor should we find surprising the example given a long time ago by Angell (1964, pp. 377-79), in the context of discussing arguments with multiple independent reasons, but without so much as using the words *conductive* or *convergent*; his example was Albert Einstein's (2005, pp. 158-70) argument that his relativity principle was better than Isaac Newton's gravitation. See also, M. Salmon 2002, pp. 260-65; W.C. Salmon 1984, pp. 127-39; Scriven 1976, p. 217.

not even inductively probable or instances of the standard inductive forms, such as induction by enumeration, inference to the best explanation, causal inference, etc. However, she is concerned with distinguishing conductive from convergent arguments.

In fact, she has a subargument designed to show that [G14] conductive arguments should not be *equated* to convergent ones. Of course, it is true, by definition, that [G141] all conductive arguments are convergent. However, the converse does not hold: [G142] not all convergent arguments are conductive. For "[G142a1] it is possible to offer an argument which exemplifies the convergent support pattern, but in which there are several different premises, each of which, taken alone, deductively entails the conclusion. [G142a11] This is rather uncommon, but may occur, either because the arguer expects that some of his premises will be contested or because he is not aware that the entailment relationships hold and make some premises logically redundant" (1987b, p. 70).[9] Similarly, "[G142b1] some inductive arguments use the convergent support pattern, particularly [G142b11] if a number of distinct, and apparently unrelated cases, are cited to support a generalization" (1987b, p. 70). That is, such arguments would be convergent, but some deductively valid and some inductively probable; hence, they would violate the first ("nonconclusiveness") clause of the definition, and so they would not be conductive.

It must be pointed out that, in her published work, Govier does not give or construct actual examples of such arguments, with the properties of being convergent, but deductively valid or inductively strong, and so not conductive. She does not do so, not only when she first advances the argument (1987b, p. 70), but also in later editions of her textbook, where the argument is repeated in a footnote for instructors (2001, p. 411n2; 2010, p. 376n2).[10] I believe what is needed here is to find real or realistic[11] examples of such arguments, as a way of testing the existential claims in the subargument. The failure to find them would considerably weaken this argument. In such an inquiry it might also happen that we find candidates for such examples, but that a careful analysis reveals that they are not, after all, convergent or deductively valid or inductively probable. And this in turn would undermine the key thesis (proposition G14) in this subargument, namely the distinction between convergence and conduction. However, in terms of the overall account, this would only mean that the first two conditions (G111 and G112) of the definition are not distinct and should be collapsed into one. I am not sure the damage would be any greater than that.

Finally, like Wellman, but elaborating and amplifying, Govier argues that [G15] conductive arguments can be appraised. After all, they are arguments, and like all arguments [G151] we can evaluate the acceptability of each premise. Similarly, [G152] we can assess the relevance of each premise. And, as usual, [G153] we should try to determine the strength of each relevant premise as a reason for the conclusion. Then, moving in the direction of the more distinctive and specifically relevant manner of evaluation, [G154] we

---

[9] Govier repeats this argument in an instructors' footnote in the latest edition of her textbook (2010, p. 376n2).

[10] In private communication, Govier has proposed the following: "an example of an argument with convergent support that I would not be inclined to call conductive would be one that was inductive, but had separately relevant premises ... Consider—James went to Western Canada high, the same school as Mary; James went to the University of Calgary, as did Mary; James was a high achiever at the U. of C., as was Mary; these are reasons to think that James is acquainted with Mary." However, the difficulty here is that although we can agree that this is a convergent inductive argument, to deny it conductive status begs the question. To me, this example seems to be as conductive as Govier's (1999b, pp. 168-69) much discussed example of the good-manager argument.

[11] With these words ("real or realistic") I want to echo Govier's (2000, pp. 289-90) own approach, which I have independently advocated (Finocchiaro 1980, pp. 293-431; 2005a, pp. 21-91), as have others (e.g., Fisher 1988, 2004).

should try to determine the collective or cumulative strength of all premises taken together as support for the conclusion. Next, assess [G155] "whether any counterconsiderations acknowledged by the arguer are negatively relevant to the conclusion" (2010, p. 365); [G156] "what additional counterconsiderations, not acknowledged by the arguer, are negatively relevant" (2010, p. 365); and [G157] "how strong is each of the counterconsiderations as a reason against the conclusion" (1999b, p. 170). Finally, [G158] "reflect on whether the premises, taken together, outweigh the counterconsiderations, taken together, and make a judgment. [G159] Try to articulate good reasons for that judgment" (2010, p. 364).

In elaborating these principles, Govier is clear that her goal is to steer a judicious middle course between two opposite and unsatisfactory extremes. On the one hand, we have the claim that there is nothing one can do to appraise a conductive argument than to think the argument through again and again. Sometimes Wellman is taken to be making this unhelpful claim, but we have seen above that his account does include more: he is explicit in formulating the guideline that the pros outweigh the cons (proposition W16b11); and he elaborates a hefting model of weighing (W16b15), which is very helpful. On the other hand, there is the other extreme of thinking that the strength of each premises and each counterconsideration can be measured; that the cumulative strength of each set can be added up; and that the two can be subtracted from one another to arrive at the net positive support or negative disconfirmation. Some of Govier's own language may give this impression, for example the talk of strength, of positive and negative relevance, and the distinction of the individual and the cumulative assessment of strength. However, her commentary on these rules makes it clear that she is rejecting this quantitative and mechanistic model (1999b, p. 170).

Nevertheless, some questions arise. Some of these will be taken up when I discuss the critiques advanced by other philosophers. For now I want to raise the following point, which I do not think has been previously raised. Govier's principles of appraisal seem to contain an asymmetry between the treatment of positively relevant reasons and the treatment of negatively relevant counterconsiderations: whereas for the case of counterconsiderations one is supposed to think of other considerations besides those acknowledged by the arguer (proposition G155), before performing the balancing act of weighing the pros and the cons, for the case of favorable reasons there is no requirement to think of and take into account additional ones not stated by the arguer. Her justification for this asymmetry is this:

> [T]o reflect on whether there are further considerations—not stated in the argument—that would count in favor of the conclusion and would outweigh any counterconsiderations ... takes you beyond appraising the stated argument. It moves you to a new stage where you are amending or reconstructing that argument ... when your real interest is whether you should accept the conclusion and not merely whether the conclusion is well supported by the particular argument you are evaluating. (Govier 2010, p. 366)

In short, finding and taking into account additional evidence is not relevant to the evaluation of the original argument, but to the evaluation of the acceptability of the conclusion. However, this justification presupposes that finding and taking into account counterevidence is relevant to the evaluation of the original argument, and not merely to the eventual evaluation of the conclusion. And then the issue becomes why this assumption should be accepted: why taking into account additional counterevidence is relevant, but taking into account additional evidence is not relevant, to the assessment of the original argument as given; why taking into account additional evidence is relevant only to the evaluation of the acceptability of the conclusion, but taking into account additional counterevidence is not limited in the same way. I don't think this issue has been properly addressed in the literature. I believe further work is needed to determine whether this asymmetry holds, and if so why.

5. Allen's critiques

Some important critiques of Govier's argument have been advanced by Derek Allen. In his critical study of her *Problems in Argument Analysis and Evaluation*, he elaborates a powerful criticism of Govier's anti-deductivist claim, proposition G13, and the supporting subargument. And since this subargument has three parts, so does the criticism. Here, Allen's key claim is that [A1] Govier's proposition G13 has not been justified, i.e., that the supporting subargument is not successful, or not cogent: "a reconstructive deductivist will take the enthymeme approach to conductive arguments ... Govier has not demonstrated that this approach is always mistaken. Nor has she demonstrated that we will always be in a better position to assess conductive arguments if we reject the enthymeme approach in favor of her own" (1990, p. 58). Allen's argument is the following.

For the purpose of this discussion, Allen asks us to [A111] focus on the same example that had been considered by Govier and Wellman: (a) you should return the book because (b) you promised to do so. [A112] The deductivist could reconstruct this argument by adding two other premises: (c) other things being equal, you should keep your promises, and (d) other things are equal. [A113] Note that premise (c) is not a categorical universal generalization, which would have been false, but that it is qualified by the *ceteris paribus* clause; however, premise (d) asserts that this clause holds in this case. [A114] The expanded, and qualified, argument is now deductively valid, but admittedly we may not always be in the position of knowing that premise (d) is true or acceptable. However, [A115] if we do not know whether in this case the other things are equal, then we are in no position to claim that the original argument, interpreted as a conductive argument, is conductively adequate, for, in Allen's clear and succinct reformulation, [A1151] conductive adequacy means, that "the premise outweighs ... any stated or unstated counterconsiderations ... that are negatively relevant to its conclusion" (1990, p. 56). On the other hand, [A116a1] if we have enough information to be able to say that the other things are equal, that would make the reconstructed argument one with acceptable premises, and thus sound or cogent (on account of the deductive validity); but [A116a2] the same information would also enable us to asses the original argument as conductively adequate. Allen concludes that [A11] "it matters not" (1990, p. 56), "it ... makes no difference" (1990, p. 57) whether we interpret and assess the argument conductively or deductively. That is, [A1] Govier has not shown that her approach is better than the deductivist one.

What I would add is that, as long as we do not claim Allen to have shown that the deductivist approach is better, his counterargument is cogent. In other words, Allen has shown that the inferential adequacy of a conductive argument corresponds to the acceptability of some of the premises in a properly nuanced deductivist approach. Thus, from the point of soundness or cogency, which involves both strength of the inference and acceptability of the premises, there is no advantage in either approach, unless or until we consider other factors. The situation is analogous to the deductivist reconstruction of traditional inductive arguments, which has long been known to be possible, but whose desirability or preferability has to be judged on other grounds (see, e.g., W.C. Salmon 1984, p. 18). And this leads to the other grounds on which Govier bases her anti-deductivist claim.

As we saw above, another reason she gives is that the deductivist reconstruction of a conductive argument turns one argument into several (proposition G13c1). Allen (1990, pp. 57-58) argues cogently that [A2] this is not true. [A211] Consider a conductive argument with two premises: Ra1; Rb1; so C. Here [A212] Ra1 does not entail C, and Rb1 does not entail C. [A213] Suppose we give a deductivist reconstruction, which adds two premises: Ra2 such that Ra1 and Ra2 entail C; and Bb2 such that Rb1 and Rb2 entail C. The reconstructed deductive argument is: "Ra1 and Ra2; Rb1 and Rb2; so C." [A21] The reconstruction is no more two arguments than the original was. [A214] It is true, of course, that in the original argument, Ra1 and Rb1 are separately relevant and cumulative in weight, whereas in the reconstruction some of the premises are not separately relevant (e.g., Ra1 and Ra2, Rb1 and Rb2), and none are cumulative or mutually reinforcing. But [A215] this means that the original argument is, and the reconstruction is not, a conductive argument. [A216] It does not mean that the reconstruction is two arguments; to so conclude "is a *non-sequitur*" (1990, p. 58).

With another powerful argument, Allen (1993, pp. 116-18) has objected that [A3] Govier's definition of conductive argument should be amended to stipulate that each premise should not be deductively relevant to the conclusion, where deductive relevance means: a premise P is deductively relevant to the conclusion C if and only if P's relevance depends on another proposition Q such that P&Q entail C. This amendment may be included in the fourth main clause of Govier's definition, proposition G114. In fact, I have already included it in my reconstruction above, where that fourth clause includes a miscellaneous cluster of notions, such as non-empirical, a priori, conceptual, criterial, and normative. I was led to so include it by the fact that Govier (1999b, pp. 157, 178n6) has explicitly accepted Allen's amendment. For this reason, and also because of the difficulty and complexity of Allen's argument, here I shall omit presenting a reconstruction.

Finally, Allen (1993, pp. 109-11) raises another insightful objection which I would interpret as another amendment to Govier's definition, regarding the counterconsiderations clause, proposition G113, but which she does not even mention, let alone accept. That clause stipulates, as we have seen, that there may be counterconsiderations; that is, explicit counterconsiderations may be present, but if they are not, implicit counterconsiderations are presupposed. Indeed, the distinctive conductive adequacy of such arguments depends on whether the favorable reasons outweigh the counterconsiderations; and normally the evaluation of such arguments involves explicit argumentation about what outweighs what. Now, when the counterconsiderations are explicit in the original argument, sometimes the argument may contain also an explicit justification of such a balance-of-considerations claim. This is especially true when there is just one explicit favorable reason and one explicit counterconsideration. Allen gives examples of this situation, taken from a decision of the Canadian Supreme Court declaring unconstitutional a rape-shield law (barring the admissibility of evidence about the previous sexual activity of a plaintiff in a rape trial); and the examples involve opinions in which different judges balance and weigh the value of protecting the victim and the value of ascertaining the truth. Now, Allen's key point is that [A4] such arguments need not, and, I would add, normally would not, be conductive; for [A41] these are arguments concluding that one value or factor outweighs another in importance, not arguments concluding the presence of a value or factor after assuming that it outweighs the other. In Allen's words: "According to Govier, conductive reasoning frequently involves the weighing of pros and cons ... reasoning of that sort is *based on* the judgment that one factor, or set of factors, outweighs another, which is to say that some such judgment *underlies* the inference to the reasoning's conclusion—rather than being itself the conclusion ... But it is worth adding that arguments that involve [or to be more precise: arguments that conclude with] the weighing of one factor, or set of factors, against another need not be conductive" (Allen 1993, p. 110, my italics).

This issue has already arisen above, in one of Wellman's subarguments justifying his anti-deductivist claim (W14a). There he argued that the deductivist reconstruction of conductive arguments includes premises whose justification cannot be purely deductive but must include some conductive reasoning. In a sense, there Wellman is making a point which is the reverse of the one in Allen's last considered objection (A4). Allen is arguing that some conductive reasoning has parts that are not conductive; Wellman is arguing that some deductive reasoning has parts that are nondeductive but conductive.

At the moment, I am not ready to decide this issue. The question seems to be what type of arguments, if any, can be used to justify claims that one reason outweighs a counterconsideration. These are claims that are normally presupposed in conductive arguments; often explicitly stated in such arguments; sometimes explicitly justified in these arguments; and always to be explicitly assessed in the evaluation of them. Although this is an open question, if we recall my working hypothesis formulated in the introduction above, and if we note the nuanced character of that formulation, we can see that Allen's fourth criticism seems to confirm the first part; that is, the claim that an essential characteristic of conductive arguments is a *balance-of-considerations claim* that must be implicitly made, explicitly formulated, or critically justified for the construction, interpretation, or evaluation of conductive arguments.

6. Ennis's critiques

Another philosopher who has advanced some noteworthy critiques of Govier's account is Robert Ennis (2001, 2004). One criticism is that [E1] "the definition of 'conduction' is needlessly narrow" (Ennis 2004, p. 38), because [E11] "the convergence requirement seems unduly narrow" (2004, p. 35). For [E111] this requirement "eliminates a large number of arguments, including all that I have so far considered in this paper" (2004, p. 33); that is, cases of qualified reasoning such as [E111a] Ennis's raccoon argument, [E111b] Toulmin's Petersen argument, [E111c] Weddle's rain-prediction argument, and [E111d] Plantinga's Frisian-lifeguard argument. Ennis's raccoon argument is this: "raccoons rarely attack a human when they do not feel threatened and do not feel that their young are threatened. The raccoon that is ambling across the yard does not feel threatened by us, and it does not feel that its young are threatened—its young are not around. So the raccoon will probably not bother you, even though you are within fifteen feet of it" (2004, p. 25).

It might seem that this objection is analogous to Govier's own objection (G2) to the individual-case requirement of Wellman's definition, and that Ennis is in effect suggesting that the convergence requirement be dropped from the definition of a conductive argument. Or perhaps he is suggesting that we drop the language of "conductive" arguments, and instead talk of "qualified" reasoning. In either case, Ennis argument is committed to claiming that [E1121] qualified-reasoning arguments have all the essential characteristics of what Govier calls conductive arguments, and hence [E112] should be treated or categorized in the same way. This subargument can and should be added to or grafted onto the one reconstructed in the last paragraph, and may be regarded as a tacit part of that argument.

These are "formal" similarities between this objection by Ennis to Govier (E1) and the earlier objection by Govier to Wellman (G2). However, evaluatively speaking, one can raise the question whether Ennis's objection is relevant: whether it is true that qualified-reasoning arguments have all the essential characteristics of conductive argument, and whether we can conclude that the two classes of arguments should be categorized or treated in the same way. A key point I would make is that the examples of qualified-reasoning arguments mentioned here are cases or variations of "statistical syllogism," that is, arguments that apply an inexact, qualified, or statistical generalization to an individual case to reach a conclusion about that individual case. This is an extremely common and important type of argument because it is connected with questions of stereotyping, profiling, and prejudice (see Schauer 2003; Scriven 1976, pp. 205-10). And it even shares a significant similarity with conductive arguments, insofar as the inferential adequacy of statistical syllogisms depends on the so-called requirement of total evidence,[12] and this requirement is analogous to the one requiring that counterconsiderations be taken into account, which is the key factor in conductive adequacy. However, I regard this problem as an open question, deserving of further study.

Ennis's second criticism argues that [E2] Govier's definition of conduction is difficult to apply because [E21] the convergence requirement is difficult to apply (Ennis 2004, p. 35). For [E211] when an argument is such that more than one reason support the conclusion, often there is no indication "whether each reason is an INUS condition or an independent condition" (2004, p. 34); here, [E212] an INUS condition is an acronym Ennis adopts from John Mackie (1993) to mean a condition that is an *i*nsufficient but *n*ecessary member of an *u*nnecessary but *s*ufficient set.

That is, consider the argument: C because P, Q, and R. An instance might be Govier's own example: "she would be a good manager because she has considerable experience, she is very good at dealing with people, and she knows the business well" (1999b, pp. 156, 168). Govier starts by interpreting P, Q, and R as separately or independently relevant to C. And then, since they are mutually reinforcing, she concludes that the argument is convergent; and given the nonconclusiveness, she takes the argument to be conductive. Ennis is questioning the initial interpretation of the reasons as independently supportive: "each could be an INUS condition … all three together constituting the set, making these conditions dependent on each other" (2004, p. 34).

I believe Ennis's question is well-taken because the argument as stated does not convey the separation of the reasons as explicitly as would be done by another possible formulation, namely "C because P, because Q, and because R." Repeating the connective "because" would make it clear that one intended to treat each reason separately and independently. But as it stands, the meaning is ambiguous. Thus, Ennis's second criticism seems cogent.

Lastly, Ennis has another criticism that is longer and more complex to justify, but easy to state. The objection is that [E3] Govier's attitude toward deductive standards is inconsistent. That is, "although she apparently eschews the use of deductive standards in conduction, she needs them to show the relevance" (2004, p. 35) of the reasons. In particular, this criticism can be taken as directed at Govier's key anti-deductivist claim, proposition G13.

The argument is this. In evaluating the strength of reasons (proposition G153), and the same would also apply to counterconsiderations (G157), Govier claims that "what helps us to evaluate the strength of reasons is that reasons must have a degree of generality" (1999b, p. 171); such generality is qualified by means of the clause "other things being equal"; "by spelling out qualified universals … we are able to move beyond the apparently irreducible claim that 'P1 is relevant to C'" (1999b, p. 171); and "a strong reason is one where the range of exceptions is narrow. A weak reason is one where the range of exceptions is large" (1999b, p. 171). Ennis is pointing out that Govier explains the relevance of a reason in terms of whether it together with a qualified universal would deductively entail the conclu-

---

[12] As acknowledged by Govier herself (2010, pp. 269, 371); see W.C. Salmon 1984, pp. 96-97.

sion when the qualifier is removed; and she explains the strength of a reason in terms of the number of exceptions that are covered by the qualification (the more exceptions, the weaker the reason; the fewer, the stronger). Schematizing further, Govier seems to conceive strength as follows:

Original conductive argument:	P, so C.
Reconstruction for evaluation purposes:	P.
	Other things being equal, if P then C.
	Probably, other things are equal.
	So, probably C.

The strength of P is being correlated to the degree of probability of the third premise in this reconstruction. Now, Ennis notes (2004, p. 34) that such a reconstruction is to be contrasted with one where the qualified universal would read, "Other things being equal, if C then P." This alternative reconstruction might seem strange and idiosyncratic, but it can be made more familiar and plausible by noting that it would conform to the form of reasoning called abductive, or inference to the best explanation. Thus, Ennis seems to be making a forceful point, and this criticism seems to have some cogency.

7. Zenker's criticism of *ceteris paribus*

A more radical criticism of Govier's method for evaluating the strength of reasons has been advanced by Frank Zenker. His own critical conclusion is that [Z1] "*ceteris paribus*, c-p generalizations are irrelevant to evaluating conductive argumentation" (Zenker 2009d, p. 11), where a *c-p generalization* is an obvious abbreviation meaning a generalization qualified by means of the clause *ceteris paribus* or *other things being equal*. Zenker advances four reasons against Govier's method of evaluating the strength of reasons in terms of the number of exceptions to the c-p generalization.

First, [Z11] this method says nothing about the comparative evaluation of the strength of the pro reasons as a whole and the con reasons as a whole; it only pertains to the comparative strength of reasons within each group (Zenker 2009d, pp. 3-4).

Second, [Z12] Govier's method presupposes an incorrect analysis of c-p generalizations. [Z121] Govier's presupposition is that c-p generalizations sometimes warrant and sometimes do not warrant transitions from the particular reason to the particular conclusion. But [Z122] the correct analysis is that they do not allow such transitions unless pertinent objections are answered (Zenker 2009d, pp. 4-6).

Thirdly, [Z13] the introduction of c-p generalizations is not necessary. Rather, [Z131] it is better to introduce the individualized associated conditional. [Z1311] Then, working at this individual level, a strong reason will be one embedded in an argument that meets the objections advanced against it (Zenker 2009d, pp. 6-8).

Finally, [Z141] working at the same individual level, it can happen that a reason is stronger than another even if the former has a larger class of exceptions. Thus [Z14] the strength of a reason in a conductive argument cannot be a function of only the exception class (Zenker 2009d, pp. 8-9).

This criticism does show, in my opinion, that the concept of a c-p generalization and its connection to conductive arguments deserve more and deeper analysis than that provided by Govier. Furthermore, it seems likely that the analysis is to be carried out along a different direction than that pursued by Govier. Indeed it is not surprising that someone who has carried such a comprehensive study of *ceteris paribus* (Zenker 2009b) would discover such limitations. However, the other side of this coin is that such criticism of Govier's account seems somewhat unfair insofar as it focuses a very small part. This is the part pertaining to proposition G153, the elaboration of which I did not include in my reconstruction above, precisely because it did not seem to be sufficiently important or central to Govier's account.

On the other hand, two other aspects of Zenker's criticism seem to reinforce certain aspects of Wellman's original account that were modified or not elaborated by Govier. For example, when Zenker says that c-p generalizations allow the inference of the conclusion from the reason if and only if the pertinent objections are answered (proposition Z122), this is reminiscent of (although not identical to) Wellman's definition of validity, proposition W16a1 above: "to say that an argument is valid is to claim that, when subjected to an indefinite amount of criticism, it is persuasive" (Wellman 1971, p. 110). Similarly, when Zenker emphasizes the individualized associated conditional and case by case reasoning, this corresponds to Wellman's (1971, pp. 73-82) stress on reasoning without rules and without criteria, reflected even in the fourth clause of his definition of conduction, proposition W11 above.

The upshot of my considerations is that Zenker's criticism is not as negative and destructive as it may seem at first, but rather reflects an approach to conductive arguments different from Govier's. The alternative nature of the criticism is even more marked and striking in Harald Wohlrapp's (1995, 1998, 2008a) critique, to which I now turn.

8. Wohlrapp's dynamical approach to conduction

Referring to Govier's account, Wohlrapp claims that "there are at least two reasons to [WO1] reject this view. First, [WO1a1] it contains a misunderstanding of the relationship between deductive schemes and other possibilities for passing from sentences to other sentences. [WO1a11] Deduction is not just one possibility among others, but is fundamental in the sense that it is presupposed by all other inference schemes like inductions, etc., whereas these are not presupposed by deduction" (Wohlrapp 1998, pp. 341-42). There seems to be no explicit elaboration of this subargument in Wohlrapp's English-language publications, although the deductivist character of his alternative account (to be summarized below) is relatively obvious.

Wohlrapp's second reason to reject Govier's account is that "[WO1b1] this view fixes argumentation theory in a quasilogical and nondynamic perspective, [WO1b2] viz. in an unfruitful dichotomy of structural and procedural perspectives. [WO1b11] The process of argumentation seems here to be no more than a sequence of inference steps, where each step can be isolated and analyzed by itself. [WO1b3] I want to plea for a more differentiated and realistic view in which procedural and structural elements of argumentative speech are integrated and where premises and conclusion of an argumentation form a 'retroflexive' system of mutual support" (Wohlrapp 1998, p. 342).

Wohlrapp then goes on to sketch his dynamic account, thus providing an articulation and justification of the claim just made (proposition WO1b3). However, before reconstructing this dynamic account, let us mention a third criticism, pertaining to Govier's method of evaluating the strength of a reason based on the size of the class of exceptions to the associated c-p generalization. He too finds it unsatisfactory, but it is revealing that he expresses his criticism in terms of it being unfruitful, at least relatively speaking, namely relative to his alternative dynamic approach: "[WO1c1] The question 'how many exceptions-to-be-respected are there for the argument's associated general principle?' is not productive ... [WO1c11] The exceptions are not countable and [WO1c12] if an intuitive estimate shall suffice, then it remains unclear what is the significance of such an estimate. [WO1c13] If we disregard all these puzzles for a moment: how would we proceed with these somehow determined numbers ? ... would we really calculate them arithmetically?" (Wohlrapp 2008a, pp. 11-12). For Wohlrapp, these are rhetorical questions.

Let us now reconstruct Wohlrapp's more "differentiated," and "realistic," and "fruitful" account that "dynamically" combines "structural" and "procedural" elements. The key thesis is that [WO2] a conductive argument (as usually defined, i.e., a pro-and-con argument) should be interpreted as a temporary stage in the process of argumentation that needs to be completed and modified in various ways to result in a good and more stable argument. Or in his own words, "as long as we have to deal with a construction featuring open counterarguments, the thesis [i.e., the conclusion] either is not a valid orientation, or we have not yet completed the argumentation ... A conductive argument is nothing but a state of argumentation assessed at some point in time" (Wohlrapp 2008a, p. 21).

The completion and modification processes are distinct from each other and internally multi-faceted. [WO21] A conductive argument should be "completed" in three ways (Wohlrapp 2008a, pp. 16-17): one way is [WO211] to pair each pro reason with a con reason, searching for unstated ones if need be; another is [WO212] to check the acceptability of each pro and con reason, reconstructing the supporting subarguments if need be; the third way is [WO213] to elaborate the point of view (called the "frame") of each reason, by reconstructing the unstated assumptions and latent structure if need be. [WO22] Furthermore, a conductive argument should be "modified" in four ways aimed at integrating the points of view (the "frames") used in the pro and con reasons (Wohlrapp 2008a, pp. 17-18): one way is to [WO221] criticize and if necessary replace a given frame or point of view; another is to [WO222] rank the various frames for their importance, if possible; a third is to [WO223] harmonize, if possible, the various frames so that they are no longer incompatible, but still remain distinct; the fourth way is to [WO224] elaborate a combination or synthesis of the frames. Wohlrapp (2008a, p. 17) is at pains to point out that [WO225] such a frame integration should not be merely a "reconciliation" of interests and differences, in the sense that "existing" interests and differences are "negotiated," but rather a critical reconciliation that involves evaluation and modification.

The rest of Wohlrapp's main constructive argument consists of an analysis of two of Govier's own examples, the nanny argument in the dialogue between husband and wife, and the euthanasia-legalization argument. The analysis is designed to show that [WO3] these two conductive arguments can be completed and modified in accordance with the various principles just stated, i.e., propositions WO211, WO212, WO213, WO221, WO222, WO223, WO224, and WO225.

In a sense, the analysis of those two arguments does illustrate and support these "dynamical" principles. The analysis is insightful and plausible, and so Wohlrapp's argument has some cogency, and his dynamical account receives some confirmation. However, does the argument show that his dynamical account is "more realistic" than Govier's, as claimed in proposition WO1b3? Taking realism to mean at least empirical adequacy, this claim is questionable. In fact, I believe Wohlrapp (1998, p. 347) is correct when he himself admits that "this is not the normal case. Usually, we hang around halfway and we comfort ourselves with the quantitative metaphor having produced a reasonable balance of so many arguments." That is, in cognitive practice conductive arguments as such have a reality which the dynamical approach perhaps fails to capture, or at least captures less faithfully than the static approach. Thus, my conclusion is that more empirical work is needed to test whether the dynamical account is sufficiently descriptive and not excessively prescriptive.

Finally, Wohlrapp advances a claim that may be regarded as a corollary of what I have called his key thesis above, proposition WO2. The corollary is that [WO4] in conductive argumentation, "the conclusion reached with the arguments [i.e., reasons] presented is not the result of a weighing, whatever that be. The result was reached via an evaluation that arranged the arguments [reasons] into a thetical construct and, by means of continuing their discussion, examined them with respect to their suitability for supporting the thesis [i.e., conclusion]" (Wohlrapp 2008a, p. 21). The term "thetical construct" is, of course, both a neologism and obscure. The German phrase, *thetischen Konstruktion*, is slightly clearer insofar as "construction" (*Konstruktion*) seems more appropriate than "construct." The adjective "thetical" (*thetischen*) suggests a meaning of pertaining to "thesis" (*These*).[13] Thus, I decipher this corollary claim, WO4, as follows. I believe "thetical construct" refers to a network or structure of logically or probatively interrelated propositions; the "discussion" consists of the processes of completion and integration that make up his alternative procedure for the evaluation of whether or to what extent the conclusion is thereby supported; and the procedure is the one mentioned in propositions WO21 and WO22 above. In fact, in another place Wohlrapp (1998, p. 349) gives this other formulation of what I take to be the same claim: [WO4] "the secret of a successful argumentative conduction is frame unification. The nature of the inference step is the formulation of ... a (complex) frame which integrates, on the one hand, our positions and, on the other, the different realms in which we place" the issue of the argument. This corollary thesis represents Wohlrapp's interpretation of the nature of conductive inference: the crucial element is not a "weighing" of the pro and con reasons, but an evaluation of them ideally carried out in accordance with the dynamical principles sketched. The only thing I would add here is that this thesis is also in need of further empirical support.

9. Brooks on the health-care bill

It is now time to examine some relevant empirical material, namely some conductive ground-level argumentation, so to speak. On December 18, 2009, the *New York Times* published two op-ed columns about the health-care reform bill that had been widely discussed the whole year and would be voted upon in the U.S. Senate a few days later. One opinion was in favor of the bill and was authored by Paul Krugman (cf. Appendix 2). The other was against the bill and was authored by David Brooks (cf. Appendix 1). Besides the obvious difference in substantive content, the two arguments make an interesting and instructive contrast in argumentative style, structure, and power, so much so that they would reward close study on the part of informal logicians and argument theorists. However, given our present focus on conductive arguments, I shall limit myself to Brooks's argument.

Brooks's column is reproduced verbatim in Appendix 1. However, for convenience of analysis, and to facilitate reference, I have added in brackets a label for each paragraph, from the letter 'a' to 'q'. As is customary for newspapers, each paragraph is very short, consisting of either just one sentence or at most a few. Thus, it will also be convenient to assign a label to each sentence within a given paragraph, consisting of the paragraph letter plus a numeral corresponding to the place of the sentence in the sequence within the paragraph. For example, the fifth and last sentence of paragraph 'g', "but if you've got cancer, you want surgery, not nasal spray," will be given the label 'g5'. However, note that I have not actually inserted these numerals in Appendix 1, because I did not want to overburden the eye of the reader, and the work can be quickly done in one's head with the mind's eye.

It is worth saying at the outset, that whatever one may think of the substantive content of Brooks's conclusion, and of the strength of his argument, his essay is a model of clarity.

---

[13] In private communication, Wohlrapp has confirmed this particular suggestion.

It is equally obvious, from the context, the style, and the structure, that here we have a conductive argument, indeed a paradigm example of conductive argument.

Before we get involved into the details, let us have a quick glimpse at the whole. Brooks is recommending rejection of the bill, on the basis of several reasons to oppose the bill, but with an awareness that there are also several reasons to favor the bill, and in light of a judgment that the bad aspects of the bill outweigh the good ones. However, note that since Brooks's conclusion is a negative recommendation, the premises *supporting* his conclusions are the reasons *against* the bill; the counterconsiderations or objections to his conclusion are the reasons *for* the bill; and the balance-of-considerations claim that the strength of the argument's premises outweighs the strength of the objections is equivalent to the claim that the reasons *against* the bill outweigh the reasons *for* it. In short, there is a kind of reversal of sign that must be kept in mind depending on whether we take the point of view of the pros and cons of Brooks's conclusion or the point of view of the pros and cons of the bill.

With these preliminaries and clarifications in mind, Brooks's argument may be reconstructed as follows.

[B] The Senate health care bill should not be passed (cf. p1), for although [B1] there are at least four reasons for passing the bill, [B2] there are at least six reasons for not passing it, and [B3] the latter outweigh the former, i.e., the reasons for not passing outweigh the reasons for passing the bill (cf. p2).

The main reasons to favor the bill are: first, [B1a] "it would provide insurance to 30 million more Americans" (a1); second, [B1b] the bill addresses "the deficit issue seriously" (b1), relatively speaking; third, [B1c] the bill contains very many "little ideas in an effort to reduce health care inflation" (d1); and fourth, [B1d] "if this fails, it will take a long time to get back to health reform" (f1).

The first one of these reasons is left unsupported, being uncontroversial in the context of these discussions. But the other three are supported by subarguments that are themselves relatively complex, and some of which may themselves be conductive. For example, Brooks claims that [B1b] relatively speaking, the bill takes "the deficit issue seriously" because [B1ba] it is much more fiscally responsible than the prescription drug benefit passed during the Bush administration (b2); [B1bb] the extra costs to cover the uninsured are partly offset by Medicare cuts and tax increases (b3); and [B1bc] "the bill won't explode the deficit" (c3); but [B1bd] "the bill is not really deficit neutral" (b1). This seems to be an attempt to support the bill's fiscal seriousness nonconclusively by means of three separately relevant and jointly cumulative considerations, while acknowledging one objection.

The main reasons to oppose the bill are: first, [B2a1] "it does not fundamentally reform health care" (g1); second, [B2b1] "it will cause national health care spending to increase faster" (i1); third, [B2c1] "the bill sets up a politically unsustainable situation" (j1); fourth, [B2d1] the bill regulates about 17% of the economy, and [B2d2] "you can't regulate 17% of the U.S. economy without a raft of unintended consequences" (l); fifth, [B2e1] "it will slow innovation" (m1), since [B2e11] "government regulators don't do well with disruptive new technologies" (m2); sixth and finally, [B2f1] "if this passes, we will never get back to cost control" (n1).

These considerations are premises meant to support Brooks's negative recommendation not to pass the bill. Like the counterconsiderations, and even more so, these premises are individually part of relatively complex subarguments designed to justify them. Some of this structure I have already included, being relatively straightforward, as in B2d and B2e. Let us look at the other more complex subarguments.

To show why [B2a1] the bill does not really reform health care, Brooks argues as follows. [B2a11] The current system is financially opaque, insofar as patients are insulated from the cost of their medical decisions. [B2a12] It contains perverse financial incentives, insofar as providers are rewarded for providing more services and penalized for being more efficient. [B2a13] These aspects of the system are the root cause of the increase and acceleration of health care costs. [B2a14] The bill does not change these aspects of the system because [B2a141] it embodies a gradualist "Burkean" approach, [B2a142] which is effective for minor imperfections, but [B2a143] not for essential flaws.

In Brooks's second subargument against the bill, the reason he mentions, i.e.., the acceleration of health care spending (B2b1), involves only an intermediate effect. The end result will be that [B2b2] health care spending will squeeze out all other government spending, especially at the state level (i3).

Brooks's third subargument tries to justify his third reason against the bill, that [B2c1] it will produce "a politically unsustainable situation" (j1). That is, "[B2c1111] the demand for health care will rise sharply. [B2c1112] The supply will not … As a result, [B2c111] prices will skyrocket while efficiencies will not. [B2c11] There will be a bipartisan rush to gut reform" (j2, 3, 5, 6).

Finally, Brooks's sixth subargument is a two-step argument, one of which is an argument by analogy. [B2f111] Health care reform for American society is like developing proper eating habits for children; for example, expanding medical coverage is like eating dessert, while cost control is like eating spinach (n2). [B2f112] Children are motivated to first eat beneficial but tasteless food like spinach by being allowed to later eat less beneficial but more tasty food like dessert; they could not be motivated to eat spinach later by first eating dessert (n3). So, [B2f11] American society cannot be motivated to control costs later by expanding coverage first. But, [B2f12] the bill amounts to first expanding coverage and expecting to control costs later. So, [B2f1] "we will never get back to cost control" (n1).

In the reconstruction above, the third premise immediately supporting the main conclusion is the balance-of-considerations claim that [B3] the reasons for not passing outweigh the reasons for passing the bill. A striking feature of Brooks's argument is that this claim is explicitly made by the arguer when he states that if the bill is passed "the few good parts of the bill will get stripped out and the expensive and wasteful parts will be entrenched" (p2). Equally striking, is the fact that Brooks does not explicitly argue in support of this claim; instead he seems to suggest that the claim involves a pure or irreducible judgment call (o3). Moreover, he also seems to suggest that the difference of weight is small, when he says "I flip-flop week to week and day to day" (o2).

On the other hand, implicitly, he seems to have an argument in mind when in the context of this claim he calls attention to the fact that this is "a health care bill without systemic incentives reform" (p2). I believe this is a reference to the lack of fundamental reform, elaborated in the first subargument against the bill (B2a). So the argument is perhaps that the bill's lack of fundamental reform causes its drawbacks to overwhelm its advantages. That is, the bill's cons outweigh the bill's pros because the bill lacks fundamental reform and without it the cons will prevail over the pros. The bill's pros are: [B1a] expanded insurance coverage, [B1b] relative fiscal responsibility, [B1c] numerous promising piecemeal experiments, and [B1d] the attempt to break self-fulfilling cycle of failure. The bill's cons are: [B2b] tendency to monopolize government expenses, [B2c] political unsustainability, [B2d] unintended consequences, [B2e] slowing of innovation, and [B2f] reversed motivational sequence.

Then the main argument would perhaps have the following structure: [B'] the bill should not be passed because [B'1] it does not fundamentally reform health care and [B'2] without it the bad aspects of the bill will prevail over its good aspects. [B'21] The bad aspects are: [B'21a] tendency to monopolize government expenses, [B'21b] political unsustainability, [B'21c] unintended consequences, [B'21d] slowing of innovation, and [B'21e] reversed motivational sequence; [B'22] the bill's lack of fundamental reform will tend to strengthen these. [B'23] The good aspects are: [B'23a] expanded insurance coverage, [B'23b] relative fiscal responsibility, [B'23c] numerous promising piecemeal experiments, and [B'23d] the attempt to break self-fulfilling cycle of failure; [B'24] the bill's lack of fundamental reform will tend to weaken these.

There are problems with this reconstruction. First, this reconstruction (B') is not a conductive argument. The final subargument (B'1 and B'2 to B') has two premises that are not separately relevant but rather dependent on each other. Second, the justification of the second premise (B'2) has four premises that are also interdependent and not separately relevant. This B'2 subargument seems to be a predictive argument that reaches a conclusion on the basis of an analysis of conflicting trends and consequences. It is the type of argument on which Allen's fourth critique (A4) focused.

However, this is not really a problem for this reconstruction, for there is no reason why Brooks's argument has to be a conductive argument. Instead it could be taken to be a problem for Wellman's and Govier's definitions of conductive argument. But even that is questionable, since it is obvious that their definitions do not have to apply to all arguments; conductive arguments may be common, but they are certainly not the only type of argument. Brooks's argument may very well be one of these other types. But perhaps a trace of a problem remains, insofar as Brooks's argument seems to have the typical or essential characteristics of a conductive argument, and yet this reconstruction does not exhibit them.

A more serious problem with this reconstruction (B') emerges if we focus on the justification of the strengthening claim [B'22] and the weakening claim [B'24]. It is easy to see, in the context of this discussion, that the bill's lack of fundamental reform would strengthen its tendency to monopolize government expenses, its political unsustainability, and the reversed motivational sequence. On the other hand, the points about unintended consequences and the slowing of innovation seem to be independent of the lack of fundamental reform, and indeed Brooks's corresponding subarguments above exhibit this independence. Similarly, it is easy to see that the bill's lack of fundamental reform will tend to weaken its relative fiscal responsibility and the numerous promising piecemeal experiments, but the expanded insurance coverage and the breaking of the self-fulfilling cycle of failing to reform are effects or features of the bill that are independent of the lack of fundamental reform. I suppose the issue here could be formulated by saying that the B' reconstruction violates the principle of charity.

Thus, let us try another reconstruction that avoids this uncharitable flaw. Brooks's argument is best reconstructed as follows: [B''] The bill should not be passed. Admittedly, [B''a1a] it will expand insurance coverage and [B''a1b] would represent a break with the self-fulfilling cycle of failing to reform, and [B''a1c] these are good things. However, [B''a2a] the bill lacks fundamental reform, [B''a2b] will have massive unintended consequences, and [B''a2c] will slow innovation; [B''a2d] these are bad things, and [B''a3] they outweigh the good. Moreover, [B''b1] without fundamental reform the bill's *other* bad aspects will prevail over the bill's *other* good aspects. [B''b11] The other bad aspects are: [B''b11a] its tendency to monopolize government expenses, [B''b11b] its political unsustainability, and [B''b11c] the reversed motivational sequence; [B''b12] these will be strengthened by the lack of fundamental reform. [B''b13] The other good aspects are:

[B″b13a] its relative fiscal responsibility and [B″b13b] the numerous promising piecemeal experiments; and [B″b14] these will be weakened by the lack of fundamental reform.

In this reconstruction, there are two independent subarguments, B″a and B″b, supporting the main conclusion B″. The second (B″b) subargument has the same structure as that of the previous main argument B′, and so it is not a conductive argument. But the first (B′a) subargument is a conductive argument, essentially identical in structure to the final step of the original (B) reconstruction. This (B′a) subargument uses and explicitly states, but does not justify, the balance-of-considerations claim (B″a3). Notice that the aspects of the bill are not only being subdivided into pros and cons, but that each of these groups is being subdivided into those that are not affected by the lack of fundamental reform and those (the "others") that are. A conductive argument is being given involving the former, whereas the latter are involved in a predictive argument based on the analysis of conflicting trends and consequences.

10. Other views: Conduction under various aliases

The discussion so far makes it obvious that Wellman's account of conductive arguments has been influential insofar as it has generated a considerable body of literature. Moreover, the discussion leaves no doubt of the importance of the concepts defined, principles formulated, and issues raised in this literature. The details of my discussion, however tedious at times, make it clear that this literature contains novelties, insights, and promises that merit further dissemination, elaboration, and research.

On the other hand, a number of caveats are in order. First, it is obvious that although Wellman may have invented the notion of conduction, he did not invent the practice of conductive argumentation, any more than the theorists of prose and other literary genres were the first to actually speak prose. Second, it would be a mistake to think that nowadays, after the growth of such philosophical work on conductive arguments, good conductive argumentation can occur only if one explicitly uses the technical terminology and conceptual framework of conduction. The example of Brooks's health-care argument, and its elegance, sophistication, and brilliance (whatever one may think of the acceptability of his conclusion) provide an antidote against such a mistake.

Thirdly, and more importantly in the present context, we should not pretend that Wellman and his followers are the first or only ones to have theorized about or studied conductive arguments. To do so would lead us to neglect other scholarly work which, without so much as using the word conduction and its cognates, contains contributions to the same area of cognitive reality. Some of these contributions deserve mention here.[14]

One classical source would be John Stuart Mill, in particular the theory of argument in his essay *On Liberty*, especially chapter 2 entitled "Of the Liberty of Thought and Discussion." One strand of his argument there involves the view that "on every subject on which difference of opinion is possible, the truth depends on a balance to be struck between two sets of conflicting reasons" (Mill 1951, p. 128). This view is elaborated in the context of an attempt to show the importance of considering objections to one's own conclusions, besides the supporting reasons (cf. Finocchiaro 2007c).

---

[14] Other contributions which deserve further study from this point of view, but which here cannot be even summarized and must be merely cited, are: Perkins (1985, 2002); Perkins, Allen, and Hafner (1983); Perkins, Farady, and Bushey (1991); Pollock (1974, pp. 33-49, 300-340; 1995, pp. 38-42, 85-140); Slob (2006); Verheij 2006, pp. 194-98; and Voss et al. 1991.

Other sources are closer and more current. One is Scriven's (1981) account of the "weight and sum" methodology for evaluating such things as programs, products, proposals, and personnel. In the typical case, several distinct "dimensions" are involved and need to be weighted, and for each dimension the entry being evaluated is "scored" for its "performance." Both the dimension weights and performance scores are assigned numbers, such as 1-5 or 1-10. Then "the total score for each entry is obtained simply by multiplying the weights by the performance scores and summing them" (Scriven 1981, p. 86).

Scriven is concerned to point out that this methodology is extremely important and useful, but also extremely "tricky." For example, care is needed regarding questions such as the following: the numbers used in the two scales and the relationship between them; the number of dimensions, the cumulative effect of small differences in performance scores, the possible existence of big differences within a given dimension, and the relationship among these three things; the possible need to lump some dimensions together or to subdivide others, before the evaluation process is completed; the possibility that some dimension embodies a necessary condition, whose non-satisfaction pre-empts and swamps all the other weights; and the difference between pairwise comparison and general comparison of entries.

It seems obvious to me that the problems Scriven is dealing with overlap to a large extent with the ones examined by writers on conductive arguments. In other words, what Scriven calls evaluative arguments correspond to what Wellman and his followers call conductive arguments, and the methodology of former overlaps with the methodology of the latter.

Another nearby and current source is Johnson's account of the dialectical tier of argumentation and of the dialectical obligations of arguers. Although he (Johnson 2000a, pp. 84-88, 92-95) has explicitly attempted to elaborate his own critical appreciation of Govier's account of conductive arguments, it seems to me that the most crucial point has been left unsaid. It is this. Suppose one follows[15] Johnson is analyzing the nature of argumentation in such a way that, besides having an illative core consisting of reasons supporting the conclusion, arguments possess a dialectical tier consisting of replies to objections and criticism of alternative positions. And suppose one again follows Johnson in conceiving the appraisal of argumentation as consequently requiring the appraisal of the dialectical tier, involving such questions as: exactly what objections must an arguer reply to; exactly what alternative positions must one criticize; must an arguer, for example, anticipate objections? It seems to me that such a dialectical approach to the analysis and appraisal of argumentation is one designed precisely to deal with what Wellman and Govier call conductive arguments. In effect, given his dialectical definition of argument, Johnson is treating all arguments (in his sense) as conductive arguments (in Govier's sense). The overlap is so deep and pervasive that he does not need to examine conductive arguments in a particular section of his theory; they lurk everywhere throughout his account.

Actually, Johnson (2009a, pp. 92-95) comes close to admitting as much, although not in such words. This occurs when he articulates his appreciation that "the truth behind conductivism" is that argumentation is a special case of reasoning (studied in informal logic), but distinct from entailment (studied in formal deductive logic) and from inference (studied in inductive logic). However, my main point here is that Johnson's theory of argument is a good example of a contribution that deals with the same problems examined by conductive

---

[15] Of course, one need not follow Johnson completely, but may do so partially, as I have argued in Finocchiaro 2005a, pp. 292-326. However, those differences are not relevant to the present issue.

theorists, but without using the conductive terminology; instead it uses dialectical terminology.

Another such significant and current example is the work of Christian Kock (2003, 2007b, 2007c, 2007d). He has studied what he calls "deliberative argumentation," which he defines as argumentation about "proposals." Unlike propositions, proposals are neither true nor false, but rather right or wrong, or more or less good. Such arguments are common in political debates and, indeed, in all practical argumentation. Kock claims that deliberative argumentation has properties such as the following: "There will always be several good but contradictory arguments. Contradictory arguments do not cancel each other. A good argument never entails a policy by necessity or inference. Contradictory arguments often rely on plural values which are not objectively commensurable. Contradictory arguments must nevertheless be compared for choices to be made. Choices rely on individuals' value commitments and are subjective. Debates between exponents of opposite policies cannot be expected to lead towards agreement, but must help other individuals consider and compare the pro and con arguments relating to a policy" (Kock 2007d, p. 238). These claims make it obvious that, as Kock himself has pointed out, his account is similar to that of Wellman and Govier, although of course there are differences. Clearly, Kock's work exemplifies well the possibility of an account of conductive arguments that uses different terminology but shares conceptual and substantive content.

Finally, there is the instructive case of the literature on two-sidedness, as distinct from one-sidedness. Such literature spans a very broad spectrum, ranging from pedestrian and formulaic empirical studies by marketing, consumer, and communication researchers to lofty and sublime[16] analyses by philosophers. Starting with the former, one might begin by noting that if conductive arguments are as ubiquitous and effective as claimed by their proponents, then they should have been discovered and exploited also by advertisers. And indeed, this happens to be the case. The terminology used is "two-sided advertising"; this is advertising in which some negative information, and not only positive information, about a product is given in the advertisement. The practice has also become the subject of an extensive social-science literature. Fortunately, there are at least two so-called "meta-analyses" that draw their conclusions based in part on an interpretive summary of the literature. Eisend (2006) reviews twenty-five studies of two-sided vs. one-sided advertising, and also does a so-called "regressive analysis" of them. O'Keefe (1999) is a more ambitious review, examining eighty-nine studies of two-sided vs. one-sided messages in both advertising and non-advertising contexts; he focuses on a so-called "random-effects analysis."

One of Eisend's general conclusions is that two-sided advertising is more persuasive that one-sided advertising. Some quotations will give us an idea of nuances and qualifications to this general conclusion, as well as give us a flavor of the potential relevance to conductive argumentation: "Two-sided messages work, particularly they enhance source credibility, reduce negative cognitive responses, and have positive impact on brand attitude and purchase intention ... Two-sided messages help to mainly improve source credibility and to reduce negative cognitions, whereas the impact on attitudes and purchase intentions proved to be weaker" (Eisend 2006, pp. 195-96). On the other hand, O'Keefe argues that this is true only in the context of advertising messages. However, in non-advertising contexts, two-sided messages are not always more persuasive. It depends on whether they are refutational or nonrefutational, refutational two-sided messages being those which not only mention the negative information or opposing arguments, but also refute or criticize them.

---

[16] Here I have in mind the Hegelian concept of dialectic, which can be connected with the idea of avoiding one-sidedness (see Finocchiaro 1988, pp. 143-230); but obviously even a summary of this connection would beyond the scope of the present chapter.

In fact, it turns out that "for non-advertising messages, refutational two-sided messages are significantly more persuasive than one-sided messages, and nonrefutational two-sided messages are significantly less persuasive than one-sided messages" (O'Keefe 1999, p. 231). Although there are many more details and nuances, and although a philosopher would want to adopt a critical stance toward such empirical work, it is clearly suggestive and one can ignore it only at one's own risk.

Moving on to a philosophical example, Dale Jacquette has also studied conductive arguments without using Wellman's terminology of conduction, and has done so in the context of an examination of the tactics of the ancient Greek sophists. Jacquette discusses the problem of whether there are two sides to any issue, and what to make of the sophists' practice of switching sides. His resolution is, I believe, insightful and correct. It is this: "what is objectionable is that ... the sophist argues pro and then argues con, and leaves it at that, omitting any assessment of the strengths and weaknesses of the arguments ... This is the sophists' error, that they defend a proposition, and then criticize it and defend its negation, as though the two were always in an even standoff" (Jacquette 2007, pp. 125-26).

In the spirit of such investigations, which are relevant to the study of conductive arguments but do not use the conductive terminology, I would next like to summarize and adapt some of my own work relating to Galileo (Finocchiaro 1980, esp. pp. 27-45; 1997, pp. 1-7, 309-56; 2010a, esp. pp. xiii-xliii, 1-134). I hope to be able to show that it has obvious relevance to conductive arguments.

11. Galileo on the motion of the earth

In 1543, Copernicus published a book elaborating a world system whose key thesis was that the earth moves by rotating on its own axis daily and by revolving around the sun yearly. Copernicus's accomplishment was really to give a *new argument* in support of an *old idea* that had been considered and almost universally rejected since the ancient Greeks. He demonstrated that the known facts about heavenly motions could be explained in quantitative detail if the universe is structured geokinetically and heliocentrically; and further that this explanation was more coherent (and also simpler and more elegant) than the geostatic account.

Despite its novelty and significance, however, as a proof of the earth's motion Copernicus's argument was inconclusive. First of all, his argument was clearly an abductive one, i.e., an inference to the best explanation. Moreover, there were many powerful arguments against terrestrial motion that had accumulated for two millennia. In summary, the earth's motion seemed epistemologically absurd because it flatly contradicted direct sense experience. It seemed empirically false because it had astronomical consequences that were not observed to happen: for example, similarities between the earth and the planets; phases for the planet Venus; and annual parallax in the fixed stars. The earth's motion also seemed physically impossible because it supposedly contradicted the laws of motion of the available (Aristotelian) physics, and the most incontrovertible mechanical phenomena (such as vertical fall). And it seemed religiously heretical because it conflicted with the literal meaning of Scripture, such as the passage about the miracle of stopping the sun, in Joshua 10: 12-13.

Thus, the Copernican Revolution required much more than Copernicus's own argument. First, the geokinetic hypothesis had to be supported not only with new arguments, but also with new evidence. Galileo's telescopic discoveries provided such novel evidence.

Second, the earth's motion had to be not only constructively supported with new arguments and evidence, but also critically defended from the host of powerful old and new objections. Galileo answered the observational astronomical objections by showing that almost all the empirical consequences implied by Copernicanism were visible with the telescope, although still invisible with the naked eye. He answered the scriptural objections by arguing that Scripture is not a scientific authority, and so scriptural passages should not be used to invalidate astronomical claims that are proved or provable. And he answered the physical mechanical objections by articulating a new physics centered on the principles of conservation and composition of motion.

Third, the defense of the geokinetic hypothesis required not only the destructive refutation of those objections, but also the appreciative understanding of their strength. Galileo was keen on this, and so in his writings we find the anti-Copernican arguments stated more clearly and incisively than in the works of Aristotelians advocating the geostatic system.

Fourth, Galileo also realized that his case in favor of Copernicanism was not absolutely conclusive or decisive because, for example, his telescope failed to reveal an annual parallax of the fixed stars, which was a consequence of the earth's annual revolution around the sun.

In short, Galileo's key contribution to the Copernican Revolution was to elaborate an argument for the geokinetic thesis that stressed reasoning and observation judiciously guided by the ideals of rational-mindedness, open-mindedness, and fair-mindedness. Galileo presented such an argument in his book *Dialogue on the Two Chief World Systems, Ptolemaic and Copernican* (1632). And he not only constructed, presented, and published such a piece of argumentation, but he showed a rare and keen awareness of what he was doing and of the desirability of doing so.

I want to illustrate this meta-cognitive awareness by quoting his explicit formulation of the three key principles just mentioned. What I label rational-mindedness is the principle that when one is considering a new doctrine "one [should] examine with the utmost severity what the followers of this doctrine know and can advance [in its favor], and that nothing be granted them unless the strength of their arguments greatly exceeds that of the reasons for the opposite side" (Galilei 2008, p. 165). What I label open-mindedness is the attitude exemplified by the Copernicans insofar "the followers of the new system [of the world] produce against themselves observations, experiments, and reasons much stronger than those produced by Aristotle, Ptolemy, and other opponents of the same conclusions" (Galilei 2008, pp. 216-17). And what I call fair-mindedness is the principle prescribing that "when one presents arguments for the opposite side with the intention of confuting them, they must be explained in the fairest way and not be made out of straw to the disadvantage of the opponent" (Galilei 2008, p. 283).

Expressed in the terminology of the present subject, my claim can be expressed by saying that I have been arguing (however cryptically and succinctly) that the main argument in Galileo's *Dialogue* is a conductive argument. For Galileo justifies the conclusion that the earth moves (1) nonconclusively by means of (2) several distinct and separately relevant subarguments that (3) cumulatively reinforce each other and that are formulated in the context of a (4) strong acknowledgment of counterconsiderations and objections. Moreover, I would also claim that Galileo's argument is conductively adequate, although here I have not given reasons to justify this claim.

Furthermore, however convinced I am of my interpretation and however strong my meta-argument may be, it would be ironic if in the present context I forgot that the field in which I am presently operating is that of interpretive studies, and that arguments supporting interpretations are typically conductive arguments. Additionally, besides being in a context of interpretive studies, I am dealing here with a question of classification: how to classify Galileo's own main argument in the *Dialogue*. Finally, since the issue is whether his argument is a conductive one, I am interested in exploring a definition of conductive argument that would be analogous to Freeman's definition of deductive and inductive arguments, mentioned above. This would be a conductive definition of conductive argument, where the various requirements to be satisfied are not individually necessary and jointly sufficient conditions, but rather separate indices the accumulation of which can adequately justify our interpretive conclusion, without guaranteeing its truth or rendering it inductively probable. Thus, I feel it is only prudent to give some other reasons of a different sort, as well as to acknowledge some opposing reasons.

So far, I have given two separately relevant (sets of) reasons. One is that many facts about the Copernican Revolution and about Galileo's work can be explained or understood in terms of the interpretation that his key contribution to that episode was to have advanced a conductive argument for the geokinetic thesis. Another reason is that on several occasions, by explicitly formulating the principles of rational-mindedness, open-mindedness, and fair-mindedness, Galileo showed that he was reflectively aware that what was needed and all that was possible at the time was to give a conductive argument for the earth's motion.

A third reason is one which I appropriate from another scholar, named Filippo Soccorsi (1947), who did not even mention the word 'conduction' and advanced his interpretation in the 1940's. This was long before Wellman and his followers, as well as long before the present writer, whose background in both argumentation studies and Galileo studies makes it unsurprising and predictable that he would explore the potential interpretation of Galilean arguments by means of informal-logic categories. Translated into conductive terminology, Soccorsi's interpretation amounts to the claim that many features about the Inquisition trial and condemnation of Galileo in 1633 (starting with the very fact the trial occurred at all) can be understood if we construe the argument in the *Dialogue* as a self-conscious conductive argument, because this type of argumentation was bound to be misunderstood by the Church authorities and manipulated by his enemies. Here we must recall that the *Dialogue* is the book published in 1632 that triggered the trial and condemnation by the Inquisition the following year. Keeping my terminological translation in mind, Soccorsi's words are worth quoting precisely for their lack of loaded logical and informal-logical terminology, which lack makes the substance of his insight even more striking. Referring to Galileo's arguments in the *Dialogue*, Soccorsi claims:

> If no one of the arguments constituted a rigorous demonstration, still their combination ... was not devoid of persuasive force, especially for a mind that could comprehend the synthesis and penetrate it with the new point of view of the new mechanics ... This observation allows us to explain how it was possible that there was a profound misunderstanding between Galileo and those old-fashioned minds ... which ... at most were concerned with asking the experts whether any one of the proofs was conclusive: in this manner they missed the persuasive force of Galileo's arguments. (Translated and quoted in Finocchiaro 2005b, p. 291.)

A fourth and final reason for my interpretation comes from the full title of Galileo's book. As was customary in the seventeenth century, books tended to have very long titles that were descriptive of the content and form of the work. The full title of Galileo's *Dialogue* is very revealing since it contains many words and phrases that may be taken as conductive indicators. It reads: *Dialogue by Galileo Galilei, Lincean Academician, Extraordinary Mathematician at the University of Pisa, and Philosopher and Chief Mathematician to the Most Serene Grand Duke of Tuscany; where in meetings over the course of four days* one discusses the *Two Chief World Systems, Ptolemaic and Copernican*, proposing indeterminately the philosophical and natural reasons for the one as well as for the other side (see Finocchiaro 1980, pp. 12-18; 1997, pp. 359-60; 2005b, p. 133). Here, Galileo's "indeterminately" is equivalent to the "nonconclusively" of Wellman and his followers. And the Galilean talk of "reasons for the one as well as for the other side" is equivalent to the reasons and counterconsiderations, or pros and cons, of the conductive theorists.

Of course, such language was connected with the historical fact that Galileo had been prohibited by officials and institutions of the Catholic Church to hold or defend the geokinetic thesis. Moreover, such a title had fateful historical repercussions. That is, during the proceedings of the 1633 Inquisition trial, Galileo was charged and convicted in part for having tried to give the misleading impression that his argumentation was "indeterminate," but in reality favoring the Copernican side. In conductive terminology this means that he was blamed for not having limited himself to presenting the pros and cons of the geokinetic thesis, but for having dared to make the judgment that the strength of the pros outweighed the strength of the cons, and indeed for having argued convincingly to justify this judgment. Using Jacquette's terminology mentioned above, we can say that one alleged crime of the *Dialogue* for which Galileo was convicted was that he refused to be a sophist!

Finally, I am aware that various reasons have been given to try to show that Galileo's argument is not conductive, but rather deductive. For example, some scholars begin by stressing the fact that (1) the book's most prominent argument in favor of the earth's motion is one based on the existence and properties of the tides and on trying to show that they are caused by the earth's motion; (2) originally Galileo wanted to entitle the book *Dialogue on the Tides*, but (3) Church authorities objected to such a title, forcing him to adopt the title mentioned above. These scholars then go on to (4) explain this fact by saying that (5) he regarded this argument to be conclusive ([6] as one can gather from many passages in the book), and (7) originally he wanted to mention the tides in the title in order to give an indication that the book contained a demonstrative proof of the earth's motion. And so the book's original but ultimately discarded title is evidence that its main argument is deductive.

Now, the factual claims (1, 2, 3) made in this argument are indeed correct, but the explanation of them lies elsewhere; indeed the claims (5, 6, 7) making up the *explanans* are untenable. For Galileo did not regard the tidal argument as conclusive and deductive; the book's passages usually mentioned as examples of deductive indicators merely indicate that he regarded this argument as very strong, indeed his strongest. Instead he was keenly aware that the tidal argument was an inference to the best explanation; his original title was meant to stress precisely the hypothetical and explanatory nature of the book. In light of the restrictions under which he was operating, including a prohibition to defend the earth's motion, a stress on hypothetical or explanatory reasoning was much more prudent, reasonable, and innocuous. Moreover, although the tidal argument is prominently displayed and highly regarded by Galileo, the book makes it crystal clear that it is only one of several arguments in favor of the earth's motion, and the context of multiple argumentation is an indication that no one particular argument is being advanced as conclusive. I think such a connection between multiple and conductive argumentation is, *ceteris paribus*, a sound general principle of interpretation, and its soundness has been recognized by several scholars in other contexts, especially in purely philosophical argumentation such as the mind-body problem (Dauer 1974, p. 131; Govier 1980a, p. 14).

Another reason against the conductive status of Galileo's argument involves the fact that the earth's motion contradicted many biblical passages when literally interpreted (e.g., Joshua 10: 12-13). Then some scholars claim that in such cases of conflict, the operative hermeneutical principle was the one stipulating that biblical passages about natural phenomena must be interpreted literally unless there is a conclusive scientific proof to the contrary. Presumably the *Dialogue* was trying to provide the conclusive proof required by this principle in light of the contradiction between the earth's motion and the literal interpretation of Scripture. An inconclusive, conductive argument would not have been sufficient.

However, Galileo did not really accept this hermeneutical principle in the form just stated, which amounts to a biconditional. That is, it claims that if there is a conclusive proof of a natural phenomenon, then biblical passages to the contrary should be interpreted nonliterally; and if there is no such proof, then relevant biblical passages must be interpreted literally. He did accept the first conditional, making conclusive proof a sufficient condition for nonliteral interpretation; indeed this sufficiency principle was universally accepted, and had been applied centuries earlier to the case of the earth's shape, which was demonstrably spherical, rather than flat as stated or implied in many biblical passages. However, he rejected the other conditional, making conclusive proof a necessary condition for nonliteral interpretation. His critical argument (see Finocchiaro 2010a, pp. 243-48) began with the universally accepted sufficiency principle. Then he went on to ask for an explanation why such a principle holds, why in cases of conflict between a conclusive physical proof and the letter of a biblical text, priority is given to the former. His explanation was basically that Scripture is not a scientific (or astronomical) authority, but only an authority on matters of faith and morals. But then Galileo went on to consider what follows from the denial of the scientific authority of Scripture. What follows is that biblical statements have no probative weight in scientific investigation, and hence scientists ought to be free to search for natural truth by engaging in argumentation, presenting all available evidence, and determining what is the conclusion supported by the better arguments. Thus, the *Dialogue* did not have to be a conclusive proof, a deductive argument, and if the state of inquiry enabled one to formulate an inconclusive, conductive argument, there was nothing wrong with that. In particular, there was nothing wrong with weighing the evidence, to see whether one side or theory was stronger than the other. And as discussed earlier, this is precisely what Galileo did.

12. Conclusions: Progress, problems, prospects

A main strand of this chapter has been a discussion of the views on conductive arguments by Wellman, Hitchcock, Govier, Allen, Ennis, Zenker, and Wohlrapp. By and large, I interpreted Hitchcock's and Govier's views as constructive elaborations of Wellman's; Allen's, Ennis's, and Zenker's views as a series of mostly negative criticisms of Govier's views; and Wohlrapp's views as consisting partly of negative criticism, but primarily of a constructive alternative position. In accordance with my historical-textual approach, I interpreted and reconstructed all their views as a series of arguments. Moreover, since their arguments are theoretical, they obviously constitute meta-arguments, and hence my analysis was also a case study in meta-argumentation. Now, let us recall that a meta-argument was defined as an argument about one or more arguments, as distinct from a ground-level argument, which is about a subject matter other than argument. Then it is useful to explicitly coin the term 'conductive meta-argument' and define is as "a meta-argument that is about one or more conductive arguments," or as "a meta-argument that is itself conductive." These notions enable us to conceive this strand of this chapter as a historical-textual study of conductive meta-argumentation.

My meta-argumentative reconstructions attempted to be quite comprehensive and well-documented, by including all the relevant views of these scholars as well as appropriate references and quotations. By contrast, my evaluation of these reconstructed meta-arguments was more selective, indirect, implicit, incomplete, and tentative. Nevertheless, the results of my evaluation are perhaps more interesting, important, and suggestive than the results of my interpretation.

For example, despite the impression conveyed by many commentators on Wellman, including his followers, he does have a guideline for the evaluation of conductive arguments, namely the model of comparing the weight of bodies by lifting them with one's hands; and this deserves further exploration. Moreover, Wellman's has two arguments for his anti-deductivist claim (W14) that raise important and relatively open questions: one about the justification of balance-of-considerations claims (subargument W14a), the other about the non-convergence of deductive arguments (subargument W14b).

Out of Hitchcock's meta-arguments, there emerge two problems for further investigation. One is whether it is possible to give a definition of conductive adequacy as a type of appraisal that would define it independently of the definition of the conductive type of argument. The other issue is that more work needs to be done to explore the possibility of a conductive definition of conductive argument; this would be analogous, but of course substantively different, from Freeman's conductive definition of 'deductive' and 'inductive argument.'

Out of Govier's meta-arguments, besides the critiques by other scholars to be highlighted presently, two points deserve to be stressed. One is her claim that some significant scientific arguments, those justifying theory choice, are conductive; this is important, insightful, and correct. But there is also the problem of the asymmetry between positively relevant reasons and negatively relevant counterconsiderations: her principles of evaluation seem to assume that counterconsiderations not mentioned in an argument are relevant for its evaluation, but unmentioned positive reasons are not relevant to the evaluation of the argument, but only to the evaluation of the acceptability of the conclusion; the problem is that it's not clear why there should be such an asymmetry.

Combining one of Allen's, of Ennis's, and of Wohlrapp's meta-arguments, we have a reaffirmation of the deductivist approach. Allen's first criticism is a cogent argument that Govier's justification of her anti-deductivist claim is not cogent. Ennis has a cogent argument that she uses deductive standards in her evaluation of the strength of reasons, which is inconsistent with her attempt to avoid deductivism. And I also reported Wohlrapp's claim, but not his supporting argument, that she fails to appreciate that deduction is presupposed by induction and by conduction, but not vice-versa.

Next, we can combine one of Wellman's important subarguments (W14a), one of Allen's critiques (A4), one of the main strands of Wohlrapp's alternative account, and one main point emerging from my analysis of Brooks's health-care argument. I believe we get a confirmation of my working hypothesis, adumbrated in the introduction, to the effect that conductive arguments have a crucial and irreducible meta-argumentative aspect, namely a *balance-of-considerations claim* that must be implicitly made, explicitly formulated, or critically justified for the construction, interpretation, or evaluation of conductive arguments. Of course, the status, use, and justification of balance-of-considerations claims is problematic. It is not exactly clear how one justifies such claims; what type of arguments one would use in such a justification, in particular whether they would be conductive arguments; and consequently, whether in a conductive argument, if the argument is to remain of the conductive type, we must limit ourselves to merely using such claims, and not get involved in a non-conductive justification. Obviously more work needs to be done in this regard.

Another important open question is that of the relationship among conduction, convergence, and multiple argumentation. This emerges from Wellman's subargument (W14b) that deduction allows no place for the convergence of evidence, from Govier's subargument (G14) that not all convergent arguments are conductive, and from Allen's criticism (A2) of Govier's thesis that a deductivist reconstruction of a conductive argument turns one argument into several.

A common criticism of Govier's account has focused on her method for evaluating the strength of reasons in terms of the range of exceptions to the corresponding c-p generalization. Ennis objected that this method presupposes a deductivism which she seems generally to want to reject. Zenker objected that this method is misconceived because c-p generalizations have nothing to do with conductive arguments. And Wohlrapp finds the method unfruitful, at least as compared to his alterative account, which bypasses such specific estimates of strength. Although I do not think the method was intended to be taken seriously, after such criticisms, it is difficult to so take it.

Another strand of this chapter has been the analysis of some actual important examples of conductive ground-level arguments, in accordance with my historical textual approach. Brooks's argument against the U.S. Senate health-care bill is an obvious example of a conductive argument. Its conductive character is obvious both from its subject matter and from its form. Its elegance and sophistication make it deserving of further interpretation, evaluation, and analysis. This is especially true if we contrast his argument with that of Paul Krugman. On the other hand, Galileo's argument for the motion of the earth, has been widely studied for about four centuries. It is of epoch-making importance both for its role in the Copernican Revolution and in the Galileo affair. Although it has never been interpreted as a conductive argument, I have argued that it can be so interpreted; and although I have no hesitation in characterizing this meta-argument of mine as a conductive one, I believe it is very strong. Brooks's and Galileo's arguments show that the practice of conductive argumentation is prior to, is relatively independent of, and perhaps has primacy vis-à-vis the theory of conductive argumentation.

Similarly, the theory of conductive arguments has much to learn from other studies which examine the same cognitive phenomena under different labels. For this claim seems a well justified conclusion from the third strand of this chapter, which briefly examined Mill's plea for liberty of argument in *On Liberty*, Scriven's 'weight and sum' methodology, Johnson's account of the dialectical tier and dialectical obligations, Kock's account of deliberative argumentation, Eisend's and O'Keefe's meta-analyses of the social-scientific literature on one-sided vs. two-sided messages and advertising, Jacquette's discussion of the problem of two sides to any issue, and my study of open-mindedness and fair-mindedness in Galileo's work. Admittedly, I had had this hunch all along, since the beginning of this investigation; that is, the hunch that conductive argumentation, besides being practiced before and independently of conductivist studies, had also been studied without the conductive terminology. This hunch was another working hypothesis, so to speak, and it too is now reinforced.[17]

---

[17] I thank Albert DiCanzio, Trudy Govier, Harald Wohlrapp, and Frank Zenker for substantive comments on various parts or versions of the paper from which this chapter originated, and Frank Zenker and Tom Fischer for bibliographical assistance. An earlier version was first presented in April 2010 at a symposium on conductive arguments at the Center for Research in Reasoning, Argumentation and Rhetoric, University of Windsor; I thank its Fellows and especially its then Director Hans Hansen for their encouragement, hospitality, and support.

Appendix 1 "The Hardest Call" by David Brooks *The New York Times*, December 18, 2009.

[a] The first reason to support the Senate health care bill is that it would provide insurance to 30 million more Americans.

[b] The second reason to support the bill is that its authors took the deficit issue seriously. Compared with, say, the prescription drug benefit from a few years ago, this bill is a model of fiscal rectitude. It spends a lot of money to cover the uninsured, but to help pay for it, it also includes serious Medicare cuts and whopping tax increases—the tax on high-cost insurance plans alone will raise $1.3 trillion in the second decade.

[c] The bill is not really deficit-neutral. It's politically inconceivable that Congress will really make all the spending cuts that are there on paper. But the bill won't explode the deficit, and that's an accomplishment.

[d] The third reason to support the bill is that the authors have thrown in a million little ideas in an effort to reduce health care inflation. The fact is, nobody knows how to reduce cost growth within the current system. The authors of this bill are willing to try anything. You might even call this a Burkean approach. They are not fundamentally disrupting the status quo, but they are experimenting with dozens of gradual programs that might bend the cost curve.

[e] If you've ever heard about it, it's in there—improved insurance exchanges, payment innovations, an independent commission to cap Medicare payment rates, an innovation center, comparative effectiveness research. There's at least a pilot program for every promising idea.

[f] The fourth reason to support the bill is that if this fails, it will take a long time to get back to health reform. Clinton failed. Obama will have failed. No one will touch this. Meanwhile, health costs will continue their inexorable march upward, strangling the nation.

[g] The first reason to oppose this bill is that it does not fundamentally reform health care. The current system is rotten to the bone with opaque pricing and insane incentives. Consumers are insulated from the costs of their decisions and providers are punished for efficiency. Burkean gradualism is fine if you've got a cold. But if you've got cancer, you want surgery, not nasal spray.

[h] If this bill passes, you'll have 500 experts in Washington trying to hold down costs and 300 million Americans with the same old incentives to get more and more care. The Congressional Budget Office and most of the experts I talk to (including many who support the bill) do not believe it will seriously bend the cost curve.

[i] The second reason to oppose this bill is that, according to the chief actuary for Medicare, it will cause national health care spending to increase faster. Health care spending is already zooming past 17 percent of G.D.P. to 22 percent and beyond. If these pressures mount even faster, health care will squeeze out everything else, especially on the state level. We'll shovel more money into insurance companies and you can kiss goodbye programs like expanded preschool that would have a bigger social impact.

[j] Third, if passed, the bill sets up a politically unsustainable situation. Over its first several years, the demand for health care will rise sharply. The supply will not. Providers will have the same perverse incentives. As a result, prices will skyrocket while efficiencies will not. There will be a bipartisan rush to gut reform.

[k] This country has reduced health inflation in short bursts, but it has not sustained cost control over the long term because the deep flaws in the system produce horrific political pressures that gut restraint.

[l] Fourth, you can't centrally regulate 17 percent of the U.S. economy without a raft of unintended consequences.

[m] Fifth, it will slow innovation. Government regulators don't do well with disruptive new technologies.

[n] Sixth, if this passes, we will never get back to cost control. The basic political deal was, we get to have dessert (expanding coverage) but we have to eat our spinach (cost control), too. If we eat dessert now, we'll never come back to the spinach.

[o] So what's my verdict? I have to confess, I flip-flop week to week and day to day. It's a guess. Does this put us on a path toward the real reform, or does it head us down a valley in which real reform will be less likely?

[p] If I were a senator forced to vote today, I'd vote no. If you pass a health care bill without systemic incentives reform, you set up a political vortex in which the few good parts of the bill will get stripped out and the expensive and wasteful parts will be entrenched.

[q] Defenders say we can't do real reform because the politics won't allow it. The truth is the reverse. Unless you get the fundamental incentives right, the politics will be terrible forever and ever.

Appendix 2 "Pass the Bill" by Paul Krugman   *The New York Times*, December 18, 2009.

A message to progressives: By all means, hang Senator Joe Lieberman in effigy. Declare that you're disappointed in and/or disgusted with President Obama. Demand a change in Senate rules that, combined with the Republican strategy of total obstructionism, are in the process of making America ungovernable.

But meanwhile, pass the health care bill.

Yes, the filibuster-imposed need to get votes from "centrist" senators has led to a bill that falls a long way short of ideal. Worse, some of those senators seem motivated largely by a desire to protect the interests of insurance companies—with the possible exception of Mr. Lieberman, who seems motivated by sheer spite.

But let's all take a deep breath, and consider just how much good this bill would do, if passed—and how much better it would be than anything that seemed possible just a few years ago. With all its flaws, the Senate health bill would be the biggest expansion of the social safety net since Medicare, greatly improving the lives of millions. Getting this bill would be much, much better than watching health care reform fail.

At its core, the bill would do two things. First, it would prohibit discrimination by insurance companies on the basis of medical condition or history: Americans could no longer be denied health insurance because of a pre-existing condition, or have their insurance canceled when they get sick. Second, the bill would provide substantial financial aid to those who don't get insurance through their employers, as well as tax breaks for small employers that do provide insurance.

All of this would be paid for in large part with the first serious effort ever to rein in rising health care costs.

The result would be a huge increase in the availability and affordability of health insurance, with more than 30 million Americans gaining coverage, and premiums for lower-income and lower-middle-income Americans falling dramatically. That's an immense change from where we were just a few years ago: remember, not long ago the Bush administration and its allies in Congress successfully blocked even a modest expansion of health care for children.

Bear in mind also the lessons of history: social insurance programs tend to start out highly imperfect and incomplete, but get better and more comprehensive as the years go by. Thus Social Security originally had huge gaps in coverage—and a majority of African-Americans, in particular, fell through those gaps. But it was improved over time, and it's now the bedrock of retirement stability for the vast majority of Americans.

Look, I understand the anger here: supporting this weakened bill feels like giving in to blackmail—because it is. Or to use an even more accurate metaphor suggested by Ezra Klein of *The Washington Post*, we're paying a ransom to hostage-takers. Some of us, including a majority of senators, really, really want to cover the uninsured; but to make that happen we need the votes of a handful of senators who see failure of reform as an acceptable outcome, and demand a steep price for their support.

The question, then, is whether to pay the ransom by giving in to the demands of those senators, accepting a flawed bill, or hang tough and let the hostage—that is, health reform—die.

Again, history suggests the answer. Whereas flawed social insurance programs have tended to get better over time, the story of health reform suggests that rejecting an imperfect deal in the hope of eventually getting something better is a recipe for getting nothing at all. Not to put too fine a point on it, America would be in much better shape today if Democrats had cut a deal on health care with Richard Nixon, or if Bill Clinton had cut a deal with moderate Republicans back when they still existed.

But won't paying the ransom now encourage more hostage-taking in the future? Maybe. But the next big fight, over the future of the financial system, will be very different. If the usual suspects try to water down financial reform, I say call their bluff: there's not much to lose, since a merely cosmetic reform, by creating a false sense of security, could well end up being worse than nothing.

Beyond that, we need to take on the way the Senate works. The filibuster, and the need for 60 votes to end debate, aren't in the Constitution. They're a Senate tradition, and that same tradition said that the threat of filibusters should be used sparingly. Well, Republicans have already trashed the second part of the tradition: look at a list of cloture motions over time, and you'll see that since the G.O.P. lost control of Congress it has pursued obstructionism on a literally unprecedented scale. So it's time to revise the rules.

But that's for later. Right now, let's pass the bill that's on the table.

PART V – AFTERWORD

Chapter 16

Conductive Arguments: Overview of the Symposium

TRUDY GOVIER

1. Introduction[1]

As one who has been interested in conductive arguments off and on for some years, I am gratified to find this interest is shared by a substantial number of intelligent and energetic people. To those who have worked through some of my earlier efforts on this and related topics, I would like to express my appreciation. At one point during the eighties, Anthony Blair contacted Carl Wellman to inquire whether he would like to participate in the debate among informal logicians about the notion of conductive argument. Wellman had apparently moved on to other topics and declined. But had he been able to participate in the recent conference and consider the papers collected here, I am sure he would have appreciated the considerable attention given to his work.

2. Historical and philosophical background

I once suspected that one reason that Wellman's work in general, and his notion of conductive argument in particular, received relatively little attention from philosophers was that it appeared at the same time as John Rawls' *A Theory of Justice*. Be this as it may, I suspect another reason too. Suppose we understand conductive arguments as arguments in which premises are put forward as separately and non-conclusively relevant to support a conclusion, against which negatively relevant considerations may also be acknowledged. Suppose we allow that there are many arguments of this type, used in significant theoretical and practical contexts. Wellman attended mostly to ethical contexts. Others, including myself, have argued for the importance of conductive arguments in other contexts, including historical, interpretive, and scientific argumentation. If we allow these points and we further allow that there are no general rules for the assessment of conductive arguments, which are content- and context-dependent, we acknowledge definite limits to the philosopher's expertise. To many philosophers, acknowledging such limits will be unwelcome, and it will seem preferable to think simply of deductive and inductive arguments, finding sources for assessment along broadly positivistic lines in formal deductive logic and mathematics, on the one hand, and probabilistic reasoning towards empirical conclusions, on the other. I maintain, as I have long maintained, that any such escape should be temporary.

If we define the term "inductive" so broadly that all arguments that fail to be deductive count as inductive, we will then locate within the inductive category such diverse sorts of arguments as analogies, statistical syllogism, enumerative inductions, inference-to-the-best explanation (abductive) arguments, arguments based on authority, arguments based on tes-

---

[1] Aside from the cited works, all references here are to conference papers in the present volume or to points that arose in conference discussion. Versions of essays used here are those submitted for the conference, as presented and discussed, as distinct from the revised versions that were submitted after May, 2010.

timony, and what many of us, following Wellman, now call conductive arguments.[2] Arguments of all these sorts will require analysis and evaluation. A classification can be made to disappear by definitional shifts, but the existence of these arguments will remain a reality and questions about their structure and evaluation will persist, albeit under some other label.

That's why any escape from the problems of conduction should be only temporary. But of course the escape may seem permanent if one is prepared to be resolutely unempirical in one's approach to argumentation—as, apparently, many people are. But this is not the time to dwell on such issues. In the present context, talented and energetic people have gathered precisely because they are interested in conductive arguments and especially in those conductive arguments characterized by the presence of both "pros" and "cons." As urged by many participants but put forward with special emphasis by Christian Kock and Harald Wohlrapp, public discussion of policy issues characteristically requires and receives debate characterized by pros and cons, and sensitive participants in such discussions will recognize relevant support for contending positions, hence recognizing the significance of counter-considerations.

Discussants have been using conductive arguments for centuries. That is to say, in defence of claims and decisions, they have put forward distinct and independent factors as supporting reasons for conclusions recognized to be defeasible, and have often while doing so acknowledged factors that count against their conclusion. Hans Hansen usefully includes a discussion of the eighteenth century theorist George Campbell, and Campbell's observations to the effect that in moral reasoning there are often multiple *considerations*. There may be a combination of distinct themes, each point contributing to the credibility of the conclusion; and a number of independent points converge on a conclusion and contrary evidence may also be considered. Fred Kauffeld also favors the term "considerations" as referring to factors that bear on a conclusion, having a potentially good claim for our thought and attention. When we seek to assess these considerations, to determine how sound a claim is in the light of all of them, we are trying to 'balance' and 'weigh' independently relevant factors in a deliberative context. Kauffeld describes a significant illustration from the eighteenth century debates about the United States Constitution. This example serves as an important and historically significant reminder that conductive arguments have been around for a long time, even though theorizing about them by philosophers and logicians is relatively scanty.

Our interest in Wellman should not restrict us from moving beyond his beginnings, and one important way to do this is to consider the importance of conductive arguments outside the context of moral reasoning. As argued by myself and emphasized in recent papers by James Freeman and Maurice Finocchiaro, conductive arguments are prominent in interpretive disciplines including history and literary analysis, evaluative contexts in addition to those of ethics and policy discussion, and theoretical reasoning in science. In the most recent editions of my textbook, I have argued that abductive arguments require a conductive sub-argument. A key premise in any abductive argument is a claim to the effect that the hypothesis or theory being defended is the *best explanation*[3] of a given fact or set of facts. Such a claim requires support in a sub-argument. Given that there are various distinct and independent factors relevant to the explanatory merits of a hypothesis or theory (coherence with existing theory, simplicity, richness for further research, plausibility, breadth…) such

---

[2] Such arguments have sometimes been referred to as "good reasons arguments" or as "cumulation of consideration" arguments.
[3] Strictly speaking, one should say "best available explanation."

an argument will have to be conductive in nature. All this is fully in accord with standard philosophy of science.

Frank Zenker usefully points out that if one assimilates conductive arguments to inductive ones, one will lose the distinction between (conductive) cases in which accepted premises are considered or weighed for their importance as they bear on a case and may bear upon it with differential significance, and those (inductive) cases in which they are accepted *simpliciter* and not judged as to their comparative importance. Zenker also notes that the importance of a premise is not to be identified with its probability. Here is a simple example to illustrate this point: the probability that a job applicant speaks with a slight accent may be near 100%, and the quality of her speech may be relevant to her suitability for a position, while nevertheless this aspect is nevertheless relatively unimportant compared to another qualification, the technical expertise required to do the job (my example). If we acknowledge several factors supporting a given conclusion, K, we may and often do deem one of those factors of greater importance than the other. A weighing or estimation of importance is characteristic of conductive reasoning, but not, Zenker points out, of inductive reasoning. Douglas Walton recommends sorting supporting "pros" from negative "cons," emphasizing that at many points reasoning structures may be made clearer by adding statements regarded as implicit premises. Using this device, different possible structurings of conductive argumentation emerge. Walton also usefully emphasizes how valuations may be expressed through such terms as 'disgrace' and 'punishment.' By using attitudinally weighted words, speakers and writers may dodge the need to give reasons for their claims and judgments. This phenomenon is important in the context of conductive argument, as it is elsewhere, and deserves further attention. One might say, as Walton did in discussion, that an *argument* is somehow implicit in the use of a word with positive or negative connotation. I would prefer to say that *claims* are implicit in such words. I would maintain that such use of attitudinally weighted language is one kind of packing strategy, through which people avoid direct acknowledgement of difference and convey judgments contestable in the context without arguing for them at all (see Govier 1999, p. 48).

3. Measurability and weighing

Wellman was unable to propose any general method for evaluating conductive arguments; nor have subsequent theorists been sufficiently bold as to do that. Wellman advised that one should think through an argument again try to determine its "validity." (He used 'validity' in a way more general than deductive validity, a practice not followed here.) One can find some considerations convincing; obviously one's thinking them so does not make them so. To determine whether considerations really are relevant and constitute good supporting reasons for a conclusion, what can one do? One can only think the matter through again. Logical force has to be understood as psychological force after reflection.

Many, including myself, have employed such metaphors as "weight" and "balance" and "strength" in discussing the comparative significance of various considerations. Wohlrapp, Kock, and Zenker have elsewhere objected to such metaphors, deeming them to have misleading overtones of measurement and quantitative objectivity. In conference discussions, they did not return to this concern and seemed reconciled to them as dead metaphors devoid of significant quantitative overtones. In fact, such terms as *weight* and *balance* and *strength* are so standard that it seems futile to object to them, though it remains important not to presume measurability.

Wellman employed the notion of "hefting" as a way of describing our sense of the comparative significance or strength of pro and con factors, and that aspect of his work has been largely neglected. Thomas Fischer suggests usefully that the term "hefting" is useful as providing some inter-subjective, though not quantitative, sense of significance. If you and I lift two bags of flour and I find the first to be significantly heavier than the second, there is every likelihood that you will do so as well. Using this hefting procedure, without weighing the bags so as to obtain numerical weights, we are able to get a sense of whether one is heavier than, lighter than, much heavier than, only a little lighter than another, and so on. Within limits we can come to know which bag weighs more. The matter, being *inter-subjective*, then counts as *objective* in a sense in which tastes and impressions are not objective. Fischer argues that the notion of hefting can be of some assistance in understanding premise "weight" and appreciating a sense in which the weighing of premises can be regarded as objective. I have to confess, however, that I find somewhat obscure his claim that "heft-weight is a very plausible literal basis for the metaphor of premise weight." I have some difficulty understanding what it would mean for something to be a *literal basis for a metaphor*.

In several contexts, I have claimed that in assessing the importance (or weight or strength) of a reason as a consideration for or against a conclusion, one should think in terms of *ceteris paribus* (other things being equal, sometimes also referred to as *pro tanto*) and attend to the universality of reasons.[4] The *ceteris paribus* aspect has not, to my knowledge, received much negative attention. But the matter is otherwise with the aspect of universality. I assumed, and continue to assume, that if R is a reason *ceteris paribus* for K in case C, then R is a reason for K *in any other case that is relevantly similar* to C. In conductive reasoning we are considering non-sufficient (defeasible) reasons for a decision or conclusion: a reason for K does not by itself suffice to prove that K is true or to fully justify accepting K, nor is it put forward as doing so; it just offers some support. But this fact of non-sufficiency and defeasibility does not eliminate the *universality* of reason. Universality is a feature here just as it would be in a deductive case. There, if R proves K in one case, it proves K in any relevantly similar case.

As Derek Allen pointed out in conference discussions, the universality (in this sense) of reasons is presumed in legal reasoning, which could hardly exist in its absence. Past cases are brought to bear on a current case in order to test the significance of facts and precedents.

My results with regard to *ceteris paribus* reasons in the context of assessing conductive arguments have been criticized elsewhere as unhelpfully complex and (through universality) leading to a need to consider further cases of dubious relevance for the topic at hand. (They have been received more sympathetically in other quarters, as we may see here in Robert Pinto's paper.) Zenker, for example, has maintained that if we are reasoning about the significance of R for some particular case, C, the bearing of R on some other case, D, is irrelevant and will only lead us astray and into further complications. A case is to be considered on its own and often will give us plenty to worry about, just considered as itself. (This recalls Wellman's restriction of conductive reasoning to particulars, a restriction I have long resisted.) I accept that my proposals may be somewhat cumbersome and would not pretend to know just how to weigh or "weigh" the significance of positive and negative considerations. However, I do not accept a non-universalistic interpretation of what it is to give a reason.[5]

Sharon Bailin and Mark Battersby offer an account of reaching a reasoned judgment about some issue where there are pros and cons involved. Bailin and Battersby are con-

---

[4] As I recall, the original impulse for this account came from David Hitchcock; he, however, claims not to recall this, so we do not know whether the some of the credit or blame should lie with him.
[5] Pinto, in this volume, notes further complications and subtleties with regard to the 1999 essay.

cerned with reasoning and argumentation concerning substantial public issues such as capital punishment and not with brief arguments about whether to rent an apartment or hire one babysitter rather than another. It is important to distinguish these contexts. This is an aspect I have not generally emphasized. I recognize here that it does make a difference whether one is considering a short argument about some manageable practical matter or summing up a substantial public debate on a public issue such as capital punishment or abortion. In the second sort of case a "consideration" tends to be more like a line of reasoning in which the supporting or negative consideration is itself the result of considerable prior substantial debate and argumentation. There we would be especially likely to find the kind of hybrid argumentation pointed out by Pinto.

As does Harald Wohlrapp in his book-length treatment of argumentation, Bailin and Battersby allow that there is often a certain dynamism in dealing with issues of this sort. Back-and-forth debate and discussion, and the recognition of aspects that count against one's favored view may lead to qualifications even in cases where one's initially favored conclusion is maintained.

4. Counter-considerations

Most symposium participants were interested primarily in those conductive arguments in which both positively relevant (pro) and negatively relevant (con) factors are put forward by an arguer. In a conductive argument of this type, an arguer seeks to support a conclusion by citing a number of premises that count, or are taken to count, in its favor. He or she also acknowledges negatively relevant factors that count against the conclusion. These are here called counter-considerations. I will concentrate here on comments on Wellman and on my own previous work, particularly as in my 1999 essay and the seventh edition of my textbook (Govier 2010).

I distinguish in the text between cases in which the arguer strongly acknowledges counter-considerations, in the sense of allowing that these are points that really do count against the conclusion, and those in which the arguer weakly acknowledges them as points viewed by others as counting against the conclusion. One might explore further the difference between strong acknowledgement and weak acknowledgement and recast weak acknowledgement as something like "many people think that X and think that X counts against K; these people might be right; therefore there is some argument against K, grounded on the claim that these people take X as a counter-consideration." The underlying assumption here would be that if some people think that X, X could just be true. But this is not going to lead to an important counter-consideration, and I will not pursue the matter further here.

In acknowledging counter-considerations while at the same time putting forward supporting premises, and asserting the conclusion to be supported by good reasons, an arguer is committing himself or herself to the claim that the *supporting considerations "outweigh" the counter-considerations* and render the conclusion acceptable. (I will return to this theme later.) There is no claim that the conclusion is demonstrated to be true; clearly it is put forward as defeasible in the light of further considerations.

As Zenker clearly points out, in a conductive argument, the information content of the conclusion goes beyond that of the premises. In this respect, conductive arguments resemble inductive ones and fail to resemble valid deductive ones. James Freeman suggests that counter-considerations be regarded as rebuttals; he proposes to understand rebuttal broadly as being any contra consideration. This view seems to make "contra consideration" a generic term under which we could subsume both the objections a challenger might make to an argument (rebuttals) as one class, and any counter-considerations (points negatively relevant to the acceptability of the conclusion and acknowledged by the arguer himself) as another. Counter-considerations conceded by an arguer would, Freeman suggests, be considered along with premises, conjunctively. The model becomes highly complex, as Freeman develops it using resources from the Toulmin model. I would prefer to emphasize a firmer distinction between objections and criticisms of an argument by a challenger and counter-considerations recognized by the arguer himself.

This seems a suitable point to discuss another matter concerning counter-considerations, a matter raised by Ralph Johnson and also argued by Rongdong Jin. Johnson points out that in the seventh edition of my text I equate the terms 'counter-consideration' and 'objection' (see p. 375). He argues that this is a mistake. I concede that he is correct on this point. The definition I offer of 'objection' in *The Philosophy of Argument* in 1999 was better and does not involve this confusion, which slipped into the textbook as I was trying to explain, in a discussion at the end of a long book, that it is not only against the premises and reasoning of *conductive* arguments that objections may be made.

The equation of counter-considerations and objections was a mistake: I do wish to distinguish counter-considerations from objections. Counter-considerations, as explained above, are claims negatively relevant to the acceptability of the conclusion. Here we are dealing with those counter-considerations that are acknowledged by the arguer. The arguer himself or herself is allowing these negatively relevant points, and indeed the counter-considerations are part of his or her case. Objections to an argument, on the other hand, are not integral parts of that argument and are not part of the arguer's case. If, after being raised in a dialectical context, they come to be incorporated into an adapted version of an arguer's case, they could at that point play the role of counter-considerations. Thus the same point might be couched as an objection by someone other than the arguer and come to be acknowledged by the arguer as a counter-consideration.[6]

Objections are claims raised against the premises, conclusion, or supportive inferences of an argument, with the implication that there is something doubtful or unsatisfactory about one or more of these elements. Johnson is concerned not to depart too far from ordinary language; at the same time he notes that ordinary language may not allow us to fix the definitions of philosophically sensitive terms as tightly as we might wish. For the most part, Johnson and I seem to have similar sensitivities on these matters. Nevertheless I find the idea of identifying a request for clarification or a question about fact related to a case with an *objection* to be an implausible and potentially confusing departure. I would prefer to say that a question or request amounts to an objection only to the extent that it can be plausibly interpreted as a claim in an objector's *argument* to the effect that some aspect of the arguer's original argument is incorrect. For example, if a speaker is arguing that all religions involve a belief in the supernatural and someone raises his hand and asks the speaker how he defines 'supernatural,' his query does not at this point amount to an objection unless the questioner says or implies that no clear definition of the term can be given, where the speaker's account would require one. So far as explicit discourse is concerned, an objection may be expressed by someone simply making a claim or asking the question, as Johnson would have it; however I would maintain, as against Johnson, that such a claim or question amounts to an *objection* only if posed in such a way and in such a context that there is an accompanying *implication* that it reveals something wrong with the arguer's case. Thus, while I agree with Johnson's important point that counter-considerations should be distinguished from objections, I wish to resist his proposed account of objection as too broad. An objection should not be identified with a counter-consideration.

---

[6] Lowell Ayers emphasized this point, in private discussion.

In preparing the seventh edition of my text (Govier 2010), I would have done better to keep to the definition of 'objection' offered in *The Philosophy of Argument* (Govier 1999). That definition reads as follows:

> (a) an objection is any claim alleging a defect in the argument or in its conclusion; (b) which, insofar as it does not compete for the same intellectual and social space as that conclusion, does not constitute an alternative position to the conclusion; and is either (c) raised by the audience to which the argument is addressed or (d) might plausibly be raised by that audience' or (e) might plausible be raised by a rational person to whom the argument might plausibly be addressed. (p. 229)

Taking counter-considerations seriously points to another definitional problem, this time relating to convergence. As Jin notes, we need to qualify our understanding of what it is for premises to be put forward as convergently supporting a conclusion. In the seventh edition of *A Practical Study of Argument*, convergent support is defined as follows:

> convergent support: a kind of support where premises work together in a cumulative way to support the conclusion but are not linked. The bearing of one premise on the conclusion would be unaffected if the other premises were removed; however the argument is strengthened when the premises are considered together, since more evidence is then offered. (p. 55)

Jin asks, in effect: if an arguer incorporates into his or her argument counter-considerations, how is the support of the premises for the conclusion affected if one or more of those counter-considerations is removed?

Here is how I would respond to this question. If premises were positively relevant before, they remain positively relevant. Any other counter-considerations that were negatively relevant remain negatively relevant. To be sure, supportive premises would count more or "weigh more heavily" if the counter-considerations are removed, so in that sense we cannot say that their support for the conclusion would be unaffected. To fix the problem, I need to clarify the expression "the bearing of one premise on the conclusion" so as to indicate that what is referred to is the relevance of the premise to the conclusion. Its *relevance* is unaffected; its significance or weight will increase if one or more counter-considerations ar removed.

5. Further qualifications and amendments

I want to acknowledge here some difficulties with regard to my own earlier accounts. As Jin clearly states, one cannot simultaneously say that arguments are composed of premises and conclusions, while also claiming that counter-considerations are parts of some arguments although they are neither premises nor conclusions. (The problem is diminished and will ultimately dissolve, given that I said that premises and conclusion were the *basic* elements of arguments.) Hansen clearly shows that counter-considerations should not be regarded as premises, as background knowledge, as qualifications with regard to the conclusions, or as "anti-premises." I certainly do not wish to consider counter-considerations to be premises: they are not put forward as supportive of the conclusions claimed by arguers, but are acknowledged to count against those conclusions. That, of course, is just what makes it apt to term them counter-considerations. Wellman used a very broad notion of premises so that any consideration counting or thought to count *for or against* a conclusion would count as a premise. But like Jin I find this account misleadingly non-standard and too broad.

The definitional problem identified by Jin should be addressed by adapting the standard definition of 'argument.' I propose to do this by stating that (a) in an argument, premises are claims put forward in an effort to provide reasons or evidence for some further claim, the conclusion, and (b) that premises and conclusion are the basic and essential components of any argument. Some of these may be implicit but to interpret any bit of discourse as an argument is to interpret it as claiming one or more premises and a conclusion such that the former are put forward as evidence or reasonable support for the latter. In addition to these basic elements, (c) arguments may include as integral and important parts other elements including, significantly, (c.i) counter-considerations and (c.ii) indicator words. Counter-considerations are claims that count, or are deemed to count, against the conclusion in the broad sense of indicating that there may be something wrong with it. They are thought to be (and often are) negatively relevant so far as the acceptability of the conclusion is concerned, and acknowledged to be so by the arguer. As is widely recognized in textbooks and elsewhere, indicator words such as 'since,' 'because,' 'therefore,' 'thus,' and the like, may precede premises or conclusions and serve to indicate the direction of the argument.

Once we allow in our definitions that counter-considerations are integral elements of some arguments, we should supplement the standard lists of premise and conclusion indicators with words that indicate counter-considerations and other words that indicate a return to the main line of argument after counter-considerations have been acknowledged.[7] In the former category are words and phrases such as 'even though,' 'despite the fact that,' and 'although'; in the former are phrases such as 'it is still,' 'yet,' 'however,' 'even so,' and 'nevertheless.' Clearly this is a rich area for further exploration. Once counter-considerations are incorporated as an element in some arguments, we should amend the standard definition of argument to account of that fact, and I would propose to do it as above. While premise(s) and conclusion are basic and essential elements of any argument, counter-considerations and indicator words are integral elements of some arguments.

6. Dialogue and criticism

Blair raises the question of whether it would be useful to model conductive reasoning (and, I assume, argument) as dialogue. While it might be interesting to pursue this possibility, I am rather resistant to the suggestion, given the basic understanding of counter-consideration as explained here. In a dialogue, there are two or more parties. If we consider pros and cons in a dialogue context, we are very likely to suppose that "pros" are on a side identified with one participant and "cons" are on a side identified with the other. We are likely to think of dialogue as a binary matter, involving a proponent and an opponent in an actually or potentially adversarial context. The "dialogue" construction may lapse into adversariality if we construe the pros as *against* the cons, and one dialogue participant as arguing *against* the other. Something has been added in this interpretation, namely the element of adversariality suggested by 'against.' And something has been lost, namely the incorporation of both positively and negatively relevant factors into a single view. It is this element of balance, of fairness, of recognition that there are alternate views on behalf of which reasonable points can be made, that has for many been an especially important and intriguing aspect of pro and con conductive arguments.

---

[7] I incorporated these themes in the seventh edition of *A Practical Study of Argument* (Govier 2010). See pp. 356 and 357.

When it comes to the assessment of conductive arguments, several conference participants note an asymmetry in my 1999 and 2010 accounts. The asymmetry comes in that I recommend that to appraise a conductive argument it is not necessary to explore whether there are further supportive premises, but it is necessary to consider whether there are further counter-considerations in addition to those acknowledge by the arguer. Clearly there is an asymmetry between negative and the positive here. This was noted by Maurice Finocchiaro, by Blair, and by Jin. I allow that this asymmetry exists; either justification or amendment is called for. The source of the asymmetry lies in an understanding of criticism. My underlying assumption was that it is the duty of the critic to find out whether there is anything wrong with an argument, while it is not his or her duty to improve an argument. I assumed, especially in pedagogical contexts, that in teaching critical thinking, one is not trying to teach students to improve on the arguments they study. By "anything wrong" in this context, I allude to anything that would undermine either the credibility of the premises or the support they could lend to the conclusion. On this understanding of criticism, asymmetry is justified and is to be expected. On a broader understanding, it might not be warranted. What the most plausible account of argument criticism is, I leave to others to consider.

7. Structure and diagrams

Important difficulties about structure and diagramming are raised in several papers, especially Jin and in Hansen. Given the complexity of these matters, it is worth reviewing some of their central points here.

Hansen notes that premises and counter-considerations may all be true at once. If this were not the case, an arguer could not consistently acknowledge them. (Zenker at one point denies this; I think he is wrong to do so.) A conductive argument admitting of both pros and cons is called by Hansen a "balance of considerations" argument or "BC" argument. In such an argument, to reach a conclusion K we need to judge that *the supporting considerations outweigh the counter-considerations*. In other words, when we arrive at the conclusion K we are saying that there are both pros and cons and that when we assess the significance of these pros and cons, the pros count for more than the cons; hence the conclusion K should be upheld. Hansen maintains that the judgment that pros outweigh cons is presupposed for a judgment "K even though CC"; in that judgment, K is deemed correct *even though* the counter-considerations are also deemed to hold and to count against K. Because of the need for a judgment (the on-balance judgment) that the support outweighs the counter-considerations, Hansen argues for a sub-argument structure. At the first stage are the supporting (separately relevant, distinct, and as maintained by myself and others, converging) premises, and from those premises the conclusion "K even though CC_1–CC_n" (the counter-considerations) is reached but only because an added OB or (on-balance) premise is added.

That OB premise is taken by Hansen to have been implicit in the original, and it states that the specific positively relevant premises cited, taken together, outweigh the counter-considerations, which are specifically mentioned after the words "even though." (There is a somewhat anomalous asymmetry here; the counter-considerations are sort of "phased in" at the point of the conclusion, and the OB premise precedes the explicit acknowledgment of these counter-considerations.) In this model, the added OB premise allows the arguer to infer from the stated supporting premises a claim to the effect that K even though CC_1–CC_n. That's the first stage of the argument. Hansen adds a second stage, in which simply K is inferred from the first conclusion. In other words, from "K even though CC_1–CC_n" we infer simply, K. Hansen maintains that the OB premise is needed in order for the reasoning to go forward to the "even though" conclusion (which in his model is the conclusion of a sub-argument). (Zenker makes the same point, as do Pinto, Finocchiaro, and Jin.)

Hansen acknowledges two difficulties with regard to his model. The first is that it would require a revision in the long-accepted idea that the structure of conductive arguments is convergent: in Hansen's model the supporting premises and the deemed-to-be-implicit OB premise have to *link* to support the conclusion at the first stage. At the next stage, when *K simpliciter* is inferred from this first conclusion, "*K* even though CC_1–CC_n," there is no call for either linkage or convergence, since there is only one premise. Hansen notes the disappearance of convergence as a problem, and responds that even with this revisionary implication, his account preserves another notion essential to conduction, namely that of defeasibility.

A second problem with regard to inference rules and the OB premise was raised by Kevin Possin (2010) on an earlier occasion when Hansen presented his views. Possin is one who resists the notion of conductive argument altogether; he would count conductive arguments as inductive and represent each of what others have taken to be convergently supporting premises as single reasons in separate arguments. He recommends the strategy of assessing each separate argument on its own. Possin does speak of *stronger* and *weaker* points, and admits that at some point one will have to judge the net impact of all the arguments for or against some conclusion *K* and seek to sum up the impact of what have been understood to be a number of distinct arguments. As explained earlier, my response to this sort of position would be to insist that unless one simply refuses to be interested in this problem, one will only find that it will surface later under another name and at another stage.

Now with regard to Hansen's model, Possin argues that the OB premise sought by Hansen (and deemed necessary by Jin and by Zenker) recalls the sort of regress problem argued by Lewis Carroll. He claims that it constitutes an unnecessary writing-in of rules and methodological assumptions into one's premises. Possin quotes Carroll at length and interprets him as having shown that some degree of logical competence is required in order to formalize an argument and employ an inference rule. An argument should not be understood as expressing an inference rule as any one of its premises. Possin says, "We don't and can't formally represent all the aspects of the rules and practices of our inferences while they are in progress. That's why they have the status of critical thinking *skills*." Possin claims that to be rational in our judgments about actions, values, and beliefs, we commit ourselves to adopting the position that has the strongest reasons in its favor and the fewest or weakest criticism plaguing it; we don't need a *premise* telling us that that is what we are doing.[8] Using Carroll, Possin is emphatically reminding us that inference rules, background assumptions, and aspects of one's logical and argumentative practices are presupposed in reasoning and argumentation and should not, at pain of infinite regress, be regarded as premises.

I agree entirely with this claim, as a general point. And there is a sense in which I would like to apply it in the present context, since by doing so I could protect some points of my analysis. Our question, however, concerns how well the Carroll analogy applies to the present case. And the answer, I think, supports Hansen.

Hansen responds to Possin with two lines of argument. He argues that (a) the OB premise is not an inference rule and could not be one, given that it is particular in character (it

---

[8] Kevin Possin (2010), "What the Tortoise Said to Hans." I thank Possin for providing me with a copy of his paper.

states that positively relevant considerations outweigh negatively relevant considerations *in this case*). Hansen argues further that (b) the OB premise is not introduced *ad hoc* or out of any misconstrued notion of deductive completeness but rather to solve a the problem of how to relate the premises of a pro and con argument to the conclusion and counter-considerations. I think both (a) and (b) here are important and plausible. I will further discuss (a).

Let us imagine a simple case: we are considering whether Mary should be hired as an office receptionist, and as reasons supporting her hiring we cite (1) she is reliable (2) she is efficient (3) she is friendly and (4) she has good recommendations from a similar previous position. These are considerations that would support a decision to hire her. We acknowledge that there are some reasons against hiring her, these being (5) Mary may be so competent as to be likely to leave the job for a better position and (6) Mary speaks English with a slight accent. We consider all these things, decide that the first four factors outweigh the last two, and come to a decision that we should hire Mary for the position. What Hansen is recommending is an OB premise that will amount to the following:

> *OB(Mary)*: Mary's being reliable, efficient, and friendly and having good recommendations from a previous position outweigh in importance her having a slight accent in English and the possibility that she will leave this job for a better position.

Hansen says that OB(Mary) cannot be an inference rule since it is a judgment about what outweighs what in this particular case. This is correct; we are not going to have an inference *rule* or any other principle of method that is just about this particular matter. Clearly a rule cannot just be about Mary. Considering the universality of reason, we can produce a more general claim, one that may seem more promising for the kind of point Possin wants to make.

> *OBU(Mary)*: A person's being reliable, efficient and friendly and having good recommendations from a previous position outweigh in importance his or her having a slight accent in English and the possibility that he or she will leave a job for a better position.

But even here, content specificity seems too great for the claim to plausibly represent any inference *rule* of principle of method. Possin's analysis tempts me a little, since it would enable me to preserve key elements of earlier accounts. However, I think that on the matter of the OB premise Hansen is correct and Carroll-derived objections do not work.

However, I find other reasons to be less than fully content with Hansen's analysis. I am not happy with the way convergence disappears in this model. Convergence is a striking and long-recognized feature of conductive arguments, one that is of considerable significance for their assessment, given that one positively relevant consideration can continue to provide support for a conclusion even if another is deleted. Nor am I happy with Hansen's proposed sub-argument structure, which yields the somewhat awkward result that every pro and con conductive argument (OB argument, in his terminology) has two conclusions. If Hansen were to deem this a problem, he could solve it with relative ease. A statement of the form "*K* even though *CC*" does assert *K*. Accordingly, if he wished to do so, Hansen could revise his model so as to omit its second stage, leaving the conclusion in the "even though" form. If we conclude "*K* even though *CC*," we are still concluding "*K*."

Jin also notes problems with structure and diagramming and works hard to address them. He states that in pro and con arguments, the pros and cons work cooperatively to lead to the conclusion, although the individual considerations either support or oppose the conclusion independently.[9] If (1), (2), (3), and (4) are all supporting considerations, (1) and (4) can continue to provide some reasons for K even if (2) and (3) are removed. This feature is characteristic of convergence. When we come to sum up,[10] to assess the total impact of pros and cons, we have to bring the various considerations together. If we wish to assert K, in the light of the support we have for it, we are in effect making the judgment that the pro factors outweigh the (acknowledged) cons. To accept the conclusion of such an argument on the basis of the support revealed in it, the most crucial thing is to know whether the supporting factors do outweigh the opposing one. I have noted this point in my accounts in 1999 and 2010, but have a model that does not supply a specific *premise* articulating it. Like Hansen and others, Jin would like to have this judgment expressed in a premise.

Jin points out that my textbook diagrams do not capture the fact that such a judgment is required to reason forward to the conclusion. And like Hansen, he maintains that linkage seems to be required at this point. If one reasons that four points support K and two points oppose K, and concludes that K, one has in effect judged that *the supporting points outweigh the opposing ones* in significance. In other words, *on balance*, there is more to be said in favor of K than against it. Like Hansen and unlike Possin, Jin thinks that there has got to be an OB premise expressing that on-balance judgment. The argument after the weighing stage will be "Factors 1,2,3,4 ....support K; *and* factors 5,6 ...oppose K; *and* 1,2,3,4 outweigh 5,6; *therefore* the most reasonable conclusion is K." The "ands" in this construction indicate a linked structure at this stage.[11] In this structure the convergence of separately and distinctly relevant supporting and opposing considerations has disappeared, as it has in Hansen's account. But convergence appears at the earlier stage in which the positively relevant support and negative relevant counter-considerations are taken into account. This first level of the argument can be understood as in my textbook diagrams, which Jin deems clear and useful for that purpose. Straight lines indicate supporting considerations, pointing separately and distinctly, and convergently, to K. Wavy lines indicate negatively relevant considerations that point separately and distinctly to K, showing by their waviness that they are counter-considerations. But after that point, according to Jin, we need a linked structure.

So we seem to have two stages or levels here and indeed Jin was willing to speak in these terms. There is *convergence* when we consider how the positively or negatively relevant factors support or oppose the conclusion, and there is *linkage* when we sum up these factors and reason to a conclusion, employing in our reason the judgment that some factors outweigh others.

Jin speaks of levels here, and to me, there is something intuitive about this usage. Within the "pro" side we have considerations cited as separately relevant and within the "con" side, the negative considerations are also separately relevant; that is convergence. Jin suggests diagrams of increasing complexity; he includes my diagrams, which are simple (an aspect that was important and sensible, given their textbook context) but arguably incomplete, given that they do not display anything corresponding to the second stage, at which the OB premise appears.

Here we may wish to consider some deeper issues about argument diagrams. Why do we need or want them, and how much should they show? We need to reflect on such mat-

---

[9] I defend and clarify this point on pp. 172-177 in *The Philosophy of Argument*.
[10] It is just this summing up that we would have to do if we insisted on breaking the conductive argument down so that each positive reason and each negative reason would be given a place in its own single premise argument.
[11] More than bare conjunction is at stake, as we will see later.

ters to have a reasonable view as to whether it is a problem that some aspects are not shown on a diagram.[12] The purpose of the diagrams will depend on the context for which they are intended, and how much should be shown will be similarly dependent. My diagrams were designed for use in a textbook intended for first and second year university students, and aspects of this context are relevant here. I would claim for these diagrams that they are clear and vivid and show the independent relevance of considerations, and the possibility or actuality of acknowledged counter-considerations, these being importantly distinct from supporting premises. These are important features of conductive arguments. I acknowledge that these diagrams do *not* show the presence of an on-balance judgment (an implicit OB premise according to Jin and Hansen), despite the fact that on my own account, such a judgment *is* required to proceed to the conclusion.

In fact, Jin's own proposed diagrams do not show the linked structure in which the OB premise is incorporated, and which he reveals and explains so clearly. They show the pros and cons (using the wavy line technique as in my textbook) and a shunting aside representing the implicitly claimed "outweighing" by supporting considerations of counter-considerations.

A key problem here is that there are two levels or stages, one requiring convergence and the other requiring linkage, and we do not seem to be able to show both stages on the same diagram. Hearing Jin present his account, I thought of transparencies. I imagined a sheet of paper showing convergence and pro and con considerations, as in my textbook, and then, held above it, a plasticized transparency in a distinct color, which would represent a kind of linkage. Here we envisage a physical correlate of the two levels. On the paper, convergence would be represented. On the transparency, the OB premise and linkage would be represented. Somehow to understand and represent pro and con reasoning, we need both. I think Hansen and Jin have both helped to provide analytic understanding, but there is as yet no diagram that adequately represents all the relevant aspects.

Aspects of my own proposed model display convergence, the distinctness of the support, and the pros and cons. The model also displays a stage incorporating the on-balance premise (OBP), the typically implicit claim that supporting considerations outweigh counter-considerations. We can see that from this model that (1) there are reasons to accept K, and *although* (2) there are reasons not to accept K, *nevertheless* (3) the supporting considerations outweigh the counter-considerations, so (4) K. (Or, if you like, some variation such as "it is reasonable to accept K.")

It should be noted that the linkage here is expressed not through the word "and" but by using the words "although" and "nevertheless" so as to indicate that more than bare conjunction is intended here. Roughly, more than a purely conjunctive "and" is at stake. The words 'although' and 'nevertheless' allow us to express that "more." Let us define "bare conjunction" to be that form of conjunction that is standard in classical propositional logic. If we state "p and q" in a bare conjunction, we are simply asserting p as true and asserting q as true. There is no implication of any relationship between the claims p, q other than the bare fact of their truth. For instance, the claim p could be "there are three major ethnic groups in Bosnia" and the claim q could be "rarely do universities offer third year courses in critical thinking." Any other true claims could serve together as components of a bare conjunction: there, only the truth of claims is at issue. In English (and, I would expect, oth-

---

[12] I owe this point to discussions with Lowell Ayers.

er natural languages) there is typically some relation of connection of topic or theme when two claims are asserted together. We would be most unlikely to conjoin facts about Bosnia with facts about critical thinking pedagogy. Often there is a temporal implication as well. For example "The two met each other and became friends" makes perfect sense whereas "The two became friends and met each other" does not unless we shift the meaning of 'met' to mean "got together" instead of "made each other's acquaintance." (In this case, the connection suggested by 'and' is that of temporal sequence; 'and' is taken to mean "and then.") Given that in ordinary life and ordinary language we are often dealing with more than bare conjunction, it should be no surprise that in conductive arguments admitting of counter-considerations, we encounter a type of linkage that is something over and above bare conjunction.

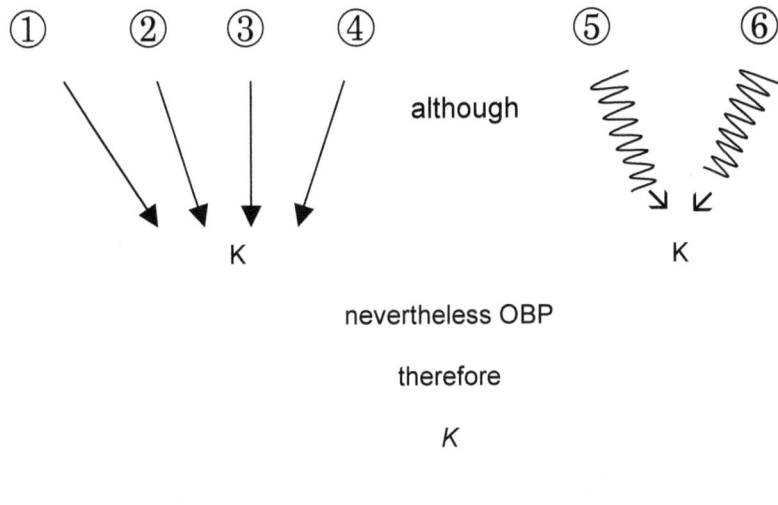

Figure 1.0

The supporting considerations are stated (1) and it is then stated that *although* (2) there are counter-considerations, *nevertheless*, it is reasonable to accept the conclusion (4) *because* (3) (the implicit OB premise) the pros outweigh cons. There is a sense in which the three basic steps link here but they do not link with bare conjunction. The word 'although' introduces counter-considerations and the word 'nevertheless' indicates a return to the main line of thought: *notwithstanding* these counter-considerations, *K*. (Obviously, I owe a debt to Hansen at this point.) Figure 1.0 provides my best efforts toward a diagram for a case in which there are four supporting considerations and two counter-considerations. I do not claim that this model is perfect, but hope that it resolves at least some of the problems indicated by Jin, Hansen, and others. There is inductive evidence to suggest that it will, at least, provide grist for the mill.

8. Conclusion

I would like again to thank all the contributors to the May, 2010 conference on conductive arguments for their hard work and good-hearted energy over two long days. The participation of persons from outside North America—China, Denmark, and Germany—was a special honor. In the present discussion, I have not been able to do justice to all the important considerations and arguments introduced in the papers in this volume, much less to claims argued elsewhere. To those who might feel that their work has received insufficient attention here, I can only express my regret and hope that any ideas insufficiently considered here will receive attention elsewhere. It should be manifestly obvious that those who do not chose to ignore the existence of conductive arguments, or dismiss them as unimportant due to their content-dependence, will have plenty to think about and work on.

THE CONTRIBUTORS

Derek Allen is Professor of Philosophy at the University of Toronto and Vice-Provost & Dean of Arts at Trinity College there. He has taught informal logic courses for some thirty years, and has been President of the Association for Informal Logic & Critical Thinking since 2007. His publications include "Assessing Inferences," in R.H. Johnson & J.A. Blair (Eds.), *New Essays in Informal Logic*, Informal Logic Publications, University of Windsor, 1994, pp. 51-57 and "Attributed Favourable Relevance and Argument Evaluation," *Informal Logic*, Vol, 18, No. 2 & 3, Summer & Fall 1996, pp. 183-201.

Sharon Bailin is a Professor Emeritus in the Faculty of Education at Simon Fraser University. She has written extensively on critical thinking and on creativity, focusing particularly on critical thinking as inquiry and on the creative dimensions to critical thinking. She and Mark Battersby are co-authors of the recent book, *Reason in the Balance: An Inquiry Approach to Critical Thinking*, which takes a conductive approach to reasoning. She is also one of the originators of a conception of critical thinking which has formed the foundation of a major curriculum project for K- 12 schools both in North America and internationally.

Mark Battersby received his BA in philosophy from NYU and his PhD from UBC. He is a philosophy professor at Capilano University. He recently published two books: *Is that a Fact?* (Broadview 2009) and, with Sharon Bailin, *Reason in the Balance: An Inquiry Approach to Critical Thinking* (McGraw Hill 2010). The latter book takes a conductive approach to reasoning. He has published numerous articles on informal logic particularly focusing on the concept of applied epistemology. His research interests include informal logic, argumentation, philosophy of science, statistics, curriculum reform, democratic participation, political economy and environmental ethics.

J. Anthony Blair is a graduate of McGill and Michigan; a Senior Fellow at the Centre for Research in Reasoning, Argumentation and Rhetoric; University Professor (Emeritus) at University of Windsor; co-editor of the journal *Informal Logic*, of many Proceedings of the Amsterdam ISSA and the Windsor OSSA conferences, of *Informal Logic, First International Symposium* (Edgepress) and *New Essays in Informal Logic* (IL Press); co-author of *Logical Self-Defense* (IDEA Press) and *Reasoning, A Practical Guide* (Prentice-Hall); author of *Groundwork in the Theory of Argumentation* (Springer); and author of numerous theoretical papers on argumentation, informal logic and critical thinking.

Maurice Finocchiaro is a graduate of MIT and UC Berkeley; Distinguished Professor of Philosophy (Emeritus), University of Nevada, Las Vegas; recipient of fellowships and grants from the Guggenheim Foundation, National Science Foundation, National Endowment for the Humanities, and American Council of Learned Societies; and author of numerous publications in logical theory and the history and philosophy of science. Among his books are *Arguments about Arguments* (Cambridge University Press, 2005) and *Defending Copernicus and Galileo* (Springer, 2010). He is currently working on a book entitled *Meta-argumentation*.

Thomas Fischer received his Ph.D. in Philosophy from the University of Texas at Austin. From 2006 to present, he has been teaching critical thinking at the University of Houston Downtown. He has also attended and presented at numerous international conferences on informal logic, critical thinking, and theory of argument.

The Contributors

James Freeman is Professor of Philosophy at Hunter College of The City University of New York. His research includes logic, both formal and informal, argumentation theory, and epistemology. His papers appear in various journals, especially *Informal Logic* and *Argumentation,* and in collections on argument theory. He is the author of *Thinking Logically: Basic Concepts for Reasoning* (Prentice- Hall, 1988, 1993), *Dialectics and the Macrostructure of Arguments* (Foris Publications, a division of Walter de Gruyter, 1991), *Acceptable Premises: An Epistemic Approach to an Informal Logic Problem* (Cambridge University Press, 2005), and *Argument Structure: Representation and Theory* (Springer, 2011).

Trudy Govier is Professor of Philosophy at the University of Lethbridge in Lethbridge, Alberta, Canada. She is the author of the widely used textbook, *A Practical Study of Argument* (Wadsworth, Seventh Edition 2010) and several monographs in the field of argumentation theory. These include *Problems in Argument Analysis and Evaluation* (1987) and *The Philosophy of Argument* (1999). She has enjoyed working for several non-governmental organizations. Govier's interests extend also to topics in social philosophy, including social trust, forgiveness, and reconciliation. She is currently beginning a new project concerning the relationship between narrative and argument.

Hans Vilhelm Hansen (Ph.D. Wayne State) was born in Copenhagen. He is now a member of the Philosophy Department in the University of Windsor. He is the co-editor of two anthologies (*Fallacies*, 1995, and *Reason Reclaimed*, 2007). His essays about argumentation and logic have appeared in *Synthese*, *Logique et Analyse*, *Philosophy and Rhetoric*, and *Argumentation*, as well as *Informal Logic*. He wrote the entry on Rhetoric and Logic for *Blackwell's International Encyclopaedia of Communication* (2008). From 2009-2011 he was Director of the Centre for Research in Reasoning, Argumentation and Rhetoric, in the University of Windsor.

Rongdong Jin is professor in the Department of Philosophy at East China Normal University (Shanghai, China), where he received his Ph.D. in 1998. He has published widely on language and logic in ancient China, philosophy of logic, argumentation theory, and philosophy of history. During the year from 2009 to 2010 he worked at the Centre for Research in Reasoning, Argumentation and Rhetoric (University of Windsor, Canada) as a Visiting Research Fellow. He is the coordinator of the research project "Informal Logic and Its Philosophical Foundation" supported by Ministry of Education of China.

Ralph H. Johnson is a Senior Fellow at the Centre for Research in Reasoning Argumentation and Rhetoric, and University Professor Emeritus in Department of Philosophy at the University of Windsor, Ontario. Johnson's main areas of research and publication are informal logic, the theory of argument and critical thinking. In 2000, he published *Manifest Rationality* (Lawrence Erlbaum). That same year he was awarded the Distinguished Research Award by the International Society for the Study of Argumentation. In 2003, he was elected a Fellow of the Royal Society of Canada. Johnson is listed in *Who's Who in Canada.*

Fred J. Kauffeld was educated at the University of Kansas and the University of Wisconsin. He studies argumentation from a rhetorical perspective, which is informed by the work of J. L. Austin, Paul Grice, and related inquiries in the philosophy of language. He has published essays on the nature of presumptions, the genesis of probative obligations in various speech acts, rational adequacy and the persuasive force of reasons, the parameters of probative obligations in day-to-day argumentation, etc. and has mounted a sustained defense of Grice's analysis of utterance-meaning. Professor Kauffeld teaches at Edgewood College in Madison, Wisconsin.

Christian Kock is Professor of Rhetoric and Head of the Division of Rhetoric at the Department of Media, Cognition, and Communication at the University of Copenhagen. With a background in literary studies, he has published and taught in English and Danish on argumentation, political debate, credibility, political journalism, the history of rhetoric, American literature, Romanticism, literary aesthetics, reception theory, versification, musical aesthetics, and writing pedagogy. He is a frequent commentator on political debate and journalism in Danish national media. His latest book *De Svarer Ikke* ("They Are Not Answering", 2011) dissects the regrettable state of political debate in Denmark.

Robert C. Pinto has his Ph.D. in philosophy from the University of Toronto, is Professor Emeritus in the Department of Philosophy at the University of Windsor and a Senior Fellow of the Centre for Research on Reasoning, Argumentation and Rhetoric. He is author of *Argument, Inference and Dialectic* (Kluwer), co-author with J.A. Blair *of Reasoning: A Practical Guide* (Prentice-Hall), and co-author with Hans V. Hansen *of Fallacies: Classical and Contemporary Readings* (Pennsylvania State Press) and of *Reason Reclaimed* (Vale Press). In addition, he is a member of the editorial boards of *Informal Logic* and of *Argumentation*.

Douglas Walton holds the Assumption University Chair in Argumentation Studies, and is Distinguished Research Fellow at the Centre for Research in Reasoning, Argumentation and Rhetoric, at the University of Windsor. He serves on the editorial boards of several journals, including *Informal Logic*, *Argument and Computation*, and *Artificial Intelligence and Law*. He is the author of at least forty-five books and three hundred refereed papers in the areas of argumentation, logic and artificial intelligence. The books include *Witness Testimony Evidence*, Cambridge University Press, 2008, *Fundamentals of Critical Argumentation*, Cambridge University Press, 2006, and *Legal Argumentation and Evidence*, Penn State Press, 2002.

Harald Wohlrapp is a pupil of the German philosopher Paul Lorenzen (Dialogue Logic). He taught philosophy at the University of Hamburg from 1970 through 2009 and is presently engaged in research about the analysis of "the embryo debate." He has published about Hegelian and Marxist philosophy, philosophy of science, interculturalism and argumentation theory. His latest monograph is: *Der Begriff des Arguments. Über die Beziehungen zwischen Wissen, Forschen, Glauben, Subjektivität und Vernunft* (The Concept of Argument. Relations between Knowledge, Research, Belief, Subjectivity and Reason), 2nd ed. Würzburg: Königshausen & Neumann 2009.

Frank Zenker is a researcher at Lund University Sweden, Departments of Philosophy and Cognitive Science, and a fellow at the Helsinki Collegium for Advanced Studies, Finland. He works in Social Epistemology and the Philosophy of Science. His current projects concern motivated halting points of pro/con argumentation, modeling scientific change within a geometric model of conceptual knowledge, and the specification of the boundary between dialectics and epistemology. Frank holds an M.A. in Discourse and Argumentation Studies from the University of Amsterdam, The Netherlands, and a Ph.D. in Philosophy of Science from the University of Hamburg, Germany.

References

Adler, J.E. (1992) Even arguments, explanatory gaps and pragmatic scales. *Philosophy and Rhetoric* 25: 22-44.

Alchourón, C., Gärdenfors, P. & Makinson, D. (1985). On the logic of theory change: Partial meet contraction and revision functions. *Journal of Symbolic Logic* 50: 510-530.

Allen, D. (1990). *Trudy Govier's Problems in Argument Analysis and Evaluation. Informal Logic* 12: 43-62.

Allen, D. (1993). Relevance, conduction and Canada's rape-shield decision. *Informal Logic* 15: 105-122.

American Heritage Dictionary of the English Language. (1994). 3rd ed. Boston: Houghton Mifflin (1994).

Angell, R.B. (1964). *Reasoning and Logic.* New York: Appleton.

Anonymous (1993). A revolution effected by good sense and seliberation. In B. Bailyn (Ed.), *The Debate on the Constitution: Federalist and Antifederalist Speeches, Articles, and Letters During the Struggle over Ratification* (Vol. 1, pp. 9-11). New York: Library Classics of the United States. [A newspaper editorial, originally published in the *Daily Advertiser*, a New York newspaper, September 24, 1787.]

Anscombe, G.E.M. (1957). *Intention.* Oxford: Basil Blackwell.

Aqvist, L. (2007). An interpretation of probability in the law of evidence based on pro-et-contra argumentation. *Artificial Intelligence and Law* 1: 391-410.

Aristotle (1984). *Nicomachean Ethics.* In Jonathan Barnes (Ed.), *The Complete Works of Aristotle*, Vol 2, pp. 1729-1867. Princeton: Princeton University Press.

Arrow, K.J. (1950). A difficulty in the concept of social welfare. *Journal of Political Economy* 58: 328–346.

Atkinson, K., Bench-Capon, T. & McBurney, P. (2006). Computational representation of practical argument. *Synthese* 152: 157-206.

Austin, J.L. (1962). *A Plea for Excuses.* Cambridge, MA: Harvard University Press.

Austin, J.L. (1953). How to talk—some simple ways. *Proceedings of the Aristotelian Society* 53: 227-46.

Bailin, S. & Battersby, M. (2010). *Reason in the Balance: An Inquiry Approach to Critical Thinking.* Whitby, ON: McGraw-Hill Ryerson.

Bailin, S. & Battersby, M. (2009). Inquiry: A dialectical approach to teaching critical thinking. In H.V. Hansen, *et al.* (Eds.), *Argument Cultures*, CD-ROM (pp.). Windsor, ON: OSSA.

Ball, W.J. (1995). A pragmatic framework for the evaluation of policy arguments. *Review of Policy Research* 14: 3-24.

Banning, L. (1989). Virginia: Sectionalism and the general good. In M.A. Gillespie & M. Lienesch (Eds.), *Ratifying the Constitution*, pp. 261-299. Lawrence, KA: University Press of Kansas.

Barrett, T. (2008). Is carbon tax political poison? Dion and Campbell might have just sold it badly: pollster. *TheTyee.ca*, Oct. 20.

Battersby, M. (2006). Applied epistemology and argumentation in epidemiology. *Informal Logic* 26.1: 41-62.

Bench-Capon, T. (2001). Review of *The Notion of an Ideal Audience in Legal Argument. Artificial Intellligence and Law* 9: 59-71.

Bench-Capon, T. (2003). Persuasion in practical argument using value-based argumentation frameworks. *Journal of Logic and Computation* 13: 429-448.

Bench-Capon, T. and Sartor, G. (2000). Using values and theories to resolve disagreement in law. In J. Breuker, R. Leenes & R. Windels (Eds.), *Legal Knowledge and Information Systems. Jurix 2000: The Thirteenth Annual Conference*, pp. 73-84. Amsterdam: IOS Press.

Bench-Capon, T. & Atkinson, K. (2009). Abstract argumentation and values. In I. Rahwan & G. Simari (Eds.), *Argumentation and Artificial Intelligence*, pp. 45-64. Berlin: Springer.

Bickenbach, J.E. & Davies, J.M. (1997). Conductive reasoning. In *Good Reasons for Better Arguments. An Introduction to the Skills and Values of Critical Thinking*, pp. 321-326. Peterborough, ON: Broadview Press.

Blair, J.A. (1992). Everyday argumentation from an informal logic perspective. In W.L. Benoit, *et al.* (Eds.), *Readings in Argumentation*, pp. 357-376. New York: Foris Publications.

Blair, J.A. (1998). The lsimits of the dialogue model of argument. *Argumentation*. 12: 325-339.

Blair, J.A. (2007). The "logic" of informal logic. In H.V. Hansen, *et. al.* (Eds). *Dissensus and the Search for Common Ground*. Windsor, ON: OSSA, CD-ROM.

Brandom, R. (1994). *Making it Explicit: Reasoning, Representing and Discoursive Commitment*. Cambridge, MA: Harvard University Press.

Brandom, R. (2000). *Articulating Reasons: An Introduction to Inferentialism*. Cambridge MA: Harvard University Press.

Brockriede, W. & Ehninger, D. (1960). Toulmin on argument: An interpretation and application. *Quarterly Journal of Speech* 46: 44-53.

Brooks, D. (2009). The hardest call. *New York Times*, December 18.

Canadian Charter of Rights and Freedoms. http://laws.justice.gc.ca/en/charter/1.html

Cantlon, J., Libertus, M., Pinel, P., Dehaene, S., Brannon, E., Pelphrey, K. (2009). The neural development of an abstract concept of number. *Journal of Cognitive Neuroscience*, 21.11: 2217-2229.

Carroll, L. (1895). What the Tortoise said to Achilles. *Mind* 4: 278-80. [widely reprinted.]

Cayrol, C. and Lagasquie-Schiex, M. (2009). Bipolar abstract argumentation systems. In I. Rahwan & G.R. Simari (Eds.), *Argumentation in Artificial Intelligence*, pp. 65-83. Dordrecht: Springer.

Christie, G. (2000) *The Notion of an Ideal Audience in Legal Argument*. Dordrecht: Kluwer Academic Publishers.

Cohen, L.J. (1986). *The Dialogue of Reason: An Analysis of Analytical Philosophy*. Oxford: Clarendon Press.

Cohen, L.J. (1989). *An Introduction to The Philosophy of Induction and Probability*. Oxford: Clarendon Press.

Copi, I.M. (1982). *Introduction to Logic*, 6th ed. New York: Macmillan.

Copi, I.M. & C. Cohen (1990, 2001). *Introduction to Logic* (8th, 9th eds.). New York: Macmillan.

Cornfield, J., *et al.* (1959). Smoking and lung cancer: Recent evidence and a discussion of some questions. *Journal of the National Cancer Institute* 22: 173-203.

Dauer, F. (1974). The diagnosis of an argument. *Metaphilosophy* 5: 113-32.

Ducrot, O. (1996). *Slovenian Lectures: Argumentative Semantics*. S. McEvoy (Trans.). Ljubljana: Institute for Humanistic Studies.

Eemeren, F.H. van & Grootendorst, R. (1984). *Speech Acts in Argumentative Discussions: A Theoretical Model for the Analysis of Discussions Directed towards Solving Conflicts of Opinion*. Dordrecht/Berlin: Foris/Mouton de Gruyter.

Eemeren, F.H. van, Grootendorst, R. & Kruiger, T. (1984). *The Study of Argumentation*. New York: Irvington.
Eemeren, F.H. van & Grootendorst, R. (1992). *Argumentation, Communication, and Fallacies: A Pragma-Dialectical Perspective*. Hillsdale, NJ: Lawrence Erlbaum.
Eemeren, F.H. van & Grootendorst, R. (2004). *A Systematic Theory of Argumentation: The Pragma-Dialectical Approach*. Cambridge: Cambridge University Press.
Einstein, A. (2005). *Relativity: The Special and General Theory*. New York: Pi Press.
Eisend, M. (2006). Two-sided advertising: A meta-analysis. *International Journal of Research in Marketing* 23: 187-98.
Ennis, R.H. (2001). Argument appraisal strategy: A comprehensive approach. *Informal Logic*, 21.2: 97-140.
Ennis, R.H. (2004). Applying soundness standards to qualified reasoning. *Informal Logic* 24: 23-39.
Fahnestock, J. & Secor, M. (1985). Toward a modem version of stasis. In C.W. Kneupper (Ed.), *Newspeak: Rhetorical Transformations*, pp. 217-226. Arlington, TX: Rhetoric Society of America.
Fahnestock, J. & Secor, M. (1988). The stases in scientific and literary argument. *Written Communication* 5: 427-443.
Fahnestock, J. & Secor, M. (2003). *A Rhetoric of Argument: Text and Reader*, 3rd ed. New York: McGraw-Hill Higher Education.
Feteris, E.T. (2008). Weighing and balancing in the justification of judicial decisions. *Informal Logic* 28: 20-30.
Finocchiaro, M.A. (1980). *Galileo and the Art of Reasoning: Rhetorical Foundations of Logic and Scientific Method*. Boston Studies in the Philosophy of Science, vol. 61. Dordrecht: Reidel [now Springer].
Finocchiaro, M.A. (1981). Remarks on truth, problem-solving, and methodology. *Studies in History and Philosophy of Science* 12: 261-68.
Finocchiaro, M.A. (1986). Judgment and reasoning in the evaluation of theories. In: A. Fine & P. Machamer (Eds.), *PSA 1986: Proceedings of the 1986 Biennial Meeting of the Philosophy of Science Association* (vol. 1), pp. 227-235. East Lansing, MI: Philosophy of Science Association.
Finocchiaro, M.A. (1988). *Gramsci and the History of Dialectical Thought*. New York: Cambridge University Press.
Finocchiaro, M.A. (Trans. & Ed). (1997). *Galileo on the World Systems: A New Abridged Translation and Guide*. Berkeley: University of California Press.
Finocchiaro, M. (2003). Dialectics, evaluation, and argument. *Informal Logic*: 23.1: 19-50.
Finocchiaro, M.A. (2005a). *Arguments about Arguments: Systematic, Critical, and Historical essays in Logical Theory*. New York: Cambridge University Press.
Finocchiaro, M.A. (2005b). *Retrying Galileo, 1633-1992*. Berkeley: University of California Press.
Finocchiaro, M.A. (2007a). Arguments, meta-arguments, and metadialogues: A reconstruction of Krabbe, Govier, and Woods. *Argumentation* 21: 253-68.
Finocchiaro, M.A. (2007b). Famous meta-arguments: Part I, Mill and the tripartite nature of argumentation. In H.V. Hansen, C.W. Tindale, J.A. Blair, R.H. Johnson & D.M. Godden (Eds.), *Dissensus and the Search for Common Ground*, Windsor: Ontario Society for the Study of Argumentation, CD-ROM.
Finocchiaro, M.A. (2007c). Mill on liberty of argument. In H.V. Hansen & R.C. Pinto (Eds.), *Reason Reclaimed*, pp. 121-34. Newport News, VA: Vale Press.

Finocchiaro, M. A. (2009). Meta-argumentation in Hume's critique of the design argument. In J. Ritola (Ed.), *Argument Cultures: Proceedings of OSSA 09*, CD-ROM, pp. 1-12. Windsor, ON: Ontario Society for the Study of Argumentation.

Finocchiaro, M.A. (2010a). *Defending Copernicus and Galileo: Critical reasoning in the two affairs*. Boston Studies in the Philosophy of Science, vol. 280. Dordrecht: Springer.

Finocchiaro, M.A. (2010b). Meta-argumentation: Prolegomena to a Dutch project. In F.H. van Eemeren, B. Garssen, D. Godden & G.R. Mitchell (Eds.), *Proceedings of the Seventh International Conference of the International Society for the Study of Argumentation*, Amsterdam: Sic Sat.

Fischer, T. (2011). Weighing considerations in conductive pro and contra arguments. (This volume)

Fisher, A. (1988, 2004). *The Logic of Real Arguments* (1st & 2nd eds.). Cambridge: Cambridge University Press.

Floridi, L. (2005). Semantic Conceptions of Information. In E.N. Zalta (Ed.), *The Stanford Encyclopedia of Philosophy*. Summer 2009 edition. <http://plato.stanford.edu/entries/information-semantic/>.

Freeman, J.B. (1983). Logical form, probability interpretations, and the inductive / deductive distinction. *Informal Logic* 5.2: 2-10.

Freeman, J.B. (1988). *Thinking Logically*. Englewood Cliffs, NJ: Prentice-Hall.

Freeman, J.B. (1991). *Dialectics and the Macrostructure of Arguments: A Theory of Argument Structure*. Berlin & New York: Foris Publications.

Freeman, J.B. (1995). The appeal to popularity and presumption by common Knowledge. In H.V. Hansen & R.C. Pinto (Eds.), *Fallacies: Classical and Contemporary Readings*, pp. 263-273. University Park, PA: The Pennsylvania State University Press.

Freeman, J.B. (2001). Argument structure and disciplinary perspective. *Argumentation* 15: 397-423.

Freeman, J.B. (2005a). *Acceptable Premises*: An Epistemic Approach to an Informal Logic Problem. Cambridge: Cambridge University Press.

Freeman, J.B. (2005b). Systematizing Toulmin's warrants: An epistemic approach. *Argumentation* 19: 331-346.

Freeman, J.B. (2009). Is epistemic probability Pascalian? Presented at the Association for Informal Logic and Critical Thinking Group Session, American Philosophical Association Eastern Division Meetings, New York, NY, December 30, 2009. Available at http://www.hunter.cuny.edu/philosophy/repository/essays-articles-by-james-freeman/is-epistemic-probability-pascalian.pdf.

Freeman, J.B. (2011). Evaluating conductive arguments: Critical questions in light of the Toulmin model. This volume, Ch. 9.

Freeman, J. B. (201x). *Argument Structure: Representation and Theory*. Dordrecht, The Netherlands: Springer (forthcoming).

Gabbay, D.V., Johnson, R.H., Holbach, H.J. & Woods, J (Eds.). (2002). *Handbook of the Logic of Argument and Inference: The Turn Toward the Practical*. Amsterdam: Elsevier/North-Holland.

Galilei, G. (2008). *The Essential Galileo*. M.A. Finocchiaro (Trans. & Ed.). Indianapolis: Hackett.

Gärdenfors, P. (1984). Epistemic importance and minimal changes of belief. *Australasian Journal of Philosophy* 62: 136-157.

Gärdenfors, P. (1988). *Knowledge in Flux: Modeling the Dynamics of Epistemic States*. Cambridge, MA: MIT Press.

Gärdenfors, P. (Ed.). (2003). *Belief Revision*. (Cambridge Tracts in Theoretical Computer Science 29). Cambridge: CUP.

Gärdenfors, P. (2005). *The Dynamics of Thought*. (Synthese Library, Vol. 300). Dordrecht: Springer.
Goddu, G.C. (2007). Walton on argument structure. *Informal logic*. 27: 5-25.
Goffman, E. (1974). *Frame Analysis*. Cambridge, MA: Harvard University Press.
Goldfarb, W. (2003) *Deductive Logic*. Indianapolis: Hackett.
Gordon, T.F. & Walton, D. (2009). Legal reasoning with argumentation schemes. In C.D. Hafner (Ed.), *12th International Conference on Artificial Intelligence and Law*, pp. 137-146. New York: ACM Press.
Govier, T. (1980a). Carl Wellman's *Challenge and Response*. *Informal Logic Newsletter* 2.2: 10-15.
Govier, T. (1980b). More on deductive and inductive arguments. *Informal Logic Newsletter* 2.3: 7-8.
Govier, T. (1980c). Assessing arguments: what range of standards?" *Informal Logic Newsletter* 3.1: 2-4.
Govier, T. (1985, 1992, 2001a, 2005, 2010a) *A Practical Study of Argument* (1st, 3rd, 5th, 6th and 7th eds.). Belmont, CA: Wadsworth.
Govier, T. (1987a). *Problems in Argument Analysis and Evaluation*. Dordrecht: Foris Publications.
Govier, T. (1987b). Two unreceived views about reasoning and argument. In T. Govier, *Problems in Argument Analysis and Evaluation*, pp. 55-80. Dordrecht: Foris.
Govier, T. (1987c). Beyond induction and deduction. In F.H. van Eemeren, *et al.* (Eds.), *Argumentation: Across the lines of discipline*, Proceedings of the conference on argumentation 1986, pp. 57-64. Dordrecht: Foris.
Govier, T. (1995). Critical study of *New Essays in Informal Logic*. *Informal Logic* 17: 407-19.
Govier, T. (1999a). *The Philosophy of Argument*. Newport News, VA: Vale Press.
Govier, T. (1999b). Reasoning with pros and cons: Conductive arguments revisited. In T. Govier, *The Philosophy of Argument*, Ch. 10. Newport News, VA: Vale Press.
Govier, T. (2000). Critical review of Johnson's *Manifest Rationality*. *Informal Logic* 20: 281-291.
Govier, T. (2001b). Conductive arguments and counterconsiderations. In T. Govier, *A Practical Study of Arguments*, 5th ed., pp. 392-412.
Govier, T. (2009). More on dichotomization: Flip-flops of two mistakes. In J. Ritola (Ed.), *Argument Cultures: Proceedings of OSSA 09*, CD-ROM, pp. 1-10. Windsor, ON: OSSA.
Govier, T. (2010b). Conductive arguments and counterconsiderations. In T. Govier, *A Practical Study of Arguments*, 7th ed., pp. 352-77.
Habermas, J. (1984). *The Theory of Communicative Action*, vol.1. Boston: Beacon Press.
Halberda, J., Mazzocco, M. & Feigenson, L. (2008). Individual differences in non-verbal number acuity correlate with maths achievement. *Nature* 455 (2 October): 665-668.
Hamilton, A. (1993). Alexander Hamilton's conjectures about the new constitution. In B. Bailyn (Ed.), *The Debate on the Constitution: Federalist and Antifederalist Speeches, Articles, and Letters During the Struggle over Ratification* (Vol. 1, pp. 9-11). New York: Library Classics of the United States.
Hamilton, A., Madison, J., & Jay, J. (1961). *The Federalist Papers*. New York: New American Library.
Hansen, H.V. (2002). An exploration of Johnson's sense of 'argument.' *Argumentation* 16.3: 263-276.

Hansen, H.V. (2010). The structure of balance-of-consideration arguments. Association for Informal Logic and Critical Thinking session, American Philosophical Association Central Division meeting, Chicago, February.
Hansen, H.V. (2010b). Notes on balance-of-consideration arguments. This volume, Ch. 3.
Hastings, A.C. (1963). *A Reformulation of the Modes of Reasoning in Argumentation*. Evanston, Illinois: Ph.D. Dissertation, Northwestern University.
Hempel, C.G. (1966). *Philosophy of Natural Science*. Englewood Cliffs, NJ: Prentice-Hall.
Hitchcock, D. (1980). Deductive and inductive types of validity. *Informal Logic Newsletter* 2.3: 9-10.
Hitchcock, D. (1981). Deduction, induction, and conduction. *Informal Logic Newsletter* 3.2: 7-15.
Hitchcock, D. (1983). *Critical Thinking: A Guide to Evaluating Information*. Toronto: Methuen.
Hitchcock, D. (1985). Enthymematic arguments. *Informal Logic* 7: 83-97.
Hitchcock, D. (1994). Validity in conductive arguments. In R.H. Johnson & J.A. Blair (Eds.), *New Essays in Informal Logic*, pp. 58-66. Windsor, Ontario: Informal Logic.
Hitchcock, D. (2000). Statement on practical reasoning. http://citeseerx.ist.psu.edu/viewdoc/download?doi=10.1.1.29.6897&rep=rep1&type=pdf, downloaded Jan. 16, 2010.
Hitchcock, D. (2003). Toulmin's warrants. In F.H. van Eemeren, *et al.* (Eds.), *Anyone Who Has a View: Theoretical Contributions to the Study of Argumentation*, pp. 69-82. Dordrecht/Boston/London: Kluwer Academic Publishers.
Hitchcock, D. (2007). Informal logic and the concept of argument. In D. Jacquette (Ed.), *Philosophy of Logic*, pp. 101-131. Amsterdam: Elsevier B.V.
Hitchcock, D. & Vereij, E. (Eds.). (2006). *Arguing on the Toulmin Model: New Essays in Argument Analysis and Evaluation*. Dordrecht: Springer.
Husserl, E. (1976), *Ideen zu einer reinen Phänomenologie und phänomenologischen Philosophie I*. K. Schumann (Ed.). *(Husserliana Vol. III/I)* Den Haag: Martinus Nijhof.
Irwin Toy Ltd. v. Quebec (Attorney General), (1989) 1 S.C.R. 927. http://scc.lexum.umontreal.ca/en/1989/1989scr1-927/1989scr1-927.pdf
Jacquette, D. (2007). Two sides of any issue. *Argumentation* 21: 115-27.
Johnson, R.H. (2000a). *Manifest Rationality: A Pragmatic Theory of Argument*. Mahwah, NJ: Erlbaum.
Johnson, R.H. (2000b). More on arguers and dialectical obligations. In C.W Tindale, H.V. Hansen & E. Sveda (Eds.), *Argumentation at the Century's Turn*. St. Catherines, ON: Ontario Society for the Study of Argumentation. ISBN 0-9683461. (CD-ROM).
Johnson, R.H. (2002). Manifest rationality reconsidered: Reply to my fellow symposiasts. *Argumentation*. 16: 311-331.
Johnson, R.H. (2003). The dialectical tier revisited. In F.H. van Eemeren, J.A Blair, C.A. Willard & A.F. Snoeck Henkemans (Eds.), *Anyone Who has a View: Theoretical Contributions to the Study of Argumentation*, pp. 41-54. Dordrecht: Kluwer.
Johnson, R.H. (2007). Anticipating objections as a way of coping with dissensus. In H.V. Hansen, *et al.* (Eds.), *Dissensus and the Search for Common Ground*, CD-ROM, pp.1-16. Windsor, ON: OSSA.
Johnson, R.H. (2009). Revisiting the logical/dialectical/rhetorical triumvirate. In J. Rutolo (Ed.), *Argument Cultures*, CD-ROM. Windsor, ON: OSSA.
Johnson, R.H. & Blair, J.A.. (1977, 1983, 1993). *Logical Self-Defense* (1st, 2nd, 3rd eds.). Toronto: McGraw-Hill Ryerson. [(1994) 1st U.S. ed. New York: McGraw-Hill.] [(2006) 1st U.S. ed. reissue. New York: IDEA Press.]

Johnson, R.H. & J.A. Blair (2000). Informal logic: An overview. *Informal Logic* 20: 93-107.
Jonsen, A. & Toulmin, S. (1988). *The Abuse of Casuistry*. Berkeley: University of California Press.
Kagan, S. (1989*)*. *The Limits of Morality*. Oxford: Clarendon Press.
Kahneman, D., Slovic, P. & Tversky, A. (1982). *Judgment Under Uncertainty: Heuristics and Biases*. Cambridge: Cambridge University Press.
Kaminski, J.P., & Saladino, G.J. (Eds.). (1988). *Ratification of the Constitution by the States: Virginia* (Vol. VIII-X). Madison: State Historical Society of Wisconsin.
Kauffeld, F.J. (2002). Pivotal issues and norms in rhetorical theories of argumentation. In F.H. van Eemeren & P. Houtlosser (Eds.), *Dialectic and Rhetoric: The Warp and Woof of Argumentation Analysis*, pp. 97-119. Dordrecht: Kluwer.
Kay, P. (1990) Even. *Linguistics and Philosophy* 13: 59-111.
Kenny, A. (1966). Practical inference. *Analysis* 26: 65-75.
Kenny, A. (1979). *Aristotle's Theory of the Will*. London: Duckworth.
Kenyon, C.M. (Ed.). (1966). *The Antifederalists*. Boston: Northeastern University Press.
Kienpointner, M. (1992). *Alltagslogik. Struktur und Funktion von Argumentationsmustern*. Stuttgart-Bad Cannstatt: Frommann-Holzboog.
Kock, C. (2003). Multidimensionality and non-deductiveness in deliberative argumentation. In F.H. van Eemeren, J.A. Blair, C.A. Willard, A.F. Snoeck Henkemans (Eds.), *Anyone Who Has a View: Theoretical Contributions to the Study of Argumentation*, pp. 155-171. Dordrecht: Kluwer.
Kock, C. (2006). Multiple warrants in practical reasoning. In D. Hitchcock & B. Verheij (Eds.), *Arguing on the Toulmin Model: New Essays on Argument Analysis and Evaluation*, pp. 247-259. Dordrecht : Springer Verlag,.
Kock, C. (2007a). Is practical reasoning presumptive? *Informal Logic* 27: 1-18.
Kock, C. (2007b). The domain of rhetorical argumentation. In F.H. van Eemeren, J.A. Blair, C.A. Willard & B. Garssen (Eds.), *Proceedings of the Sixth Conference of the International Society for the Study of Argumentation*, pp. 785-89. Amsterdam: Sic Sat.
Kock, C. (2007c). Norms of legitimate dissensus. *Informal Logic* 27: 179-196.
Kock, C. (2007d). Dialectical obligations in political debate. *Informal Logic* 27: 233-247.
Kock, C. (2009a). Choice is not true or false: the domain of rhetorical argumentation. *Argumentation* 23: 61-80.
Kock, C. (2009b). Constructive controversy: Rhetoric as dissensus-oriented discourse. *Cogency* 1: 89-115.
Krugman, P. (2009). Pass the bill. *New York Times*, December 18.
Laudan, L. (1983). *Science and Values*. Berkeley: University of California Press.
Libertus, M. & Brannon, E. (2009). Behavioral and neural basis of number sense in infancy. *Current Directions in Psychological Science* 18.6: 346-351
Lorenzen, P. (1969). *Normative Logic and Ethics*. Mannheim, Zürich: Bibliographisches Institut.
Mackie, J.L. (1993). Causes and conditions. In E. Sosa & M. Tooley (Eds.), *Causation*, pp. 33-55. Oxford: Oxford University Press.
Mann, T. (1977). *Argument Assessment for Design Decisions*. Dissertation, University of California, Berkeley.
McBryde Johnson, H. (2003). Unspeakable conversations. *New York Times*, February 16. http://www.nytimes.com/2003/02/16/magazine/unspeakable-conversations.html?ref=petersinger. Accessed July 30, 2011

McBurney, P., Hitchcock, D. & Parsons, S. (2007). The eightfold way of deliberation dialogue. *International Journal of Intelligent Systems* 22: 95-132.

Meiland, J.W. (1981). *College Thinking: How to Get the Best out of College.* New York: New American Library.

Mill, J.S. (1951). *Utilitarianism, Liberty, and Representative Government.* New York: Dutton.

Naess, A. (2005). Surveys of arguments for and against a standpoint. In H. Glasser, *et al.* (Eds.), *The Selected Works of Arne Naess* (vol.7), pp. 75-95. Dordrecht: Springer.

O'Keefe, D.J. (1977). Two concepts of argument. *Journal of the American Forensic Society.* 13: 121-128.

O'Keefe, D.J. (1999). How to handle opposing arguments in persuasive messages: A meta-analytic review of the effects of one-sided and two-sided messages. *Communication Yearbook* 22: 209-49.

Pera, M. (1994). *The Discourses of Science.* Chicago: University of Chicago Press.

Perelman, Ch. (1982). *The Realm of Reason.* Notre Dame, IN: University of Notre Dame Press.

Perelman, Ch. and Olbrechts-Tyteca, L. (1958). *La Nouvelle Rhétorique: Traité de l'Argumentation.* Paris: Presse Universitaires de France.

Perkins, D.N. (1985). Postprimary education has little impact on informal reasoning. *Journal of Educational Psychology* 77: 562-71.

Perkins, D.N. (2002). Standard logic as a model of reasoning. In D.V. Gabbay, R.H. Johnson, H.J. Holbach & J. Woods (Eds.), *Handbook of the Logic of Argument and Inference: The Turn Toward the Practical* pp. 187-224. Amsterdam: Elsevier/North-Holland.

Perkins, D.N., Farady, M. and Bushey, B. (1991). Everyday reasoning and the roots of intelligence. In J.F. Voss, D.N. Perkins & J.W. Segal (Eds.), *Informal Reasoning and Education*, pp. 83-105. Hillsdale, NJ: Lawrence Erlbaum.

Perkins, D.N., Allen, R. & Hafner, J, (1983). Difficulties in everyday reasoning. In W. Maxwell (Ed.), *Thinking, the Expanding Frontier*, pp. 177-89. Philadelphia: The Franklin Institute Press.

Pinto, R.C. (2001). Cognitive science and the future of rational criticism. In R.C. Pinto, *Argument, Inference, and Dialectic*, pp. 113-125. Dordrecht: Kluwer

Pinto, R. C. (2006). Evaluating inferences: The nature and function of warrants. *Informal Logic* 26: 287-317. Reprinted in D. Hitchcock & B. Verheij (Eds.), *Arguing on the Toulmin Model*, pp. 115-143. Dordrecht: Springer.

Pinto, R. C. (2007). Understanding 'probabily' and other modal qualifiers. In Proceedings of OSSA 2007 (Ontario Society for the Study of Argumentation, University of Windsor, Windsor Ontario). This paper is currently under revision—a link to the most recently revised version can be found at http://web2.uwindsor.ca/courses/philosophy/pinto/papers.htm .

Pinto, R.C. (2009). Argumentation and the force of reasons. In J. Ritola (Ed.), *Argument Cultures: Proceedings of the 8th OSSA Conference*, CD-ROM, pp. 1-23. Windsor, ON: OSSA.

Pinto, R.C. (2009). Argumentation and the force of reasons. *Informal Logic* 29.3: 268-295.

Pinto, R.C. (2011). Weighing evidence in the context of conductive reasoning (this volume).

Pinto, R.C. & Blair, J.A. (1993). *Reasoning: A Practical Guide.* Englewood Cliffs, NJ: Prentice-Hall.

Pollock, J.L. (1974). *Knowledge and Justification.* Princeton: Princeton University Press.

Pollock, J.L. (1995). *Cognitive Carpentry: A Blueprint for How to Build a Person.* Cambridge, MA: MIT Press.

Pollock, J.L. (2002). Defeasible reasoning with variable degrees of justification. *Artificial Intelligence* 133: 233-282. An expanded version of this paper in PDF format is available at http://oscarhome.soc-sci.arizona.edu/ftp/publications.html. References in the text are to the PDF version of this paper.

Pollock, J.L. (2008). Defeasible reasoning. In J.Adler and L. Rips (Eds.), *Reasoning: Studies of Human Inference and its Foundations*, pp. 451-470. Cambridge University Press. This paper is available in PDF format at
 http://oscarhome.soc-sci.arizona.edu/ftp/publications.html. Quotations are from the PDF version of this paper.

Pollock, J.L. (2010). Defeasible reasoning and degrees of justification. *Argument and Computation* 1: 7-22.

Possin, K. (2010). What the tortoise said to Hans. Session of the Association for Informal Logic and Critical Thinking, Central Division of the American Philosophical Association Meetings, Chicago, February.

Prakken, H. An exercise in formalizing teleological case-based reasoning. In J. Breuker, R. Leenes and R. Windels (Eds.), *Legal Knowledge and Information Systems. Jurix 2000: The Thirteenth Annual Conference*, pp. 49-57. Amsterdam: IOS Press.

Prakken, H. (2006). Formal systems for persuasion dialogue. *The Knowledge Engineering Review* 21: 163-188.

Quine, W. van O. (1952) *Methods of Logic*. London: Routledge and Kegan Paul.

R. v. Keegstra. (1990). 3 S.C.R. 697. http://csc.lexum.umontreal.ca/en/1990/1990scr3-697/1990scr3-697.pdf

R. v. Oakes. (1986). 1 S.C.R. 103. http://scc.lexum.umontreal.ca/en/1986/1986scr1-103/1986scr1-103.pdf

Rawls, J. (1971). *A Theory of Justice*. Cambridge, MA: Harvard University Press.

Reed, C. & Walton, D. (2003). Argumentation schemes in argument-as-process and argument-as-product. In J.A. Blair, *et al.* (Eds.), *Informal Logic @ 25: Proceedings of the Windsor Conference, 2003*, CD-ROM. Windsor, ON: OSSA.

Rehg, W. (2009). *Cogent Science in Context: The Science Wars, Argumentation Theory and Habermas*. Cambridge, MA: The MIT Press.

Rescher, N. (1977). *Dialectics: A Controversy-Oriented Approach to the Theory of Knowledge*. Albany: State University of New York Press.

Ross, W.D. (1930). *The Right and the Good*. Oxford: The Clarendon Press.

Rubin, R. & Young, C.M. (1989). *Formal Logic, A Model of English*. Mountain View: Mayfield.

Russell, B. (1967). *The Autobiography of Bertrand Russell*, Vol. I (1872-1914). London: George Allen and Unwin.

Salmon, M. (2002). *Introduction to Logic and Critical Thinking* (4th ed.). Belmont, CA: Wadsworth.

Salmon, W.C. (1984). *Logic* (3rd ed.). Englewood Cliffs, NJ: Prentice-Hall.

Schank, R.C. & Abelson, R.P. (1977). *Scripts, Plans, Goals and Understanding*. Hillsdale, New Jersey: Lawrence Erlbaum.

Schauer, F. (2003). *Profiles, Probabilities, and Stereotypes*. Cambridge, MA: Belknap Press of Harvard University Press.

Scheuer, O., Loll, F., Pinkwart, N. & McLaren, B.M. (2009). Computer-supported argumentation: A review of the state of the art. *International Journal of Computer-Supported Collaborative Learning* 5.1: 1-67.

Scriven, M. (1976). *Reasoning*. New York: McGraw-Hill.

Scriven, M. (1981). The "weight and sum" methodology. *American Journal of Evaluation* 2: 85-90.
Scriven, M. (1991). *Evaluation Thesaurus* (4th ed.) Newbury Park, CA: Sage.
Searle, J.R. (1975). A taxonomy of illocutionary acts. In K. Gunderson (Ed.), *Language, Mind and Knowledge*, pp. 344–369. Minneapolis: University of Minnesota Press. Repr. in Searle, J. R. (1979). *Expression and Meaning*, pp. 1-29. Cambridge: Cambridge University Press.
Searle, J.R. (1983). *Intentionality: An Essay in the Philosophy of Mind*. Cambridge: Cambridge University Press.
Singh, P., Lin, T., Mueller, E.T., Lim, G., Perkins, T., & Zhu, W.L. (2002). Open mind common sense: Knowledge acquisition from the general public. *Proceedings of the First International Conference on Ontologies, Databases, and Applications of Semantics for Large Scale Information Systems*, Lecture Notes in Computer Science. Heidelberg: Springer Verlag.
Sinnot-Armstrong, W. & Fogelin, R.F. (2010). *Understanding Arguments. An Introduction to Informal Logic* (8th ed). Belmont, CA: Wadsworth Cenage Learning.
Skyrms, B. (1966, 1975, 1999). *Choice and Chance, An Introduction to Inductive Logic* (1st, 2nd, 4th eds.) Belmont, CA: Dickenson.
Slob, W.H. (2006). The voice of the other: A dialogico-rhetorical understanding of opponent and Toulmin's rebuttal. In D. Hitchcock & B. Verheij (Eds.). (2006). *Arguing on the Toulmin Model: New Essays in Argument Analysis and Evaluation*, pp. 165-180. Dordrecht: Springer.
Snoeck Henkemans, A.F. (1992). *Analysing Complex Argumentation*. Amsterdam: Sic Sat.
Snoeck Henkemans, A.F. (2000). State-of-the-art: The structure of argumentation. *Argumentation* 14: 447-473.
Snoeck Henkemans, A.F. (2001). Argumentation structures. In F.H. van Eemeren (Ed.), *Crucial Concepts in Argumentation Theory*, pp. 101-134. Amsterdam: SicSat.
Soccorsi, F. (1947). *Il processo di Galileo*. Rome: Edizioni La Civiltà Cattolica.
Stevenson, C.L. (1944). *Ethics and Language*. New Haven: Yale University Press.
Stich, S. (1990). *The Fragmentation of Reason*. Cambridge, MA: MIT Press.
Thomas, S.N. (1973, 1981). *Practical Reasoning in Natural Language*. (1st, 2nd eds.). Englewood Cliffs, NJ: Prentice-Hall.
Toulmin, S.E. (1958). *The Uses of Argument*. Cambridge: Cambridge University Press.
Tyaglo, A. (2002). How to improve the convergent argument calculation. *Informal Logic* 22.1: 61-71.
Verheij, B. (2006). Evaluating arguments based on Toulmin's scheme. In D. Hitchcock & B. Verheij (Eds.). *Arguing on the Toulmin Model: New Essays in Argument Analysis and Evaluation*, pp. 181-202. Dordrecht: Springer.
Vorobej, M. (1994). The TRUE test of linkage. *Informal Logic* 16: 147-157.
Vorobej, M. (1995). Hybrid arguments. *Informal Logic* 17: 289-296.
Vorobej, M. (2006). *A Theory of Argument*. New York: Cambridge University Press.
Voss, J.F., Perkins, D.N. & Segal, J.W. (1991). *Informal Reasoning and Education*. Hillsdale, NJ: Lawrence Erlbaum.
Walton, D. (1996). *Argument Structure: A Pragmatic Theory*. Toronto, ON: University of Toronto Press.
Walton, D. (1996). *Argumentation Schemes for Presumptive Reasoning*. Mahwah, NJ: Lawrence Erlbaum.
Walton, D. (2008). Three bases for the enthymeme: a dialectical theory. *Journal of Applied Logic* 6: 361-379.
Walton, D. (2011). Defeasible reasoning and informal fallacies. *Synthese* 179.3: 377-407.

Walton, D. & Krabbe, E.C.W. (1995). *Commitment in Dialogue*. Albany: State University of New York Press.
Walton, D., Reed, C. & Macagno, F. (2008). *Argumentation Schemes*. Cambridge: Cambridge University Press.
Walton, D., Atkinson, K., Bench-Capon, T.J.M., Wyner, A. & Cartwright, D. (2010). Argumentation in the framework of deliberation dialogue. In C. Bjola 7 M. Kornprobst (Eds.), *Arguing Global Governance*, pp. 210-230. London: Routledge.
Walzer, A.E. (2003) *George Campbell: Rhetoric in the Age of the Enlightenment*. Albany: SUNY Press.
Wellman, C. (1963). The ethical implications of cultural relativity. *The Journal of Philosophy* 60: 169-184.
Wellman, C. (1964). Judgments of value and obligation. *Ethics* 74: 143-149.
Wellman, C. (1968). Emotivism and ethical objectivity. *American Philosophical Quarterly* 5: 90-99.
Wellman, C. (1971). *Challenge and Response: Justification in Ethics*. Carbondale, IL: Southern Illinois University Press.
Wellman, C. (1975a). Ethical disagreement and objective truth. *American Philosophical Quarterly* 12: 211-221.
Wellman, C. (1975b, 1988). *Morals and Ethics* (1st, 2nd eds.). Englewood Cliffs, NJ: Prentice-Hall.
Wellman, C. (1976). The justification of practical reason. *Philosophy and Phenomenological Research* 36: 531-546.
Wellman, C. (1999). Relative moral duties. *American Philosophical Quarterly* 36: 209-223.
Wilson, J. (1993). Everything which is not given, is reserved. In B. Bailyn (Ed.), *The Debate on the Constitution: Federalist and Antifederalist Speeches, Articles, and letters During the Struggle over Ratification* (Vol. 1, pp. 63-69). New York: Library Classics of the United States.
Wittgenstein, L. (1969). *Philosophische Untersuchungen*. In L. Wittgenstein, *Schriften* Bd. 1. Frankfurt am Main: Suhrkamp.
Wohlrapp, H. (1995). Resolving the riddle of the non-deductive argumentation schemes. In F.H. van Eemeren, R. Grootendorst, J.A. Blair & C.A. Willard (Eds.), *Proceedings of the Third ISSA Conference on Argumentation, Vol. II*, pp. 55-62. Amsterdam: SicSat.
Wohlrapp, H. (1997). Some remarks on non-deductive argument. In J.F. Klumpp (Ed.), *Argument in a time of Change: Proceedings of the Tenth NCA/AFA Conference on Argumentation*, pp. 24-30. Washington, DC: National Communication Association.
Wohlrapp, H. (1998). A new light on non deductive argumentation schemes. *Argumentation* 12: 341-350.
Wohlrapp, H. (2007). *A Philosophical Concept of Argument*. Unpublished.
Wohlrapp, H. (2008). Section 6.4 The pro- and contra-discussion (A critique of Govier's "conductive argument") in *Der Begriff des Arguments*. Wurzburg: Konigshausen und Neumann. F. Zenker Section 6.4 translation. Retrieved from www.frankzenker.de. http://www.frankzenker.de/downloads/Zenker_2008_Translation%20of%20Wohlrapp%202008%20Pro%20Con%20Discussion_GER_ENGL.pdf .
Wohlrapp, H. (2008, 2009). *Der Begriff des Arguments. Über die Beziehungen zwischen Wissen, Forschen, Glauben, Subjektivität und Vernunft* (1st, 2nd eds.). Würzburg: Königshausen und Neumann.
Woods, J. (2010). Defeasible reasoning. In C. Tindale & C. Reed (Eds.), *Dialectics, Dialogue and Argumentation. An Examination of Douglas Walton's Theories of Reasoning and Argument*, pp. 239-261. London: College Publications.

Zenker, F. (2007). Complexity without insight: *Ceteris Paribus* clauses in conductive argumentation. In S. Jacobs (Ed.), *Concerning Argument* (Proceedings of the 2007 NCA/AFA Conference on Argumentation), pp. 810-818. Washington, DC: National Communication Association. The version of this paper cited here is from http://www.frankzenker.de/downloads/ZENKER_ALTA_2007.pdf .

Zenker, F. (2009a). "On the other hand" — Towards a dialectically adequate model for pro/contra argumentation. Unpublished manuscript.

Zenker, F. (2009b). *Ceteris paribus in Conservative Belief Revision. On the Role of Minimal Change in Rational Theory Development* (Ph.D. Thesis, University of Hamburg). Berlin: Peter Lang.

Zenker, F. (2009c). The pro contra discussion. Translation of Wohlrapp, H. (2008) pp. 316-334. Unpublished manuscript, in <http://www.frankzenker.de/downloads/Zenker_2008_Translation%20of%20Wohlrapp%202008%20Pro%20Con%20Discussion_GER_ENGL.pdf>.

Zenker, F. (2009d). Complexity without insight: *Ceteris paribus* clauses in conductive argumentation. In S. Jacobs (Ed.), *Concerning Argument: Proceedings of the 2007 NCA/AFA Conference on Argumentation, Alta, Utah*, pp. 810-818. Washington, DC: National Communication Association. Independently paginated version available at: http://www.frankzenker.de/academia.html.

Zenker, F. (2010a). Analyzing social policy argumentation: A case study of the 2007 majority opinion of the German National Ethics Council regarding an amendment of the stem cell law. *Informal Logic* 30: 62-91.

Zenker, F. (2010b). Deduction, induction, conduction: An attempt at unifying natural language argument structure. *Proceedings of the Wake Forest Conference on Argumentation*. The version of this paper cited here is from http://www.frankzenker.de/downloads/Zenker%202009%20Deduction%20Induction%20Conduction.pdf . See also this volume, Ch. 6.

Zimmer, C. (2009). The Math Instinct. *Discover Magazine*. November: 28.

Index of Names

A

Abelson, R.P. 198
Adler, J. 44-7
Alchourón, C. 76
Allen, D. 5, 74, 156, 211, 224, 238-40, 256, 257, 265
Allen, R. 249
Angell, B. 226, 235
Anscombe, G.E.M. 73
Aqvist, L. 75
Aristotle 62-3, 67, 87, 205, 253
Arrow, K.J. 75-6
Atkinson, K. 199
Austin, J.L. 52-4, 73, 159
Ayers, L 267, 274

B

Baier, K. 235
Bailin, S. 2, 7, 146, 265-6
Ball, W.J. 75
Banning, L. 163
Bar-Hillel, Y. 76
Battersby, M. 2, 7, 146, 265-6
Bench-Capon, T. 93-4, 102, 200
Bickenbach, J. 74, 224
Blair, J.A. 24, 30, 106, 147, 218, 224, 262, 269, 270
Boswell, J. 32
Brandom, R. 111-12
Brooks, D. 8, 224, 245-9, 257-8
Bushey, B. 249

C

Campbell, G. 4, 31-3, 263
Cantlon, J. 86, 88
Carnap, R. 76
Carroll, L. 271
Cartwright, N. 95
Cayrol, C. 94
Chandler, R. 97
Christie, G. 92, 101
Cicero 75
Cohen, C. 11
Cohen, L.J. 137, 234
Copernicus 252
Copi, I. 2, 11
Cornfield, J. 156-7

D

Dauer, F. 255
Davies, J. 74, 224
DiCanzio, A. 258
Dickson, B. 167, 169, 171-4, 177, 179-81, 184, 185
Ducrot, O. 44-6

E

Eemeren, F.H. van 76, 214, 226
Einstein, A. 235
Eisend, M. 224, 251, 258
Elliot, G. 102
Ennis, R. 224, 232, 232, 240-2, 256-7

F

Fahnestock, J. 63
Farady, M. 249
Feteris, E. 74
Finocchiaro, M. 2, 7, 8, 61, 211, 224-6, 232, 234, 236, 249-52, 256, 262, 269-270
Fischer, T. 7, 8, 258, 265
Fisher, A. 236
Floridi, L. 76
Fogelin, R. 74
Franklin, B. 99
Freeman, J.B. 2, 4, 6, 7, 25, 30, 131, 132, 138, 167, 175-7, 187-90, 196, 226, 232, 235, 263-7

G

Galileo, G. 224, 252-6, 258
Gärdenfors, P. 75-6
Goddu, G. 27
Goffman, E. 216
Goldfarb, W. 43, 45-6
Goodwin, J. 43
Gordon, T. 115
Govier, T. 4, 6, 7, 10, 11, 15, 18-24, 26-8, 30, 33, 35-6, 38, 42, 52-6, 59, 68-70, 74-5, 86-91, 94-5, 97-9, 102, 104-6, 111, 115-17, 119, 122, 130, 133, 136-8, 144-5, 158, 177, 188, 196, 210-11, 218, 224, 233-44, 250-1, 255-8, 264, 266, 268
Griffin 120
Grootendorst, R. 76, 214, 226

Index of names

H

Habermas, J. 24
Hafner, C.D. 249
Hansen, H.V. 4, 6, 8, 27, 55, 80, 158, 209, 258, 262, 267, 269-74
Hamilton, A. 8, 17, 161-3
Hegel, G.W.F. 214
Hempel, C. 96, 119
Henry, P. 164-5
Heraclitus 214
Hitchcock, D. 8, 10, 13-18, 21-6, 30, 94, 117, 128-9, 133, 135-7, 148-9, 204, 209, 211, 219, 223-4, 230-1, 233, 235, 256, 259, 265
Hudon, R. 49
Hume, D. 31
Hurka, T. 105, 120
Husserl, E. 216

J

Jacquette, D. 224, 251-2
Jay, J. 8, 162
Jefferson, T. 8
Jin, R. 6, 267-75
Johnson, B. 151
Johnson, R.H. 5, 30, 138, 147, 224, 250, 258, 266

K

Kagan, S. 7
Kahneman, D. 151
Kaminski, J.P. 163-5
Kauffeld, F. 8, 161, 211, 262
Kienpointner, M. 210
Keegstra, J. 170-1
Kenny, A. 64-5, 67-8
Kenyon, C.M. 161
Kock, C. 5, 75-6, 100-2, 154, 209, 216, 224, 250-1, 258, 262-3
Krabbe, E.C.W. 191, 214
Krugman, P. 245, 258
Kruiger, T. 226

L

Lagasquie-Schiex, M. 94
Laudan, L. 234
Laurenzen, P. 223
Lee, H. 164

Lim, G. 197
Lin, T. 197

M

Macagno, F. 191, 198, 199
Mackie, J. 241
Madison, J. 162-164
Makinson, D. 76
Mann, T. 84
Marshall, J. 164
Mason, G. 165
McBurney, P. 199, 204, 223
McKenzie, J. 170
McLachlin, B. 167, 169, 171, 174-5, 177, 179, 182-6, 189-90
Meiland, J. 54
Mill, J.S. 224, 249, 258
Monroe, J. 165
Mueller, E.T. 197

N

Naess, A. 10

O

O'Keefe, D.J. 24, 224, 251, 258

P

Parmenides 214
Parsons, S. 204, 223
Patterson, S. 209
Paul, R. 102
Pera, M. 234
Perelman, Ch. 210
Perkins, D.N. 197, 249
Pinto, R.C. 7, 30, 33, 79, 94, 99, 113, 206, 264, 270
Plantinga, A. 240
Plato 214
Pollock, J. 37, 60, 79, 95, 108-11, 113, 122, 137, 249
Possin, K. 42, 270-2
Prakken, H. 93, 204
Ptolemy 253

Q

Quine, W. van O. 43, 45-6

R

Rawls, J. 223, 261
Reed, C. 191, 198-9
Rehg, W. 74
Rescher, N. 140-1
Ross, W.D. 4, 8, 133
Russell, B. 214

S

Saladino, G.J. 163-5
Salmon, M. 235
Salmon, W.C. 235, 238, 241
Schafer-Landau 120
Schank, R.C. 197
Schelling, T. 120
Scheuer, O. 191, 241
Scriven, M. 17, 74, 76, 115, 224, 226, 235, 241, 249, 250, 258
Searle, J. 58, 73
Secor, M. 63
Singer, P. 151
Singh, P. 197
Sinnot-Armstrong, W. 74
Skinner, B.F. 120
Skyrms, B. 5, 231
Slob, W.H. 249
Snoeck Henkemans, A.F. 74, 226
Soccorsi, F. 254
Solomon, R. 120
Stevenson, C.L. 203
Stitch, S. 57

T

Thomas, S. 23, 235
Toulmin, S.E. 4, 27, 62, 92, 94, 131, 133-4, 139-41, 167, 176, 187-90, 210, 240, 266
Trebbe-Johnson 105, 120
Tversky, A. 151
Twain, M. 218
Tyaglo, A.V. 95

V

Verheij, B. 249
Voss, J.F. 249

W

Walton, D. 8, 116, 191, 197-9, 202-3, 214, 264
Walzer, A.E. 32
Weddle, P. 240
Wellman, C. *passim*
Whitaker, W. 97
Wilson, J. 161
Wittgenstein, L. 58, 62, 216
Wohlrapp, H. 8, 10, 24, 80-1, 86, 91, 95, 99-100, 102, 109, 159, 213-14, 216-17, 220, 222, 224, 243-5, 256-8, 263-4, 266
Woods, J. 79

Z

Zenker, F. 5, 8, 10, 19, 21, 26-7, 95-8, 101-2, 106-108, 114-15, 148, 219, 224, 242-3, 256-8, 264-6, 271
Zhu, W.L. 197

Index of Terms

A

Abductive argument, reasoning 73, 106, 210, 218, 242, 252, 262-63
Accumulation of considerations, reasons 75, 99, 224, 227, 263
Alternative:
  action(s), approach 198, 204
  claim(s), position(s) 54, 55, 57, 59-60, 148, 150, 153, 155, 157, 250, 256, 269
  conditions 186
Argument,
  conductive *passim*
  definition(s) of 10, 14, 36, 225, 228, 269
  evaluative 93, 250
  practical 62, 64, 73
  pro and con(tra) 4-7, 10-30, 52-61, 70, 81-2, 84-5, 86-103, 149, 159, 161, 166, 192, 204-5, 208-9, 219, 221, 251, 269, 272
  strength 7, 17, 22, 32-3, 35, 41, 44-5, 53, 60, 68, 76-8, 80, 86, 88-9, 91, 100-01, 104, 107-10, 112-20, 122, 136-7, 148-9, 152-5, 158, 205, 214, 218-19, 227, 236-8, 241-3, 245-6, 248, 252-3, 255, 257-8, 264-5, 268
Argumentation practice(s) 99-100, 147, 159, 178, 244, 249, 258, 271
Argumentative praxis 212-13, 216-17, 223
Argumentation, inference, reason(ing) schemes 92, 110, 112, 117, 192, 194-5, 197-204, 206-7, 211, 220, 222, 243
Argumentation theory 1, 21, 55, 62, 69, 73, 87-8, 99, 102-3, 210, 212-14, 216, 219, 223, 225, 243, 249-50, 258
Associated universal conditional, generalization 128, 238, 242-3
Assumption(s) 36, 40, 44-5, 57, 110-11, 121, 151, 197, 209, 215, 225, 234, 237, 244, 271
Audience(s) 11, 18, 47, 55, 56, 60, 68, 70, 101-2, 188, 215, 268

B

Backing 62, 129-133, 144, 175-9, 181-2, 184, 186-90
Background assumptions, information, knowledge, material 25, 36, 39-40, 45, 77, 148, 268, 271
Balance of considerations (BC) 10, 13-19, 22, 27, 31-51, 52, 86, 99, 134, 151-2, 155, 158-66, 225, 233, 239-40, 246-7, 249, 257, 263-4, 270
Bayesianism 115
Burden of proof 89, 150, 153, 155, 163-4, 182, 198

C

Ceteris paribus 80, 90-1, 95-8, 116, 129 136, 139-41, 143-4, 176-9, 181-4, 187-8, 230, 233, 238, 242, 255, 265
Claim(s) 14-15, 18-21, 33, 36, 39, 46, 48, 50, 52, 55-7, 59-60, 62-73, 75-77, 82, 84-5, 103, 131, 146-7, 149-53, 184, 186-8, 214-15, 225-8, 231, 234, 238, 240-1, 263-4, 267
Commensurability 69, 162
Computational approaches 115
Conductive argument, reasoning, *passim*
  definition(s) of 1-2, 104-6, 191, 227-8, 231-3, 239-40, 250, 254, 257, 268-70, 272, 274-5
  pattern(s) of 3-7, 10, 12-16, 19, 22-3, 26, 31, 33, 51, 91, 94, 112, 127, 129, 133, 175-7, 179-81, 183, 186, 188-9, 192, 211, 227-8, 236
Connection adequacy 129, 131, 135, 137
Consideration(s) 1, 3-4, 6-7, 11-29, 33, 38, 41, 44, 56, 69-72, 75, 81-2, 84, 86, 91, 93-4, 97, 99, 102, 105, 109, 110-26, 127, 133-4, 136-8, 145-8, 150-1, 153-7, 166-7, 175, 177, 185-8, 190, 205, 218, 221, 230-1, 263-6, 269, 272-5
  overriding 3, 7, 124-5, 160-2
  negative(ly relevant) 3, 10, 12, 17, 19, 22, 110, 127, 129, 133-8, 149, 167, 186, 262, 266, 272-3
  multiple 3-4, 12, 94, 97, 113, 115, 161, 235, 263

pro and con(tra)   1, 6, 107-8, 112-14, 119-25, 133, 137, 145, 158, 191, 227, 265, 274
Contraconsideration(s)   (see counterconsideration(s))
Convergent argument, reasoning, support   4, 6, 13-15, 21-4, 26-7, 29-30, 32, 34, 35, 40-1, 95, 105, 143, 176, 215, 218, 234, 236, 241, 258, 268, 271, 273
Counter argument(s), counterargument(s)   20, 54-5, 58-60, 149, 198
Counterconsideration(s), counter-consideration(s)   10, 12-24, 31, 33-42, 44, 52-4, 58-9, 61, 74-5, 80-1, 84-5, 99, 104-8, 112-114, 116, 118, 122-3, 137, 139, 140, 146, 158, 179, 188, 190, 218, 234, 237-9, 241, 246, 253, 255, 257, 263, 266-70, 272-5
definition(s) of   21, 25, 52-61, 268-9
vs objections   267
Counterexample   117, 135-6
Counterrebuttal   140-2, 144
Cumulative reasoning, support   6, 16, 22, 17, 29, 103, 106, 115, 230, 234, 237, 239, 246, 250, 253, 268

D

Deductive argument, inference, reasoning   3-6, 12, 32-3, 36, 40, 52, 64, 68, 73-85, 97, 103-4, 110, 117, 129, 135-6, 148, 191, 210-11, 218-19, 227-8, 232-5, 238-41, 243, 254-7, 262, 265-6, 272
Deductivist approach   231, 235, 238-41, 243, 257-8
Decision (making)   1-3, 5, 62, 64-5, 68, 71-2, 89, 92-4, 100, 102, 118, 126, 151, 153, 156, 161, 169, 172, 179-82, 193, 202, 204-6, 208, 218, 221, 263, 265, 272
Defeasible argument, inference, reasoning   4, 5, 41, 42, 51, 60, 79, 93, 104-5, 108-11, 137, 191, 198, 203-5, 209, 265-6
Defeat(er)   41, 104, 108-10, 113-14, 116-17, 137
rebutting   108-10, 117, 137, 141
undercutting   108-9, 117, 137, 141
Deliberation, deliberative argumentation   64, 67-9, 72, 74-5, 89-9, 157, 163-6, 191-3, 202-6, 208-9, 222, 251, 258, 263

Diagrams, diagramming   1, 5-6, 10, 13, 17-18, 22-4, 27-31, 35-8, 40, 95, 138-43, 191-6, 201, 206-7, 210, 213, 222, 226, 229-30, 270, 272-5
Dialectic(al)   57-61, 80, 99, 102, 147-9, 153, 210, 250-1, 258, 267
environment   58, 61, 148
space   149
tier   5, 25, 52-61, 95, 138, 250, 258
Dialogue approach, model   1, 6-7, 11, 18, 24, 196, 204-5, 214, 221, 269
Dimensions (of the activity of arguing)   213, 216, 221
objective   213, 215, 221
procedural   213-14, 218, 220
structural   213
subjective   213, 215, 220
Diminisher   108-10

E

Enthymemes, enthymematic argument(s)   129, 194, 235
Epistemic/epistemological, claims, issues, values, etc.   7, 61-2, 69, 73, 81, 95, 97, 114, 129, 132, 137-8, 140, 144, 177, 187-8, 216, 252
"Even" arguments, relation   45-8
"Even though" arguments, relation   31, 36, 37, 39-42, 44-5, 47-9, 51
Ethics, ethical   2, 5, 8, 67-72, 75, 94, 112, 119-20, 130, 133-5, 147, 150-1, 156, 191-3, 202-6, 208-9, 212, 224, 227, 234, 262-3

F

Fallacy, fallacies, fallacious   33, 62, 102, 148, 150, 152-4, 191, 208,
Federalist Papers, Party, position   161-6
Field dependent(-ce)   62, 129, 176, 188, 224, 227
Formal (deductive) logic   76, 94, 98, 129, 131, 145, 176, 200, 218-19, 250, 262, 271
Formal disputation   140-1
Frame(s), framing, frame structures, framework   80, 99, 100, 144, 151, 154, 157, 162-5, 199, 204, 209, 214, 216, 218, 244-5
criticism   217

Frame(s) (cont'd)
  harmonizing 217
  ranking 217
  synthesizing 217
  unification 245

H

Heft(ing) 87, 264
Historical-textual approach 224-5, 250
Hybrid argumentation 119, 266

I

Implicit premises 194-6, 201, 264
Incommensurable (-bility) 67, 163
Independent support 16-17, 23, 26, 38, 226
Indicator words 21, 269
Inductive argument 52, 33-5, 41, 74, 76-84, 94, 103-8, 111, 114, 117, 210, 218-21, 228, 230-6, 238, 250, 262, 266, 271, 275
Inference to the best explanation reasoning 105, 232-5, 237, 242, 252-3
Information content 75, 220, 268
Informal logic (-ian) 13, 18, 21, 60, 75, 97, 210-11, 245, 250, 262
Interpretive claims 74

J

Justification 7, 47, 50, 133, 155-7, 204, 220-1
  degree(s) of 109-10, 115
  justificatory force 76

L

Legal reasoning 92, 94, 265
Linked argument 32, 41-2
Logic (-al) 11-13, 35, 42-3, 45, 62, 64-5, 67, 69, 74, 76-7, 79
  classical 218
  deductive 77, 111, 129, 131, 145, 176, 219, 250, 262
  force 8, 13, 16, 135, 264
  space 218

M

Macrostructure (-ral) 127
Measureable (-bility) 86, 115, 264
Meta-argument(s) 230, 232, 235, 253, 256-7
  conductive 224-5
  philosophical 235
Meta-level 77, 214, 220, 225
Methodology 114, 167, 177, 188-90, 249-50, 258
Monotony 77, 81
Moral reasoning 4, 31-3, 263
Multi-dimensional 63, 65
Multiple argumentation 255, 257

N

Nonconclusiveness 235-6, 241
Nonmonotonic 111, 230
Notwithstanding clause 8, 31, 36, 42, 44, 48-50

O

Objection(s) 5, 15, 16,19-21, 23-29, 52-61, 82, 146-49, 153, 155, 161-6, 205, 219-23, 239-42, 245-6, 249-53, 266-8, 272
  definition(s) of 20, 52-61, 267
On Balance Principle/Premise (OBP) 75, 80-1, 217-18, 274-5
Openminded(ness) 252
Open texture argument 120
Ordinal scale 77

P

Parity of ranking 167
Patterns of conductive argument
  (see conductive argument)
Perspectives 73, 101, 151-2, 213, 243
Persuasion dialogue 204, 210
Plausibility 42, 128, 198, 234, 263
Practical argument, inference, reasoning 62-5, 67-8, 71-3, 94, 97, 100, 119, 147, 191, 194-5, 197-200, 202-4, 250
Pragma Dialectic(s) 18

Premise,
  addition, deletion 77-8
  definition of 12, 14-15, 21, 25-6,
  weight 86-91, 94-5, 98-100, 102-3, 265
Presumption 33, 47, 49-51, 53, 80,
  137,141, 143-144, 155, 176, 189
Probability 33, 62, 78, 80-2, 95, 105, 121,
  137, 140, 165, 169, 198-200, 230-1, 242,
  264
Probative obligations, responsibilities 158,
  162-3
Problem solving 5, 234
Pro tanto 4, 7, 265

Q

Qualified reasoning 240
Qualified universals 116, 241

R

Reasoned judgment 148, 191
Reasoning,
  conductive *passim*
  deductive (see deductive reasoning)
  inductive (see inductive reasoning)
  value-based 200
Reason schemas 111
Rebuttals 24-5, 29, 134-41, 216, 266
Reflective equilibrium 222
Relevance 16, 18, 22, 26, 34, 69, 71, 97,
  105-6, 109, 111-12, 122, 131, 134, 136,
  216, 231, 234, 236, 239, 241, 252, 265,
  268, 274
  negative 59, 109, 233, 237
  of premises,
    independently relevant 3, 12-13,
    16, 17, 22-3, 26, 104, 127, 138, 139,
    175, 241, 263
    nonconclusively relevant 262
Reliability 176-7, 186-7, 213-15
Retroflexive 148, 271-2, 243
Rhetoric(al) 42-7, 49-51, 62-3, 67-8, 70,
  159, 210, 212, 215-16, 243, 256

S

Scale weight 86-8, 100
tandard of proof 150, 169
Syntactic(al) 46-7, 49-50, 213
Statistical syllogism 241-2
Strength 7, 17, 21, 32-3, 35, 40-1,44-5, 48,
  53, 60, 68, 75-8, 80, 86-9, 91, 100-1, 104,
  107-10, 112-21, 136-7, 148-9, 152-155,
  158, 161, 205, 214, 218-19, 236, 238, 241,
  243-5, 247-8, 251-4, 257, 264-5, 268
Subjective (-ivity) 78, 80-1, 89, 97, 100-2,
  121, 154, 183, 186, 203, 210, 215-16,
  220-1, 250, 265

T

Toulmin model 127, 129, 133, 139-40,
  167, 175, 180
Transsubjectivity, Principle of 216, 221,
  223
Types of argument, inference, reasoning 5,
  52, 63, 94, 104, 202, 231-3
Truth 12, 19-20, 34-5, 39, 43-4, 62-5, 67,
  72-4, 104, 106, 108,119, 128-30, 169,
  172-4, 176, 180-2, 188, 215, 218-19, 222-
  3, 228, 232-3, 239, 249-50, 253, 255, 259,
  274

U

Universal audience 70, 101, 215
Universality 101, 265, 272
Undercutter 110, 195

V

Valid(ity) 2, 6, 8, 11-12, 39-45, 63-4, 67,
  69-70, 75, 94, 104, 110, 111-12, 122, 129,
  133-6, 145, 215, 219, 221, 227-8, 230-6,
  238, 243-4, 252, 264, 266
  constitutional 167, 171, 175, 205
Value(s) 7, 72-3, 75, 91-4, 97, 99, 101,
  103, 114-15, 154, 157, 191, 193, 195-203,
  205, 207, 209, 211, 250, 271

Index of Terms

W

Warrant [n.]   4, 27, 53, 62, 73, 97, 112-14,
128-41, 144, 153, 161, 167-8, 175-81,
183, 185-90
  types of   131, 137, 176
Warrant [v.], -ed   242, 148, 152-4, 164-6
Weighing   17, 22-3, 27-9, 33, 39, 69, 70,
74, 75-6, 84, 86-7, 90, 94, 99,104,107-8,
115, 122, 133, 135-7, 145, 148, 154-7,
161, 166-7, 173, 177, 182, 186-9, 205-6,
210-11, 217, 227-8, 231, 237, 239, 244-5,
264-5, 273-274
Weight(s), (-ting)   7, 14, 16-17, 52, 56, 63,
68-71, 74, 81, 82-4, 86-91, 93-5, 98-100,
102-3, 104, 112, 114-15, 118-20, 123-5,
134, 140, 146, 148-9, 151-2, 154-7, 166,
186-8, 202, 205, 210, 219-21, 227-30,
234, 247, 249, 255-6, 258, 264-5, 268
Weight and sum   114, 249, 258
  deductive   69, 104

www.ingramcontent.com/pod-product-compliance
Lightning Source LLC
Chambersburg PA
CBHW050129170426
43197CB00011B/1769